GLOBE FEARON

American History

Civil War to the Present

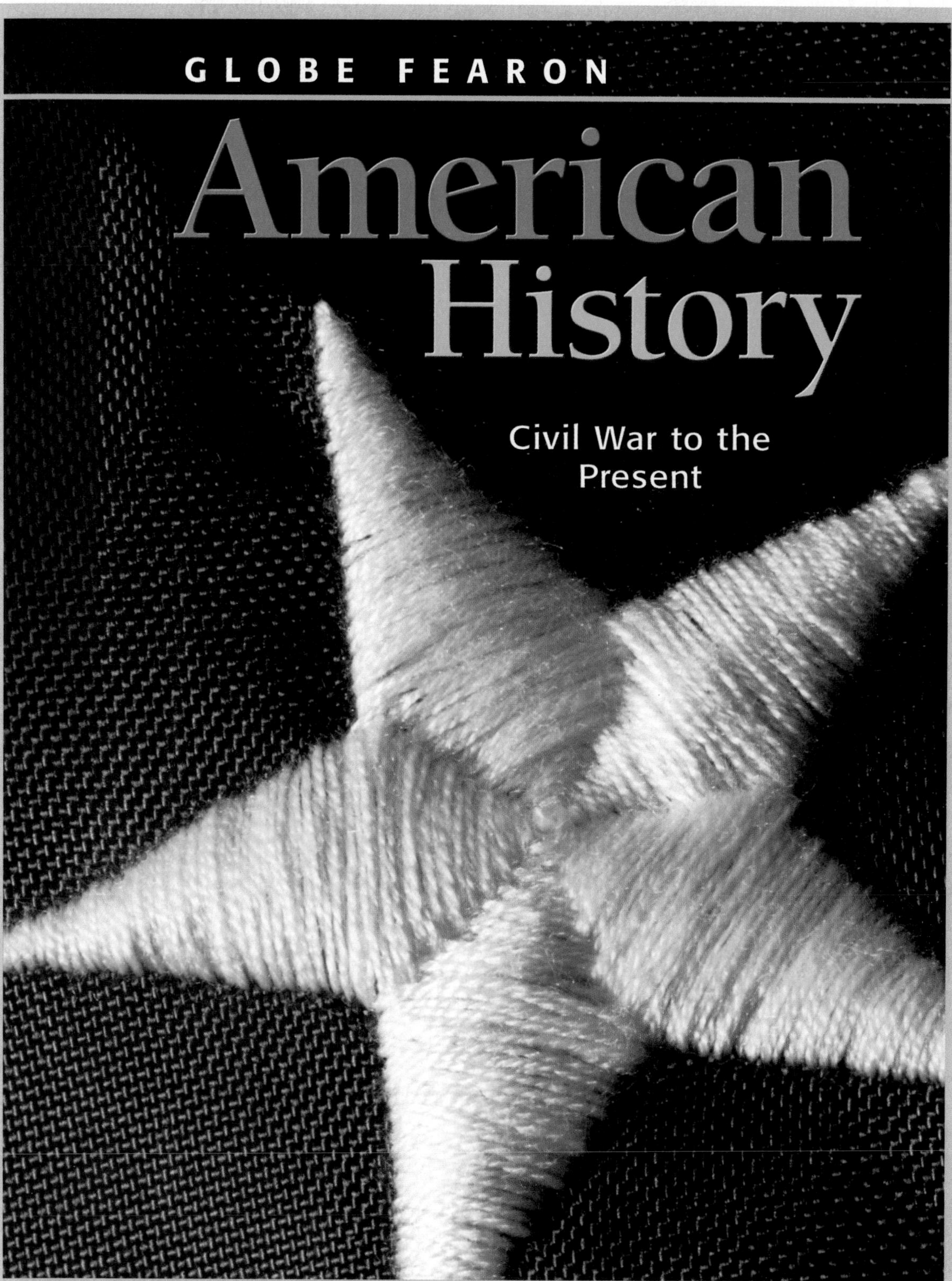

GLOBE FEARON

Pearson Learning Group

The following people have contributed to the development of this product:

Art & Design: Sharon Bozek, Sherri Hieber-Day, Jenifer Hixson, Salita Mehta, Elizabeth Nemeth, Jim O'Shea, Eileen Peters, Karolyn Wehner, Angel Weyant
Editorial: Linda Dorf, Elaine Fay, Alisa Loftus, Colleen Maguire, Jane Petlinski, Jennie Rakos, Tara Walters
Manufacturing: Nathan Kinney
Marketing: Katie Erezuma
Production: Lorraine Allen, Louis Campos, Karen Edmonds, Sue Levine, Karyn Mueller, Phyllis Rosinsky, Cindy Talocci
Publishing Operations: Travis Bailey, Kate Matracia

Acknowledgments appear on page R31, which constitutes an extension of this copyright page.

ISBN 0-13-024411-2

Printed in the United States of America
1 2 3 4 5 6 7 8 9 10   07 06 05 04

Globe
Fearon
Pearson Learning Group

1-800-321-3106
www.pearsonlearning.com

Globe Fearon gratefully acknowledges the contributions of the following consultants and reviewers.

Content Consultants

Yong Chen, Ph.D.
Associate Professor, History and
Asian American Studies
University of California, Irvine
Asian American studies

Frank De Varona, E.S.
Visiting Associate Professor
Florida International University
Miami, FL
Latino studies

Daniel J. Gelo, Ph.D.
Professor and Chair, Department of Anthropology
University of Texas at San Antonio
San Antonio, TX
Native American studies

Linda L. Greenow, Ph.D.
Chair, Department of Geography
S.U.N.Y. New Paltz
New Paltz, NY
Geography

Deborah Gray White, Ph.D.
Chair, Department of History
Rutgers University
New Brunswick, NJ
African American studies
Women's studies

Reviewers

Lawrence Broughton
Chairman, Social Studies Department
North Chicago Community High School
North Chicago, IL

Melvin Garrison
Social Studies Curriculum Specialist, K–12
Office of Curriculum Support
School District of Philadelphia
Philadelphia, PA

Flossie Baker Gautier
Social Studies Teacher
Bay High School
Panama City, FL

Floyd Kessler
Assistant Principal
Junior High School 190
Queens, NY

Charlotte Kresovich
Social Studies Teacher
School District of Philadelphia
Philadelphia, PA

Michael Mann
English and History Unified Curriculum Teacher
North Star Academy
Newark, NJ

CONTENTS

Slavery identification
badge
(page 378)

World War I magazine cover
(page 540)

Depression-era photograph
(page 590)

Vietnam War draft card
and dog tag
(page 678)

Peace button
(page 702)

Patriotic ribbon
(page 746)

Robot
(page 750)

MAPS

CHARTS AND GRAPHS

Build Your Skills

PAST to PRESENT

Connects topics in history to today

CONNECT History

Links history to other areas of study

Points *of* View

Presents two sides of important issues

They Made History

Highlights important people who made a difference

Primary Source Documents

Includes twelve key documents and speeches

Geography
HANDBOOK and ATLAS

The Hubbard Glacier stretches into the sea near a cruise ship in Alaska.

Why Study Geography?

A good place to begin your study of American history is with the study of geography. Geography is the study of the physical features of Earth and the people who live on it, including the relationship between people and their environment. Geography helps us to understand history by seeing how the characteristics of a place affect people and events.

Five Geography Themes

Geographers have developed five themes to show the connection between history and geography. These themes are location, place, region, movement, and human interaction.

Location Street signs in New York City

Location

When you study events in history, you need to know exactly where in the world they take place. The theme of location answers the question "Where is it?" To know precisely where a place is located, geographers have come up with a grid system of imaginary lines on maps. These are called lines of latitude and lines of longitude. You will learn more about this grid system on page GH7.

Sometimes, it is useful to know where an area is in relation to another area. For example, New York City is in the northeast corner of the United States, close to New Jersey and Connecticut. A specific location in New York City could be the intersection of 6th Avenue and West 52nd Street.

Place The peaks of the Rocky Mountains behind Aspen, Colorado

Place

Geographers help us to find out what a place is like. Every place on Earth has its own features that makes it different from every other place.

If you asked geographers to describe Aspen, Colorado, they would point out physical features such as rivers, hills, and mountains. They might also give its population, and describe the kind of buildings people have constructed there. So, a description of a place includes not only its geographical features, but also how people have shaped that place over time.

Region

Because the world is so vast, it is sometimes convenient to think about it in terms of regions. A region is an area that has similar features and characteristics. These can include similar landforms, the type of climate the region has, or even its own particular culture. For example, the Great Plains of the United States is a region because it is an area with a great deal of level land that is good for farming. The states in this region also share a similar climate that includes very cold winters.

Movement

In early America, people moved around to hunt or gather food. Later, they traveled to explore, to conquer, and to gain riches. Some people left their homes to find good farmland, more space, or better jobs.

Today, movement has become a daily part of our lives. People use planes, trains, cars, buses, and subways to move from one place to another. Ships and planes crisscross the globe as goods and resources are exchanged among nations. When we study history, we look at the movement of people, ideas, and goods to understand the changes that have occurred.

Human Interaction

In the study of history, we look at the interaction between people and their surroundings. We might ask: How does the environment of a place affect how people live? The weather and resources of a place, for example, will determine how people use the land for business and recreation, as well as the types of houses people build. The North Carolina coast has been developed to allow people to take advantage of the water resources around them for business and leisure activities such as sailing and fishing.

Region Wheat harvesting in the Great Plains

Movement Airport in Seattle, Washington

Human Interaction Houses along the North Carolina coastline

Reading a Map

To understand geography, you need to know how to read a map and understand its parts.

Maps are drawings of places on Earth. To help you read maps, mapmakers—or cartographers—include certain elements on most maps they draw. These include the title, the key, the compass rose, the locator map, and the scale.

Many of the maps you see are general-purpose maps that give political or physical information. A political map shows boundaries as well as capital cities and major cities. A physical map shows natural features, such as rivers and oceans. Special-purpose maps show specific kinds of information. For example, a climate map is a special-purpose map that shows the temperature of a place or region.

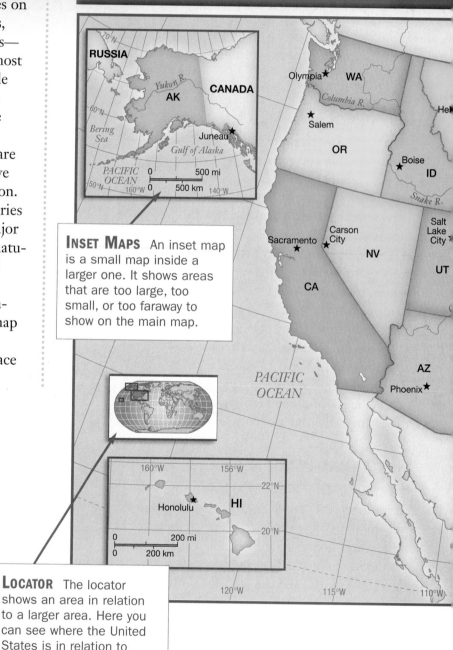

The United States

RUSSIA

70°N

Yukon R.

CANADA

AK

60°N

Bering Sea

Juneau ★

Gulf of Alaska

PACIFIC OCEAN

50°N

160°W   140°W

0   500 mi

0   500 km

Olympia ★   WA

Columbia R.

Salem ★

OR

He

Boise ★

ID

Snake R.

Sacramento ★   Carson City ★

NV

Salt Lake City ★

UT

CA

AZ

Phoenix ★

PACIFIC OCEAN

160°W   156°W

22°N

Honolulu ★   HI

20°N

0   200 mi

0   200 km

120°W   115°W   110°W

INSET MAPS An inset map is a small map inside a larger one. It shows areas that are too large, too small, or too faraway to show on the main map.

LOCATOR The locator shows an area in relation to a larger area. Here you can see where the United States is in relation to the world.

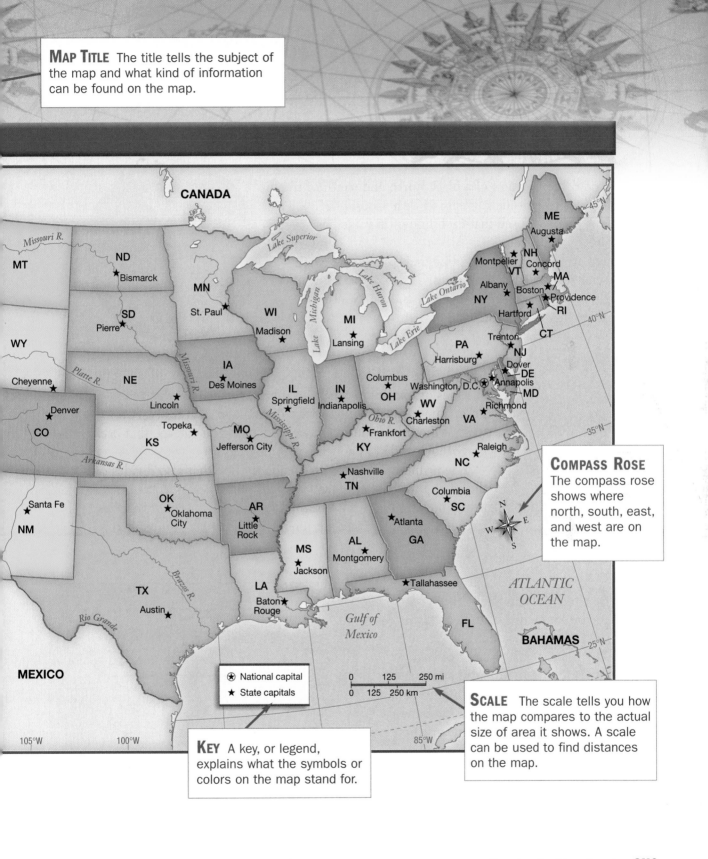

MAP TITLE The title tells the subject of the map and what kind of information can be found on the map.

CANADA

MEXICO

ATLANTIC OCEAN

BAHAMAS

Gulf of Mexico

Missouri R.
Lake Superior
Lake Michigan
Lake Huron
Lake Ontario
Lake Erie
Ohio R.
Mississippi R.
Missouri R.
Platte R.
Arkansas R.
Brazos R.
Rio Grande

MT
ND ★Bismarck
MN
★St. Paul
SD ★Pierre
WY
Cheyenne★
Denver★
CO
WI
Madison★
IA ★Des Moines
NE
Lincoln★
Topeka★
KS
MO ★Jefferson City
MI ★Lansing
IL Springfield★
IN ★Indianapolis
OH Columbus★
KY ★Frankfort
TN ★Nashville
Santa Fe★
NM
OK ★Oklahoma City
AR ★Little Rock
MS ★Jackson
AL Montgomery★
GA
★Atlanta
SC Columbia★
NC ★Raleigh
VA ★Richmond
WV ★Charleston
PA Harrisburg★
ME ★Augusta
NH ★Concord
VT ★Montpelier
MA Boston★
NY Albany★
Trenton★ NJ
★Providence RI
Hartford★ CT
DE ★Dover
MD ★Annapolis
Washington, D.C.⊛
TX Austin★
LA Baton Rouge★
FL ★Tallahassee

45°N
40°N
35°N
25°N
105°W 100°W 85°W

⊛ National capital
★ State capitals

0   125   250 mi
0 125 250 km

COMPASS ROSE The compass rose shows where north, south, east, and west are on the map.

N
W · E
S

SCALE The scale tells you how the map compares to the actual size of area it shows. A scale can be used to find distances on the map.

KEY A key, or legend, explains what the symbols or colors on the map stand for.

Geography Handbook **GH6**

Latitude and Longitude

Mapmakers have created a special kind of grid system to help us find the exact location of any place on Earth.

Lines of Latitude

Latitude is the position of a place north and south of the equator. Lines of latitude run east to west around the globe. On the map, you can see that each line of latitude has a measurement in degrees (°).

The equator is an imaginary line that divides the earth into two halves, called hemispheres. The Northern Hemisphere lies north of the equator, and the Southern Hemisphere lies south of it.

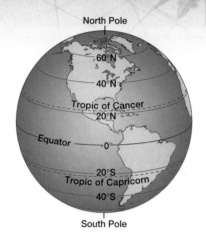

Lines of Longitude

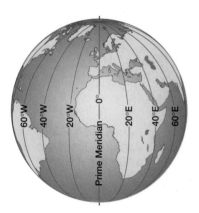

Lines of longitude run from the North Pole to the South Pole. They are used to measure distance in degrees east and west of the prime meridian. On the map, you can see that each line of longitude has a measure in degrees (°).

The prime meridian is an imaginary line that also divides the earth into hemispheres. The half that lies west of the prime meridian is the Western Hemisphere. The half that lies to the east of the prime meridian is the Eastern Hemisphere.

Using Latitude and Longitude

Once you know the latitude and longitude of a place, you can locate it quickly on a map. The point at which lines of latitude and longitude meet is the grid address, or coordinates, of an exact location. For example, the city of New Orleans, Louisiana, is located at 30°N/90°W. This means that New Orleans is 30° north of the equator and 90° west of the prime meridian. Use the map to find the approximate coordinates of Philadelphia, Pennsylvania.

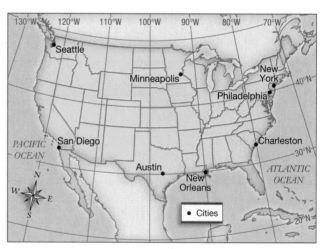

Map Projections

A map projection is a way of showing the round Earth on a flat surface.

To locate places, geographers use maps and globes. Because a globe is the same shape as the earth, it shows the sizes and shapes of the earth's features accurately. Even though a globe has this advantage, flat maps are more convenient. A flat map allows you to see all of the earth's surface at the same time. The disadvantage of a flat map is that it distorts how the earth really looks.

To solve this problem, mapmakers have developed different map projections. No map projection shows the earth correctly in every way. Some projections show the sizes of continents correctly but distort their shapes. Others show the correct shape of the landmasses but distort their sizes.

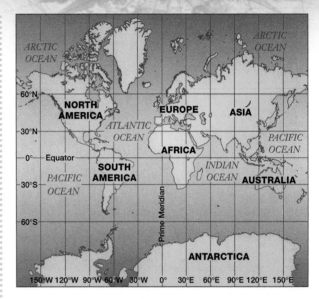

Mercator Projection

The Mercator projection shows the true shapes of landmasses, but distorts their sizes. On the Mercator projection, the actual curved lines of latitude and longitude are shown straight. Because the lines are straight, lands on either side of the equator must be stretched in size.

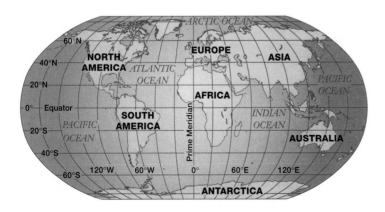

Robinson Projection

Today, many people use another kind of map projection called the Robinson projection. The lines of latitude and longitude are curved to show the curve of the earth's surface. The Robinson projection shows land and ocean sizes accurately, but the shapes of the land are slightly distorted.

Geography Dictionary

1. **Bay** a part of an ocean or lake that is partially enclosed by land

2. **Canyon** a narrow, deep valley with steep sides

3. **Delta** a triangular area of land formed from deposits at the mouth of a river

4. **Desert** a dry area where few plants grow

5. **Glacier** a large ice mass that moves slowly down a mountain or over land

6. **Harbor** a sheltered area of water where ships can anchor safely

7. **Island** an area of land completely surrounded by water

8. **Lake** a body of water that is almost completely surrounded by land

9. **Mountain peak** the very top part of a mountain

10. **Mountain range** a series of connected mountains

11. **Peninsula** a body of land jutting into a lake or ocean, surrounded on three sides by water

12. **Plain** an area of level land, usually at low elevation and often covered with grasses

13. **Plateau** a broad, flat area of land higher than the surrounding land

14. **River** a large natural flow of water that runs through the land

15. **Strait** a narrow strip of water connecting two larger bodies of water

16. **Swamp** an area of land that is saturated by water

17. **Valley** a long, low area of land that is between hills or mountains

18. **Volcano** an opening in the earth, usually raised, through which gases, lava, and hot ashes escape from the earth's interior

Atlas ★ The World

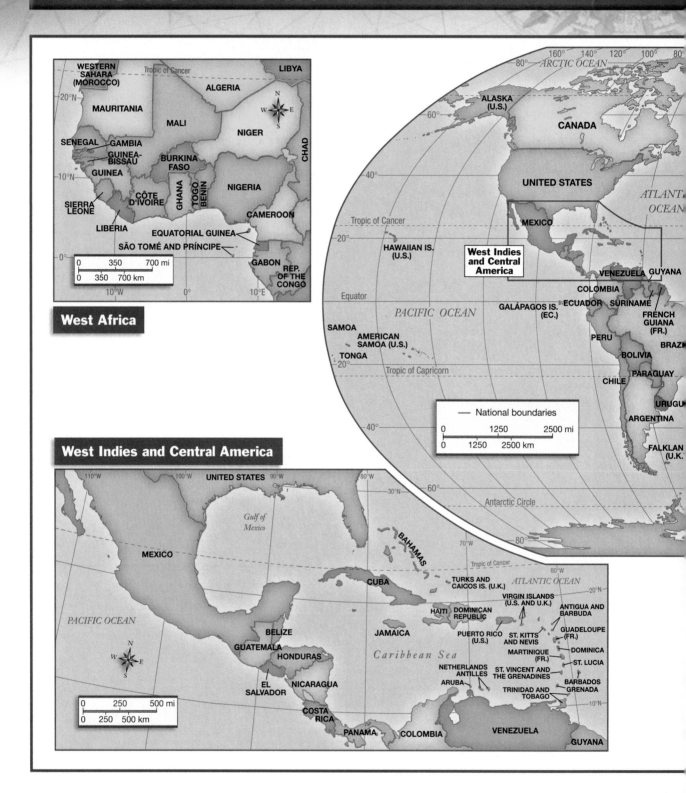

West Africa

WESTERN SAHARA (MOROCCO)
Tropic of Cancer
LIBYA
ALGERIA
20°N
MAURITANIA
MALI
NIGER
SENEGAL
GAMBIA
GUINEA-BISSAU
BURKINA FASO
GUINEA
10°N
SIERRA LEONE
CÔTE D'IVOIRE
GHANA
TOGO
BENIN
NIGERIA
CHAD
CAMEROON
LIBERIA
EQUATORIAL GUINEA
SÃO TOMÉ AND PRÍNCIPE
0°
GABON
REP. OF THE CONGO
10°W
0°
10°E

0 350 700 mi
0 350 700 km

West Indies and Central America

160° 140° 120° 100° 80°
80° ARCTIC OCEAN
ALASKA (U.S.)
60°
CANADA
40°
UNITED STATES
ATLANTIC OCEAN
Tropic of Cancer
MEXICO
20°
HAWAIIAN IS. (U.S.)
West Indies and Central America
VENEZUELA GUYANA
COLOMBIA
Equator
GALÁPAGOS IS. (EC.)
ECUADOR SURINAME
FRENCH GUIANA (FR.)
PACIFIC OCEAN
SAMOA
AMERICAN SAMOA (U.S.)
PERU
BRAZIL
TONGA
BOLIVIA
20°
Tropic of Capricorn
PARAGUAY
CHILE

— National boundaries
0 1250 2500 mi
0 1250 2500 km

URUGUAY
ARGENTINA
40°
FALKLAN (U.K.)
60°
Antarctic Circle
80°

West Indies and Central America

110°W
100°W
UNITED STATES
90°W
80°W
30°N
60°
Gulf of Mexico
70°W
MEXICO
BAHAMAS
Tropic of Cancer
60°W
CUBA
TURKS AND CAICOS IS. (U.K.)
ATLANTIC OCEAN
20°N
VIRGIN ISLANDS (U.S. AND U.K.)
ANTIGUA AND BARBUDA
PACIFIC OCEAN
HAITI
DOMINICAN REPUBLIC
GUADELOUPE (FR.)
BELIZE
JAMAICA
PUERTO RICO (U.S.)
ST. KITTS AND NEVIS
DOMINICA
GUATEMALA
MARTINIQUE (FR.)
ST. LUCIA
HONDURAS
Caribbean Sea
NETHERLANDS ANTILLES
ST. VINCENT AND THE GRENADINES
BARBADOS
GRENADA
EL SALVADOR
NICARAGUA
ARUBA
TRINIDAD AND TOBAGO
10°N
COSTA RICA
PANAMA
COLOMBIA
VENEZUELA
GUYANA

0 250 500 mi
0 250 500 km

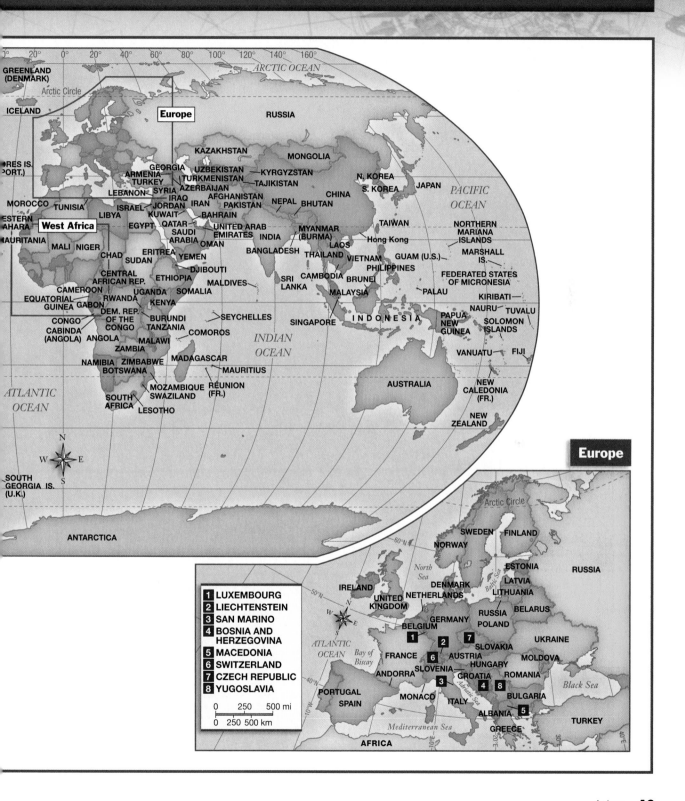

GREENLAND (DENMARK)

Arctic Circle

ICELAND

RES IS. PORT.)

Europe

ARCTIC OCEAN

RUSSIA

KAZAKHSTAN

MONGOLIA

GEORGIA
ARMENIA   UZBEKISTAN   KYRGYZSTAN
TURKEY   TURKMENISTAN
           AZERBAIJAN   TAJIKISTAN
LEBANON   IRAQ   AFGHANISTAN   CHINA   N. KOREA
SYRIA   S. KOREA   JAPAN   PACIFIC
           IRAN   PAKISTAN   OCEAN
MOROCCO   JORDAN   NEPAL   BHUTAN
TUNISIA   ISRAEL   KUWAIT   BAHRAIN
ESTERN   LIBYA   TAIWAN   NORTHERN
AHARA   EGYPT   QATAR   UNITED ARAB   MARIANA
West Africa   SAUDI   EMIRATES   INDIA   MYANMAR   ISLANDS
AURITANIA   ARABIA   OMAN   (BURMA)   Hong Kong
MALI   NIGER   ERITREA   YEMEN   BANGLADESH   LAOS   GUAM (U.S.)   MARSHALL
         CHAD   SUDAN   THAILAND   VIETNAM   IS.
         CENTRAL   DJIBOUTI   CAMBODIA   FEDERATED STATES
CAMEROON AFRICAN REP. ETHIOPIA   MALDIVES   SRI   BRUNEI   OF MICRONESIA
EQUATORIAL   UGANDA   SOMALIA   LANKA   PALAU   KIRIBATI
GUINEA GABON RWANDA KENYA   MALAYSIA
         DEM. REP. BURUNDI   NAURU   TUVALU
CONGO   OF THE   TANZANIA   SEYCHELLES   SINGAPORE   I N D O N E S I A   PAPUA   SOLOMON
CABINDA CONGO   NEW   ISLANDS
(ANGOLA) ANGOLA MALAWI   COMOROS   INDIAN   GUINEA
         ZAMBIA   OCEAN   VANUATU   FIJI
NAMIBIA ZIMBABWE MADAGASCAR
BOTSWANA   MAURITIUS
         MOZAMBIQUE RÉUNION   AUSTRALIA   NEW
ATLANTIC SWAZILAND (FR.)   CALEDONIA
OCEAN   SOUTH   (FR.)
         AFRICA   LESOTHO
                                                                     NEW
                                                                     ZEALAND

N
W   E
S

SOUTH
GEORGIA IS.
(U.K.)

ANTARCTICA

Europe

1 LUXEMBOURG
2 LIECHTENSTEIN
3 SAN MARINO
4 BOSNIA AND
  HERZEGOVINA
5 MACEDONIA
6 SWITZERLAND
7 CZECH REPUBLIC
8 YUGOSLAVIA

0   250   500 mi
0   250 500 km

Arctic Circle

SWEDEN   FINLAND
NORWAY

North
Sea

IRELAND
UNITED   NETHERLANDS   DENMARK   ESTONIA
KINGDOM   LATVIA
                                     LITHUANIA   RUSSIA
BELGIUM   GERMANY   RUSSIA   BELARUS
                      POLAND
ATLANTIC 1   2   7   SLOVAKIA   UKRAINE
OCEAN   FRANCE 6 AUSTRIA   MOLDOVA
Bay of   SLOVENIA HUNGARY
Biscay   ANDORRA   3   CROATIA   ROMANIA
                            4   8   Black Sea
PORTUGAL   MONACO   BULGARIA
SPAIN   ITALY   ALBANIA   5
                                       TURKEY
         Mediterranean Sea   GREECE

AFRICA

North America

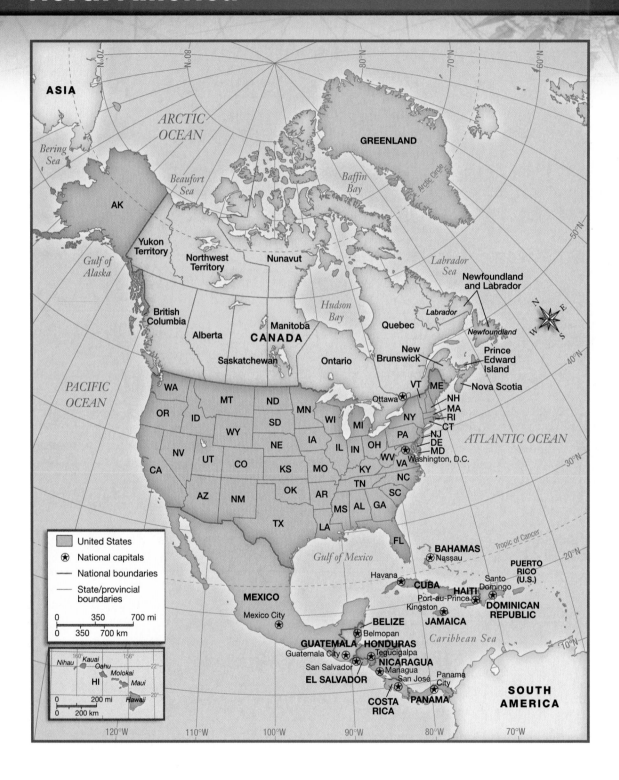

ASIA

ARCTIC OCEAN

Bering Sea

Beaufort Sea

GREENLAND

Baffin Bay

AK

Yukon Territory

Northwest Territory

Nunavut

Arctic Circle

Gulf of Alaska

Labrador Sea

Newfoundland and Labrador

British Columbia

Hudson Bay

Labrador

Alberta

Manitoba

Quebec

Newfoundland

Prince Edward Island

CANADA

New Brunswick

Saskatchewan

Ontario

Nova Scotia

PACIFIC OCEAN

WA

MT

ND

MN

VT ME

Ottawa ⊛

NH

WI

MI

NY

MA RI

OR

ID

SD

PA

CT

WY

NE

IA

IL IN

OH

NJ

DE

MD

ATLANTIC OCEAN

NV

UT

CO

MO

WV

VA

Washington, D.C.

CA

KS

KY

NC

AZ

NM

OK

AR

TN

SC

MS AL

GA

TX

LA

FL

BAHAMAS

⊛ Nassau

Tropic of Cancer

Gulf of Mexico

PUERTO RICO (U.S.)

Havana

CUBA

Santo Domingo

HAITI

Port-au-Prince

MEXICO

Kingston

DOMINICAN REPUBLIC

Mexico City ⊛

BELIZE

JAMAICA

⊛ Belmopan

GUATEMALA

HONDURAS

Caribbean Sea

Guatemala City ⊛

⊛ Tegucigalpa

San Salvador ⊛

NICARAGUA

EL SALVADOR

Managua ⊛

Panama City

SOUTH AMERICA

San José ⊛

COSTA RICA

PANAMA ⊛

Legend

- United States
- ⊛ National capitals
- — National boundaries
- — State/provincial boundaries

0   350   700 mi
0   350   700 km

Nihau Kauai Oahu Molokai Maui
HI
Hawaii

0   200 mi
0   200 km

A3

South America

Caribbean Sea

ATLANTIC OCEAN

N
W   E
S

CENTRAL
AMERICA

Maracaibo•
•⊛ Caracas
VENEZUELA
Georgetown
•⊛ Paramaribo
Bogotá
•⊛
GUYANA
⊛ Cayenne
Cali•
⊛
COLOMBIA
French Guiana
(FR.)

Quito•
ECUADOR
⊛
•Guayaquil
SURINAME

Equator   0°

Negro
Amazon

Madeira
Tapajós
Xingu
Tocantins

PERU
BRAZIL

Lima•
São Francisco
10°S

Lake
Titicaca   BOLIVIA
•⊛ La Paz
Arequipa•   •Santa Cruz
⊛   Brasília ⊛
Sucre   20°S

PARAGUAY
São Paulo•
Concepción•   Tropic of Capricorn
⊛ Asunción

PACIFIC OCEAN   CHILE

Valparaiso•   Rosario   Salto•
•   •   URUGUAY   30°S
Santiago ⊛ ARGENTINA   •⊛
Buenos Aires•   •Montevideo   ATLANTIC OCEAN

⊛ National capitals
• Cities
— National boundaries

0   250   500 mi

0 250 500 km   40°S

Strait of
Magellan
Falkland (Malvinas)
Islands (U.K.)   50°S

100°W   90°W   80°W   70°W   60°W   50°W   40°W   30°W   20°W

20°N

10°N

10°S

Europe

National capitals ⊛
National boundaries —

0   250   500 mi
0   250   500 km

ICELAND
Reykjavik

Arctic Circle

60°N

Norwegian Sea

SWEDEN
FINLAND
NORWAY
Oslo
Helsinki
Stockholm
Tallinn
ESTONIA

RUSSIA

Moscow

North Sea

Baltic Sea

DENMARK
Copenhagen
Riga LATVIA
LITHUANIA
Vilnius
Minsk

IRELAND
Dublin
UNITED KINGDOM
NETHERLANDS
London
Amsterdam
Berlin
GERMANY
RUSSIA
Warsaw
POLAND
BELARUS
Kiev

50°N

ATLANTIC OCEAN

Brussels
BELGIUM
1 Luxembourg
Paris
Prague 7
SLOVAKIA
Vienna Bratislava
AUSTRIA Budapest
HUNGARY
UKRAINE

Bay of Biscay

FRANCE
2
6 Bern
SLOVENIA Ljubljana
Zagreb
CROATIA
ROMANIA
Bucharest
Chisinau
MOLDOVA

40°N

ANDORRA
Monte Carlo
3
Sarajevo
4 Belgrade
8
BULGARIA
Sofia
Black Sea

PORTUGAL
Madrid
MONACO
Rome
ITALY
Adriatic Sea
Skopje
MACEDONIA

Lisbon
SPAIN
ALBANIA 5
Tiranë

ASIA

10°W

Strait of Gibraltar

GREECE
Athens
Aegean Sea

AFRICA

Valletta
MALTA
Mediterranean Sea

0°
10°E
20°E
30°E

1	LUXEMBOURG
2	LIECHTENSTEIN
3	SAN MARINO
4	BOSNIA AND HERZEGOVINA
5	MACEDONIA
6	SWITZERLAND
7	CZECH REPUBLIC
8	YUGOSLAVIA

Africa

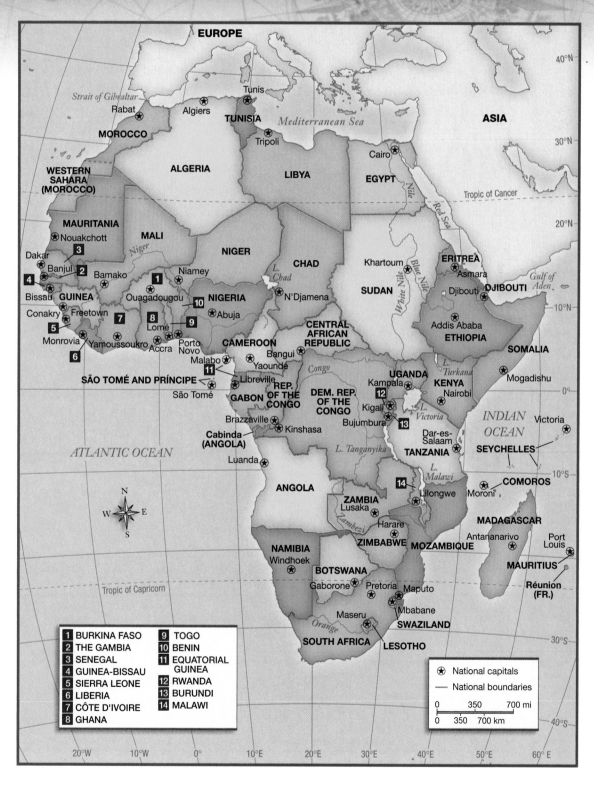

EUROPE

Strait of Gibraltar

Rabat ✪
Algiers ✪
Tunis ✪

MOROCCO

TUNISIA

Tripoli ✪

Mediterranean Sea

ASIA

Cairo ✪

WESTERN SAHARA (MOROCCO)

ALGERIA

LIBYA

EGYPT

Tropic of Cancer

40°N

30°N

20°N

Nile

MAURITANIA

Nouakchott ✪

MALI

Niger

3

Dakar ✪
Banjul ✪ **2**
4

Bamako ✪

1

Niamey ✪

NIGER

L. Chad

CHAD

Khartoum ✪

SUDAN

White Nile

Blue Nile

Red Sea

ERITREA

Asmara ✪

Djibouti ✪ **DJIBOUTI**

Gulf of Aden

10°N

Bissau
GUINEA
Conakry ✪ Freetown ✪ **7**
5
Monrovia ✪ **6**
Yamoussoukro ✪

Ouagadougou ✪
10
8
Lomé ✪ **9**
Accra ✪ Porto Novo ✪

NIGERIA

Abuja ✪

N'Djamena ✪

CENTRAL AFRICAN REPUBLIC

CAMEROON

Bangui ✪

Addis Ababa ✪

ETHIOPIA

SOMALIA

Mogadishu ✪

Malabo ✪ **11**

Yaoundé ✪

Congo

UGANDA

Kampala ✪

L. Turkana

SÃO TOMÉ AND PRÍNCIPE

São Tomé ✪

Libreville ✪

REP. OF THE CONGO

DEM. REP. OF THE CONGO

12
Kigali ✪

KENYA

Nairobi ✪

0°

GABON

Brazzaville ✪

Kinshasa ✪

Bujumbura ✪ **13**

L. Victoria

Dar-es-Salaam ✪

INDIAN OCEAN

Victoria ✪

Cabinda (ANGOLA)

TANZANIA

SEYCHELLES

ATLANTIC OCEAN

Luanda ✪

L. Tanganyika

L. Malawi

10°S

ANGOLA

14

Lilongwe ✪

Moroni ✪ **COMOROS**

ZAMBIA

Lusaka ✪

Zambezi

Harare ✪

MADAGASCAR

Antananarivo ✪

Port Louis ✪

NAMIBIA

Windhoek ✪

ZIMBABWE

MOZAMBIQUE

MAURITIUS

Réunion (FR.)

BOTSWANA

Gaborone ✪

Pretoria ✪

Maputo ✪

Mbabane ✪

Maseru ✪

SWAZILAND

30°S

Orange

SOUTH AFRICA

LESOTHO

N
W E
S

Tropic of Capricorn

1 BURKINA FASO	**9** TOGO
2 THE GAMBIA	**10** BENIN
3 SENEGAL	**11** EQUATORIAL GUINEA
4 GUINEA-BISSAU	
5 SIERRA LEONE	**12** RWANDA
6 LIBERIA	**13** BURUNDI
7 CÔTE D'IVOIRE	**14** MALAWI
8 GHANA	

✪ National capitals
— National boundaries

0   350   700 mi
0   350   700 km

40°S

20°W   10°W   0°   10°E   20°E   30°E   40°E   50°E   60°E

Asia and The Middle East

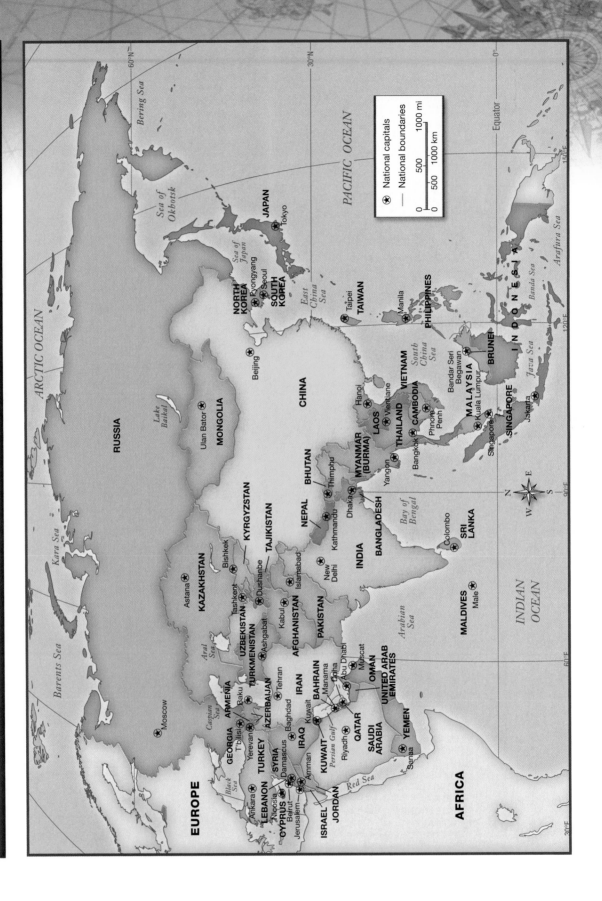

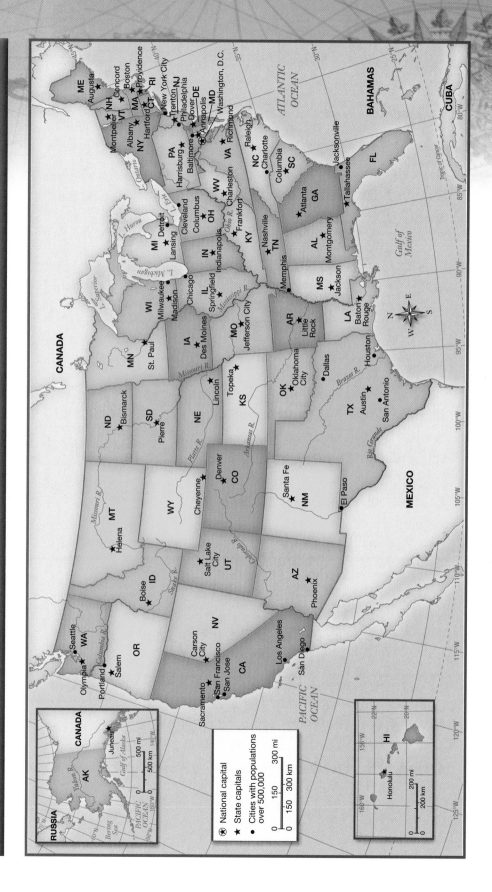

The United States

The United States

National capital ✪
State capitals ★
Cities with populations over 500,000 ●

Prologue: A Look Back

CHAPTER 1 ★ A Look Back

The First Americans Prehistory–1570

The Big Idea
The story of our nation begins thousands of years ago, during the Ice Age. Nomads from Asia spread throughout North and South America. In time, great civilizations developed in Central and South America. Other cultures developed in North America. By the 1500s, Native Americans lived in most of what is now the United States. Their cultures depended on the environment in which they lived.

Early Peoples
Scientists think that there was a land bridge between Asia and North America. Hunters crossed from one continent to the other. When the Ice Age ended, glaciers melted, and the land bridge was covered with water. Thousands of people lived in the Americas by that time. Native Americans found a great deal of variety in the Americas. They found mountains and valleys, rivers and forests. They hunted and gathered food to survive. People learned to farm about 5000 B.C. They began to settle in groups. Religion was an important part of their life.

Ruins of an ancient Anasazi village

Civilizations in the Americas
Complex societies developed in Central and South America. The Olmecs built huge temples. The Maya used writing and created a calendar. The Aztecs ruled millions of people. The Incas built 14,000 miles of roads. In North America, the Adena-Hopewell people built mounds for burial sites. The Mississippians were mound builders, too. In the Southwest, the Hohokam developed irrigation. The Anasazi lived in dwellings that were similar to apartment buildings.

Native Americans
Native Americans lived in areas with different kinds of lands and climates. They developed ways of life that were suited to each area. Native Americans established farming communities in the Northeast and Southeast. They hunted and gathered food on the Plains. They learned to grow crops in the dry Southwest. In the polar regions, they hunted and fished. Native Americans of the Northwest coastal areas depended on fish for food. They used trees to make clothing and shelters.

★ **How did the first Americans adapt to their surroundings?**

Anasazi pot

Early Exploration 1000–1535

Christopher Columbus

The Big Idea

Starting in the early 1000s, people on the continents of Africa, Europe, and Asia began to look outward. Africa had rich resources. Trading kingdoms developed, based on these resources. European explorers came in contact with Africa in the Middle Ages. Trade sprang up between Europe and Asia, too. Portugal led the way in finding a sea route to Asia.

West African Trading Kingdoms

Gold and salt are important African resources. People wanted to trade these resources. Trade routes developed to make this happen. The Muslims of North Africa traded with people from West Africa, Europe, and Asia. Trading kingdoms arose in West Africa. These kingdoms were Ghana, Mali, and Songhai. Outside of trading, most Africans were farmers. Communities were based on kinship.

Early European Expeditions

Through the Middle Ages, Europeans had little contact with other peoples. After 1095, the Crusades took Europeans to the Holy Land. They began to trade with Muslims. Marco Polo traveled to China. He wrote about its riches in 1298. European rulers wanted the riches of Asia and Africa. However, land routes were controlled by Venetian and Muslim merchants. Nations began to look for a sea route. The Portuguese found a sea route around Africa. In 1498, the explorer Vasco da Gama sailed to India.

Columbus arriving in
North America

Major Voyages to the Americas

The Vikings were the first Europeans to reach North America and establish a settlement. Their settlement did not last, however. In the late 1400s, countries were looking for a sea route to Asia by sailing west. Christopher Columbus was an Italian explorer. In 1492, he sailed west for the Spanish rulers. He landed on an island in the Caribbean Sea. Columbus thought he was in Asia. He called the people Indians. They were really Native Americans. Other explorers followed Columbus's direction. Pedro Cabral claimed Brazil for Portugal. John Cabot claimed Newfoundland for England. Giovanni da Verrazano and Jacques Cartier explored for France.

★ **Why did European explorers sail west?**

New Settlements in the Americas
1512–1682

The Big Idea

The Spanish explorer Hernándo Cortés conquered the Aztecs of Mexico. Francisco Pizarro conquered the Incas in Peru. Spanish settlements followed. The Spaniards also explored North America. They established settlements in present-day Florida and New Mexico. The Dutch and the French settled parts of North America. The English founded Jamestown in 1607.

Spanish Conquest and Colonies

In 1519, the Spanish explorer Cortés landed in Mexico. There, he found the Aztec civilization. He wanted its great wealth. By 1521, the Spaniards had conquered the Aztecs. In a similar way, Pizarro and members of his expedition conquered the Incas by 1533 in what is now present-day Peru in South America. Spain gave Spaniards large pieces of land in New Spain. Native Americans worked for the Spanish settlers. Most of the workers died from overwork and disease. Other Spanish explorers traveled through what is now present-day Florida, Texas, and the Southwest of the United States. They claimed these lands for Spain.

Painting of the
Jamestown colony

Other European Settlements

In the 1600s, other European countries sent explorers to parts of North America. Henry Hudson claimed the area in present-day New York for the Netherlands. Samuel de Champlain founded Quebec for France. Robert de La Salle explored the Mississippi River valley for France. The English founded Jamestown, Virginia, in 1607. It was the first permanent English settlement in North America. Jamestown suffered hard times at first. Life improved when settlers began to grow tobacco as a cash crop.

Slavery in the Americas

Slavery was a part of all European colonies in the Americas. The Portuguese began to use African slaves in the 1430s. The enslaved people endured terrible conditions during the trip, or passage, across the Atlantic Ocean. Once in the Americas, life for slaves was very hard. African slaves in the Caribbean worked on sugar plantations. Enslaved people in American colonies planted and harvested crops such as tobacco, rice, cotton, and indigo.

Pocahontas helped
protect the settlers
at Jamestown from
the Algonquins.

★ **What sources did Europeans use for labor in the Americas?**

Founding Colonial America 1607–1733

Metacomet, Chief of the Wampanoag people

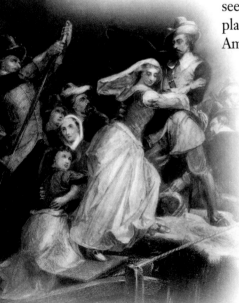

The arrival of English settlers in America

The Big Idea

In North America, small settlements grew into towns. Towns became colonies. Historians group the colonies into three geographic regions. These groups are the New England colonies, the Middle colonies, and the Southern colonies. Between 1630 and 1640, more than 200,000 people from England sailed to the American colonies.

New England Colonies

The Pilgrims sailed for America in 1620. They founded the Plymouth Colony so that they might worship freely. The Puritans, who arrived in 1630, founded the Massachusetts Bay Colony. Roger Williams founded Rhode Island as a place for those who disagreed with Puritan beliefs. Connecticut was settled in 1636 by a Puritan minister. Two merchants started the colonies of Maine and New Hampshire in 1629. Settlers in the American colonies often pushed into Native American lands. Fights broke out between settlers and Native Americans.

Middle Colonies

Dutch colonists settled New Netherland. In 1664, the English Duke of York sent ships to New Netherland and forced the Dutch to surrender their colony. New Netherland then became New York. Two friends of the Duke of York took control of the colony of New Jersey. Swedish people, who first settled Delaware, also came under English control. William Penn founded Pennsylvania. He was a Quaker, a religious group seeking freedom from persecution. Pennsylvania was founded as a safe place for people of all religious beliefs. Penn bought land from Native Americans. As a result, he had good relations with them.

Southern Colonies

Settlers in Virginia began to establish large farms called plantations. In 1624, King James of England made Virginia a royal colony. The colony of Maryland was started in 1632. There, Catholics could worship in peace. The colony of Carolina began in 1663. In 1729, it split into North Carolina and South Carolina. Georgia was the last English colony. It was established in 1733 as a home for debtors. For the most part, the Southern colonies developed a farming economy based on slave labor.

★ **Which colonies were founded for religious reasons?**

CHAPTER 5 ★ A Look Back

The Thirteen Colonies 1650–1775

The Big Idea

The thirteen colonies grew quickly. By 1750, more than 1 million people lived in eastern North America. From the 1600s, farming was an important part of life in all the colonies. Different industries arose in the three regions. England tried to control trade in the colonies. The Enlightenment thinkers of Europe influenced the colonists. The Great Awakening stressed the importance of religion. Slavery took root in the Southern colonies.

The Colonial Economy

A varied economy developed in the thirteen American colonies. Colonists farmed throughout the colonies. However, farming on a small New England farm differed from farming on a large Southern plantation. In New England, fishing, lumber, and shipbuilding were major industries. The mining of iron ore and the fur trade helped the economy of the Middle colonies. Cotton and tar were important in the South. The new English Navigation Acts placed limits on colonial trading. Many colonists ignored these English laws, however.

Life in the Colonies

Most people settled in the colonies to improve their lives. Social classes gave structure to the society. Married women worked alongside their husbands. They had few legal rights, however. Children helped their families, especially on family farms. The Enlightenment led to interest in science and learning. Benjamin Franklin was the most famous colonial scientist. Colonists established schools for higher learning. Freedom of the press was important. The Great Awakening brought many people back to their faiths.

Slavery in the Colonies

The growth of the plantation system in the Southern colonies resulted in an increased number of enslaved people who were used as laborers. African slaves were brought to the colonies in trading ships. Many died on this terrible trip, called the Middle Passage. Enslaved Africans worked on large tobacco and rice plantations. There were some free Africans as well. Slave codes were laws that limited slaves' rights. Sometimes slaves rebelled against their condition. These uprisings were always put down.

 Why was slavery important to the economy of the Southern colonies?

Philadelphia, Pennsylvania, in 1702

Butter churn

Roots of Rebellion 1689–1763

A soldier's powderhorn used to hold gunpowder

The Big Idea

People in England gained more rights in the 1600s and 1700s. American colonists wanted the same rights. New France developed differently from England's American colonies. It was based more on trade than on settlement. As American colonists moved westward, they came in conflict with French traders and trappers. France and England fought wars in North America. After the French and Indian War, France gave up New France.

England's Colonial Rule

The English monarchy grew more limited over time. In 1689, the Glorious Revolution gave Parliament greater powers. The colonists liked John Locke's contract theory of government. Colonial government consisted of a governor, a council, and an assembly. Voting was limited to males who owned property. In the 1700s, colonial assemblies began to gain more power. At the same time, the English government kept out of colonial affairs. The colonists became accustomed to governing themselves.

Conflict With the French

New France was a wilderness empire. Trappers and traders roamed great distances. The fur trade depended on good relations with Native Americans. The Iroquois, however, were not friendly with the French. Conflicts with the Iroquois made trade difficult for the French. English colonists also challenged the French fur trade. France built a series of forts to defend its empire. England and France fought three wars between 1689 and 1739.

British troops storming Quebec in 1759

The French and Indian War

England, Scotland, and Wales joined to form the nation of Great Britain in 1707. In North America, the British and French began to fight over the Ohio River valley. Great Britain wanted colonists to settle there. France wanted the land for its fur trade. Both countries sent troops to North America. The French and Indian War broke out. The French won early battles. However, the British captured Quebec in 1759. The Treaty of Paris ended the war. France gave up its land in North America.

★ **Which events in the 1600s and 1700s could be viewed as roots of rebellion?**

Road to Independence 1763–1776

The Big Idea

The French and Indian War left the British with a huge debt. The British government wanted the American colonies to pay a share of the debt. In addition, Great Britain wanted to avoid conflicts with Native Americans on the new frontier. They looked to the colonists to help them. As time went on, the colonists decided to declare their independence from Great Britain. In 1775, the first battles in the war for independence were fought.

Engraving of the
Boston Massacre

Resistance to British Taxes

King George issued the Proclamation of 1763. It said that colonists could not settle west of the Appalachian Mountains. Then, Parliament passed the Quartering Act in 1765. It forced colonists to feed and house British soldiers. Parliament also taxed the colonies. Colonists opposed these taxes. They cried, "No taxation without representation!" They refused to buy British goods. Parliament repealed the hated acts.

Growing Tensions

The problems between Great Britain and its colonies only grew worse. In 1767, new taxes were placed on common products. Again, the colonists resisted. In 1770, British soldiers in the colonies fired on protesters in Boston. This event became known as the Boston Massacre. People in Boston formed the Committee of Correspondence to keep people in the Massachusetts colony informed of British actions in Boston. Parliament then passed the Tea Act. In Boston, colonists dumped tea into the harbor. Parliament responded with the Intolerable Acts.

A Declaration of Independence

The First Continental Congress met in 1774. Delegates from 12 colonies wrote the British king a petition. The king did not listen. Neither side would compromise. Colonists began to arm for war. The Second Continental Congress met in May 1775. It sent another petition to King George, which he ignored. The Congress decided to declare independence from Great Britain. The Declaration of Independence was approved and signed on July 4, 1776.

Tea from the
Boston Tea
Party

★ **How did the colonists try to resolve their differences with Great Britain before they declared independence?**

The Revolutionary War 1776–1783

British crown

The Big Idea

The Revolutionary War lasted five years. People who supported the war were called Patriots. Americans who did not want independence from Great Britain were called Loyalists. Congress chose George Washington to command the Continental army. At first, the Patriots suffered defeats. The American victory at the Battle of Saratoga in New York brought French support into the war. In 1781, the Revolutionary War ended.

The Early Years of War

The Continental army faced a big challenge as the war began. They were fighting a world power. British soldiers were well trained. The British controlled the seas. The Patriots had the advantage of fighting on their own land. They also had excellent leaders. The British captured New York City in July 1776. Washington retreated to Pennsylvania. He led a surprise attack on December 25, 1776, and took Trenton and Princeton in New Jersey. These victories gave hope to both soldiers and citizens.

The War Expands

The British developed a plan to capture the Hudson River valley. British General William Howe's force was to march north from New York City. Instead he attacked Philadelphia, Pennsylvania. Washington's troops retreated to Valley Forge. There they suffered through a hard winter with little food. In the meantime, another force of Patriots won a battle at Saratoga, New York. The French recognized the new nation. France sent troops and supplies.

An Independent Nation

American and French forces trapped British forces in Yorktown, Virginia. The British surrendered. The victory at Yorktown ensured American independence. The Treaty of Paris was signed in 1783, and Great Britain recognized the United States as an independent nation. The United States now faced new challenges. Congress needed to build confidence in the new government. Still, the United States was a model for people everywhere seeking liberty.

★ **How did French support help the Americans win the Revolutionary War?**

George Washington crossing the Delaware

Forming a Government 1777–1791

The Big Idea

The Second Continental Congress created a plan for a national government in 1777. This plan was called the Articles of Confederation. However, the national government was too weak under the Articles. In 1787, the Philadelphia Constitutional Convention met. Months later, they had worked out a new plan of government. This plan is the United States Constitution.

Signing of the
U.S. Constitution

The First Government

Every state set up its own state government. All of the states' constitutions included a section, known as the bill of rights, that defined people's basic rights. The Second Constitutional Congress appointed a committee to develop a national government. This plan became the Articles of Confederation. It gave more power to the states than to the federal government. The national government had no president or king. There was no national court system. By 1781, all 13 states had ratified, or approved, the Articles of Confederation.

Problems in the New Nation

The new federal government could not solve problems in foreign policy. British troops remained in forts south of the Great Lakes. There was a border dispute with Spain. The Articles worked well, however, in deciding how to settle western lands. The Northwest Territory was established. Congress passed a plan for accepting new states. Money was the most difficult issue under the Articles. Congress could not pay its debts to foreign governments. In Massachusetts, the state placed such high taxes that a rebellion broke out. People began to question whether the Articles were strong enough to solve the problems the nation faced.

The U.S. Constitution and the Bill of Rights

A constitutional convention met in 1787. Delegates, called the Founding Fathers, created a good plan for government—the U.S. Constitution. The Constitution created a framework for the government. It included ideas about government from several sources. It called for a President and a national court system. Some states would not ratify the Constitution without a description of basic rights. The first ten amendments to the Constitution became the Bill of Rights.

Benjamin Franklin, the nation's first postmaster

 Why were the Bill of Rights so important to the colonists?

A Government for a New Nation
1789–1800

Abigail Adams,
wife of President
John Adams

The Big Idea

George Washington was elected the first President of the United States. He and Congress worked to define their jobs. They thought of ways to solve the nation's financial problems. Washington solved problems on the western frontier, too. John Adams was elected President in 1796. He faced problems both in foreign affairs and at home.

George Washington as President

Americans had never had a President before. They did not know how to address President Washington. They decided to use "Mr. President." The new country counted its citizens in the first census. Washington chose a group, or Cabinet, of advisors. Congress passed a law to organize the country's court system. To raise money, Congress decided to tax imported goods. Congress also created a national bank.

Early Challenges

Political parties started to form soon after the new government began its work. Members of the Federalist Party believed in a strong national government. They wanted the United States to become a great power with large cities. Alexander Hamilton led this group. Thomas Jefferson and James Madison led the Democratic-Republicans. They wanted stronger state governments. They saw the United States as a nation of small farms and villages. President Washington showed strong leadership when he sent troops to put down an uprising called the Whiskey Rebellion. He settled conflicts with Native Americans. He also avoided another war with Great Britain.

Washington traveling
to his inauguration

The Presidency of John Adams

In the election of 1796, candidates ran as party members. This system strengthened political parties in the country. John Adams faced problems as soon as he took office as the new U.S. President. France objected to the treaty the United States had signed with Great Britain. The two countries almost went to war over it. Federalists passed two acts that limited freedoms—the Sedition Act and the Alien Acts. Adams was not re-elected in 1800.

★ **What points of view did the first political parties represent?**

An Era of Expansion 1800–1815

The Big Idea
The election of 1800 brought Thomas Jefferson and the Democratic-Republicans into office. Jefferson believed in a weak central government. In 1803, Jefferson bought the vast Louisiana Territory from France. Problems with Great Britain led to the War of 1812. The war increased nationalism in the United States.

Jefferson as President
The election of 1800 produced a tie between Thomas Jefferson and Aaron Burr. The House of Representatives had to break the tie. Finally, Jefferson became President. The Twelfth Amendment kept this problem from happening again. Jefferson wanted the national government to be small. He decreased the size of the army and navy. His policies contrasted with John Marshall's. John Marshall was the Chief Justice of the Supreme Court. In the 1803 legal case called *Marbury* v. *Madison*, Chief Justice Marshall ruled that the Supreme Court decides if a law is constitutional.

British troops attacking Washington, D.C. in 1814

The Louisiana Purchase
Pirates from the Barbary States of North Africa kidnapped American citizens in 1803. The United States finally agreed to pay a ransom. British troops also took sailors from American ships. Congress stopped shipping trade with European countries. Perhaps Jefferson's most noteworthy act was the Louisiana Purchase. The United States suddenly doubled its size. The explorers Meriwether Lewis and William Clark headed an expedition to survey the new land. They returned with a great deal of information about its wonders.

The War of 1812
British forces continued to help Native Americans raid settlements in the Northwest Territory. They also continued to kidnap American sailors. Finally, the U.S. Congress declared war. The War of 1812 began. British troops burned Washington, D.C., in 1814. They also attacked Baltimore, Maryland. On this occasion, Francis Scott Key wrote "The Star-Spangled Banner." The war ended with no clear winner. Heroes such as Andrew Jackson emerged from the conflict.

★ **Why might people see the Louisiana Purchase as Jefferson's most important act?**

Sacagawea, a Shoshone guide on the Lewis and Clark expedition

The Nation Grows 1810–1842

Cartoon showing "King" Andrew Jackson

Cherokees being forced on the Trail of Tears

The Big Idea

Americans were proud of their nation's accomplishments. New tariffs and improved transportation led to more growth. The United States expanded its boundaries by purchasing Florida from Spain. The Monroe Doctrine strengthened the United States as a world power. Andrew Jackson changed the presidency while in office. He made democratic reforms, or changes. A belief in states' rights began to conflict with nationalism.

The Rise of Nationalism

The American System was a plan to make the United States self-sufficient. It had three main points—raise tariffs, or taxes, form a national bank, and improve roads. This period was known as the Era of Good Feelings. Only one political party was active. The Supreme Court kept enlarging the government's powers. The United States bought Florida from Spain. The Monroe Doctrine stated that European countries could not start or take over colonies in the Western Hemisphere.

Jacksonian Democracy

Andrew Jackson was elected President in 1828. He made many changes in American politics. He had unofficial advisors called the "kitchen cabinet." Jackson also helped develop the convention system of nominating candidates as well as increasing the power of the presidency. He vetoed a bill to recharter the national bank. He threatened to force states to obey national law. The economy weakened at the end of Jackson's presidency. It continued to suffer for the next five years.

U.S. Policies Toward Native Americans

Americans continued to move westward. Settlers asked the federal government to remove Native Americans from their land. President Monroe set up an Indian Territory. President Jackson ordered Native Americans to give up their land east of the Mississippi River. They would have to move to the Indian Territory. The Cherokees in Georgia did not want to move. Jackson sent soldiers to force them to leave. Cherokees called their 800-mile journey the Trail of Tears.

★ **How did Andrew Jackson change American politics?**

Life in the North and the South
1789–1860

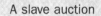

A slave auction

The Big Idea

The Industrial Revolution changed the way Americans manufactured goods. Interchangeable parts and better transportation sped up the manufacturing process. New inventions changed the process as well. Manufacturing was centered in the Northeast. In the South, cotton became the main crop. The increase in cotton farming led to a greater demand for slaves. Slave codes, or laws, were enforced in the South. Enslaved African Americans developed a distinct culture.

The Industrial Revolution

The Industrial Revolution in the United States began in 1789. A British mechanic built a cotton-spinning machine in a factory in Rhode Island. Soon, the number of factories in the Northeast skyrocketed. Eli Whitney's idea of interchangeable parts also changed manufacturing. New canals, roads, and railroads made it cheaper and faster to ship resources and finished goods.

Cotton Is King

Eli Whitney's other invention changed the course of American history. This invention was the cotton gin. It increased cotton production in the South. In a short time, cotton gins appeared all across the South. Planters throughout the South grew cotton as a cash crop. The South's economy depended on the millions of bales of cotton produced yearly. Farms of all sizes produced cotton.

The Slave System

Slavery was a major part of the social and economic system in the South. Slave codes protected the interests of slave owners. They denied slaves basic freedoms. Most slaves worked from dawn to dusk, and were not paid for their labor. Enslaved African Americans developed strong family ties. Their distinct culture combined both African and American traditions. Some slaves tried to escape to freedom. Some joined slave rebellions, but these rebellions were always put down.

 How did Eli Whitney help the economies of both the North and the South?

Cotton gin

The Spirit of Change 1800–1850

Frederick Douglass

New York City
in the 1800s

The Big Idea

As the 1800s unfolded, a uniquely American culture was emerging. In part, this was due to the growth of cities. Immigrants fueled this growth. Free public education became available to more people. American writing and art stressed the individual and nature. Americans also made advances in the sciences. They were caught up by the spirit of reform. They believed that individuals could improve society. Ending slavery and getting rights for women were two movements for reform.

Cities and a Growing Population

People moved to cities to be near factories. Cities were exciting places in which to live and work. Cities had problems, too, such as dirty conditions and disease. Many immigrants settled in cities in the Northeast. They lived in their own neighborhoods. Some Americans resented the many new immigrants coming into the country. Cities also became centers of culture. They began to offer free public education to all. Many colleges were founded at this time.

New Ideas Take Shape

American writers began to publish more of their works in the 1830s. Some writers encouraged individualism. Other writings reflected American life. American art and music developed at this time, as well. Thinkers such as John Audubon and Louis Agassiz made contributions to scientific knowledge.

Reforming Society

The spirit of reform took root with the Second Great Awakening. Preachers urged people to live according to God's laws. They wanted people to try to improve society. Americans responded. They worked for better treatment of the mentally ill. Some tried to improve conditions in prisons. Some worked to help people with hearing or vision impairments. Communes and the temperance movement attracted others. One of the most important efforts was the antislavery movement. The fight for equal rights for women grew out of the struggle to end slavery.

★ **How was the antislavery movement related to the Second Great Awakening?**

Westward Expansion 1821–1853

The Big Idea

Americans' drive westward continued through the mid-1800s. Settlers moved to Texas while it was part of Mexico. They won its independence and then asked for Texas to be part of the United States. War broke out with Mexico over Texas's boundaries. After the war, the United States claimed the land that is now the Southwest and California. The United States negotiated with Great Britain to gain part of the Oregon Territory. A religious group called the Mormons began to settle in present-day Utah.

The journey west in covered wagons

Texas Wins Independence

Stephen Austin led a group of American settlers to Texas in 1821. They soon came into conflict with Mexican leaders. In 1836, Texans declared independence. At the Alamo, Mexican troops killed the Texan soldiers. However, Texans won independence at the Battle of San Jacinto. Texans wanted to join the United States. In 1845, the U.S. Congress gave Texas statehood.

War With Mexico and the Movement West

War broke out with Mexico in 1846. American forces defeated Mexican troops. Mexico gave up Texas and the Mexican Cession for a payment of $15 million from the United States. Once again the United States gained a huge territory. In 1846, the United States and Great Britain agreed to split the Oregon Territory. Shortly after, Mormons began moving to present-day Utah. They were seeking freedom to follow their religion.

Settlement in California

The Spaniards set up settlements called missions in California. They hoped to introduce Christianity and a new way of life to the Native Americans there. The missions were abandoned after Spanish rule ended in 1821. Gold was discovered in California in 1848. By 1853, almost 250,000 people lived in California. Most of them were looking for gold. Towns sprang up and were abandoned when the gold ran out. California became the thirty-first state in 1850.

★ **What territories were added to the United States during this period of westward expansion?**

Advertisement encouraging Americans to move to Texas

A House Divided

"... General Sumner had a fight with the rebels this morning. He drove them towards the river, and then our gunboats opened on them, and they cut the rebels all to pieces. They ran and left everything behind them."

—from a letter by Christian Geisel, a Union soldier, in 1862

LINK PAST AND PRESENT Many people today re-enact historical events. In this photograph, people recreate a battle as it was fought in the Civil War.

★ What do the quotation and the photograph tell about how the Civil War was fought?

377

CHAPTER 16

The Road to War 1820–1861

I. **The Question of Slavery in the West**
II. **Deepening Divisions Over Slavery**
III. **Challenges to Slavery**
IV. **Breaking Away From the Union**

*S*olomon Northup worked on a cotton plantation in Louisiana. He described a typical day:

> " An hour before day light the horn is blown . . . the fears and labors of another day begin; and until its close there is no such thing as rest . . . "

By 1820, there were 1,530,000 people who, like Solomon Northup, were enslaved. The plantations they worked on were mainly in the South. Most plantation owners saw nothing wrong with forcing people to work without pay. Other Americans disagreed. They asked themselves the following questions: Wasn't our nation founded on the principles of freedom and liberty? How, then, can slavery be allowed? More and more, people would argue about whether slavery should continue.

Identification badges

U.S. Events	1815			1825		1835
Presidential Term Begins		1817 James Monroe		1825 John Quincy Adams	1829 Andrew Jackson	
World Events	1815			1825		1835

1820
Missouri Compromise is proposed.
Harriet Tubman is born about this year.

1836
Texas declares its independence.

1821
Peru, Mexico, and Guatemala win independence from Spain.

1825
First public railroad operates in England.

1833
Slavery is outlawed in British colonies.

VIEW HISTORY This painting by Eastman Johnson is called *A Ride for Liberty—The Fugitive Slaves*. In Charleston, South Carolina, African Americans were forced to wear badges (left).

★ What can you infer from these badges about the effect of the slave system on the lives of African Americans?

Get Organized

CAUSE-AND-EFFECT CHAIN

Recognizing the causes and effects of events helps you to understand history. Use a cause-and-effect chain as you read this chapter. List each important event in the box. In the ovals, fill in a cause and an effect. Here is an example from this chapter.

CAUSE
Missouri applies for statehood.

EVENT
The Missouri Compromise is passed.

EFFECT
Tension increases between North and South.

1852
Harriet Beecher Stowe's novel, *Uncle Tom's Cabin*, is published.

1854
Republican Party is formed.

1860
South Carolina leaves the Union.

1845
Texas becomes a state.

1850
Compromise of 1850 is passed.

1858
Lincoln-Douglas debates occur.

1861
Civil War begins.

1845

1855

1865

1837 Martin Van Buren | 1841 William Harrison 1841 John Tyler | 1845 James Polk | 1849 Zachary Taylor 1850 Millard Fillmore | 1853 Franklin Pierce | 1857 James Buchanan | 1861 Abraham Lincoln

1845

1855

1865

1848
Slavery ends in French West Indies colonies.

1854
Last of the slaves in Venezuela are freed.

1861
Serfs in Russia are freed.

I The Question of Slavery in the West

Terms to Know

popular sovereignty control by the people

fugitive a person who has run away

secede to withdraw from or leave

Main Ideas

A. Congress approved the Missouri Compromise to keep a balance of power between free and slaveholding states.

B. The debate over slavery centered on new territories and states in the West.

C. The Compromise of 1850 was another attempt to satisfy both the North and the South.

Active Reading

PREDICT
When you predict, you use what you know to guess what might happen next. As you read this section, use the facts provided in order to predict how the issue of slavery would be settled in the new territories.

A. Slavery in an Expanding Nation

In the early 1800s, thousands of people moved to territories in the West. The question arose: When these territories join the Union—the United States—should they be slaveholding or free states? Differences of opinion between the North and the South would divide the country. Congress would have to decide.

An illustration for an anti-slavery publication

Balance in the Senate

Many settlers from the South were slaveholders. They believed that the territories in the West should be admitted to the Union as slave states. Many people from the North wanted those territories to join as free states. They wanted slavery to be banned.

In 1819, there were 11 free states and 11 slaveholding states in the United States. Each state was represented by two senators. The power in the Senate between the North and the South, therefore, was evenly balanced. When Missouri asked to join the Union as a slaveholding state, this balance was threatened. Missouri's admission to the Union would give the South more power in the Senate.

The Missouri Compromise

Leaders in Congress argued about Missouri's statehood for months. In 1820, Henry Clay from Kentucky, the Speaker of the House of Representatives, proposed a plan. It had the following three main points:

1. Missouri would join the Union as a slave-holding state. That would please the South.
2. Maine, which had also applied for statehood, would be admitted as a free state. That would please the North.
3. An imaginary line at latitude 36°30' would be drawn across the territory gained in the Louisiana Purchase. South of the line, slavery was permitted. North of the line, slavery was banned—except in Missouri.

Congress approved the plan called the Missouri Compromise. It was enacted in 1821. The plan kept the balance of power between the North and the South even in the Senate, as shown in the chart. For the time being, the question of slavery seemed settled.

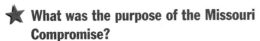 **What was the purpose of the Missouri Compromise?**

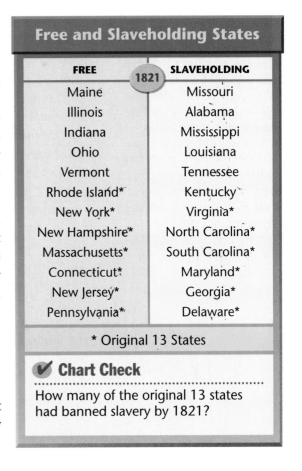

Free and Slaveholding States

FREE	1821	SLAVEHOLDING
Maine		Missouri
Illinois		Alabama
Indiana		Mississippi
Ohio		Louisiana
Vermont		Tennessee
Rhode Island*		Kentucky
New York*		Virginia*
New Hampshire*		North Carolina*
Massachusetts*		South Carolina*
Connecticut*		Maryland*
New Jersey*		Georgia*
Pennsylvania*		Delaware*

* Original 13 States

✔ **Chart Check**

How many of the original 13 states had banned slavery by 1821?

B. More Lands, More Questions

The Missouri Compromise applied only to land that had been part of the Louisiana Purchase. The slavery debate was still to be settled in other territories.

Texas, California, and New Mexico

Texas applied for statehood after gaining its independence from Mexico in 1836. At the time, slavery was permitted in Texas. In 1845, after years of debate in Congress, Texas was admitted into the United States as a slaveholding state.

The issue of slavery remained a question in the land that was won from Mexico, including California and New Mexico. Great debates arose in Congress. In 1846, Representative David Wilmot of Pennsylvania called for a law that banned slavery in these lands. This bill, which never passed, was called the Wilmot Proviso.

In the Senate, John C. Calhoun of South Carolina believed, as did many Southerners, that government did not have the authority to ban slavery. He said that enslaved people were "property" that owners could take anywhere.

Other lawmakers, including Senator Stephen Douglas from Illinois, were more middle-of-the-road. They favored the idea of **popular sovereignty**, or letting the people of a territory decide. The people in a new territory could vote to settle the issue of slavery. The right to vote, however, was not extended to enslaved people.

Do You Remember?

In Chapter 15, you learned that the United States declared war on Mexico in 1846. After Mexico lost the war, it had to give up much of its land to the United States.

Then & Now

Third parties continue to play an important role in national politics. In the 2000 presidential election, the two leading candidates were Democrat Albert Gore Jr. and Republican George W. Bush. A third candidate, Ralph Nader of the Green Party, appealed to voters who were not satisfied with either major party. The Green Party stood for strong environmental protections and other reforms.

The Free-Soil Party

As the nation continued to debate the issue of slavery, sectionalism grew. Some Americans were more loyal to the North or to the South than they were to the entire country.

The leaders of the two major political parties—the Democrats and the Whigs—did not take a strong stand against slavery in the new territories. They did not want to lose the support of the South. This angered many voters. In 1848, some antislavery members of both parties formed the Free-Soil Party.

Free-Soilers, mainly Northerners, believed in the right of all citizens to control their own labor. They feared that slaves would take the place of paid workers, causing "free labor" to disappear. The party's motto was Free-Soil, Free Speech, Free Labor, Free Men. Its goal was to ban slavery in the new territories. Included in the party were abolitionists, who believed African Americans had a right to freedom.

In the presidential election of 1848, Zachary Taylor, a hero of the war in Mexico, was the Whig candidate. Lewis Cass, a senator from Michigan, was nominated by the Democrats. The Free-Soilers chose former President Martin Van Buren.

Zachary Taylor won the election by appealing to voters in both slaveholding states and free states. Although Taylor won, the Free-Soil Party received 10 percent of the popular vote and gained a number of seats in Congress. Slavery had become a major national issue.

★ **Why did some Whigs and Democrats form a new political party?**

ANALYZE PRIMARY SOURCES

DOCUMENT-BASED QUESTION What does this political cartoon depict about Free-Soilers' attitudes toward slavery?

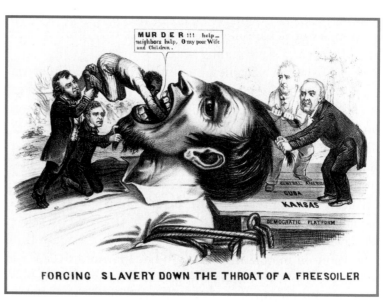

FORCING SLAVERY DOWN THE THROAT OF A FREESOILER

This political cartoon was published in the New York City newspaper *Harper's Weekly* in 1856.

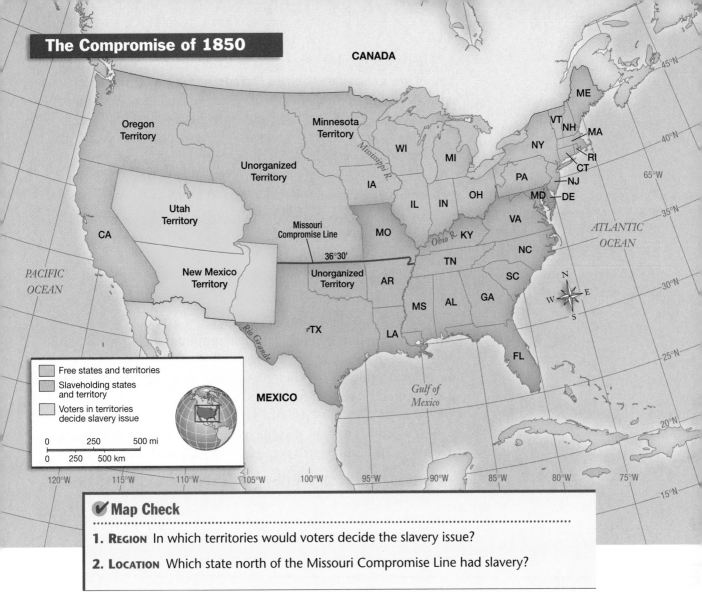

The Compromise of 1850

CANADA

Map legend:
- Free states and territories
- Slaveholding states and territory
- Voters in territories decide slavery issue

0   250   500 mi
0   250   500 km

✔ **Map Check**

1. **REGION** In which territories would voters decide the slavery issue?

2. **LOCATION** Which state north of the Missouri Compromise Line had slavery?

C. The Compromise of 1850

By 1849, there were 15 free states and 15 slaveholding states. When California asked to join the Union, the balance of power became a concern once again.

Clay, Calhoun, and Webster Debate

Henry Clay once more laid out a plan to satisfy both sides. In this plan, California would be admitted as a free state. Also, the slave trade would end in Washington, D.C. To please the South, Clay proposed a law that would help capture slaves who were **fugitives**, or runaways, who escaped to the North. The new law would force people in free states to help recapture escaped slaves. Finally, Clay proposed that popular sovereignty would decide the issue of slavery in the territories of Utah and New Mexico.

The plan was debated for eight months. Senator John C. Calhoun, too ill to address the Senate, asked another senator to read his speech. Calhoun warned that if southern interests were not respected, the South would **secede**, or withdraw, from the Union.

Senator Daniel Webster of Massachusetts defended Clay's plan. He wanted, above all, to keep the Union together. He said,

 I wish to speak today not as a Massachusetts man, nor as a northern man, but as an American. . . . I speak for the preservation of the Union. . . . There can be no such thing as a peaceable secession. Peaceable secession is an utter impossibility. **"**

ANALYZE PRIMARY SOURCES

DOCUMENT-BASED QUESTION
What do you think Webster's opinion of sectionalism would be?

Compromise Is Reached

Finally, Senator Stephen Douglas proposed a plan to unify the North and the South. His idea was to divide Clay's plan into a series of bills. Members of Congress could vote for the bills they approved and not vote for the bills they opposed. The new laws, known as the Compromise of 1850, were passed by Congress.

Many people thought that the compromise would settle the issue of slavery. It did prevent a war—but for only ten years.

★ **Why did Senator Henry Clay propose the Compromise of 1850?**

I Review

Review History
A. How did the Missouri Compromise keep the balance of power in the Senate?
B. Why were the debates in Congress centered on territories in the West?
C. How did the Compromise of 1850 satisfy the North and the South?

Define Terms to Know
Provide a definition for each of the following terms.
popular sovereignty, fugitive, secede

Critical Thinking
Why did tension between the North and the South increase despite compromises?

Write About History
Write an editorial about the debate in Congress leading to the Compromise of 1850. Use a northern or southern point of view.

Get Organized
CAUSE-AND-EFFECT CHAIN
Think about the main events in this section. Use your cause-and-effect chain to link these events together. For example, what were some causes and effects of the Compromise of 1850?

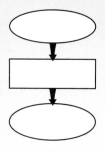

Build Your Skills

CLASSIFY INFORMATION

People often waste time looking for items. Classifying can save time and help people to remember where objects belong. Imagine trying to find a CD in a music store if the CDs were not classified by type of music and musical group. Think about how helpful it is to know exactly where to find the CD you want. Classifying means organizing items into categories that make sense.

When you read about history, you can classify information to help you find, examine, and remember it. It is helpful to classify information when you are reading, when you are studying for a test, or when you are preparing to write a paper. For example, you might choose to classify historical information by person, place, event, idea, or date.

Here's How

Follow these steps in order to classify historical information.

1. Identify the information that you want to classify.

2. Decide on the categories you will use to classify your information.

3. Make a chart of the information.

Here's Why

You have just read about the question of slavery in the West. Suppose you had to write an essay about the people who played important roles in the debate over slavery. Classifying would help you to organize the information and to write the essay.

Practice the Skill

Copy the chart on a sheet of paper. Read Section I again, and add names from it to Column 1. Fill in the second and third columns.

Extend the Skill

Write a brief essay about the leaders and their contributions that are listed in your chart.

Apply the Skill

As you read the remaining sections of this chapter, think of ways in which you can classify information. For example, as you read Section II, you might make a chart that contains the following categories: Issue or Event, Northern View, and Southern View. Use your chart as a study tool.

LEADER	STATE	CONTRIBUTION OR IDEA
Henry Clay	Kentucky	Missouri Compromise; Compromise of 1850
David Wilmot		
John C. Calhoun		

II Deepening Divisions Over Slavery

Terms to Know

extremist a person whose opinions are very different from those of most people

civil war a war between people of the same country

Main Ideas

A. The Fugitive Slave Law hardened northern attitudes against slavery.

B. The practice of popular sovereignty caused violence in Kansas.

C. The Dred Scott decision legalized slavery in the western territories.

Active Reading

CONTRAST POINTS OF VIEW
When you contrast points of view on an issue, you look at differences of opinion. As you read this section, contrast points of view on the Fugitive Slave Law and the Dred Scott case.

A. Changing Ideas in the North

Slavery no longer existed in the North. Therefore, many Northerners did not take a side in the slavery debate. Only a small number of people in the North were abolitionists. They continued to help enslaved people escape to freedom by using the Underground Railroad. Attitudes changed after the Compromise of 1850, when many Northerners realized that they must take one side or the other.

The Fugitive Slave Law

One part of the Compromise of 1850 was the Fugitive Slave Law. The law required Northerners to help capture escaped slaves and return them to slaveholders in the South. People who broke the law could receive a six-month jail term and a $1,000 fine.

Before the Fugitive Slave Law went into effect, an enslaved person might escape to freedom along the Underground Railroad to free states. Now, there would be no escaping to safety anywhere in the United States. Even free African Americans might be rounded up in error and sent to slaveholders. If captured, African Americans were not even allowed to tell their story to a jury.

Many Northerners were upset about the law. It forced them to be part of the slave system even though they did not support it. In response, riots broke out in several northern cities.

This advertisement offers a reward for the return of a fugitive slave.

$100 REWARD

Ran away from the subscriber, living near the Anacostia Bridge, on or about the 17th November, negro girl ELIZA. She calls herself Eliza Coursy. She is of the ordinary size, from 18 to 20 years old, of a chestnut or copper color. Eliza has some scars about her face, has been hired in Washington, and has acquaintances in Georgetown.

I will give fifty dollars if taken in the District or Maryland, and one hundred dollars if taken in any free State; but in either case she must be secured in jail so that I get her again.

JOHN. P. WARING.

Nov. 28, 1857.

Uncle Tom's Cabin

By 1852, it was impossible for Northerners to avoid the discussion of slavery. In that year, Harriet Beecher Stowe's novel *Uncle Tom's Cabin* was published. Stowe's book told the story of an enslaved African American named Uncle Tom who is at the mercy of the brutal slaveholder Simon Legree. This story reached millions of people, not only in book form, but also in stage presentations. *Uncle Tom's Cabin* helped people in many parts of the world understand that slavery was a human problem.

When *Uncle Tom's Cabin* appeared in 1852, it was a bestseller—with more than 300,000 copies sold in its first year. Many white Southerners complained that *Uncle Tom's Cabin* did not present a fair or accurate picture of the lives of enslaved African Americans. They argued that Stowe had seen little of slavery firsthand. They claimed that *Uncle Tom's Cabin* was filled with insults and lies. However, the book made many Americans ask if it was right for one human being to own another human being.

★ **Why did some Northerners oppose the Fugitive Slave Law?**

They Made History

Harriet Tubman 1820–1913

Harriet Tubman was born into slavery in Maryland about 1820. When she was almost 30 years old, she feared that she might be sold away from her family, so she escaped to the North. There, Tubman joined the Underground Railroad's secret network of abolitionists who helped runaway slaves. Between 1850 and 1860, Tubman made 19 dangerous journeys to rescue family members and others. She led more than 300 enslaved African Americans to freedom in the United States and Canada. In fact, Tubman was so successful that southern slave catchers offered a reward of $40,000 for her capture!

Harriet Tubman

Black Heritage USA 13c

The photograph (above) shows Harriet Tubman, far left, with some of the people she helped escape. The stamp (left) of Harriet Tubman was issued in 1995.

Critical Thinking Why was Harriet Tubman so determined to help slaves escape to freedom?

ANALYZE PRIMARY SOURCES

DOCUMENT-BASED QUESTION Why would people from Missouri come to Kansas to try to vote?

B. Kansas Becomes a Battleground

The Fugitive Slave Law and *Uncle Tom's Cabin* increased Northerners' opposition to slavery. Then, after the passage of the Kansas-Nebraska Act, the growing divide between Northerners and Southerners erupted into violence.

The Kansas-Nebraska Act

Senator Stephen Douglas of Illinois wanted to encourage people to settle in the West. In 1854, he sponsored the Kansas-Nebraska Act, which created the new territories of Kansas and Nebraska. In these territories, popular sovereignty would be used to determine the issue of slavery. The settlers would vote whether to allow slavery.

Both territories were north of latitude 36°30'. According to the Missouri Compromise, slavery was banned in territories north of this line. The Kansas-Nebraska Act would cancel the Missouri Compromise. Some Northerners felt betrayed by Douglas, a senator from a northern state.

Bleeding Kansas

Nebraska lay just west of Iowa, a free state. Kansas, which was farther south, bordered slaveholding Missouri. Because it was so close to other slaveholding states, Kansas soon became a battleground over the issue of slavery. The settlers' votes would decide whether Kansas would be a slaveholding territory or a free territory. Proslavery and antislavery settlers rushed to the area. Each side was determined to have the majority.

Just before the vote in 1855, thousands of proslavery Missouri residents, called "border ruffians," rode across the border into Kansas. These people were **extremists**, or people who held opinions not agreed on by the vast majority of people. A witness described the scene:

> 66 . . . before the polls were opened, some 300 to 400 Missourians and others were collected in the yard . . . where the election would be held, armed with bowie-knives, revolvers, and clubs. They said they came to vote and whip the [Northerners]. . . . Some said they came to fight. 99

The border ruffians voted illegally and helped to elect a proslavery government. In response, the antislavery settlers set up their own government. Kansas now had two different governments claiming authority. It became a territory in turmoil.

In May 1856, a group of border ruffians attacked Lawrence, Kansas, a town of many antislavery settlers. The border ruffians destroyed homes, businesses, and printing presses. The ruffians expected the people of Lawrence to fight back immediately, but they did not.

Three days later, however, a group of men—led by the abolitionist John Brown—dragged five proslavery men and boys from their homes and killed them. Proslavery forces struck back with more killings.

By late 1856, many people had died in the fighting in Kansas. This violence won the territory the grim nickname Bleeding Kansas. Some Americans called the fighting a **civil war**, or a war between people of the same country.

★ **Why was there so much violence in Kansas?**

C. Attention Turns to the Capital

Soon after the fighting erupted in Kansas, many Americans turned their attention to Washington, D.C. There, the Supreme Court was hearing a case involving the freedom of Dred Scott.

The Dred Scott Case

In the 1830s, Dred Scott, an enslaved African American, was taken by his slaveholder from Missouri, a slaveholding state, to the free state of Illinois and then to the free territory of Wisconsin. In 1846, Scott and his wife, Harriet, sued for their freedom. He argued that once having lived in free areas, they were no longer slaves.

Dred and Harriet Scott sued for their freedom. The case eventually went to the Supreme Court.

Roger Taney wrote the Supreme Court decision that created further tension between slave-holding and free states.

In 1856, the nine justices of the U.S. Supreme Court heard the case. On March 6, 1857, Chief Justice Roger B. Taney announced the decision of the Court. The main parts of the decision were as follows:

1. Scott could not file a lawsuit because African Americans were not citizens.
2. The Constitution protects a citizen's right to own property. Slaves, considered property, could be taken anywhere by owners.
3. The U.S. Congress had no right to outlaw slavery in a territory. Therefore, the Missouri Compromise was unconstitutional.

Effects of the Dred Scott Case

The Dred Scott decision pleased many southern slaveholders. It meant that slavery was legal in all the territories. The decision gave white Southerners a right they had been demanding for years.

In the North, African Americans held meetings to criticize the ruling. White Northerners were also angered by the decision. Many of them had hoped that slavery would die out if it was not permitted in the territories. Now, slavery seemed likely to spread westward as the nation expanded.

 What were three parts of the Supreme Court's decision in the Dred Scott case?

II Review

Review History

A. Why did northern attitudes toward slavery change after the passage of the Fugitive Slave Law?

B. How did popular sovereignty lead to violence in Kansas?

C. How did the Dred Scott case answer the question of slavery in the West?

Define Terms to Know

Provide a definition for each of the following terms.
extremist, civil war

Critical Thinking

How do you think John Brown might have reacted to the Dred Scott decision?

Write About History

Write a paragraph about the Dred Scott decision in which you contrast two points of view.

Get Organized

CAUSE-AND-EFFECT CHAIN
Use your cause-and-effect chain to link the events of this section together. For example, what was one cause of changing attitudes toward slavery in the North? What was one effect?

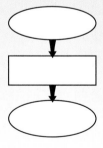

Points of View

Harriet Beecher Stowe and *Uncle Tom's Cabin*

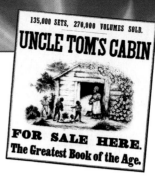

Advertisement for *Uncle Tom's Cabin*

Harriet Beecher Stowe (1811–1896) was the daughter of Lyman Beecher, a well-known Congregational minister and educator. In 1836, Harriet married Calvin Stowe. They had seven children.

Throughout much of her life, Stowe fought against slavery. In the 1830s and 1840s, the Stowe family helped slaves escape to freedom on the Underground Railroad. Stowe also taught formerly enslaved African American children in her family's school.

Stowe wrote a novel about the evils of slavery called *Uncle Tom's Cabin*. The book was published in 1852. The following passages are from book reviews of *Uncle Tom's Cabin*.

> ❝ . . . *Uncle Tom's Cabin* is an antislavery novel. It is a caricature [exaggeration] of slavery. It selects for description the most odious [distasteful] features of slavery–the escape and pursuit of fugitive slaves, the sale and separation of domestic slaves, the separation of husbands and wives, parents and children, brothers and sisters. It portrays the slaves of the story as more moral, intelligent, courageous, elegant and beautiful than their masters and mistresses. . . . ❞
>
> —From *Southern Press Review,* 1852

> ❝ . . . *Uncle Tom's Cabin* . . . is stamped on every page with genius. . . . It proves that . . . Mrs. Stowe has the high ability of looking on both sides of one question. With feelings and principles equally opposed to slavery . . . she is yet able to paint the slaveholder. . . . with no touch of bigotry [prejudice]. . . . No southerner need be ashamed of the noble, kind and generous St. Clare [a slaveholder in the novel] or the angel-child, his daughter. ❞
>
> —From *Boston Morning Post,* 1852

ANALYZE PRIMARY SOURCES

DOCUMENT-BASED QUESTIONS

1. What is the point of view of the writer from the *Southern Press Review*?

2. What is the point of view of the writer from the *Boston Morning Post*?

3. **Critical Thinking** Examine how each review describes the characters in the novel who support slavery. What similarities and differences did you find between these two reviews?

III Challenges to Slavery

Main Ideas

A. The Republican Party was formed to block slavery's expansion in the West.

B. The debate over slavery sometimes erupted into violence.

C. The issue of slavery affected both Democrats and Republicans as they prepared for the 1860 election.

 Active Reading

PROBLEM SOLVING
Efforts were made to find solutions to the country's problems before the Civil War erupted. As you read this section, identify problems between the North and the South. Then, identify solutions that were suggested to deal with those problems.

A. Founding a New Political Party

The issue of slavery continued to divide the two major political parties—the Democrats and the Whigs—in the early 1850s. Eventually, the Whig Party would disappear, destroyed by disagreements over slavery. A new party, the Republicans, would emerge.

Organizing the Republican Party

With the repeal of the Missouri Compromise, antislavery forces from the Democrats and the Whigs joined with Free-Soilers to form the Republican Party. Overall, the Republicans wanted to stop the expansion of slavery in new territories of the West. However, the party also included abolitionists who wanted to **emancipate**, or free, enslaved people throughout the country. Many Republicans wanted to give western lands to settlers free of charge. Many favored improvements such as railroads to help the economy grow.

The Republican Party was formed in 1854. In elections that year, party candidates won many seats in Congress, as well as several governorships in northern states.

The Election of 1856

The Republican Party participated in a presidential election for the first time in 1856. The party's nominee for President was John C. Fremont. The Republicans clearly opposed the expansion of slavery into any territory. The Democrats nominated James Buchanan.

Do You Remember?
In Chapter 14, you learned that the antislavery movement differed from the abolition movement. Abolitionists wanted an immediate end to slavery. Antislavery supporters took a more cautious approach. They wanted to work to end slavery slowly.

Although Fremont's name did not appear on ballots in any slave states, he carried the electoral votes in 11 free states. If he had won just one more state, Republicans would have won the election.

Southern Democrats realized how important they were to their party. Many wanted to ask the national party to support slavery in the next election. Northern Democrats realized that their party could not win in the North if it supported slavery.

★ Who came together to form the Republican Party?

B. The Debate Over Slavery

By the 1850s, slavery was the main political issue in the country. Emotions intensified on both sides. A civil war between the North and the South was brewing, and there was no turning back.

The Sumner-Brooks Affair

In the Congress, feelings on both sides of the slavery issue ran high. In May 1856, violence broke out in the Senate following a speech by Charles Sumner of Massachusetts. In his speech the anti-slavery senator harshly criticized proslavery senators, especially Andrew Butler of South Carolina. Three days later, Representative Preston Brooks, a relative of Senator Butler, entered the Senate and struck Senator Sumner on the head with a gold-topped cane. Brooks continued beating Sumner until he was unconscious and bleeding.

Almost immediately, Sumner and Brooks became heroes in their regions. Brooks resigned from the House, was immediately re-elected, and died soon after. Sumner, however, recovered slowly from the attack and eventually returned to the Senate.

Violence over the slavery issue broke out in the U.S. Congress. Here, Representative Brooks attacks Senator Sumner.

Abraham Lincoln and Stephen Douglas raced head to head in the 1858 Illinois Senate election. They would meet again in 1860 to battle for the White House.

The Lincoln-Douglas Debates

Stephen A. Douglas, a Democrat, wanted to run for President in 1860. First, he had to be re-elected to represent Illinois in the Senate. The Republicans chose Abraham Lincoln to run against Douglas in the Senate race. Lincoln was not as well known as Douglas.

Lincoln challenged Douglas to a series of public debates in different Illinois locations from August through October 1858. The debates gave voters a chance to compare the candidates' views on slavery in the territories.

During the debates, Lincoln spoke forcefully against permitting slavery in the territories. He said that the United States could not survive "half slave and half free." Douglas supported popular sovereignty, which was the right of territories to vote to allow or ban slavery within their borders. Neither man liked slavery, but they saw different ways of dealing with the issue.

The Republican Party opposed Douglas's position, but so did southern Democrats. Still, Douglas won the election and kept his Senate seat. On the other hand, Lincoln lost the election but gained a national reputation. Some Republicans began to think of this plain-speaking man as a possible presidential candidate.

John Brown at Harpers Ferry

After killing proslavery men in Kansas in 1856, John Brown left the territory. In 1859, he appeared in Virginia. Brown led a group of 18 to 21 followers, both African American and white, on a raid of the federal arsenal in Harpers Ferry. Weapons and ammunition were stored at the arsenal. Brown's plan was to give the weapons to enslaved African Americans to start a slave rebellion.

U.S. Marines led by Robert E. Lee surrounded Harpers Ferry. Ten of Brown's followers were killed, and Brown was captured. He and six other survivors were tried for treason and hanged. Treason is acting against your own country.

A hostage taken by Brown's group during the raid later wrote,

“ During the day and night I talked much with John Brown, and found him as brave as a man could be, and sensible upon all subjects except slavery. Upon that question he was a religious fanatic, and believed it was his duty to free the slaves, even if in doing so he lost his own life. ”

ANALYZE PRIMARY SOURCES
DOCUMENT-BASED QUESTION
Did Brown's actions match this description of him? Why or why not?

Brown's raid symbolized Southerners' deepest fears—that this rebellion would lead to other slave **insurrections**, or uprisings. Southerners believed that northern abolitionists supported slave uprisings. This suspicion was confirmed when documents found at Harpers Ferry showed that Brown had received money from several wealthy Northerners.

⭐ **How did the Lincoln-Douglas debates help Lincoln?**

C. Choosing a Presidential Candidate

The Democratic Party was divided over the issue of slavery. This division weakened the party. In the coming election, Democrats would face not only a challenge from the Republican Party, but also internal challenges within their own party. The political parties prepared for a tough battle for the presidency.

The Democrats Divide

The Democratic Party met in Charleston, South Carolina, to select a presidential candidate for the election in 1860. The southern and northern Democrats were split over the issue of slavery. William L. Yancey, a delegate from Alabama, asked the party to support slavery in the territories. Stephen Douglas knew he could not win the presidential election in the North if his party supported the expansion of slavery. He used his influence to defeat Yancey's proposal, which was known as the Alabama Platform. As a result, Yancey and other southern delegates left the convention.

After the Southerners walked out, the remaining Democrats voted to hold another convention in six weeks in Baltimore, Maryland. There, Northern Democrats nominated Douglas for President. Douglas and his supporters believed in popular sovereignty for deciding the issue of slavery in the territories.

Southern Democrats held their own conventions in Richmond, Virginia, and in Baltimore. They nominated John C. Breckinridge of Kentucky for President. Breckinridge and his followers supported the Dred Scott decision. They believed slaveholders should be allowed to take their slaves into any territory.

On October 18, 1859, John Brown (kneeling, at right) and his men were trapped by U.S. Marine fire at Harpers Ferry.

Republicans Nominate Lincoln

The Republican delegates met in Chicago, Illinois, to nominate their presidential candidate. They knew that the split in the Democratic Party helped their chances for victory in the 1860 election. Four Republican candidates were nominated. One of them was Abraham Lincoln of Illinois. The other three candidates were better known nationally than Lincoln. However, Lincoln's supporters promised to give them jobs in his Cabinet if Lincoln was elected.

Senator William H. Seward was the leading candidate. He had become well known for his antislavery position and his talk about a conflict between the North and the South. Lincoln seemed more moderate in his views. Although he disliked slavery and promised to fight its spread, he had assured Southerners that he would not interfere with slavery in the South. Therefore, the Republican convention chose Lincoln because he seemed to be a safer choice than Seward.

To many white Southerners, however, Lincoln was a "black Republican" who wanted to end their way of life. Southerners threatened to secede if the Republicans won the election. To prevent secession, a third party formed. Known as the Constitutional-Union Party, it nominated John Bell of Tennessee. This party of southern Whigs and others tried to ignore the issue of slavery. It hoped to prevent a Republican majority in the electoral college.

 Over what issue did the Democratic Party break apart in 1860?

III Review

Review History
A. Why was the Republican Party formed?
B. How did John Brown contribute to the violence that preceded the Civil War?
C. Who were the main candidates for President in 1860?

Define Terms to Know
Provide a definition for each of the following terms.
emancipate, insurrection

Critical Thinking
Why would the division of the Democratic Party help the Republican Party?

Write About Government
Write a speech as a delegate to the first Democratic convention in 1860. Your goal is to convince the party that it is necessary to remain united in order to defeat the Republicans.

Get Organized
CAUSE-AND-EFFECT CHAIN
You can use your cause-and-effect chain to see how one event in this section led to another. For example, what was a cause and an effect of the Lincoln-Douglas debates?

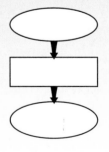

IV ★ Breaking Away From the Union

Terms to Know

Confederacy the Confederate States of America, formed in 1861 by southern states that had seceded from the Union

line item veto a veto of a portion but not all of a proposed law

provisional temporary

Main Ideas

A. Some southern states seceded from the Union when Abraham Lincoln won the presidency.

B. Southern states that seceded formed the Confederate States of America.

C. Efforts to bring the seceded states back into the Union failed.

📖 Active Reading

SEQUENCE OF EVENTS Many events led to the Civil War. Understanding the order in which these events occurred will help you to make sense of this period. As you read this section, pay attention to the events that led to the battle at Fort Sumter.

★★★★★★★
Meet
the President
★★★★★★★★★★★★★★★

Abraham Lincoln
1809–1865

Years in office 1861–1865

Political Party Republican

Birthplace Kentucky

Occupations Surveyor, Postmaster, Lawyer

Nickname Honest Abe

Did you know? Lincoln married Mary Todd In 1842. They had four sons. Only one, Robert, lived to adulthood.

Quote "I believe this government cannot endure, permanently half slave and half free."

A. Secession Splits the Nation

Southerners' worst fears came true in the election of 1860. Abraham Lincoln was elected President. Many feared that the institution of slavery was at risk.

The Election of 1860

Abraham Lincoln received only 40 percent of the popular vote. However, he earned a majority in the electoral college, which was enough to win the election. Lincoln won every free state except New Jersey, which was split between Stephen Douglas and Lincoln. John Breckinridge swept the South. John Bell took three slaveholding states between the North and the South: Kentucky, Virginia, and Tennessee. Stephen Douglas took three electoral votes in New Jersey and all the electoral votes of Missouri.

Secession in South Carolina

When the news of Lincoln's election reached South Carolina, the legislature called for a state convention to discuss leaving the Union. Delegates met in Charleston on December 20, 1860. All the delegates voted that "the union now subsisting [existing] between South Carolina and other States" was ended. The headline of the city's main newspaper, the *Charleston Mercury*, read "The Union Is Dissolved." *Union* usually refers to the entire United States. During the Civil War, however, the northern states were known as the Union, while the states that seceded were known as the **Confederacy**, or the Confederate States of America.

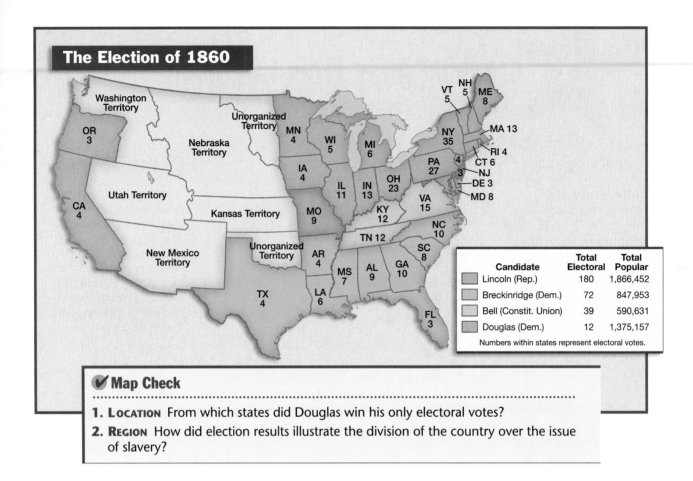

The Election of 1860

Candidate	Total Electoral	Total Popular
Lincoln (Rep.)	180	1,866,452
Breckinridge (Dem.)	72	847,953
Bell (Constit. Union)	39	590,631
Douglas (Dem.)	12	1,375,157

Numbers within states represent electoral votes.

✔ Map Check

1. **LOCATION** From which states did Douglas win his only electoral votes?
2. **REGION** How did election results illustrate the division of the country over the issue of slavery?

After South Carolina left the Union, many Americans still wanted to preserve it. Even in the South, some people were alarmed by secession. Some northern abolitionists thought it was best if the southern states left. However, many Northerners agreed with Lincoln that the southern states could not lawfully leave the Union and that the federal government should not allow them to do it.

Six More States Secede

Many Southerners believed in a state's right to secede. Some, however, wanted to wait and see if the Republicans would really take action in Congress to interfere with slavery.

Within two months, six more states seceded. They were Mississippi, Florida, Alabama, Georgia, Louisiana, and Texas. The process was delayed in Texas by Governor Sam Houston, who refused to call a convention. Delegates to an unofficial convention asked for a popular vote. Texans voted to secede after the state had already been accepted by the Confederacy. Eight other states in the South permitted slavery, but no other states seceded before Lincoln's inauguration.

★ **Which state seceded first from the Union?**

B. Organizing the Confederate States of America

The seven states that had voted to leave the Union knew that they needed to join together. They would be weak unless they stood united against the Union.

The Confederate States of America

In February, the seven states that had seceded sent delegates to a convention in Montgomery, Alabama. There, they created the Confederate States of America, or the Confederacy.

The Confederate states drew up a constitution of their own. In many ways, it was similar to the founding document of the United States—the U.S. Constitution. The new government had an executive branch that included a president. There was also a legislative branch called the congress, made up of a senate and a house of representatives. A judiciary branch, or court system, was provided for but was never fully organized.

While the Confederate constitution resembled the U.S. Constitution, there were some differences. For example, the president could serve only a single, six-year term. The Confederate constitution also did not allow the Confederate congress to spend money within the states for roads or other "internal improvements." The president also had the power of a **line item veto**. This veto meant that he could reject parts of a law without having to reject all of it. Oddly, the new constitution did not include the right to secede. Delegates seemed to take that for granted. A major difference in the constitution of the Confederacy was that it allowed slavery in the territories.

Jefferson Davis, president of the Confederacy, was a graduate of West Point and a former U.S. senator and Secretary of War.

Organizing the Confederate Government

In a meeting, delegates elected Jefferson Davis of Mississippi as the **provisional**, or temporary, president of the Confederacy. They selected Alexander H. Stephens of Georgia as provisional vice president. Both men were elected later by popular vote.

Davis appointed his cabinet immediately. Secretary of War Leroy Walker began organizing an army. Secretary of the Treasury Christopher Memminger worked on a tax system to provide the new government with funds. Secretary of State Robert Toombs worked to get other countries to recognize the Confederacy.

The Confederate government operated in Montgomery, Alabama, until Virginia seceded and joined the Confederacy. Then, the Confederate capital was moved to Richmond in May 1861.

★ How was the Confederate constitution like the U.S. Constitution?

C. Attempts at Reunification of the United States

James Buchanan was still President during the first wave of secession. Buchanan did not believe secession was constitutional. However, he did not think that he had the power to stop it. Buchanan decided to wait until Lincoln took office and let him deal with the problem.

Attempts to End Secession

Before Lincoln took office, both houses of Congress appointed committees to consider ways to restore the Union. The group appointed by the House of Representatives was known as the Committee of 33. The Senate group was called the Committee of 13.

The Committee of 33 tried to bargain with the Confederacy. They promised better enforcement of the Fugitive Slave Law. They also proposed a constitutional amendment to stop the government from interfering with slavery.

The Committee of 13 had a different solution. It included extending the Missouri Compromise line of 36°30' north latitude to the Pacific Ocean. Slavery would be permitted south of that line. The Senate committee's plan also promised payment for runaway slaves if the Fugitive Slave Law was not enforced properly. This plan was known as the Crittenden Compromise, named after its author, Senator John J. Crittenden.

A third attempt to find a compromise involved the Washington Peace Conference. Most of the delegates were elderly statesmen, such as former President John Tyler, who were no longer involved in politics. Their ideas were similar to those of Senator Crittenden.

The Point of No Return

Lincoln took office in 1861, believing that it was his duty to preserve the Union. He warned that the southern states did not have the legal right to leave the Union. Unlike Buchanan, Lincoln believed the President had the power to stop them from leaving. At the same time Lincoln talked tough, however, he pledged that there would not be a war unless the South started it. He ended his First Inaugural Address with these words about all the states:

> " . . . We are not enemies, but friends. We must not be enemies. Though passion [strong feeling] may have strained it must not break our bonds of affection. The mystic chords of memory, stretching from every battlefield and patriot grave to every living heart . . . all over this broad land, will yet swell the chorus of the Union. . . . "

ANALYZE
PRIMARY
SOURCES **DOCUMENT-BASED QUESTION**
According to Lincoln's address, what bonds did all the states share?

Yet all efforts to bring the seceded states back into the Union failed. Confederate officials demanded that federal property within their states be handed over to the Confederate government. Lincoln would not agree to that. Confederate troops began taking over federal property, such as post offices and forts. The President did not want to allow the taking of property, but if he sent troops to prevent it, he might be accused of starting a war.

By April 1861, the Union held only a few forts in Florida and one in South Carolina. Attention became focused on Fort Sumter, located in a harbor at Charleston, South Carolina. The Confederacy demanded the surrender of the fort, but the Union commander, Major Robert Anderson, refused. On April 12, 1861, Confederate forces opened fire on the fort. The shelling lasted for almost a day and a half and ended when the Union troops ran out of ammunition and Major Anderson surrendered. Many people in Charleston had watched the shelling from their rooftops. The Civil War had begun.

The bombardment of Fort Sumter signaled the beginning of the Civil War.

 How did the U.S. government work to keep the Union together?

IV Review

Review History
A. How did Lincoln's election affect South Carolina and some other slave states?
B. Why did the states that seceded form their own government?
C. How did the Civil War begin?

Define Terms to Know
Provide a definition for each of the following terms.
Confederacy, line item veto, provisional

Critical Thinking
If Lincoln was willing to keep slavery in order to preserve the Union, why do you think that the South still felt it needed to secede?

Write About History
Write a newspaper editorial about the Confederate decision to fire on Fort Sumter. Use either a northern or a southern point of view.

Get Organized
CAUSE-AND-EFFECT CHAIN
Think about the events that led to the first battle of the Civil War. What events were immediate causes of that battle? What events resulted from that battle? Use your cause-and-effect chain to link these events together.

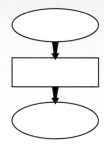

Chapter Summary

In your notebook, complete the following outline. Then, use your outline to write a brief summary of the chapter.

The Road to War

  I. The Question of Slavery in the West

    A. Slavery in an Expanding Nation
    B.
    C.

  II. Deepening Divisions Over Slavery

    A.
    B.
    C.

  III. Challenges to Slavery

    A.
    B.
    C.

  IV. Breaking Away From the Union

    A.
    B.
    C.

Interpret the Timeline

Use the timeline on pages 378–379 in order to answer these questions.

1. How long after the Compromise of 1850 did the Civil War start?

2. **Critical Thinking** Which events in the United States and the world show the growth of the antislavery movement?

Use Terms to Know

Select the term that best completes each sentence.

civil war	fugitive	secede
emancipate	insurrection	

1. People who thought slavery was wrong wanted to _____ all slaves.

2. The Underground Railroad was a secret route used by _____ slaves.

3. A _____ occurs when people in the same country fight against each other.

4. South Carolina was the first state to _____, or leave the Union.

5. A slave _____, such as the one John Brown planned, worried many Southerners.

Check Your Understanding

1. **Explain** why westward expansion caused divisions between the North and the South.

2. **Summarize** the main differences between the Missouri Compromise and the Compromise of 1850.

3. **Explain** why there was bloodshed in Kansas in the mid-1850s.

4. **Discuss** how *Uncle Tom's Cabin* changed northern opinions about slavery.

5. **Explain** why a number of southern delegates left the 1860 Democratic convention in Charleston.

6. **Identify** the reason for the formation of the Republican Party.

7. **Describe** the reaction of several southern states to President Lincoln's election.

8. **Explain** the importance of Fort Sumter.

Critical Thinking

1. **Analyze Primary Sources** Do you think that the person who drew the political cartoon on page 382 supported slavery? Explain.

2. **Draw Conclusions** Do you think that resistance to the Fugitive Slave Law surprised people in the national government? Explain.

3. **Make Inferences** How might the presidential election of 1860 eventually affect slavery?

4. **Analyze Primary Sources** Judging by Lincoln's words quoted on page 400, what did he want the states that had seceded to do?

Put Your Skills to Work
CLASSIFY INFORMATION

You have learned that classifying, or sorting, information can help you to understand the relationships between people, events, and ideas.

Copy the chart below. In the first column, write the names of five people from Chapter 16. In the second column, list something each person did. In the third column, write one effect of each person's action.

PERSON	ACTION	EFFECT
Dred Scott	He sued for his freedom.	The Supreme Court judged that the Missouri Compromise was illegal and that Congress could not regulate slavery.

In Your Own Words
JOURNAL WRITING

Harriet Beecher Stowe's book *Uncle Tom's Cabin* changed many people's opinions about slavery. Write a journal entry about a book that you have read. Choose a book that made you change your mind about something. What was the issue? Why did the book have such a strong effect on you?

Net Work
INTERNET ACTIVITY

Work with a group of classmates. Use the Internet as a resource in order to create an illustrated timeline of John Brown's life. Include key events in his life, such as his involvement in Bleeding Kansas and Harpers Ferry. Write a brief description of each event. Then, illustrate your timeline with photographs, artwork, and famous quotations. Share your timeline with the class.

For help in starting this activity, visit the following Web site: www.gfamericanhistory.com.

Look Ahead
In the next chapter, learn how the Civil War divided the nation.

CHAPTER 17

The Civil War 1861–1865

I. **The Early Days of the War**
II. **War and American Life**
III. **Victory for the North**

The Civil War split the country into two warring enemies. Sometimes, families were divided as well. Alexander and James Campbell, two brothers, found themselves on opposite sides of the war. Alexander, who lived in New York, joined the Union army. His brother James lived in South Carolina and joined the Confederate army. After learning that they fought against each other in a battle, Alexander wrote the following letter:

> **"** I was astonished to hear from the prisoners that you [were the] color Bearer of the Regiment that assaulted the Battery at this point the other day. I was in the [fort] during the whole engagement doing my Best to Beat you but I hope you and I will never again meet face to face bitter enemies on the Battlefield. **"**

The Civil War turned brother against brother and friend against friend. This division resulted in the deadliest conflict ever to occur on American soil.

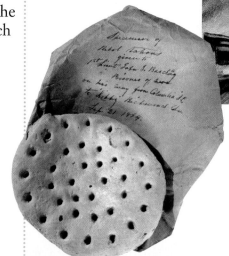

Hardtack

U.S. Events	1860	1861	1862
	1860 Lincoln wins election.	**1861** Eleven states form the Confederate States of America. The First Battle of Bull Run takes place.	**1862** The Seven Days Battles and the Battle of Antietam occur. Ironclads *Monitor* and *Virginia* clash in a sea battle.
Presidential Term Begins		1861 Abraham Lincoln	
World Events	1860	1861	1862
		1861 The czar of Russia frees peasants who had been forced to work for royalty.	**1862** The International Red Cross is proposed.

VIEW HISTORY The fighting of the Civil War is shown in this painting of General Sherman's "march to the sea." To sustain themselves during the hard days of fighting, soldiers ate hardtack (left), or crackers, and dried salt pork.

★ What do these images tell you about the life of soldiers during the Civil War?

Get Organized

CHART

When you read about history, you can classify information to help you find, examine, and remember it. Use a chart to classify two types of information as you read Chapter 17. Fill in headings to describe the information you are classifying. Here is an example of a chart showing Union and Confederate states.

Confederacy	Union	
AL	CA	MN
AR	CT	MO
FL	DE	NH
GA	IA	NJ
LA	IL	NY
MS	IN	OH
NC	KS	OR
SC	KY	PA
TN	MA	RI
TX	MD	VT
VA	ME	WI
	MI	WV

1863
Confederate troops surrender Vicksburg.
The Confederate army is defeated at Gettysburg.
Lincoln formally signs the Emancipation Proclamation.
Lincoln gives the Gettysburg Address.

1865
Lee surrenders to Grant at Appomattox Court House, and the Civil War ends.

1864
Sherman begins his "march to the sea."

1863 — 1864 — 1865

1863 — 1864 — 1865

1863
French troops capture Mexico City.

1864
French scientist Louis Pasteur develops pasteurization.

1865
Lewis Carroll's *Alice in Wonderland* is published in Britain.

I ★ The Early Days of the War

Terms to Know

border states four slave states located between the Union and the Confederacy that stayed in the Union during the Civil War

strategy a plan

blockade a barrier of ships or troops that prevents goods from entering or leaving an area

Main Ideas

A. The North and the South prepared for war.

B. Both the North and the South had important advantages.

C. The Confederacy won most of the early battles in the East.

Active Reading

EVALUATE
When you evaluate something, you examine it and try to determine its value, or worth. As you read this section, evaluate the plans for victory that the Union and the Confederacy each used.

A. The Buildup to Battle

When Abraham Lincoln was elected President in 1860, many white Southerners became convinced that their rights would no longer be protected. As a result, their thoughts turned to war.

The Confederacy Expands

Six states had seceded by February 1861. Eight other states in the South, however, still hoped that Lincoln would not interfere with slavery where it already existed. Then, the Confederates attacked Fort Sumter, South Carolina, on April 12. President Lincoln asked for 75,000 volunteers to put down the rebellion in the South.

Some of the southern states saw Lincoln's request for militia as a sign of war. So, four more undecided states—Virginia, Arkansas, Tennessee, and North Carolina—seceded from the Union. Non-slaveholding farmers in northwestern Virginia remained loyal to the Union. In 1861, they broke away from Virginia. Two years later, the new state of West Virginia was admitted to the Union.

The last four undecided states did not secede. Missouri, Maryland, Kentucky, and Delaware became known as **border states**—states on the border of the North and the South. These states stayed in the Union, but they sent soldiers to fight for both armies.

The border states were very important to both the North and the South. They had many factories and resources needed by both sides during the war. They could change the balance of power by deciding to join one side or the other. Throughout the war, President Lincoln was very careful not to do anything that might cause the border states to join the Confederacy.

Soldiers wore badges to identify their regiment, or military unit.

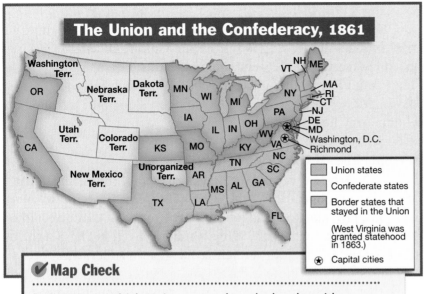

The Union and the Confederacy, 1861

Union states

Confederate states

Border states that stayed in the Union

(West Virginia was granted statehood in 1863.)

⊛ Capital cities

✔ Map Check

1. **LOCATION** Which Union states shared a border with the Confederacy?
2. **PLACE** How many states belonged to the Union in 1861?

Leadership and Strategy

Each side had its own **strategy**, or plan, to win the war. The Union army had to invade the South and defeat its army. The South would win if it could defend itself and outlast the North.

In 1861, the Union army was commanded by 75-year-old General Winfield Scott. He devised the Anaconda Plan. It was named for the tropical snake that wraps itself around its prey and squeezes the life out of it.

According to the plan, the navy would set up a **blockade**, or a line of ships that would prevent access to southern ports. This blockade would cut off all supply routes to and from the South. Land and naval forces would then seize the Mississippi River valley, cutting the South into two parts. This action would weaken the South by dividing its army and supplies. At the same time, Union soldiers would attack and capture the Confederate capital at Richmond, Virginia.

The Anaconda Plan was a sound one. However, it would take time. People in the North quickly grew impatient for victories. Many wanted to smash the Confederacy instead of slowly squeezing it to death.

The South's strategy was to fight a defensive war. Southern forces would fight only if Union forces attacked them or invaded the South. Except for a few military actions, the Confederate plan was to survive long enough for the North to lose hope and end the war.

★ **What was the Anaconda Plan?**

President Abraham Lincoln

Spotlight on
Culture

Many famous songs are connected with the Civil War. Probably the best-known of all is "Dixie," the favorite marching song of the Confederate army. Surprisingly, the song was written by a Northerner.

In 1859, Daniel Emmett of Mount Vernon, Ohio, wrote the song for a show he was appearing in. He was very upset when he learned his song had become a southern favorite. *Dixie* is a nickname for the South.

B. The Two Sides

The Union and the Confederacy had different goals in the Civil War. Northerners fought to restore the Union and, later in the war, to end slavery. Southerners supported the idea of states' rights. They fought to maintain their way of life, which included owning slaves. Many Southerners also volunteered to fight because the Union army had invaded the Confederacy.

Advantages of the Union

The North had many advantages over the South, including a much larger population. The North had more people to make weapons, provide food, and join the army or navy. About 22 million people lived in the North. Only 9 million lived in the South. Of these, about 3.5 million were enslaved African Americans.

The North had more industry and a better transportation network than the South had. As a result, supplies could be produced and transported more easily. Abraham Lincoln also was a great asset to the North. His leadership and dedication gave the Union troops strength to fight the war.

Advantages of the Confederacy

Even though it was weaker economically, the Confederacy had better military leadership during the early years of the war. Many southern military leaders had trained at West Point, the nation's leading military academy. One southern general, Robert E. Lee, had been offered command of the U.S. Army. He turned the job down because his home state, Virginia, had joined the Confederacy.

The South also had the advantage of fighting on its home soil. To win the war, the South did not have to conquer the North. It had to survive until the North realized it was impossible to defeat the South. Southerners fought bravely because they were defending their land, their homes, and their way of life.

The southern states also had an important crop, cotton. The South hoped that its cotton, needed in Great Britain and other European countries, would lead these countries to support the Confederacy in its battle for independence.

★ How was the population of the North an advantage in the war?

C. Early Battles of the War

During the first two years of the war, the South won most of the battles that were fought east of the Appalachian Mountains.

The First Battle of Bull Run

When President Lincoln called for volunteers in 1861, he expected the war to last no more than 90 days. Many Northerners agreed with him. On July 21, 1861, Lincoln ordered 37,000 soldiers under the command of General Irvin McDowell to attack a smaller force of Confederate soldiers at a creek called Bull Run, near Manassas, Virginia. Lincoln hoped they would easily win the battle and move on to capture Richmond. Many spectators from nearby Washington, D.C., followed the Union soldiers. They expected to enjoy a picnic as they watched the skirmish that would bring an end to the rebellion.

As the First Battle of Bull Run began, both sides fought well and held their ground. Then, additional Confederate troops arrived, increasing the number of Confederate soldiers to 35,000. The Confederate soldiers, commanded by General P.G.T. Beauregard, pushed toward the Union forces with a loud, frightening scream, which became known as the rebel yell. The Union soldiers panicked. They fled to Washington, D.C., along with the crowd of spectators who had come to see the fighting.

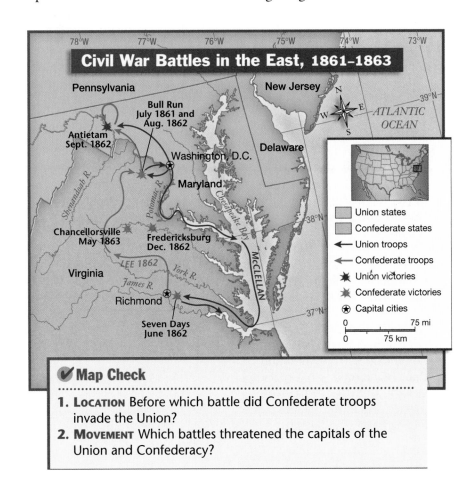

Civil War Battles in the East, 1861–1863

Pennsylvania

New Jersey

Bull Run
July 1861 and
Aug. 1862

Antietam
Sept. 1862

Delaware

ATLANTIC
OCEAN

Washington, D.C.

Maryland

Chancellorsville
May 1863

Fredericksburg
Dec. 1862

Virginia

LEE 1862

Richmond

Seven Days
June 1862

- Union states
- Confederate states
- ← Union troops
- ← Confederate troops
- ✳ Union victories
- ✳ Confederate victories
- ✪ Capital cities

0 ____ 75 mi
0 ____ 75 km

✔ Map Check

1. **LOCATION** Before which battle did Confederate troops invade the Union?
2. **MOVEMENT** Which battles threatened the capitals of the Union and Confederacy?

Robert E. Lee

Battles in the East, 1862–1863

In the spring of 1862, the Union Army of the Potomac under General George McClellan moved to an area south of Richmond, Virginia. McClellan delayed his attack while he waited for additional troops to arrive. This delay gave the Confederate forces a chance to prepare for the expected Union advance. The new Confederate commander, Robert E. Lee, struck the Union army repeatedly in a series of attacks known as the Seven Days Battles. McClellan was forced to accept defeat.

General Lee believed that the South needed to win the war quickly. He was afraid the North would soon put its great economic advantage to use. Lee planned to invade the North. He advanced into Maryland in September 1862 after defeating the Union army a second time at Bull Run. The two armies clashed on September 17 in the Battle of Antietam. It was the bloodiest day of the war, with more than 23,000 men killed or wounded. Lee lost one third of his army. To Lincoln's dismay, McClellan did not pursue Lee's retreating forces into Virginia, missing a chance to crush the Confederate army.

In December, Confederates defeated the Union army at Fredericksburg, Virginia. Lee won again at the Battle of Chancellorsville in May 1863. This victory was a bitter one, however. Lee's most valuable general, Thomas J. "Stonewall" Jackson, was shot accidentally by his own troops. He died a week later.

 Who won the first battle of the Civil War?

 **Review**

Review History
A. How did Union and Confederate plans for victory differ?
B. What advantages did the South possess?
C. What were Lincoln's hopes at the First Battle of Bull Run?

Define Terms to Know
Provide a definition for each of the following terms.
border states, strategy, blockade

Critical Thinking
In what ways did industry in the North help its war effort?

Write About History
Northerners were confident before the Battle of Bull Run that they would win a quick victory over the South. Write a letter to a friend about your feelings after the battle.

Get Organized
CHART
Create a chart to classify the information in this section. For example, classify the battles of the early years of the Civil War as Confederate victories or Union victories.

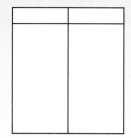

Build Your Skills

PREDICT CONSEQUENCES

When you predict consequences, you make an educated guess about something that might happen. You do this by examining what you already know. For example, when you watch a movie you get to know the personalities of the characters. You can use what you know about the characters to predict the end of the movie.

When you read about history, you can predict the consequences of decisions that people made. This helps you to better understand the events you read about. You will also learn how people's decisions have led to consequences, both in the past and today.

Here's How
Follow these steps to predict consequences.

1. Review the information you already have.

2. Look for trends and patterns. Ask yourself the following question: Based on what I already know about this and other situations, what is the most likely consequence?

3. Check your prediction. Were you correct? If not, why?

Here's Why
You have just read about the strengths and weaknesses of the North and the South. Suppose you had to predict the consequences of the North's advantages over the South.

Practice the Skill
Copy the chart on the right on a sheet of paper. In the boxes on top, write three facts from Section I about the North's advantages in the war. Think about how these facts may affect the outcome of the war. In the bottom box, predict a consequence based on this information.

Extend the Skill
Write a paragraph explaining how the information you wrote in the chart led to the consequence you predicted. After you finish reading this chapter, review your prediction to see if it was correct.

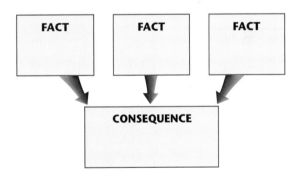

Apply the Skill
As you read the remaining sections of this chapter, predict the consequences of the actions taken by the Union and by the Confederacy. For example, in Section III, predict the consequences of General Lee's decision to invade the North again.

II War and American Life

Terms to Know

trench warfare soldiers fighting from long ditches dug in the ground

conscription the act of requiring people to serve in the military

ironclad warship metal or metal-covered steam-driven warship

Main Ideas

A. The Confederacy wanted recognition from other countries, while northern leaders worked to prevent it.

B. Advances in military technology and other developments made the Civil War the first modern war.

C. African Americans played an important role in the Civil War.

Active Reading

SUMMARIZE
When you summarize, you collect and analyze details to make a general statement. As you read this section, summarize the reasons why the Civil War is called the first modern war.

A. The South Looks for Friends

To earn money for the war, the Confederacy needed to sell its products to other countries. Northern leaders worked hard to prevent the South from reaching this goal.

A Search for Allies

Confederate President Jefferson Davis had one important goal in foreign policy. It was to convince other countries, particularly in Europe, that the Confederate States of America was a separate and independent country from the United States of America. Then, these countries might be willing to send troops to help the Confederacy win the war.

For a while, it seemed that Great Britain would formally recognize the Confederacy as a separate nation from the United States. Southern cotton was important to the British textile industry. However, some people in Britain strongly opposed slavery. For that reason they did not want to help the Confederacy. Then, British textile manufacturers discovered new sources of cotton in Egypt and India. Pressure to recognize the Confederacy weakened.

The United States wanted to prevent other countries like Great Britain from recognizing the Confederacy. The United States was represented in Britain by Charles Francis Adams. He was able to convince British leaders to remain neutral. Adams also persuaded British shipyards to stop selling ships to the Confederacy.

The Blockade

As part of the Anaconda Plan, the North's blockade kept the South from shipping cotton to Great Britain. Southerners tried to break the blockade with small, quick ships called blockade runners. These ships could travel faster than the much larger U.S. warships. Yet, the South could not make up for its loss of trade. Food shortages in the South began to reach critical levels.

★ **Why did the Confederacy want recognition from other countries?**

B. The First Modern War

The Civil War is called the first modern war. New technological developments and ideas about war shaped the way the war was fought.

New Advances in Technology

The Civil War saw the introduction of several new weapons. Before the war, American soldiers used a weapon called a musket. It had to be reloaded after firing each shot. During the Civil War, the Springfield rifle replaced the musket. It could shoot farther and more accurately. Repeating rifles, which could be loaded with several bullets at a time, were also introduced. The Minié ball, a new bullet invented in France in 1848, could be shot farther than other bullets. With it, a person could hit a target from almost a mile away. Because soldiers could shoot faster, farther, and more accurately, the casualty rate increased greatly during the war.

Trench warfare, or soldiers fighting from long, deep ditches dug in the ground, was used during the Civil War. Trenches played an important role in several battles. Trench warfare became very common 50 years later during World War I.

Soldiers defended their positions from long trenches that often stretched for miles around cities and towns.

Communications and transportation were also improved. Messages were sent by telegraph rather than by riders on horseback. Railroads were widely used to transport soldiers and supplies. Finding enemy positions was made easier by sky views from hot air balloons.

Serving in the Army

Many men were needed to fight the battles of the Civil War. At first, both sides counted on volunteers. However, this system did not produce enough soldiers. In 1862, the South passed a law that called for **conscription**, or requiring people to serve in the military. The North passed its conscription law the following year. These laws were the first national draft laws in U.S. history. A draft is the process by which people are selected for service without their expressed consent. However, the Union's law allowed people to pay a fee of $300 to avoid being drafted. This angered people who could not afford to pay to evade fighting. They felt it favored the wealthy.

Soldiers spent most of their time in temporary camps or traveling to new camps. When they arrived at a new site, soldiers often needed to cut down trees and put up tents. They had to cope with boredom, bad weather, and disease. More than twice as many men died from disease as died in battle. Food was often scarce, unsafe, or unpleasant, as one Union soldier recalled.

ANALYZE PRIMARY SOURCES

DOCUMENT-BASED QUESTION
Why do you think Civil War soldiers did not throw out unpleasant food?

> **"**It was no uncommon occurrence for a man to find the surface of his pot of coffee swimming with weevils [beetles] after breaking up hardtack in it . . . but they were easily skimmed off and left no distinctive flavor behind. **"**

After men left home for battle, many women took over their work. In the South, women learned to run plantations and farms. Others worked in factories or other businesses to support their families. Hundreds of women became wartime nurses. Clara Barton, who became famous as a nurse for the Union army, later founded the American Red Cross. Sally Louisa Tompkins created a hospital for southern soldiers. A few women served as spies, and almost 400 women disguised themselves as men so they could fight.

New arrangements were made for prisoners of war. In earlier wars, prisoners were exchanged or released soon after each battle. During the early years of the Civil War, prisoners were allowed to go home if they promised not to fight again. By 1863, however, both sides were keeping prisoners in camps to prevent them from returning to battle.

Women such as Anne Bell helped the war effort in many ways, including serving as nurses for wounded soldiers.

Most prisoners in camps were treated poorly. They were forced to live in filthy, cramped shelters and were given little food. Almost 50,000 people died in these camps. One much-feared Union camp was located in Elmira, New York. One of the best-known Confederate prison camps was in Andersonville, Georgia. Treatment of Union prisoners was so harsh that Henry Wirz, the commander of Andersonville, was executed after the war for his unjust handling of the prisoners.

The Changing Face of Sea Warfare

A new development in naval warfare was the **ironclad warship**. An ironclad was either a wooden ship covered with iron plates or a ship made mostly out of metal. The Confederates built the first ironclad. They raised a sunken Union ship named the *Merrimack*, covered it with iron plates, and renamed it the *Virginia*. It was described by A. B. Smith, a Union sailor, as a "huge, half submerged crocodile."

On March 8, 1862, the *Virginia* attacked a group of Union ships near Norfolk, Virginia. Shells from the Union ships bounced off the ironclad. After the *Virginia* sank two wooden Union ships, the North sent in its own ironclad, the *Monitor*. The two ships battled for hours, but neither could sink the other. The *Monitor* was forced to withdraw. After this battle, both sides built more ironclads to use in the war.

★ **How did policies about prisoners of war change during the war?**

One unusual feature of the *Monitor* (left) was its revolving gun turret. Cannons were rotated within this structure located on top of the ship so that enemy ships such as the *Virginia* (right) could be fired upon easily.

On January 1, 1863, Abraham Lincoln signed the Emancipation Proclamation.

As he began to sign the paper, his hand was shaking so much that he was unable to write. Feeling superstitious, he paused. Lincoln then remembered that, at the New Year's Day reception earlier, he had spent hours shaking hands with several people. That explained the trembling!

Lincoln continued to sign the document—slowly, but firmly. He signed with his full name, which was rare. Then, he said, "I never in my life felt more certain that I was doing right then I do in signing this paper."

You can read the Emancipation Proclamation on page R6.

C. Ending Slavery in the North

An important event in the history of the nation occurred on September 22, 1862. President Lincoln issued an order that would emancipate, or free, enslaved people in areas still controlled by the Confederacy. African Americans played an important part in the Civil War. Their contributions on the battlefield greatly aided the war effort.

The Emancipation Proclamation

President Lincoln had certain goals in mind when he made the decision to issue the Emancipation Proclamation. He felt that once enslaved men and women in the South heard that they had been freed, they might refuse to work. This refusal would harm the Confederacy's war effort. Lincoln also knew that many people in the North would welcome the abolition of slavery and bring renewed energy to the Union war effort.

On January 1, 1863, President Lincoln formally signed the Emancipation Proclamation. Because Lincoln was not the president of the Confederacy, no enslaved people were actually freed until Union forces took control of the southern states. In addition, Lincoln's order did not apply to enslaved people in the border states. However, the Emancipation Proclamation was a promise that slavery would end if the Union won the war. Henry Ward Beecher, a famous abolitionist, said, "The Proclamation may not free a single slave, but it gives liberty a moral recognition."

The Emancipation Proclamation had several other effects. It made the end of slavery a new goal for the North. Before this time, Union soldiers had been fighting primarily to preserve the Union. Now, it became an important goal to fight for the freedom of all enslaved people. In addition, Free Soil Party members believed that white laborers would have more job opportunities when slavery ended. Finally, the Emancipation Proclamation convinced Great Britain and France not to aid the Confederacy. Both countries strongly opposed slavery.

African American Soldiers

Early in the Civil War, Frederick Douglass and others demanded that African Americans in the North be allowed to fight. President Lincoln feared that if African Americans were allowed to join the armed forces, the border states might join the Confederacy. Lincoln eventually became convinced that African American soldiers could be a valuable resource for the Union. In 1863, free African Americans were finally allowed to enlist in the U.S. Army.

Almost 185,000 African Americans served in the Union army. More than half of these soldiers were formerly enslaved and had fled from the South to freedom in the North. About 20,000 African Americans served in the U.S. navy. African American soldiers served in separate regiments, usually commanded by white officers. One of the most famous African American regiments was the 54th Massachusetts Volunteers. The 54th fought with great courage in the attack on Fort Wagner in South Carolina in 1863.

Until June 1864, African American soldiers received lower pay than white soldiers. They had lower-quality supplies and lived in worse conditions. African American soldiers faced an added danger. The Confederacy threatened to kill or sell into slavery any captured African American soldiers and their officers.

By the end of the war, African American troops had fought in nearly 500 engagements, including 39 major battles. About 39,000 African American soldiers died, and 23 were awarded the Medal of Honor for heroism.

African American sharpshooters

 What special challenges did African American soldiers face?

 **II Review**

Review History
A. How was cotton important to the South's relationships with other nations?
B. What made the Civil War the first modern war?
C. How did African Americans contribute to the war efforts of the North?

Define Terms to Know
Provide a definition for each of the following terms.
trench warfare, conscription, ironclad warship

Critical Thinking
In what ways did advances in technology make fighting more difficult for soldiers?

Write About Citizenship
You are an abolitionist newspaper reporter living in the North. Write an article about the Emancipation Proclamation.

Get Organized
CHART
Create a chart to classify information you read about in this section. For example, classify old and new weapons and technology used before and during the war.

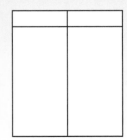

PAST *to* PRESENT

Submarines

During the Civil War, people in the North and the South raced to build a submarine. The Confederates were the first to build one—the *H.L. Hunley*. In February 1864, the *Hunley* rammed a torpedo into the wooden side of a Union ship and sank it. The explosion damaged the *Hunley* and caused it to go down as well.

Some modern submarines are almost as long as two football fields. They are powered by nuclear reactors and can hold more than 150 crew members. Sailors in the U.S. Navy volunteer to live and work in submarines for up to six months at a time.

The *Hunley's* only weapon was a torpedo on a long pole attached to its front. In this painting, the pole appears to the left. The man is standing at the back end of the submarine, near the propeller.

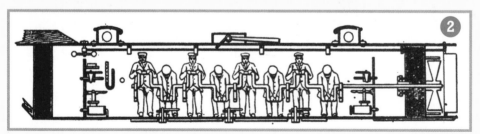

This diagram shows what the inside of the *Hunley* was like. Eight men turned the propeller by hand. A ninth man (not shown) steered the submarine.

This view inside the USS *Seawolf* shows sailors working at the main control board.

Modern submarines are much larger than those used in the Civil War. In this photograph of the USS *Seawolf*, contrast its size to the size of the men standing near its top. Now look back at the painting of the *Hunley* and compare the sizes of both submarines.

Submarine Facts

	H.L. Hunley	USS *Seawolf*
Year Built	1863	1997
Weight	7.5 tons	9,150 tons
Length	39.5 feet	353 feet
Height	4 feet 3 inches	35 feet
Width	3 feet 10 inches	40 feet
Speed	4 miles per hour	28 miles per hour
Total Crew	9	134

The chart above lists some differences between the *Hunley* and a modern submarine, the *Seawolf*.

Hands-On Activity

What is it like to live and work on a modern submarine? Where do crewmembers sleep? Can they communicate with their families? Using the Internet, "interview" a sailor who has served on a submarine. Make a list of questions, and then answer them by using the information you find. To get started, go to: www.gfamericanhistory.com.

III Victory for the North

Terms to Know

habeas corpus the right of a citizen to ask a court to decide if a prisoner is being held lawfully

censorship control of free expression

total war a war against civilians and resources as well as against armies

Main Ideas

A. The Union army won crucial victories in the West.

B. President Lincoln took some extreme measures during wartime.

C. Campaigns by Union generals Grant and Sherman ended the war.

 **Active Reading**

SEQUENCE OF EVENTS
A sequence of events is the order in which events occur. As you read this chapter, make a timeline of important events to help you understand their sequence.

A. The Turning Point

The Confederate army, battling in the East, had proven to be much stronger than anyone had thought. Yet, Union forces were winning battles in the West. These victories did not, however, cause the Confederacy to collapse. Northerners were asking, How could the Union win the war?

Ulysses S. Grant

Fighting in the West, 1861–1863

In the early years of the war, Union forces fought well west of the Appalachian Mountains. The first important Union victories came in early 1862. A Union general named Ulysses S. Grant captured the Confederate strongholds of Fort Henry and Fort Donelson in Tennessee. Grant defeated the Confederates again at the Battle of Shiloh, also in Tennessee, in April 1862. At the same time, a Union naval force under Admiral David Farragut captured New Orleans, Louisiana.

The Union forces had begun to cut the Confederacy in two. Union troops controlled most of the Mississippi River, which prevented the Confederates from moving troops and supplies. However, the mighty Confederate stronghold at Vicksburg, Mississippi, still stood. It prevented the Union from taking complete control of the river.

The Siege of Vicksburg

In May 1863, General Grant had one goal: to capture the Confederate city of Vicksburg, Mississippi. Control of Vicksburg would give the Union control of the entire Mississippi River and split the Confederacy in two. Grant had wanted to take Vicksburg since the Battle of Shiloh in April 1862. Now, he was ready.

Grant tried five times to capture Vicksburg. The first four attempts failed, but Grant's fifth plan worked. He began a six-week siege, or long attack, of the city while blocking off its supply routes.

With no source of fresh food or water, the people of Vicksburg were forced to eat mules and rats. The lack of food combined with the ongoing siege forced the Confederate troops to give up. On July 4, 1863, about 30,000 Confederate defenders surrendered Vicksburg. Five days later, Union forces took control of Port Hudson, Louisiana. Union troops now had total control of the Mississippi River. The South was now divided completely. They had accomplished one of the goals of the Anaconda Plan.

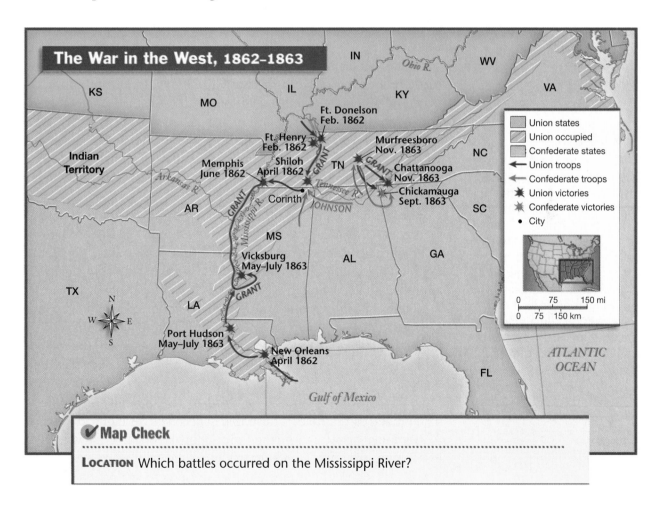

The War in the West, 1862–1863

Legend:
- Union states
- Union occupied
- Confederate states
- ← Union troops
- ← Confederate troops
- ✳ Union victories
- ✳ Confederate victories
- • City

0   75   150 mi
0   75   150 km

Ft. Donelson Feb. 1862
Ft. Henry Feb. 1862
Memphis June 1862
Shiloh April 1862
Corinth
Murfreesboro Nov. 1863
Chattanooga Nov. 1863
Chickamauga Sept. 1863
Vicksburg May–July 1863
Port Hudson May–July 1863
New Orleans April 1862

GRANT
JOHNSON

✔Map Check

LOCATION Which battles occurred on the Mississippi River?

Gettysburg was the Civil War's deadliest battle. Close to 50,000 men were killed or wounded.

The Gettysburg National Cemetery was completed in 1872 to honor the men who had fought at Gettysburg. More than 7,000 veterans are buried there, including soldiers who fought in other major wars involving the United States.

Today, the cemetery is part of a national park, which was created in 1895 as a memorial to the armies that fought there during the Civil War.

Gettysburg

At the same time that Vicksburg was falling to Grant, another battle was taking place in the East. Robert E. Lee believed that it would be necessary to win a great battle to force the North to make peace. He had invaded the Union in 1862 and had been defeated at the Battle of Antietam in Maryland. However, in the late spring of 1863, he decided that it was time to invade the North again. His target was the rich farming region of central Pennsylvania, where he hoped to find supplies for his army.

The Union army in the East, now commanded by General George G. Meade, stayed between Lee's army and Washington, D.C. The two armies met near Gettysburg, Pennsylvania. There, the fighting raged for three days. At first, neither side could gain an advantage. The key moment of the battle came on July 3, 1863.

About 15,000 Confederate soldiers followed their general, George Pickett, in an attack known as Pickett's Charge. Pickett led his soldiers across a mile of open field. Although the Confederate soldiers showed incredible bravery, the attack failed. The open field made the Confederate soldiers perfect targets for the waiting Union troops. Only about one third of the Confederate soldiers made it across the field. Those that succeeded were quickly forced to surrender or retreat. As the fighting broke off, Lee knew he had lost his chance. The Confederates retreated to Virginia. Although Lee and his army continued to battle fiercely against the Union forces, they would never again have the strength to invade the North.

Lincoln's Speech at Gettysburg

In November 1863, President Lincoln was invited to attend a ceremony in Gettysburg. The ceremony was held to honor the men who had died there and to dedicate a cemetery to their memory. The two-minute speech that Lincoln made at Gettysburg is considered one of the greatest speeches in American history.

In his Gettysburg Address, Lincoln reminded the audience of the ideals on which the United States was founded. He stated that the Civil War was being fought to preserve those very ideals. He added that soldiers had fought and died in order to prove that a nation founded on these ideals could survive and prosper. He asked the listeners to make sure that the United States experienced "a new birth of freedom."

You can read the Gettysburg Address on pages R6–R7.

★ **What was the key moment at the Battle of Gettysburg?**

B. Lincoln's Leadership

Lincoln's main goal during the war was to restore the Union. Many agreed with his goal, but others disagreed with his methods. Some began to lose faith in Lincoln during the long years of war.

Opposition to the Lincoln Presidency

From the start of his presidency, Abraham Lincoln ran into opposition from people in the North. Some people wanted him to declare the end of slavery immediately rather than move slowly toward emancipation. When Union armies lost battles early in the war, some thought that Lincoln was not managing the war well. Others, mostly Democrats, wanted to make peace with the South and allow it to secede. Some Democrats openly supported the South. These people were known as Copperheads to their enemies because a copperhead is a poisonous snake.

Lincoln felt that criticism of the war weakened the Union. To protect the country, he suspended **habeas corpus**, the constitutional protection against unlawful imprisonment. More than 13,000 opponents of the war were arrested and held in prison without being given trials. The government also closed more than 300 newspapers for criticizing the war. Some people thought this act of **censorship**, or prevention of free expression, violated citizens' First Amendment rights.

Lincoln often visited the Union army camps to discuss strategy with his generals. Here, he meets with two commanders at the Union camp on the battlefield at Antietam Creek.

The Election of 1864

As the 1864 election grew near, not all Republicans thought Abraham Lincoln should run. However, the party nominated him again. The Democrats nominated General George McClellan who had been removed from his command of the Union army.

Many people thought the Democrats would win the election. The war was dragging on with no end in sight. People doubted that President Lincoln could bring the war to a successful end. McClellan promised to end the war quickly if he was elected. Then, events took a turn for the better. News of Union victories lifted spirits in the North. Fortunately for Lincoln, this news arrived just before the election. Lincoln was re-elected by a landslide.

 **Why did Lincoln suspend habeas corpus?**

C. The End of the War

In March 1864, President Lincoln appointed General Ulysses S. Grant commander of all Union armies. His capture of Vicksburg and his later victories had convinced Lincoln that Grant was the man to beat General Robert E. Lee. After almost three long years of war, the tide finally began to turn in favor of the North.

Grant Moves Toward Richmond

Over the spring and summer of 1864, Grant marched his troops into Virginia. He believed that he could win only by waging **total war**—destroying all food, homes, farms, buildings, and other supplies that could be used by the Confederate army or by civilians. In total war, civilians suffer as much as soldiers.

As Confederates fled Richmond, Virginia, they burned much of the city so that Union forces would not benefit from its capture.

Grant and Lee fought a series of battles near Richmond known as the Wilderness Campaign. Both armies suffered huge losses. However, Grant's philosophy was different from that of earlier Union commanders who let Lee escape. Grant said, "Get at him as soon as you can. Strike at him as hard as you can, and keep moving."

In June 1864, Grant planned a major attack on Petersburg, Virginia. This city was an important railroad center just south of Richmond. Grant and Lee faced off again. As the Union troops began a siege against the city, both sides settled in trenches that stretched for miles. The siege lasted ten months before Lee finally retreated.

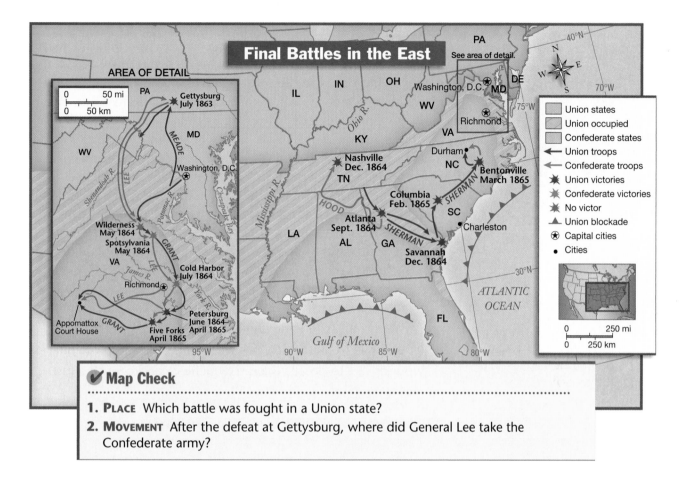

Final Battles in the East

Map legend:
- Union states
- Union occupied
- Confederate states
- Union troops
- Confederate troops
- Union victories
- Confederate victories
- No victor
- Union blockade
- Capital cities
- Cities

AREA OF DETAIL

Gettysburg July 1863
Washington, D.C.
Wilderness May 1864
Spotsylvania May 1864
Cold Harbor July 1864
Richmond
Appomattox Court House
Five Forks April 1865
Petersburg June 1864–April 1865

Nashville Dec. 1864
Durham
Bentonville March 1865
Columbia Feb. 1865
Atlanta Sept. 1864
Savannah Dec. 1864
Charleston

✔ Map Check

1. **PLACE** Which battle was fought in a Union state?
2. **MOVEMENT** After the defeat at Gettysburg, where did General Lee take the Confederate army?

Sherman Marches Across the South

As Grant and Lee battled for Petersburg, General William Tecumseh Sherman took command of Union forces in the Deep South. Like Grant, Sherman also believed in total war as a way of defeating the spirit of the Confederacy. He felt that all people who supported the southern cause were to blame for the war. He wanted them to feel the consequences of their support of the Confederacy's war efforts.

Sherman and 100,000 troops attacked Atlanta, Georgia. The Confederate forces commanded by General John B. Hood were unable to stop Sherman's troops. They captured Atlanta in September 1864. After burning the city, Sherman began his famous "march to the sea." His army sliced a path 60 miles wide through Georgia, destroying everything in its way. The soldiers burned barns and crops, killed livestock, and blew up bridges and railroads. Sherman said his goal was to "make Georgia howl!"

Sherman's army reached the Atlantic Ocean at Savannah, Georgia, in December 1864. The city surrendered without a fight. Next, he turned north, planning to meet Grant's army near Richmond.

The surrender at Appomattox Court House

ANALYZE PRIMARY SOURCES

DOCUMENT-BASED QUESTION
What were President Lincoln's goals after the end of the Civil War?

The Collapse of the Confederacy

After losing to Grant at Petersburg, Lee realized that the South's hopes for victory were lost. He knew his desperate army would soon starve. Many of his soldiers had deserted, or run away from, the army. They wanted to protect their families and homes. Lee tried to move his army west, but Grant surrounded it. On April 9, 1865, at Appomattox Court House, a village in Virginia, General Lee finally surrendered. Grant's surrender terms were generous. He even allowed Confederate soldiers to keep their own horses.

The rest of the Confederate commanders quickly surrendered, and Jefferson Davis, president of the Confederacy, was captured. The Civil War had ended. Many Americans had faith that under the wise leadership of Abraham Lincoln, the country could begin to heal. In his second inaugural address, Lincoln shared his hopes for the country's future:

> "With malice [anger] toward none; with charity for all . . . let us strive to finish the work we are in, to bind up the nation's wounds . . . to do all which may achieve and cherish a just and lasting peace. "

★ **What was Grant's plan to end the Civil War?**

III Review

Review History
A. Why were the battles of Gettysburg and Vicksburg the turning point in the Civil War?
B. Who were the Copperheads?
C. Why did General Robert E. Lee surrender?

Define Terms to Know
Provide a definition for each of the following terms.
habeas corpus, censorship, total war

Critical Thinking
Do you think a President is ever justified in restricting civil rights for security reasons in wartime? Why or why not?

Write About History
Write a paragraph explaining what impact total war had on southern soldiers and their families.

Get Organized
CHART
Create a chart to classify the information in this section. For example, classify the military leaders of the war as Union or Confederate.

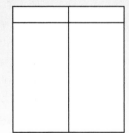

CONNECT
History & Technology

The Civil War in Photographs

During the Civil War, photography changed the way history was recorded. For the first time, war was captured in photographs. Portable darkrooms and other advances in technology allowed photographers to record the camps, the aftermath of battles, and the grim realities of the Civil War.

THE PHOTOGRAPHERS Mathew B. Brady was the best-known photographer of the Civil War period. In 1861, he decided to make a complete photographic record of the war. To do so, he hired a number of excellent photographers, including Alexander Gardner and Timothy H. O'Sullivan.

Brady stationed his photographers at various battle sites. Although he took few of the photographs himself, he supervised the operation and may have photographed the most famous battles. He also photographed Abraham Lincoln, Union generals, and Robert E. Lee.

THE TECHNOLOGY During the Civil War, photographs were limited by the technology of the day. Glass negatives were used to print images on paper. Darkroom wagons had to be on hand for developing. Exposure took between 5 and 30 seconds, much improved from the past but still time consuming. This lengthy process made it difficult to take action photos. For this reason, photographers shot mostly still or posed images, such as soldiers standing in front of their tents or wagons and regiments standing in formation.

Critical Thinking

Answer the questions below. Then, complete the activity.

1. Why was it difficult to take photographs of Civil War battles?

2. Brady is believed to have once said, "The camera is the eye of history." Do you think this is still true today? Explain.

Write About It

Use the Internet to learn more about Brady's Civil War photographs. Print out one photo. In a paragraph, describe the photo and explain why it is an important record of history. To get started, go to www.gfamericanhistory.com.

This photograph was taken by Brady after the Battle of Antietam.

Chapter Summary

In your notebook, complete the following outline. Then, use your outline to write a brief summary of the chapter.

The Civil War

I. The Early Days of the War

    A. The Buildup to Battle
    B.
    C.

II. War and American Life

    A.
    B.
    C.

III. Victory for the North

    A.
    B.
    C.

Interpret the Timeline

Use the timeline on pages 404–405 to answer the following questions.

1. How many years separate the First Battle of Bull Run from the end of the Civil War?

2. **Critical Thinking** Which event on the timeline contributed the most to the North's winning of the Civil War? Why?

Use Terms to Know

Select the term that best completes each sentence.

blockade   conscription   trench warfare
censorship   strategy

1. Soldiers in the Civil War engaged in _____ , fighting from long ditches dug in the ground.

2. In wartime _____ has been used to silence criticism of the war.

3. Both sides passed _____ laws to increase the size of their armed forces.

4. The Union created a _____ to cut off supply routes to the South.

5. The Confederacy and the Union each had a different _____ to win the war.

Check Your Understanding

1. **Identify** some of the advantages of the North.

2. **Discuss** the Confederacy's strategy for winning the war.

3. **Describe** the advances made in weapons during the war.

4. **Summarize** ways that women and African Americans contributed to the war efforts of the North and the South.

5. **Explain** the significance of the Battle of Gettysburg.

6. **Describe** the effects of total war.

Critical Thinking

1. **Make Inferences** What advice would you have given to southern leaders planning to fight in the Civil War in 1861? Explain your answer.

2. **Analyze Primary Sources** Judging from the quotation on page 414, what effects did unpleasant food have on soldiers?

3. **Analyze Primary Sources** Reread Lincoln's quotation on page 426. How would you describe Lincoln's attitude toward the South?

Put Your Skills to Work

PREDICT CONSEQUENCES

You have learned how to predict consequences based on information you already know. Predicting consequences helps you to better understand both historical and current events and what kinds of consequences might result.

Copy the following chart on a sheet of paper. Think about the last year of the Civil War. List three events that would have a lasting effect on the nation's recovery from the war. Then, predict a consequence of these events.

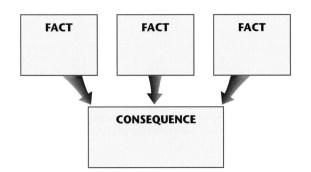

FACT   FACT   FACT

CONSEQUENCE

In Your Own Words

JOURNAL WRITING

Although the Civil War was a tragic event, it had some positive effects. For example, one result was the end of slavery in the United States. In your journal, write about a difficult experience you have had that had a positive outcome. Explain how bad things can sometimes have positive results, both intended and unintended.

Net Work

INTERNET ACTIVITY

What was life like for soldiers during the Civil War? What did they eat? What did they wear? What did they do to pass the time between battles? Working with a partner, research and create a short presentation on some part of the life of a soldier in the Union or Confederate army. Include photos, songs, letters, or journal entries—anything that would help show how soldiers lived during the war. Share your presentation with the class.

For help in starting this activity, visit the following Web site: www.gfamericanhistory.com.

Look Ahead
In the next chapter, learn how the nation struggled to rebuild after the Civil War.

CHAPTER 18

Reunion and Reconstruction 1865–1877

I. **Reuniting a Nation**
II. **Conflicts Over Reconstruction**
III. **The New South**

*T*he challenges facing the country after the Civil War were enormous. The federal government needed to reunite the nation. It also had to rebuild the South's ruined cities and shattered economy. Perhaps the greatest challenge was helping millions of newly freed African Americans make new lives. Millie Freeman, who had been enslaved, remembered how difficult it was to move forward when she said,

" It seemed like it took a long time for freedom to come. Everything just kept on like it was. "

The defeated South resisted the North's plans, especially in helping African Americans. Although the nation's wounds were beginning to heal, the scars of war would last for many years.

Primer used in the 1800s

U.S. Events	1865	1868	1871
	1865 Civil War ends. Abraham Lincoln is assassinated. Freedmen's Bureau is created. Thirteenth Amendment ends slavery.		
	1866 Civil Rights Act of 1866 is passed.	**1867** Reconstruction Act of 1867 is passed.	**1870** Fifteenth Amendment is ratified.
		1868 Fourteenth Amendment is ratified. Andrew Johnson is impeached and acquitted.	Hiram Revels and Blanche Bruce become the first African American senators.
Presidential Term Begins	1865 Andrew Johnson	1869 Ulysses S. Grant	
World Events	1865	1868	1871
	1866 Gregor Mendel begins study of genetics.	**1868** Meiji restoration in Japan occurs.	**1871** Germany is unified under Prussian leadership.

VIEW HISTORY After the Civil War, newly freed African Americans—from young children to adult men and women—attended schools in the South in order to gain an education. Supplies at these schools often included primers, or early reading books (shown left), that were donated.

★ For newly freed slaves, what were some possible social and economic advantages in learning how to read and write?

Get Organized

FLOWCHART

Understanding the order in which events happen can help you to understand the relationship that one event has with another. Create a flowchart as you read Chapter 18. List important events in the correct sequence on the flowchart. Here is an example from this chapter.

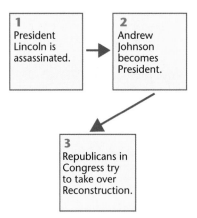

1 President Lincoln is assassinated.

2 Andrew Johnson becomes President.

3 Republicans in Congress try to take over Reconstruction.

1872
Freedmen's Bureau closes.

1877
Reconstruction ends.

1874	1877	1880

1877 Rutherford B. Hayes

1874	1877	1880

1873
Ruins of Troy, in northwestern Turkey, are discovered by archaeologists.

1876
Queen Victoria becomes empress of India.

Reuniting a Nation

Terms to Know

Reconstruction the period from 1865 to 1877 in which programs were created to reunite the South with the North

amnesty a government pardon for an offense

black codes a series of laws passed in early Reconstruction to limit the freedoms of formerly enslaved African Americans

Main Ideas

A. President Lincoln had hoped to reunite the country, but he was assassinated before he could carry out his plans.

B. Different ideas about how to reunite the nation divided President Andrew Johnson and Congress, while African Americans' rights were being challenged in the South.

 **Active Reading**

POINTS OF VIEW
How do different people feel about important issues? As you read this section, ask yourself the following question: What did President Johnson and the Republicans in Congress think about Reconstruction?

Spotlight on
Culture

Juneteenth is the oldest known celebration of the ending of slavery. It began when General Gordon Granger arrived in Galveston, Texas, on June 19, 1865, and declared the end of the Civil War and slavery. Since that time, Juneteenth has become a celebration of African American freedom.

A. Lincoln and Reconstruction

The 12 years after the Civil War are known as **Reconstruction**. During this period, the federal government looked for a way to reunite the former Confederate states with the rest of the country. There were several different plans proposed by government officials for Reconstruction. Like the war itself, Reconstruction caused conflicts between the North and the South.

The Emancipation of Slaves

One of the biggest issues of Reconstruction was the emancipation of slaves. On September 22, 1862, in the midst of the Civil War, President Abraham Lincoln had issued the Emancipation Proclamation. It stated that as of January 1, 1863 all enslaved people in Confederate states would be free. However, Confederate states ignored the Proclamation because they were no longer part of the U.S. government. Instead, Lincoln's Emancipation Proclamation served as a promise to slaves that they would be free when the North won the war.

The process of officially abolishing slavery began in April 1864, when the U.S. Senate, and later the House of Representatives, passed the Thirteenth Amendment to the Constitution. The amendment, however, needed to be ratified, or approved before it could become law. In December 1865, states loyal to the Union ratified the amendment, and slavery was officially abolished throughout the United States.

President Lincoln's Reconstruction Plan

Even before the end of the Civil War, President Lincoln had created a plan to win back the loyalty of the South. This plan was known as the Ten Percent Plan. The Ten Percent Plan would give most former Confederates **amnesty**, or a pardon, for their war actions. To gain amnesty, the states would have to meet the following requirements:

1. Promise their loyalty to the Union
2. Pledge to support the U.S. Constitution and obey laws passed by Congress
3. Accept the end of slavery

When 10 percent of a state's voters promised loyalty to the Union and the U.S. Constitution, that state would be allowed to elect a new state government. Then, the state government would have to approve the Thirteenth Amendment. However, they were not forced to give the same rights to African Americans as were given to white Americans. After approving the amendment, the state could finally re-enter the Union. In Lincoln's plan, the President would be in charge of Reconstruction.

Death of a Leader

By 1865, most Americans approved of the way President Lincoln had managed the war. They also agreed with his plan for ending slavery and healing the country. The President, however, did not live to see his plan take effect.

On April 14, just five days after Robert E. Lee's surrender at Appomattox Court House, Virginia, Lincoln was assassinated. While watching a play from his presidential box at Ford's Theater in Washington, D.C., the President was shot in the back of the head by a man named John Wilkes Booth. Lincoln died early the next morning.

Booth was both an actor and a southern sympathizer. He hated the Union and its leader. By killing Lincoln, he hoped to gain revenge for the South's defeat.

The President's death caused tremendous grief throughout the North and in the South among African Americans. His body was carried by train from Washington, D.C., back to Springfield, Illinois. As the train passed through cities, towns, and villages, millions of Americans turned out to say goodbye to their wartime President.

A large reward was offered for the capture of John Wilkes Booth after he assassinated President Lincoln. Booth was shot several days after his attack on the President.

John Wilkes Booth

Lincoln's Effect on Government

Abraham Lincoln left the federal government stronger than when he first took office. During his term, Lincoln greatly extended the powers of the presidency. He enlarged the army in order to win the war, even though the U.S. Constitution gives this job to Congress.

Lincoln also set a precedent of conduct for a U.S. President during war times. He suspended some constitutional rights for those suspected of disloyalty or those actively opposing the war. At the same time, he introduced the idea that the federal government should protect the civil rights of law-abiding citizens, especially if individual states failed to protect these rights. This idea would grow stronger over the next 100 years.

★ **How did Lincoln expand the powers of the federal government and of the presidency?**

B. Different Plans for Reconstruction

Many Republicans in Congress did not support Lincoln's plan for Reconstruction. Some of these Republicans wanted to take strong action to punish the former Confederate leaders.

Congressional Reconstruction Plan

Republicans in Congress were divided over Lincoln's plan for Reconstruction. Some supported Lincoln's plan, whereas others opposed it because they felt the plan made it too easy for the southern states to rejoin the Union.

Some of the Radical Republican leaders included (front, left to right) Benjamin F. Butler, Thaddeus Stevens, Thomas Williams, John A. Bingham, (back, left to right) James F. Wilson, George S. Boutwell, and John A. Logan.

One group, known as Radical Republicans, spoke strongly against the plan. Thaddeus Stevens and Charles Sumner were the leaders of the Radical Republicans. They wished to punish the South for rebelling against the Union. In addition, the Radical Republicans wanted to make sure former slaves gained equal rights. To accomplish their plan, they wanted Congress to control Reconstruction.

The Radical Republicans' plan for reuniting the North and the South was called the Wade-Davis Bill. This plan required that a majority, not just 10 percent, of a state's citizens pledge to support the U.S. Constitution. It also required that citizens swear they had never voluntarily supported the Confederacy. Of course, because most Southerners had sworn allegiance to the Confederacy, this requirement was impossible to meet. Although the Radical Republicans were a minority, or had fewer numbers, in Congress, they gained the support of moderate, or less radical, Republicans in order to pass their plan.

A New President

After Lincoln's death, Vice President Andrew Johnson became the seventeenth President of the United States. Johnson, who was born in North Carolina but later moved to Tennessee, was the only Southerner to remain in Congress during the Civil War. He had refused to join with his state in leaving the Union.

Johnson was nominated as Lincoln's Vice President in 1864 as a way to promote national unity. Throughout his political career, he had been a champion of the common person, standing with poor farmers against rich plantation owners. For this reason, Radical Republicans thought that Johnson would support their plan for Reconstruction.

President Johnson's Plan

President Johnson angered the Radical Republicans by adopting a Reconstruction plan similar to Lincoln's. In addition, he restored property and political rights to most former Confederate leaders. This restoration allowed many of the same people who had led the South before secession to take power again. Both moderate Republicans and Radical Republicans opposed this idea.

The battle over civil rights heated up in 1866. Early in the year, Congress passed the Civil Rights Act of 1866, which gave citizenship to all people born in the United States except Native Americans. President Johnson vetoed the bill. Republicans in Congress voted to override the President's veto.

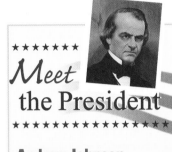

★ ★ ★ ★ ★ ★
Meet
the President
★ ★ ★ ★ ★ ★ ★ ★ ★ ★ ★ ★ ★ ★ ★

Andrew Johnson
1808–1875

Years in office 1865–1869

Political Party Democratic

Birthplace
North Carolina

Assumed office at age
57, succeeded Abraham Lincoln

Occupation Tailor

Did you know? Andrew Johnson did not know how to write until his wife Eliza taught him.

Quote "I love my country. Every public act of my life testifies that is so."

Black Codes

Beginning in 1865, southern states formed new governments based on President Johnson's Reconstruction plan. Many former Confederate leaders took positions in the new state governments.

The new governments in the former Confederate states began to find ways to limit the rights of freed African Americans. These laws were known as **black codes**. According to these laws, African Americans were not allowed to vote, hold certain types of jobs, carry weapons, or serve on juries. They also could not own or lease farms. In addition, the black codes allowed authorities to arrest and impose a monetary fine on African Americans who did not work. If a person could not pay the fine, the authorities could rent the person as a laborer to landowners until the fine was paid.

The black codes made life for freed African Americans very similar to life endured under slavery. Radical Republicans were outraged by the new laws. They believed that Southerners were trying to keep slavery in another form. As a result, the Radical and moderate Republicans decided to take control of Reconstruction.

 Under the black codes, how was life for freed African Americans similar to life under slavery?

Review

Review History

A. What was President Lincoln's plan for Reconstruction?

B. How did the Radical Republicans' plan for Reconstruction differ from Johnson's plan?

Define Terms to Know
Provide a definition for each of the following terms.
Reconstruction, amnesty, black codes

Critical Thinking
Why might Reconstruction have been frustrating for African Americans who had just received their freedom?

Write About History
Millions of Americans mourned President Lincoln's death. Write a paragraph about the contributions that Abraham Lincoln made to the country.

Get Organized
FLOWCHART
Understanding the order in which events happen helps you understand their relationship with each other. Create a flowchart of events, starting with Johnson's decision to adopt a Reconstruction plan similar to Lincoln's.

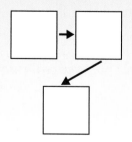

Build Your Skills

COMPARE AND CONTRAST

When you compare and contrast two items, you identify ways they are similar and ways they are different. To compare is to decide how two or more things are alike. To contrast is to find how they are different. A Venn diagram is a special kind of chart that makes it easy to compare and contrast items.

When reading about history, comparing and contrasting places, ideas, policies, or events can help you understand them better.

Here's How

Follow these steps to compare and contrast items using a Venn diagram.

1. Identify important characteristics of items you want to compare and contrast.

2. In the outer sections of the circles, write ways in which the items are different.

3. In the section shared by both circles, write ways in which the two items are alike.

4. Draw conclusions based on your diagram.

Here's Why

You have just read about different plans for Reconstruction proposed by Congress and by Presidents Lincoln and Johnson. Suppose you had to answer an essay question about comparing and contrasting these plans. Using a Venn diagram would help you organize your information and construct your answer.

Practice the Skill

Copy the Venn diagram on a sheet of paper. Review Section I, and fill in the diagram with information from the section about the different plans for Reconstruction.

Extend the Skill

Write an essay based on the following direction: Compare and contrast the combined Reconstruction plans of Presidents Lincoln and Johnson with that of the Republicans in Congress.

Apply the Skill

As you read the remaining sections of this chapter, think about ways you can compare and contrast information. For

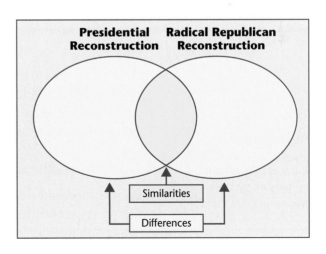

example, you could compare and contrast the lives of white Southerners before and after the Civil War.

II Conflicts Over Reconstruction

Terms to Know

carpetbagger a Northerner who moved to the South after the Civil War for political gain

scalawag a white Southerner who supported the Republicans during Reconstruction

discrimination unjust treatment of someone based on prejudice

impeachment the process of charging a high public official, such as the President, with a crime

Main Ideas

A. Disagreement over the Fourteenth Amendment led to a showdown between the President and Congress.

B. Republicans in Congress took control of Reconstruction and created new governments of southern states.

C. Republicans failed to remove President Johnson from office by a single vote.

 **Active Reading**

CAUSE AND EFFECT
A cause is a person, a thing, or an event that makes something happen. Whatever happens is called a result, or an effect. As you read this section, look for examples of causes and effects.

Do You Remember?
In Chapter 16, you read about the Supreme Court's Dred Scott decision. This decision said that Dred Scott was not a citizen and had no rights.

A. The Struggle for Control

To protect the Civil Rights Act of 1866, Republicans decided to amend the Constitution. Then, by winning most of the seats in Congress, they took control of Reconstruction.

Defining a Citizen

Because Republican leaders were afraid that the Supreme Court would rule the Civil Rights Act of 1866 unconstitutional, they passed the Fourteenth Amendment to the U.S. Constitution, which defined who a citizen was. The following ideas were included in the amendment.

1. Anyone born or naturalized in the United States (except Native Americans) and ruled by its laws is a citizen.
2. States cannot make laws that take away any rights of citizens.
3. States that limit any man's—including any African American man's—right to vote will lose representation in Congress.
4. No former Confederate leaders can hold a government office.

Congress then said that any state wishing to rejoin the Union had to ratify the Fourteenth Amendment. President Johnson, however, discouraged the states from ratifying the amendment. In the end, only Tennessee ratified it. The other 10 states of the former Confederacy refused. This disagreement about ratification of the Fourteenth Amendment set the stage for a final showdown between President Johnson and Congress.

The Election of 1866

The congressional election of 1866 became a contest between President Andrew Johnson's Reconstruction plan and the Reconstruction plan proposed by the Republicans. Johnson urged Americans to elect representatives in the House of Representatives and the Senate who supported his ideas. The voters, however, spoke out clearly for the Republicans. They won enough seats to pass any law over Johnson's veto. When the new Congress assembled in early 1867, the members were in control of Reconstruction.

★ **Why did Congress propose the Fourteenth Amendment to the Constitution?**

B. Republicans in Charge of Reconstruction

Republicans went right to work shaping Reconstruction the way they wanted it. As a result, many changes occurred in the South.

New State Governments and Constitutions

To ensure that its Reconstruction measures were carried out, Congress passed the Reconstruction Act of 1867. It placed the 10 southern states that had not ratified the Fourteenth Amendment under military rule. It also gave Congress the right to declare that state governments formed prior to 1867 were illegal. Federal troops were sent into those states to maintain law and order.

The Reconstruction Act of 1867 divided the South into five military regions and placed an army general as military governor in charge of each region. The generals registered male voters, most of whom were freed African Americans and white men who supported the Republicans. Former Confederate leaders and their supporters were not allowed to register.

Next, voters elected delegates to state conventions. Their job was to write new state constitutions supporting voting rights for African American men. Then, the voters in a state had to approve the new constitution and the Fourteenth Amendment. When all of these requirements were met, the state was allowed to be readmitted to the Union. By the end of 1870, all the states had been readmitted.

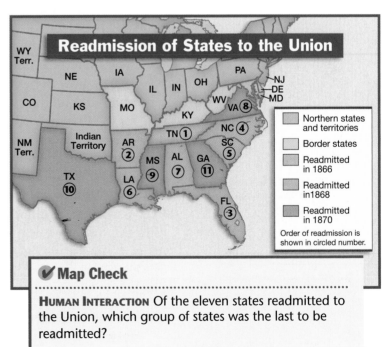

Readmission of States to the Union

Northern states and territories

Border states

Readmitted in 1866

Readmitted in 1868

Readmitted in 1870

Order of readmission is shown in circled number.

✔ **Map Check**

HUMAN INTERACTION Of the eleven states readmitted to the Union, which group of states was the last to be readmitted?

A Shift of Power

The new governments in southern states were very different from those of earlier times. They were made up of three groups: African Americans, Northerners who moved to the South, and white Southerners who sided with the Republicans. African Americans provided most of the votes to elect the new governments. However, the Northerners who moved to the South were in charge of most state governments. These Northerners became known as **carpetbaggers** because many of them traveled to the South after the war carrying cloth suitcases called carpetbags.

Most white Southerners disliked the carpetbaggers and accused them of using their government jobs to get rich. White Southerners who sided with the Republicans and the carpetbaggers were called **scalawags**. The word scalawag, used to describe a worthless farm animal, was used in the South as a term to insult people. Most white Southerners thought scalawags were traitors. However, many scalawags were farmers who had always hated slavery. Others were supporters of Republican economic policies.

Carpetbaggers were viewed by many Southerners as people who wanted to profit at the South's expense.

New Southern Governments and African Americans

The new governments made many changes. They established public schools and built roads, railroads, and hospitals. The governments also reduced the power of wealthy plantation owners. New tax laws required the rich to pay a larger share.

The new governments also eliminated property qualifications for voting and holding office, allowing many poor white men to vote for the first time. Women were not given the right to vote, but they did gain greater rights to own property. Most importantly, the new governments eliminated the black codes. **Discrimination,** or unfair treatment of a person based on race, was outlawed.

Many African Americans were elected to office during Reconstruction. Hiram Revels and Blanche Bruce of Mississippi were the first African Americans to serve as U.S. senators. Other African Americans became representatives to Congress, state officeholders, sheriffs, and mayors. One African American, P.B.S. Pinchback, became the governor of Louisiana.

★ **How did Reconstruction change the governments of southern states?**

C. A President on Trial

Although President Johnson could do little to oppose the Republicans, many still viewed him as a threat. They believed that their Reconstruction policies would be safe only if Johnson was removed from office.

Removing a President From Office

The U.S. Constitution provides a way of removing a President from office, but only if that President has committed "treason, bribery, or other high crimes and misdemeanors." Removing a President involves having the House of Representatives vote by a majority to accuse the President of a very serious crime. Then, the Senate puts the President on trial, with senators acting as jurors. It must vote by a two-thirds majority to convict. Only if the Senate convicts a President can he be removed from office. The process in which a U.S. President is accused of a crime is called **impeachment**.

In 1867, Congress passed the Tenure of Office Act, designed to limit President Johnson's power. This law made it illegal for the President to fire a Cabinet member without Senate approval. In February 1868, Johnson fired his Secretary of War, Republican Edwin Stanton, who was working with the Radical Republicans. The House voted to impeach Johnson, claiming that he had broken the Tenure of Office Act. Johnson denied the charge. Republicans, however, wanted to remove Johnson from office so that he could not oppose Reconstruction plans proposed by Congress. The impeachment trial moved to the Senate.

Impeachment Proceedings

To some observers, the Senate trial was like a circus. Admission tickets were sold. One senator, Edmund Ross of Kansas, described the scene:

> **❝**The galleries were packed. Tickets of admission were at an enormous premium. The House had adjourned and all of its members were in the Senate chamber. **❞**

Tickets for the impeachment trial of President Andrew Johnson in 1868 were eagerly sought.

ANALYZE PRIMARY SOURCES

DOCUMENT-BASED QUESTION What does the fact that ticket prices were at a premium, or selling for very high prices, tell you about people's interest in the trial?

Even before the vote took place, all the senators except one had announced how they would vote. Opponents of the President were one vote short of removing him from office. The one undecided senator was Edmund Ross. He was under tremendous pressure to vote against the President. When his name was called to vote, Ross remembered,

ANALYZE PRIMARY SOURCES

DOCUMENT-BASED QUESTION What do you think Ross meant when he said he could look down into his open grave?

 Not a foot moved, not the rustle of a garment . . . was heard. . . . Hope and fear seemed blended in every face. . . . It was a tremendous responsibility. . . . I almost literally looked down into my open grave. 🟊🟊

Ross said, "Not guilty." With that vote, President Johnson would remain in office. This decision established that only criminal actions by a President, and not political disagreements, justified removal of a President from office.

President Johnson finished his term in office. However, he lacked political influence. As a result, the Republicans continued to control Reconstruction. In 1868, Republicans nominated Ulysses Simpson Grant as their presidential candidate. The popular Civil War hero won the election easily.

★ **What action by President Johnson led to his impeachment?**

II Review

Review History
A. How did the Fourteenth Amendment protect the rights of citizens?
B. What changes did the new governments make in southern states?
C. Why did Republicans want to remove President Johnson from office?

Define Terms to Know
Provide a definition for each of the following terms.
carpetbagger, scalawag, discrimination, impeachment

Critical Thinking
Why do you think the Republicans wanted to limit the power of former Confederate leaders after the war?

Write About Government
Write a newspaper editorial that reflects your views about the fairness of the impeachment of President Johnson.

Get Organized
FLOWCHART
Understanding the order in which events happen can help you understand their relationship with each other. Create a flowchart listing events, starting with the passage of the Tenure of Office Act by Congress.

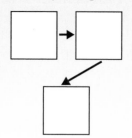

III The New South

Terms to Know

Freedmen's Bureau the federal agency created to help emancipated African Americans adjust to life as free people

sharecropping a system of farming in which farmers work another's land and use part of their crops as rent

segregation separation of the races

Jim Crow laws laws that enforced segregation in the South

Main Ideas

A. Federal programs helped freed African Americans rebuild their lives.

B. Before Reconstruction ended in 1877, white Southerners resisted it through laws that separated races and by violence.

Active Reading

GENERALIZE
When you generalize, you combine details to make an overall statement that describes a situation. As you read this section, generalize about African Americans in the South at the end of Reconstruction.

A. African Americans Build New Lives

All Southerners faced an uncertain future at the end of the Civil War. Reconstruction changed life dramatically in the South. For African Americans, freedom and the end of the war brought new opportunities and challenges.

The Freedmen's Bureau

One of the most successful programs of Reconstruction helped newly emancipated African Americans adjust to life as free people, or "freedmen." In 1865, Congress created the **Freedmen's Bureau**.

Freedmen's Bureau schools, such as this one, were established throughout the South.

This agency, led by Oliver Otis Howard, helped former slaves by finding them jobs that paid fair wages, or pay. It also set up courts to ensure justice for African Americans.

The Freedmen's Bureau had its biggest success in setting up schools. It started 4,300 schools for nearly 250,000 children and adults. The teachers at the schools were volunteers from the North. One of these teachers was Charlotte Forten, who came from a well-known African American family in Philadelphia. Forten described her school in a letter:

ANALYZE PRIMARY SOURCES

DOCUMENT-BASED QUESTION In what ways is Charlotte Forten impressed by the students at her Freedmen's Bureau School?

> **"**I never before saw children so eager to learn. . . . It is wonderful how a people who have been so long crushed to the earth . . . can have so great a desire for knowledge. **"**

The Bureau also helped establish the South's first colleges for African Americans—Howard University in Washington, D.C., Hampton Institute in Virginia, and Fisk University in Tennessee. The Freedmen's Bureau operated until 1872.

They Made History

Oliver Otis Howard 1830–1909

Oliver Otis Howard was a Union general who fought in several battles during the Civil War. In 1865, President Andrew Johnson appointed Howard to be commissioner of the Freedmen's Bureau. Howard led the Bureau until it closed in 1872. Throughout that time, he was also active in other African American causes. He helped establish Howard University in Washington, D.C., and served as its president from 1869 to 1874. Howard organized a Congregational church in Washington that included both African American and white members. Later in his life, Howard served as a peace commissioner to the Apache people. He also headed the U.S. Military Academy at West Point, New York.

General O. O. Howard led Union troops at several important battles. He was later chosen to lead the Freedmen's Bureau during Reconstruction.

Critical Thinking How does Oliver Howard's work with African Americans in the 1860s and 1870s continue to impact African Americans today?

Life after Slavery

When slavery ended, many African Americans were not prepared for the challenges of planning their own lives. Some left the plantations to make new lives in southern cities. Others used their new freedom to find long-lost family members. During slavery, families were separated and sold to different owners. After emancipation, many African Americans put ads in newspapers trying to find their brothers, sisters, parents, and children.

A new system of work, called **sharecropping**, developed during Reconstruction. In this system, many African Americans and poor white people farmed land owned by white landowners. Instead of renting the land with money, sharecroppers gave part of their harvest to the landowner.

The social life of African Americans also changed during Reconstruction. Newly freed African Americans could now openly form their own churches, which quickly became centers of community life.

Another limitation of slavery was also removed. Now, couples could be legally married. To many, legal marriage was an important symbol of freedom and equality.

Sharecroppers were constantly in debt to landowners.

⭐ **What were the accomplishments of the Freedmen's Bureau?**

B. Opposing Reconstruction

Like African Americans, white Southerners saw changes in the way they lived. Plantation output slowed, Northerners controlled state governments, and African Americans had new rights. Faced with these changes, many white Southerners fought against Reconstruction.

Secret Societies

One way in which some white Southerners opposed Reconstruction was to form secret societies, such as the Ku Klux Klan, or KKK. The Ku Klux Klan was founded in 1866 by Confederate veterans to terrorize African Americans and prevent them from voting. The group also tried to scare away Northerners and those who sympathized with them.

The Klan spread throughout the South. Its members wore white hoods and robes to scare victims and to protect their own identities.

Civil Rights Legislation During Reconstruction	
LEGISLATION	**PURPOSE**
Civil Rights Act of 1866	Gave citizenship to African Americans; protected African American rights
Fourteenth Amendment	Gave citizenship to African Americans; protected the rights of all citizens
Fifteenth Amendment	Protected the voting rights of African American men

✔ **Chart Check**

Which piece of legislation protected the voting rights of African American men?

The KKK targeted African American leaders and teachers as well as their churches, schools, and homes. Congress responded to KKK violence by passing the Ku Klux Klan Act in 1871. This outlawed the Klan's practices and allowed the government to use military force, if necessary, to stamp them out. As a result, federal troops were sent to the South, and hundreds of Klan members were arrested.

The Fifteenth Amendment

In 1870, the Fifteenth Amendment was adopted. This amendment stated that the right to vote could not be denied to any person based on race or the fact that a person had been a slave.

Although the amendment was meant to protect the voting rights of African American men, enforcement of the Fifteenth Amendment was a problem. After Reconstruction ended in 1877, southern governments found ways to sidestep this amendment. For example, some states denied the vote to people who could not read or write. This excluded many African Americans who had not been able to go to school. In other southern states, people who wanted to vote were required to pay money, called a poll tax, or show that they owned property. These laws applied to all people but affected African Americans most. However, another law, called a grandfather clause, said that if a person's father or grandfather had the right to vote before 1867, then he was now automatically allowed to vote.

Because almost no African Americans could meet this requirement or pay the poll tax, they could not vote. Despite efforts by southern governments to deprive African Americans of the right to vote, the passage of the Fifteenth Amendment made a strong statement of the federal government's position to support African American equality.

Laws to Discriminate

Some southern states wanted to achieve **segregation**, or a separation of the races, in their states. They passed a series of laws that enforced the separation of African Americans and white people in most public places. These laws came to be called **Jim Crow laws**. Jim Crow was an African American character in a popular song—a foolish old dancer who never made any trouble. *Jim Crow* became the name for any law that enforced segregation in schools, restaurants, railroad cars, and other public places.

The End of Reconstruction

After many years of Reconstruction, Americans lost interest in the South's problems. Other issues, such as hard economic times, arose. Many people believed that the government had done enough to help African Americans. They felt Reconstruction should end.

In 1876, Americans turned their attention to the presidential election, which ended up being one of the closest in history. The Democratic candidate, Samuel Tilden, received more popular votes than Republican Rutherford B. Hayes. However, Tilden was one electoral vote short of winning the election. Because the votes of several southern states were in dispute, Congress created a special group to review the election results.

Almost four months after the election, the congressional group made an agreement known as the Compromise of 1877. Rutherford Hayes would be named President. In return, the remaining federal troops in the South would be removed. Without soldiers to protect African Americans' rights, white Southerners quickly took control of their states again. Little time was wasted in returning African Americans to a life that seemed similar to slavery in many ways.

Reconstruction officially ended in 1877, and segregation tightened its grip on the South. Most Americans in the rest of the country turned their attention to other matters.

★ **What was the Compromise of 1877?**

Then & Now

In the election of 1876, the candidate who won more popular votes did not receive more electoral votes. Tilden did not become President.

This has happened several times in the nation's history, most recently in the 2000 election. Democrat Al Gore won more popular votes, but Republican George W. Bush won more electoral votes. In both elections, disputed votes caused the results of the election to be delayed by more than a month.

III Review

Review History
A. What new freedoms did emancipated African Americans gain under Reconstruction?
B. What was the purpose of the Jim Crow laws?

Define Terms to Know
Provide a definition for each of the following terms.
Freedmen's Bureau, sharecropping, segregation, Jim Crow laws

Critical Thinking
In what ways was Reconstruction successful?

Write About Culture
Volunteer teachers helped educate African Americans. Suppose you were one of these teachers. Write a letter describing your experiences in a Freedmen's Bureau school.

Get Organized
FLOWCHART
Understanding the order in which events happen can help you understand their relationship with each other. Create a flowchart to list a sequence of events, starting with the adoption of the Fifteenth Amendment.

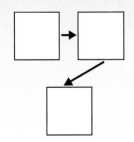

CHAPTER 18 Review

Chapter Summary

In your notebook, complete the following outline. Then, use your outline to write a brief summary of the chapter.

Reunion and Reconstruction

I. Reuniting a Nation

    A. Lincoln and Reconstruction

    B.

II. Conflicts Over Reconstruction

    A.

    B.

    C.

III. The New South

    A.

    B.

Interpret the Timeline

Use the timeline on pages 430–431 to answer the following questions.

1. Which amendment to the Constitution was ratified five years after the Civil War ended?

2. **Critical Thinking** Which events on the timeline promoted civil rights for African Americans?

Use Terms to Know

Select the term that best completes each sentence.

amnesty   segregation
discrimination   sharecropping
impeachment

1. Lincoln wanted to grant _____ , or pardon, to Confederates after the war.

2. The unfair treatment of a person based on race or religion is _____.

3. During Reconstruction, many African Americans farmed land through the _____ system.

4. Republicans used _____ to try to remove President Johnson from office.

5. A policy of _____, or separation of the races, grew in the South after the end of Reconstruction.

Check Your Understanding

1. **Explain** how slavery was abolished.

2. **Identify and describe** the ways President Lincoln's death affected the nation.

3. **Summarize** the reasons the Republicans wanted to impeach President Johnson.

4. **Explain** the significance of the Fourteenth and Fifteenth Amendments.

5. **Describe** the role of the Freedmen's Bureau.

6. **Identify** ways that white Southerners showed their resistance to Reconstruction and equal rights for African Americans.

Critical Thinking

1. **Analyze Primary Sources** According to the quote by Edmund Ross on page 442, how was the act of voting for or against impeachment a tremendous responsibility?

2. **Synthesize Information** What new groups of people became involved in the governments of the South during Reconstruction? What factors helped them gain power?

3. **Analyze Primary Sources** Reread the selection from Charlotte Forten's letter on page 444. Why do you think her students were so excited about the chance to go to school and learn?

Put Your Skills to Work

COMPARE AND CONTRAST

You have learned that using a Venn diagram to compare and contrast two items can show you how the items are similar and how they are different.

Copy the following Venn diagram on a sheet of paper. Use it to compare the lives of African Americans in the South before the Civil War and during Reconstruction. In the overlapping area, include characteristics that apply to both time periods.

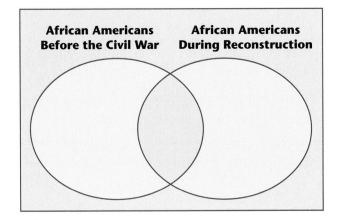

African Americans Before the Civil War

African Americans During Reconstruction

Net Work

INTERNET ACTIVITY

Abraham Lincoln is considered one of the greatest U.S. Presidents because of the way he led the country through the crisis of the Civil War. However, he is also considered a great American writer, storyteller, politician, and trial lawyer. Working with a partner, use the Internet as a resource to find sayings, speeches, or stories by the sixteenth President. Use your findings to create a class notebook called "The Wit and Wisdom of Abraham Lincoln."

For help in starting this activity, visit the following Web site: www.gfamericanhistory.com.

Look Ahead
In the next chapter, learn how many Americans joined the rush to the West.

Unit 6 Portfolio Project

Civil War Newspaper

YOUR ASSIGNMENT

It is the summer of 1865. President Lincoln was assassinated a few months ago, and Reconstruction just started. In your class, form five teams of reporters to work on a newspaper. As a class, decide where your newspaper is located. Television, radio, and computers do not exist, so people depend on your newspaper to tell them what is happening in the country and in the world.

THE STAFF MEETING

Choose Your Section Each team of reporters creates one page of the newspaper. As a team, choose one section from each list below to include on your page.

Business	Advertisements
Letters to the Editor	Cartoons and Comics
Inventions	Fashion
U.S. News	Recipes
World Events	Classified Ads

Plan Your Section Plan the articles and pictures for your page. Assign tasks to each team member. Use your textbook to find topics for your page. You may also refer to this Web site for ideas: www.gfamericanhistory.com.

THE NEWSROOM

Research and Write Use encyclopedias, other books, and the Internet to research the material for your page. Create your first draft.

Edit and Proofread Edit and proofread your articles. Make corrections and positive suggestions to your team members.

Design and Layout Paste the articles and artwork onto a large sheet of paper. Combine pages from other teams to construct the class newspaper.

Multimedia Presentation

Now, turn your newspaper into a present-day television documentary that investigates the Lincoln assassination and Reconstruction. Make cue cards that present the main points of each section. Conduct interviews of people who can contribute to the documentary. Practice your script and then rehearse the program in front of another class.

Growth at Home and Abroad

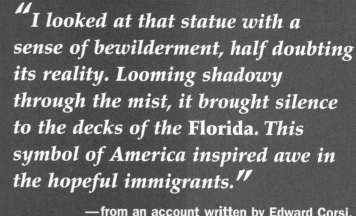

"I looked at that statue with a sense of bewilderment, half doubting its reality. Looming shadowy through the mist, it brought silence to the decks of the Florida. This symbol of America inspired awe in the hopeful immigrants."

—from an account written by Edward Corsi, an Italian immigrant in the early 1900s

LINK PAST TO PRESENT The Statue of Liberty has stood as a symbol of freedom in the United States for more than 100 years.

★ Why do you think the sight of the Statue of Liberty has had such a strong effect on immigrants coming to the United States?

CHAPTER 19

Life in the West 1858–1896

I. **Railroads, Ranchers, and Miners**
II. **Farming on the Great Plains**
III. **Native American Struggles**

*I*t was noon on April 22, 1889. Fifty thousand settlers waited impatiently along the edge of the Cherokee lands in Oklahoma. A race was about to begin—a race for free land. Suddenly, the settlers charged forward. They fanned out over the prairie. If they were the first to reach unclaimed land, they staked out a claim on which to farm and build a home.

The land rush in the West began in 1862. Within 40 years, most of the Great Plains was settled, but many newcomers were unprepared for the hard life that awaited them. A folk song from western Oklahoma expressed the feelings of many:

> Hurrah for Greer County! The land of the free,
> The land of the bedbug, grasshopper, and flea:
> I'll sing of its praises, I'll tell of its fame,
> While starving to death on my government claim.

A nineteenth-century quilt

		1862 Homestead Act and Pacific Railway Act are passed.		**1869** First transcontinental railroad is completed.
	1858 Gold is discovered near Pikes Peak, Colorado.		**1867** Grange is founded.	
U.S. Events	1855	1860	1865	1870
Presidential Term Begins	1857 James Buchanan	1861 Abraham Lincoln	1865 Andrew Johnson	1869 Ulysses S. Grant
World Events	1855	1860	1865	1870
		1863 International Committee of the Red Cross is founded.		**1867** Emperor Maximilian of Mexico is executed.

VIEW HISTORY Many western settlers, like this family in Nebraska, lived in sod houses made from chunks of grassy earth, or prairie sod. Women created quilts (left) out of small scraps of fabric.

★ **Why do you think pioneers on the Great Plains built houses like the one shown?**

Get Organized
VENN DIAGRAM

A Venn diagram helps you compare and contrast two events or items. Use a Venn diagram as you read Chapter 19. List differences in the outside sections of each circle. List similarities in the space where the circles overlap. Here is an example from this chapter.

COWHAND
- Often on the move
- Worked on horseback
- Lived in the open

- Hot, dry conditions
- Exposed to natural dangers

- Little travel
- Worked in fields
- Lived in sod houses

FARMER

1874
Farmers and ranchers begin to fence land with barbed wire.

1876
Battle of Little Bighorn takes place.

1887
Dawes Act breaks up reservations.

1890
Massacre occurs at Wounded Knee.

1892
Populist Party nominates a candidate for President.

1875	1880	1885	1890
	1877 Rutherford B. Hayes	1881 James Garfield Chester A. Arthur	1885 Grover Cleveland	1889 Benjamin Harrison

| 1875 | 1880 | 1885 | 1890 |

1876
First roller-skating rink opens in London, England.

1885
Louis Pasteur introduces rabies vaccine in France.

1889
Eiffel Tower in Paris, France, is completed.

Railroads, Ranchers, and Miners

I ★

Main Ideas

A. The railroad opened the West to increased settlement.

B. The cattle and mining industries developed and prospered in the West.

 **Active Reading**

PREDICT
When you predict, you look for clues about what might happen next. As you read this section, ask yourself the following question: Based on the information, what future events might follow?

A. Railroads and Western Settlement

After the Civil War ended, millions of Americans migrated to the region beyond the Mississippi River known as the West. Parts of California, Oregon, and Texas had already been settled. However, much of the West remained a frontier, or an undeveloped or unsettled region. The growth of railroads changed all that.

The West

Many Americans had long thought of areas of the West, especially the Great Plains, as unfit places to live. On some older maps, the whole region was labeled the "Great American Desert." In truth, the West was a diverse, though generally dry, region of grasslands, deserts, and mountains.

In the late 1800s, ranchers, miners, and farmers, all seeking opportunity, traveled west. These settlers often thought of the land as empty, but it was far from being so. Native American groups had lived there for thousands of years, and Spanish settlers had colonized it generations earlier. In addition, westward pioneers met Mexicans, French and British Canadians, Asians, and other settlers who had moved to the area as early as the 1840s.

Posters like this one advertised western lands for sale.

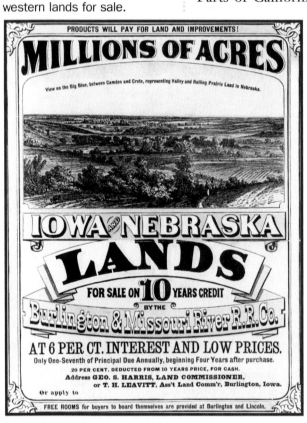

PRODUCTS WILL PAY FOR LAND AND IMPROVEMENTS!

MILLIONS OF ACRES

View on the Big Blue, between Camden and Crete, representing Valley and Rolling Prairie Land in Nebraska.

IOWA AND NEBRASKA

LANDS

FOR SALE ON **10** YEARS CREDIT

BY THE

Burlington & Missouri River R.R. Co.

AT 6 PER CT. INTEREST AND LOW PRICES.

Only One-Seventh of Principal Due Annually, beginning Four Years after purchase.

20 PER CENT. DEDUCTED FROM 10 YEARS PRICE, FOR CASH.

Address GEO. S. HARRIS, LAND COMMISSIONER,
or T. H. LEAVITT, Ass't Land Comm'r, Burlington, Iowa.

Or apply to

FREE ROOMS for buyers to board themselves are provided at Burlington and Lincoln.

Crossing the Continent

During the Civil War, Congress passed several laws to encourage westward settlement. One of these laws was the Pacific Railway Act of 1862. Under this act the federal government helped pay for the construction of a **transcontinental**, or across-the-continent, railroad. It would connect California and the East.

This law gave public land to railroad builders. Some of the land was used for laying track. Other land was sold to farmers for cash. The railroads thus became one of the biggest promoters of settlement in the Great Plains. They advertised the sale of western land not only to settlers in the United States but also in Europe.

Two companies were selected to begin building a railroad to join the East Coast and the West Coast. The Union Pacific Railroad laid track westward starting from the end of the existing railroad in Nebraska. The Central Pacific Railroad Company worked eastward from California. The two met in 1869 at Promontory Point, in present-day Utah.

On May 10, 1869, a golden spike was driven into the tracks at Promontory Point, Utah, to celebrate the completion of the transcontinental railroad.

Changing the West

The transcontinental railroad changed the West in many ways. First, it opened the region to new settlement by making it easier to travel there from the East. Second, it increased conflicts between Native Americans and settlers. Native Americans tried to defend their territory as more settlers moved into the area. Third, the railroad brought new ethnic groups to the American West, including large numbers of Chinese immigrants who built much of the western part of the railroad.

During the next several years, other transcontinental railroads were completed. By 1893, the Northern Pacific Railroad, the Southern Pacific Railroad, and the Great Northern Railroad all spanned, or extended across, the continent. Many other shorter lines—such as the Atchison, Topeka and Santa Fe; the Kansas and Pacific; and the Oregon Short Line—connected most parts of the western United States to cities in the East.

★ **What two companies built the first transcontinental railroad?**

Spotlight on History

Many men who worked for the Central Pacific Railroad Company were Chinese immigrants. They did the backbreaking and dangerous work of laying railroad tracks. Working 12-hour days, they chopped trees, built bridges, and dug through mountains. The head of the Central Pacific said, "Without them it would be impossible to complete the line on time."

Each year, herds of cattle were driven north toward the railroads to be shipped to market.

B. New Industries in the West

As railroads were making their way across the West, the cattle industry was also expanding into the region. Cattle ranchers from Texas decided that they could make money by rounding up wild cattle and driving them to railroad towns farther north. There, the herds of cattle were sold and shipped to cities in the East to meet the growing demand for beef. At the same time another major industry was developing in the West—mining. News of gold and silver strikes, or discoveries, drew waves of prospectors to the Rocky Mountains.

The Cattle Kingdom

In the 1860s, between three and six million longhorn cattle roamed wild in the brush country of South Texas. These animals were a mixture of Spanish cattle brought to the area in colonial times and English cattle that arrived with settlers from southern and midwestern states in the 1820s and 1830s. The cattle grazed on the open **range**, the huge public grasslands in the West.

In the spring of 1866, Texas cattle ranchers rounded up large herds of cattle and drove them north through Indian Territory to "cow towns" such as Kansas City, Missouri, or Dodge City in Kansas. There, the animals were loaded onto train cars and shipped to markets in cities such as Chicago, Illinois. Long cattle drives like these became annual events. Cattle were driven along routes including the Chisholm Trail, the Western Trail, and the Goodnight-Loving Trail. The same cattle that would sell for as little as two dollars each in Texas were worth 40 dollars or more in the North.

In 1866 alone, between 200,000 and 260,000 longhorns were driven more than 600 miles north for sale.

Cattle Workers

The workers of the cattle industry in the West were the **cowhands** who rode the open range. Most cowhands were young men. About 25 percent were African Americans; as many, if not more, were Mexicans and Mexican Americans. The cowhands adopted much of their clothing and their skills from the vaqueros—Mexican cowhands who had herded sheep and cattle in the Southwest and in Mexico for many years.

Cowhands spent long hours in the saddle every day. Each spring they gathered the cattle into large herds. Then, they branded new calves by burning a mark into their hides with a hot iron. This design, called a brand, was used to identify the owner of the cattle. Finally, each fall the cowhands drove the herds north. The long cattle drive usually lasted two to three months.

Many Americans in other parts of the country thought of the cowhand as a rugged, adventuresome, and free-spirited hero. This had some truth to it. However, the pay was low and the job was always tiring and often dangerous. Cowhands endured relentless heat, stampedes, storms, and swift river crossings that could drown people and animals. By day they worked amid choking clouds of dust. At night they slept on the cold bare ground. Teddy Blue, a cowhand who wrote a book about his experiences, remembered,

> " Our day wouldn't end till about nine o'clock when we grazed the herd onto the bed ground. And after that every man in the outfit . . . would have to stand two hour's night guard. . . . So I would get maybe five hour's sleep. . . . But the wagon rolled on in the morning just the same. "

The End of the Open Range

Cattle drives ended by the late 1800s. An increase in the number of cattle caused their price to fall. Then, around 1874, farmers and ranchers began to use barbed wire to fence their property. As a result, cattle could no longer roam freely. A drought in 1885 dried up water holes along the trail and turned the grassy pastures to desert. Blizzards in 1886 and 1887 killed thousands of cattle and left many more starving. Finally, added railroad routes and stops made the long drives unnecessary. By the late 1880s, cattle drives were a thing of the past, and most cattle were raised on huge, private ranches.

Then & Now

As cowhands perfected their roping and riding skills, they began to find ways to show off these skills. Shows called rodeos were developed to spotlight these skills and allow cowhands to compete against one another.

Rodeos are still an important part of the western culture of the United States. Each year, thousands of people compete in events such as bull riding, calf roping, and barrel racing.

ANALYZE PRIMARY SOURCES

DOCUMENT-BASED QUESTION Why do you think the cowhands had to stand guard at night?

Gold and Silver Mining

After the California gold rush of 1849, the search for gold and silver spread to many other parts of the West. In 1858, a gold strike occurred near Pikes Peak, Colorado. Soon after, other gold discoveries were made in present-day Idaho, Montana, and South Dakota. The last gold rush in the continental United States took place in the Black Hills of South Dakota in 1874.

Whenever a gold discovery was announced, thousands of miners swarmed to that area. They came from all parts of the country and even from overseas. Only a handful, however, ever became rich from mining gold.

Silver mining in the West became internationally famous in 1859 with the discovery of the Comstock Lode in Nevada. A lode is a mineral deposit. Silver is often embedded in rock, which could extend deep into the earth. The Comstock Lode mines sometimes reached a depth of 3,000 feet. They produced more than $300 million worth of silver and gold between 1860 and 1890.

Gold and silver were also discovered near Cherry Creek, Colorado. The prospectors who moved to this area founded the town of Denver in 1858. In present-day Montana, silver deposits led to the founding of Butte. Parts of Idaho also became a center of silver mining in the 1880s, as did southern Arizona.

 What happened at the cow towns?

Miners used shallow bowls to pan for gold in streams. They would swirl handfuls of soil or gravel in water. If gold was present, it would remain in the pan while the soil or gravel would wash over the side.

 **Review**

Review History
A. How did the railroads change the American West?
B. What was the purpose of the long cattle drives?

Define Terms to Know
Provide a definition for each of the following terms.
transcontinental, range, cowhand

Critical Thinking
Why do you think so many Americans admired the cowhand as a hero?

Write About History
You are a reporter from the East who is traveling west on the transcontinental railroad. Write a paragraph to describe your trip.

Get Organized
VENN DIAGRAM
Use a Venn diagram to compare and contrast workers in the cattle and mining industries. Consider where they worked and what their goals were.

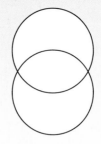

Build Your Skills

READA SPECIAL-PURPOSE MAP

There are many different kinds of maps. A special-purpose map shows more than the location of cities, states, or countries. It shows specific information such as the location of railroads and trails.

Special-purpose maps usually focus on one topic, which is identified in the title. These maps use symbols and colors to give information about that topic. You can find the meanings of the symbols and colors by studying the map key. For example, a population map might have small circles representing areas with few people and large circles to identify areas with a greater number of people. Using special-purpose maps can help you visualize information that you read.

Here's How

Follow these steps to read a special-purpose map.

1. Read the title to find out the map's topic.
2. Look for special symbols on the map. Use the map key to identify what the symbols and colors stand for.
3. Read any labels that identify special features on the map.

Here's Why

You have just read about the long cattle drives that were used to move herds of cattle to trains. Seeing a map of the cattle trails and the railroad lines can help you visualize why cattle drives were used.

Practice the Skill

Study the map at the right. Then, answer the following questions.

1. How long was the Goodnight-Loving Trail?
2. Which railroad line crossed farthest south on the Western Trail?

Extend the Skill

Using the map, write a paragraph describing the journey along a cattle trail of the West.

Apply the Skill

As you read Section III, study the map on page 467. How does this map help you understand what you read in the section?

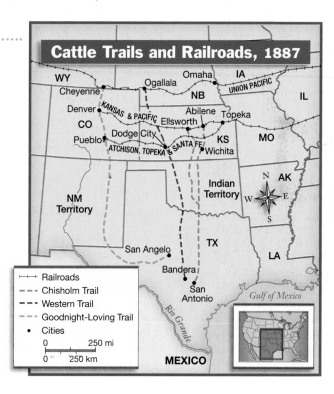

Cattle Trails and Railroads, 1887

II ★ Farming on the Great Plains

Terms to Know

homesteader a person who received land on which to build a house and farm

Exoduster an African American who moved to the Great Plains in the late 1800s

cooperative an organization that is jointly owned by those who use its services

platform a statement of a political party's policies and beliefs

Main Ideas

A. The Homestead Act encouraged people to settle the Great Plains and farm the grasslands there.

B. Life on the Great Plains was difficult because of the harsh climate and environment.

C. Farmers' Alliances and the Populist Party promoted the concerns of farmers.

 Active Reading

MAIN IDEAS AND SUPPORTING DETAILS
Identifying main ideas and supporting details can help you to understand what you read. As you read this section, identify supporting details for each main idea listed on this page.

A. Farmers Settle the Plains

Hundreds of thousands of farm families settled on the grasslands of the Great Plains. This sea of grass hid a valuable resource—a depth of about six feet of fertile topsoil. It was covered by a thick mat of roots and earth called sod. Farmers called sodbusters, used their plows to break up the sod and turn millions of acres of open range into farms.

The Homestead Act

To encourage farm settlement on the Great Plains, Congress passed the Homestead Act of 1862. For a small registration fee, this law granted 160 acres of land to anyone who agreed to live on it and farm it for five years. Those who received land, called **homesteaders**, had to be at least 21 years old. They were required to build a house with windows and plant crops.

The Homestead Act, combined with advertising by the large railroad companies, attracted millions of newcomers to the Great Plains. Most settlers were Americans who came from the East. Others, including Swedish, Norwegian, German, Irish, and Russian immigrants, traveled from Europe.

Laura Ingalls Wilder wrote about her experiences growing up on a homestead in books such as *Little House on the Prairie*. Wilder's portrayal of farm life on the Plains was quite true to life. Another homesteader recalled her high hopes for starting a new life:

Homesteaders collected buffalo chips, or droppings, from the prairie to use as fuel for cooking and warmth.

> " To me, homesteading is the solution of all poverty's problems. . . . [A]ny woman who can stand her own company, . . . [and] loves growing things, . . . and is willing to put in . . . time at careful labor, . . . will certainly succeed; will have independence, plenty to eat all the time, and a home of her own in the end. "

ANALYZE PRIMARY SOURCES

DOCUMENT-BASED QUESTION
What does the woman think a person can gain by becoming a homesteader?

African Americans on the Great Plains

African Americans from the South also sought better opportunities on the Great Plains. By 1880, about 26,000 African American men and women had migrated to Kansas. These settlers were known as **Exodusters** because they compared their journey west to the biblical Exodus of the Hebrews from slavery in Egypt.

The Exodusters founded three towns in Kansas. The largest was Nicodemus, with about 700 residents. Others settled on small tracts of land nearby. Like homesteaders elsewhere, some failed as farmers and later moved to cities. In the 1890s, more than 50,000 Exodusters established towns in Indian Territory and Oklahoma Territory.

★ Who were the Exodusters?

B. Life on the Farming Frontier

Few settlers who came to the Great Plains were prepared for the hardships they would encounter. The advertisements that lured them had promised cheap land and fertile soil, but they did not mention the harshness of the weather or the loneliness of farm life.

Hard Life on the Prairie

Scarce rainfall was one of the biggest problems for prairie farmers. Wheat was the main crop. It was best suited to the dry conditions. However, in the West, the 160 acres granted by the Homestead Act for farming wheat was not enough to support a family. Working more land required expensive equipment and additional workers, which most homesteaders could not afford.

The lack of trees for wood to build houses and make heat was another problem. Families often built their first houses out of chunks of sod. Sod houses cost little and kept out the fierce prairie winds, but they leaked dirt and could become muddy in wet weather. Later, families used other materials to build more permanent and comfortable homes.

Homesteaders could move quickly from one claim to the next by using portable shacks.

Settlers on the Great Plains burned piles of grasshoppers to prevent the insects from eating their crops.

Summers were extremely hot on the prairie, and winters were extremely cold, with temperatures as low as −40°F. Homesteaders also faced frequent natural disasters. Tornadoes could destroy homes, hailstorms could flatten wheat fields, and fires started by lightning could burn miles of prairie. Grasshoppers, which in some years swarmed in great clouds, devoured entire crops. Livestock were often killed by lightning, rattlesnakes, or blizzards.

Many homesteaders were unable to deal with the harshness of the prairie, especially those with little or no experience in farming. They returned east or moved to a nearby town. Others tried new farming techniques. Those with enough money purchased inventions such as mechanical grain harvesters and windmills, which could draw water from deep wells. Some farmers tried dryland farming, a way of tilling fields to retain moisture by covering the soil with a layer of dust.

The Grange

The loneliness of farm life was another hardship on the Great Plains. To address this problem, Oliver H. Kelley founded a social organization for farmers in 1867. It was called the Grange. In Grange Halls scattered throughout farm country, families gathered for weddings, funerals, and holiday dances. They also formed **cooperatives**, or organizations that are owned by the people who use their services. The cooperatives allowed farmers to save money by buying supplies in large quantities and selling products as a large group. By 1875, the Grange had more than 850,000 members.

★ **What were three problems faced by farmers?**

C. Farmers Unite

Farmers who joined the Grange learned that they could improve their lives by working together on common problems. In the 1870s and 1880s, farmers shifted their focus to political issues. One of their main concerns was the high prices that railroads charged for shipping their wheat to market.

Farmers' Alliances

Farmers depended on the railroads to ship their grain to eastern markets. However, the railroads often charged higher prices to ship grain than they did to ship other products. As a result, many farmers felt that the railroad industry was treating them unfairly.

To fight these and other problems, farmers organized into groups known as Farmers' Alliances. One group was organized in the Great Plains area, and another was set up in the South. By 1890, more than four million people had joined these groups. Another group, the Colored Farmers' Alliance, included more than a million African American farmers from southern states.

By 1890, the Farmers' Alliances had helped to elect many legislators that supported farmers. These legislators passed several laws regulating the railroad industry. One of these laws, the Interstate Commerce Act of 1887, created the Interstate Commerce Commission (ICC). The ICC made sure that railroads charged fair rates.

The Rise of the Populist Party

The Farmers' Alliances helped farmers gain political power. However, many farmers believed that neither the Democratic Party nor the Republican Party supported their interests. In 1891, Alliance members agreed to start a new national political party. They gathered in Omaha, Nebraska, on July 4, 1892, to adopt a **platform** for their new political party. A political party's platform is its statement of beliefs. It was called the Peoples' Party, but it was more commonly known as the Populist Party. A populist is a person who supports the rights of the common people.

This cartoon illustrates the conflict between the Grange and the railroads. The farmer, representing the Grange, warns sleeping citizens of the approaching train.

Populists were worried about the growing gap between the rich and the poor. They also believed that individual citizens were losing power to the "special-interest groups," meaning the railroads and other large companies. The Populists hoped to solve these and other problems they saw in the country. The party's platform called for the following changes:

1. Government ownership of the railroads
2. An income tax that was higher for the rich than for the poor
3. A loan program that would help farmers pay off their debts
4. Political reforms such as the direct election of senators
5. A shorter workday for laborers

The Populist Party nominated General James B. Weaver, a Civil War veteran, for President in 1892. He won several states but lost the election to Democrat Grover Cleveland. However, Populist Party members were elected to many state and local offices.

In 1896, Democrats gained the support of many Populist voters by nominating a pro-farmer representative from Nebraska named William Jennings Bryan for President. Bryan won the West and the South but lost to Ohio Governor William McKinley. After this loss, the Populist Party faded. However, its ideas lived on in reforms the country would later make.

 Why did farmers feel they needed their own political party?

II Review

Review History
A. How did the Homestead Act of 1862 encourage settlement of the Great Plains?
B. How did the Grange improve farmers' lives?
C. What reforms did the Populist Party call for?

Define Terms to Know
Provide a definition for each of the following terms.
homesteader, Exoduster, cooperative, platform

Critical Thinking
How would tighter regulation of the railroads help farmers on the Great Plains?

Write About Culture
You are a farmer on the Great Plains in the 1880s. Write a letter to a family member back East or in Europe about your experiences as a homesteader.

Get Organized
VENN DIAGRAM
Think about items you might compare in this section. Use a Venn diagram to show similarities and differences. For example, how were the Grange and the Farmers' Alliances alike and different?

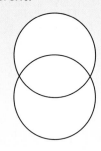

CONNECT
History & Literature

Willa Cather, *O Pioneers!*

In the 1860s, some women as well as men dreamed of owning a farm of their own. Few single women, however, had enough money to buy land. When the first Homestead Act was passed in 1862, some women took advantage of the opportunity to become property owners by staking a claim in one of the Great Plains states. Most women and girls who went west, like Willa Cather, author of *O Pioneers!*, went with their families.

WRITING FROM EXPERIENCE In 1883, Willa Cather, then nine years old, moved to Nebraska from Virginia. At first, her family tried farming on the untamed prairie; but within two years, they moved into the small village of Red Cloud. Both the town and the nearby farms were settled by Swedish, Russian, and German immigrants. The harsh but beautiful landscape, as well as the hard-working European immigrants, made a lasting impression on Cather. These experiences provided the background for Cather's novel *O Pioneers!*, which depicts life on a homestead.

A NOVEL ABOUT THE PIONEER SPIRIT The main character in *O Pioneers!* is Alexandra Bergson, the daughter of a Swedish immigrant in Nebraska. After her father dies, she takes charge of the family's farm. The land is difficult to work, but Alexandra is both determined and resourceful. She experiments with new farming methods and manages the family's money wisely. Although she faces many challenges, Alexandra fulfills her dream of success.

Critical Thinking

Answer the questions below. Then, complete the activity.

1. What might have caused families like Cather's to give up farming?

2. How does the experience of the main character in *O Pioneers!* reflect the experience of many farmers on the Plains?

Write About It

Read the first chapter of *O Pioneers!*. Then, write a paragraph explaining how Cather depicts the landscape of Nebraska. Include at least one quotation from the novel. You can find the chapter on this Web site: www.gfamericanhistory.com.

Willa Cather described life on a homestead in her novel *O Pioneers!*

III Native American Struggles

Terms to Know

extinction the death of a species

reservation public land set aside for special use, as for Native Americans

assimilate to become absorbed into a main culture

Main Ideas

A. As settlers continued to move west, the U.S. government forced Native Americans off their lands.

B. Native Americans in the southern Plains fought against settlers.

C. The Battle of Little Bighorn and the massacre at Wounded Knee were key events in the Native American wars.

 Active Reading

POINTS OF VIEW
When you contrast points of view, you examine the ways different groups of people view the same situation. As you read this section, think about how the Native Americans' view was different from that of the settlers.

A. Changes for Native Americans

Before the 1850s, the U.S. government had set aside a large region in the Great Plains as land for Native Americans. However, with the passage of the Homestead Act in 1862, the government began to encourage settlers to move to this region. As miners, ranchers, and farmers moved onto this land, Native Americans fought to preserve their way of life.

The End of the Buffalo

The Great Plains was the home of thousands of Native Americans, who followed the vast herds of buffalo throughout the region. The buffalo were very important to the Native Americans' way of life. After they were hunted and killed, buffalo were used for food, clothing, and shelter.

Approximately 15 million buffalo wandered the Great Plains in the early 1800s. A large southern herd grazed in Oklahoma, Kansas, and Texas. However, as the railroads crept steadily across the Plains, buffalo were hunted by settlers and railroad workers in increasing numbers. Some were killed to feed the railroad construction crews. Some were shot for their hides, which were in great demand in the East. Sport hunters killed many just for fun. By 1890, the buffalo had been hunted almost to **extinction**, or the dying out of the species. As the buffalo was destroyed, so was the Native Americans' hope of remaining on the Plains. Without the buffalo, it became more difficult for Native Americans to continue their way of life.

Then & Now

By the 1890s, the buffalo that remained alive were in privately owned herds or in Yellowstone National Park. In 1902, the federal government bought several hundred more buffalo from ranchers, shipped them to Yellowstone, and began raising them at a "Buffalo Ranch" in the park.

Today, about 2,000 descendants of these animals still roam Yellowstone—the largest remaining herd of buffalo in the United States.

Broken Promises

The increasing number of settlers began to change the lives of Native Americans that had lived and hunted on the Great Plains for centuries. As the western lands were settled by whites and Exodusters, the U.S. government made treaties with the Native Americans. These treaties set aside sections of land, called **reservations**, where Native American groups would live. The government promised that Native Americans would hold these lands for all time and that settlers would not be allowed on the reservations.

Many Native Americans did not want to leave the land they loved. However, their way of life was being destroyed. They could no longer roam the Great Plains in search of buffalo to hunt. The government promised to give them food, clothing, and other supplies if they moved to the reservations.

Some government officials did not follow through on their promises. They sent spoiled food to the reservations and did not provide enough supplies. They also allowed settlement on lands they had promised to set aside.

Reformers spoke out against the unfair treatment of Native Americans. In 1881, Helen Hunt Jackson wrote a book called *A Century of Dishonor*, which documented the broken promises made to Native Americans. However, by that time, most Native Americans in the West already had been forced to move onto reservations.

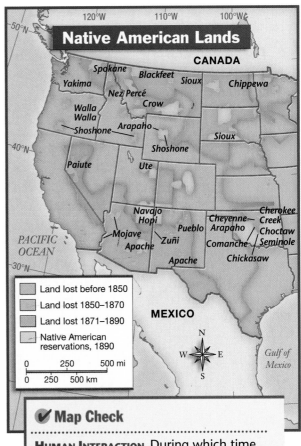

Native American Lands

Land lost before 1850
Land lost 1850–1870
Land lost 1871–1890
Native American reservations, 1890

0   250   500 mi
0   250   500 km

✔ Map Check

HUMAN INTERACTION During which time period (after 1850) did Native Americans lose the most land?

The Dawes Act

In 1887, the government of the United States further disrupted Native Americans' way of life. The U.S. Congress passed the Dawes Act to break up the reservations. Under this law, each Native American family would receive 160 acres of reservation land to own. All remaining lands would be auctioned off. This law tried to force many Native Americans to **assimilate**, or blend in with the nation's main culture. Native American families were expected to farm even if they had little experience in this way of life.

★ **What was the purpose of the Native American reservations?**

B. Battles in the West

Some Native Americans refused to move to reservations. This refusal resulted in more than two decades of scattered warfare throughout the West. Gradually, the fighting became more intense.

The Sand Creek Massacre

In 1864, the governor of Colorado Territory tried to force a group of Cheyennes and Arapahos to move to reservations. Miners wanted access to their traditional buffalo-hunting grounds. After a series of attacks led by both Native Americans and U.S. troops, peace talks were held. The Cheyennes and Arapahos were told that if they wanted peace, they should camp near a local fort. In November, Chief Black Kettle led about 450 Cheyennes and 40 Arapahos to a camp at Sand Creek, near Fort Lyon.

In spite of the Native Americans' peaceful intentions, on November 29, Colonel John Chivington led 1,200 Colorado militia in an attack on the camp. Chief Black Kettle tried to stop the attack by raising first a U.S. flag and then a white flag of surrender. The militia attacked anyway, massacring between 150 and 500 Native American men, women, and children. This attack was the beginning of a long period of warfare on the Plains.

Texas and the Southwest

Conflict between Native Americans and settlers spread throughout the West. In 1867, leaders of the Kiowas, Comanches, Cheyennes, and Arapahos signed the Treaty of Medicine Lodge Creek. In this treaty they agreed to move to reservations in present-day Oklahoma. Many members of these groups, however, did not agree with their leaders' decision and refused to move.

In 1874 and 1875, Native Americans fought U.S. soldiers in the Red River War in Texas. The army eventually trapped a group of Kiowas, Comanches, and Cheyennes in a canyon in the Texas Panhandle. Most of the Native Americans escaped, but the army burned their villages and killed more than a thousand of their horses. Without supplies or horses, many of the Native Americans were forced to surrender. The Kwahadi Comanches, led by Quanah Parker, were one of the last Native American groups to surrender. They did so in June 1875.

In Arizona and New Mexico, the Apache leader Geronimo and his group fiercely resisted the settlers until 1886. Geronimo's surrender marked the end of the wars between Native Americans and settlers on the southern Great Plains.

 What happened at Sand Creek?

C. The War in the Northwest

The Sioux people were determined to fight against the advance of settlers. The long Sioux War began when miners insisted on entering Sioux hunting grounds.

The Fetterman Massacre

To help miners reach gold and silver deposits, a road, called the Bozeman Trail, was built through the Bighorn Mountains in Wyoming. This area was part of the Sioux hunting grounds. In December 1866, the Sioux decided to fight back. They ambushed Lieutenant Colonel William Fetterman and 80 soldiers outside Fort Phil Kearney. Fetterman and all of his men were killed.

Incidents such as this one caused the federal government to work to end the fighting. In 1868, federal officials and representatives from several Sioux groups signed the Fort Laramie Treaty. In this treaty, the U.S. government agreed to abandon the Bozeman Trail. The government also created a 60 milllion acre reservation in the Dakota Territory for the Sioux. Some groups of Sioux and their leaders did not approve of the agreement. Among the leaders were Chiefs Sitting Bull and Crazy Horse. They chose to ignore the treaty and remain on their traditional hunting grounds.

The Nez Percé People

The Nez Percé people lived on lands that are now part of present-day Oregon and Idaho. They had a friendly relationship with the U.S. government until the 1860s when gold was discovered on their reservation. At first, the Native Americans cooperated with the miners. Then, federal officials drastically reduced the size of the Nez Percé reservation to give miners access to the gold mines.

Chief Joseph, one of the leaders of the Nez Percé, and about 140 fighting men resisted moving to the small reservation. Along with about 500 Nez Percé women and children, they were chased for 1,700 miles by the U.S. Army. Again and again, they fought off the army or slipped away from it as they tried to reach Canada.

Finally, just short of the border and during frigid, snowy weather, the U.S. Army attacked the Nez Percé camp in a siege that lasted six days. Chief Joseph was forced to accept defeat because his people were starving. After meeting with the commanding army officer, he declared, "I am tired; my heart is sick and sad. From where the sun now stands I will fight no more forever."

Chief Joseph

You can read Chief Joseph's speech on page R7.

The Battle of Little Bighorn

In 1875, the government permitted thousands of gold prospectors to move into the Black Hills of the Dakotas, which were sacred to the Sioux. The Sioux then left their reservation. When U.S. officials ordered them to return, the Sioux and Cheyennes united under the leadership of Sitting Bull and Crazy Horse. Some 2,500 warriors assembled on the banks of the Little Bighorn River in Montana.

Lieutenant Colonel George Armstrong Custer was sent to attack the Native Americans. In 1876, Custer led about 200 soldiers toward the camp on Little Bighorn River but was overwhelmed by Sioux and Cheyenne warriors. Custer and all of his men were killed.

Soon after, Crazy Horse was captured and killed by a government soldier. Sitting Bull fled to Canada with some of his followers. When they returned to the United States in 1881, they agreed to live on a reservation. By 1877, almost all remaining Sioux and Cheyennes had moved to reservations in Montana and South Dakota.

The Ghost Dance

In the 1880s, most Native Americans in the Northwest were living on reservations. They were deeply discouraged. Many longed for a return to their traditional ways of life. About this time, the spiritual leader Wovoka, a Paiute, offered them a vision of hope.

They Made History

Chief Sitting Bull 1831–1890

Chief Sitting Bull, or Tatanka Iyotake, was one of the great Native American leaders. In 1867, he was chosen as the head chief of the entire Sioux Nation. Sitting Bull never trusted U.S. officials, so he refused to sign treaties with the U.S. government. In 1876, Sitting Bull had a vision that his people would defeat the soldiers that came to force them off their land. Several days later, his vision came true when he led a group of Native Americans at the Battle of Little Bighorn. Eventually, Sitting Bull agreed to live on a reservation. Even there, he remained a powerful leader and often provided guidance for other Native American leaders.

Chief Sitting Bull was admired by many for his bravery and wisdom.

Critical Thinking How did the Battle of Little Bighorn relate to Sitting Bull's vision?

Wovoka preached that performing a dance called the Ghost Dance would return them to a world free of settlers and bring back Native American ancestors and the great buffalo herds.

The Ghost Dance sparked a religious revival that spread across the West. It gave Native Americans hope that someday they would once again live as their ancestors had lived.

When the Ghost Dance movement came to the Sioux reservation in South Dakota, U.S. officials became fearful. Some believed it might be a war dance. Also, some Sioux members, inspired by the Ghost Dance, began talking about leaving the reservation.

Suspecting trouble, reservation police tried to arrest Sitting Bull, but shot and killed him in the process. Afraid for their lives, about 350 Sioux fled the reservation. They camped near Wounded Knee Creek. On December 29, 1890, fighting broke out between soldiers and the Native Americans. The battle quickly turned into a massacre, as soldiers used rapid-fire cannons to kill more than 200 Sioux men, women, and children. The massacre at Wounded Knee was the end of Native American resistance in the West.

Government officials feared the meaning of the Ghost Dance, performed here by the Oglala Sioux.

 What was Custer's role in the Battle of Little Bighorn?

 **III Review**

Review History
A. Why did most Native Americans move to reservations?
B. Why did some Native Americans fight against settlers and soldiers?
C. How was the Battle of Little Bighorn different from the fighting at Wounded Knee?

Define Terms to Know
Provide a definition for each of the following terms.
extinction, reservation, assimilate

Critical Thinking
At the end of the 1800s, Native American Black Elk wrote, "We are prisoners of war." Do you agree with him or not? Explain.

Write About Citizenship
Write a paragraph explaining the causes and effects of the wars between Native Americans and the U.S. government.

Get Organized
VENN DIAGRAM
A Venn diagram can help you to compare and contrast two items. Use the following diagram to compare and contrast the life of Native Americans on the Great Plains and on reservations.

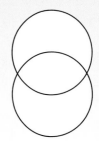

Chapter Summary

In your notebook, complete the following outline. Then, use your outline to write a brief summary of Chapter 19.

Life in the West

I. *Railroads, Ranchers, and Miners*

    A. *Railroads and Western Settlement*

    B.

II. *Farming on the Great Plains*

    A.

    B.

    C.

III. *Native American Struggles*

    A.

    B.

    C.

Interpret the Timeline

Use the timeline on pages 452–453 to answer the following questions.

1. How long after the completion of the first transcontinental railroad did ranchers begin to fence in the open range?

2. **Critical Thinking** Which U.S. event changed the lives of Native Americans the most? Explain your answer.

Use Terms to Know

Write a sentence using each of the following terms.

1. assimilate
2. cooperative
3. cowhand
4. Exoduster
5. extinction
6. homesteader
7. platform
8. range
9. reservation
10. transcontinental

Check Your Understanding

1. **Discuss** three of the factors that ended the long drives used in the western cattle industry.

2. **Summarize** the reasons that an increasing number of settlers moved west onto the frontier.

3. **Identify** the main natural resource that farmers made use of on the Great Plains and the main crop that they grew.

4. **Explain** why many homesteaders on the Great Plains gave up on farming.

5. **Summarize** how the buffalo was hunted almost to extinction.

6. **Explain** why many Native Americans resisted moving to reservations when the U.S. government ordered them to move.

Critical Thinking

1. **Recognize Relationships** How did the expansion of railroads in the West lead to the development of the Cattle Kingdom?

2. **Analyze Primary Sources** According to the quote on page 461, what qualities should a homesteader possess to succeed?

3. **Make Inferences** How would you describe Chief Joseph during his surrender?

Put Your Skills to Work

READ A SPECIAL-PURPOSE MAP

You have learned that special-purpose maps can add to your understanding of history.

Look at the map on this page. Then, answer the following questions.

1. What is the topic of this map?

2. What do the colored areas represent?

3. Where were the most silver mines?

Mining in the West

CANADA

Washington Territory • Coeur d'Alene
Montana Territory
OR
Boise
• Idaho Territory
Sacramento
WY
NV • Salt Lake City
• Carson City Utah Territory • Boulder
San Francisco
CA
Dakota Territory MN
• Deadwood
WI
IA
NE
IL
• Denver
Leadville CO KS MO
Arizona Territory
• Santa Fe OK AR TN
New Mexico Territory
MS
TX LA

PACIFIC OCEAN

MEXICO

Gulf of Mexico

N W E S

◻ Gold mining region
◼ Silver mining region
⬩ Important lode
• Cities

0   250   500 mi
0   250 500 km

In Your Own Words

JOURNAL WRITING

O Pioneers! celebrates the courage and spirit of the people who settled the Great Plains. Write a journal entry about a book that you have read. Choose a book that spotlights the courage of a person or group who overcame or endured serious hardships. Tell what the book is about and what effect it had on you.

Net Work

INTERNET ACTIVITY

Working with a group of classmates, use the Internet as a resource to create a photo exhibit of life in the West. First, select a theme for your exhibit, such as "Railroads Cross the West." Then, find photographs of related people, places, and events. Print the photographs, and write a short caption for each. Arrange your exhibit on a bulletin board for sharing with the class.

For help in starting this activity, visit the following Web site: www.gfamericanhistory.com.

Look Ahead

In the next chapter, learn about the rise of industry after the Civil War.

CHAPTER 20

The Rise of Industry 1869–1908

I. **Technology, Transportation, and Communication**
II. **Big Business and Labor Unions**
III. **Immigration**

*I*n the late 1800s, a flood of hopeful new immigrants arrived in the United States. Most came by steamship. Many ate and slept on the crowded open decks at the rear of the ship or in cramped conditions under the lowest deck. The voyage for most took about 14 days. Then, came the moment of arrival. They would step into a land far different from the one they had left. As one immigrant recalled,

> " How could it be that after having been so impatient to get there, I suddenly seemed almost frightened . . . now that we had arrived? "

The arrival of many immigrants and a growing population were not the only changes that were occurring in the United States. New inventions and businesses changed the way Americans lived.

Luggage of immigrants

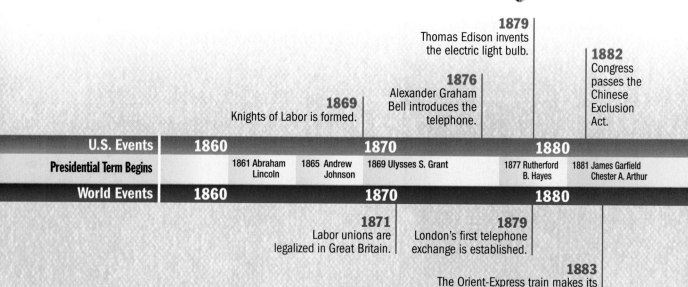

1879
Thomas Edison invents the electric light bulb.

1876
Alexander Graham Bell introduces the telephone.

1869
Knights of Labor is formed.

1882
Congress passes the Chinese Exclusion Act.

U.S. Events	1860			1870		1880	
Presidential Term Begins		1861 Abraham Lincoln	1865 Andrew Johnson	1869 Ulysses S. Grant		1877 Rutherford B. Hayes	1881 James Garfield Chester A. Arthur
World Events	1860			1870		1880	

1871
Labor unions are legalized in Great Britain.

1879
London's first telephone exchange is established.

1883
The Orient-Express train makes its first trip from Paris to Constantinople (Istanbul).

VIEW HISTORY Many immigrants looked out at the Statue of Liberty as they were about to arrive in the United States. Some immigrants brought their belongings in suitcases such as the ones pictured on the left.

★ What do you suppose these immigrants were thinking and feeling as they waited to set foot in the United States?

Get Organized

SQR CHART

SQR stands for Survey, Question, and Read. Use an SQR chart as you read Chapter 20. First, survey the chapter. Then, ask questions about what you will be reading. As you read, record notes and answers to your questions. Here is an example from this chapter.

SURVEY
This section is about changes in industry.

⬇

QUESTION
What were the major inventions at this time?

⬇

READ
Electric light bulb, Pullman car, telephone

1886
American Federation of Labor is founded.

1903
Orville and Wilbur Wright fly the first successful airplane.

1908
Henry Ford introduces the Model T automobile.

1890	1900	1910
1885 Grover Cleveland	1889 Benjamin Harrison	1893 Grover Cleveland	1897 William McKinley	1901 Theodore Roosevelt	1909 William H. Taft

| 1890 | 1900 | 1910 |

1896
First modern Olympics are held in Athens, Greece.

1898
Cuba becomes independent.

1903
Madame Curie receives the Nobel Prize for physics.

Technology, Transportation, and Communication

I

Terms to Know

Bessemer process a method for producing a stronger type of steel

patent a grant that gives an inventor the sole right to make and sell an invention for a set period of time

Main Ideas

A. New inventions made businesses more efficient and led to new industries.

B. Better railroads, automobiles, and more powerful steamships contributed to an expanding transportation network.

C. New inventions, such as the telephone and the typewriter, made communications faster.

 Active Reading

SUPPORTING DETAILS
Ideas become meaningful when they are supported by specific facts, or details. As you read this section, look for details that support the main ideas that are presented.

A. Industrial Technologies

After the Civil War ended, the United States began to change dramatically. The introduction of electricity and new inventions improved manufacturing, transportation, and communications. By 1900, the United States was no longer a nation of farmers. It was the world's leading industrial power.

Advances in the Oil and Steel Industries

Two of the industries that grew the fastest in the late 1800s were oil and steel. One of the first products to be refined, or purified, from oil was kerosene, a liquid used for lighting lamps. Gasoline, another product made from oil, would soon power the machines of the industrial age. This advance led to the creation of many new jobs.

In the 1850s, a British inventor named Henry Bessemer and an American iron manufacturer named William Kelly, working independently, developed a process for making steel quickly and cheaply. It came to be known as the **Bessemer process**. The key was blasting air into a furnace as iron was melted and transformed into steel. The air helped eliminate impurities and produced stronger steel.

By 1880, most steel produced in the United States used this faster and less-expensive method. Steel output increased and helped other industries expand. The stronger steel was used to make taller buildings, longer bridges, and miles of railroad tracks. A wealth of natural resources also helped the steel industry to expand. The United States had plenty of coal for fuel and iron ore, the raw material of steel.

Kerosene lamps

The Electrical Revolution

Another important new resource was electricity. In 1879, Thomas Edison invented the electric light bulb. Then, in 1882, he built a power plant to make electricity.

Edison developed a form of electricity known as direct current, or DC. George Westinghouse worked with Nikola Tesla, a Serbian inventor who had immigrated to the United States, to develop a more usable form of electricity than direct current. This new type of electricity, known as alternating current or AC, is used today in most homes and businesses. By 1900, electric lighting was illuminating many offices, streets, and homes in large cities. Electricity was also providing power to run streetcars and elevators.

Other Inventions

Edison and other American inventors were hard at work. Between 1865 and 1935, the U.S. government issued almost 2 million **patents**. A patent gives an inventor the sole right to make and sell an invention for a certain amount of time. Patents protect inventors from other people who want to profit from their ideas.

Many of the inventions during this period changed the way people lived. Isaac Singer invented a sewing machine that became a fixture in American households. It also provided a way to mass produce clothes and expand the garment industry. George Eastman invented and also marketed his camera. The invention of refrigerators was important to the meat industry, and cash registers and adding machines made businesses more efficient.

Inventions also led to the creation of entire new industries. For example, the development of a bottle that sealed out air allowed fruits and vegetables to be packaged safely for long-term storage. Henry Heinz was then able to bottle a tomato sauce called ketchup.

Edison's laboratory in Menlo Park, New Jersey, became the country's first industrial research center. During his lifetime, Edison received more than 1,000 patents. Edison invented the phonograph, which played music on round discs called records. He even developed a transmitter that is still used in microphones and speakers for telephones.

★ **What was the effect of the Bessemer process?**

American Inventions, 1846–1896

YEAR	INVENTION
1846	Sewing machine
1852	Elevator brake
1860	Repeating rifle
1865	Railroad sleeping car
1867	Typewriter
1867	Barbed wire
1876	Telephone
1877	Phonograph
1877	Railroad refrigerator car
1879	Electric light bulb
1879	Cash register
1882	Electric fan
1885	Adding machine
1896	Electric stove

✔ **Chart Check**

Which two inventions improved the transportation industry?

B. Expanding Transportation

Improvements in transportation were also changing the way people lived and worked. Between 1860 and 1900, railroads and steamships became important for transporting goods and people longer distances in less time. Later, inventions such as the automobile and the airplane created new methods of traveling.

The Growth of Railroads

In the late 1800s, one of the biggest users of steel was the railroad industry. Railroad companies were laying many miles of track. In 1860, about 30,000 miles of track had been laid in the United States. By 1900, more than 193,000 miles of track spread across the country.

Several developments in the late 1800s helped railroads operate more efficiently. In 1869, George Westinghouse improved the air brakes that trains used. He made it possible for trains to stop much more quickly and carry more weight safely. Train travel also became more comfortable. In the 1870s, Pullman cars, invented by George Pullman, offered reclining seats and sleeping spaces. Then, in 1886, the railroads adopted a standard gauge, or uniform distance, between the rails. This new standard allowed any train to travel on any track.

Do You Remember?

In Chapter 19, you learned that the first transcontinental railroad was completed in 1869.

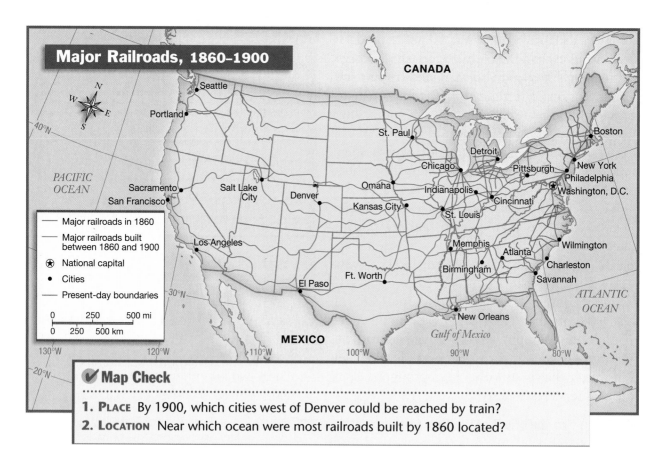

Major Railroads, 1860–1900

- —— Major railroads in 1860
- —— Major railroads built between 1860 and 1900
- ✪ National capital
- • Cities
- —— Present-day boundaries

0   250   500 mi
0   250   500 km

✔ Map Check

1. PLACE By 1900, which cities west of Denver could be reached by train?
2. LOCATION Near which ocean were most railroads built by 1860 located?

Railroads served growing industries in two important ways. First, they carried raw materials to factories. Second, they carried finished goods from factories to market. For example, railroads carried loads of iron ore from mines in Minnesota or Michigan to steel factories in Pennsylvania. Then, they hauled steel girders, or supports, from the factories to growing cities. These girders were used to construct new multistory buildings known as skyscrapers.

Orville and Wilbur Wright's airplane is pictured at the moment of the first successful flight at Kitty Hawk, North Carolina, in 1903. Orville Wright flew the plane while Wilbur Wright watched.

Ships, Cars, and Flying Machines

Larger, more powerful steam engines allowed railroad locomotives to haul more weight. These same engines, fired by coal, powered steamships on the Great Lakes and across the oceans. Steamships moved both raw materials and manufactured goods within the country and between the United States and other countries.

The first gasoline-powered automobile in the United States appeared in 1893. In 1908, Henry Ford built the first of his famous Model T automobiles. By 1917, almost 5 million automobiles were on the roads.

At the same time, brothers Orville and Wilbur Wright were experimenting with self-propelled gliders in Dayton, Ohio. In 1903, they flew the first successful airplane at Kitty Hawk, North Carolina. The first flight lasted about 12 seconds, and the airplane traveled almost 120 feet. In less than two years, the Wright brothers had improved this distance to 24 miles.

 **What methods of transportation were available by the early 1900s?**

C. Advances in Communications

Industrial growth was also fueled by advances in communications. New inventions allowed people and businesses to send messages much more quickly, which created additional new industries.

The Telegraph

The introduction of the telegraph by Samuel Morse in 1844 marked the beginning of a communications revolution. By 1900, the largest U.S. telegraph company was sending more than 63 million messages a year. A transatlantic cable laid on the Atlantic Ocean floor sent telegraph messages quickly to and from Europe. Using the telegraph, business managers could keep track of shipments around the world.

Do You Remember?
In Chapter 13, you learned that the telegraph sent messages through a system of electric pulses.

The Telephone

Alexander Graham Bell created a device that could transmit human speech—the telephone. While working on the invention one day in March 1876, Bell called to his assistant, Thomas Watson, in the next room. "Mr. Watson, come here. I want you," Bell said. Watson came rushing into the room explaining that he had heard Bell through the device's receiver. The telephone had been born.

By 1900, Bell's company had installed almost 1 million telephones in the United States. By 1920, the number had risen to nearly 10 million. The connections for telephone calls had to be made by hand on a switchboard. Jobs for switchboard operators sprang up across the country. Many women filled these jobs.

The Typewriter

Another important new communications tool was the typewriter. People communicated faster because they could now form words simply by pressing the keys on a machine instead of writing them by hand. Typewriters became essential in business. By 1886, about 1,500 typewriters were being manufactured each month.

The typewriter also provided many new jobs for women. Typing jobs paid no more than factory work, but many women preferred working in an office to working in a factory.

Alexander Graham Bell's original telephone

 What new jobs opened for women during the early 1900s?

 **Review**

Review History

A. What are three inventions that contributed to industrial growth in the 1800s?

B. How did changes in transportation help industry expand?

C. What inventions sped up communications in the second half of the 1800s?

Define Terms to Know

Provide a definition for each of the following terms.
Bessemer process, patent

Critical Thinking

How were people's lives affected by the inventions of the late 1800s and early 1900s?

Write About Culture

Which invention do you think had a greater impact on people's lives, the electric light bulb or the telephone? Write a paragraph explaining your point of view.

Get Organized

SQR CHART

Complete the SQR chart you began while reading this section. Based on the information in the section, write the answers to your questions.

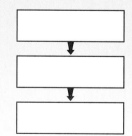

Build Your Skills

CHOOSE A RESEARCH TOPIC

One of the most important steps in writing a high-quality research report is choosing the right topic. What makes a topic right? For one thing, it should be a topic that interests you. If the topic has meaning for you, you will enjoy your task and learn more from your research.

Your topic should also be specific. If the topic is too broad, you will probably not be able to cover it effectively. If it is too narrow, you might not be able to find enough information. For example, "the railroad industry" is a very broad topic. You might not have time to explore this topic fully. A topic such as "Pullman cars" or "railroad expansion in the West" would be easier to research and write about.

Here's How
Follow these steps to choose a research topic.

1. Select two or three topics that seem interesting.
2. Check several sources of information to make sure the topic can be easily researched.
3. Narrow your topic. Look for an example or person who represents the topic, or limit the topic to a specific place or time.

Here's Why
You have just read about advances in industrial technology, transportation, and communications from the 1850s to the early 1900s. Suppose you had to write a report about a topic in one of these areas. Knowing how to narrow your topic could help you get off to a good start.

Practice the Skill
Copy the chart on a sheet of paper. Then read Section I again. Add some narrow topics for each broad topic listed.

Extend the Skill
Select one of the narrow topics and research your choice. Write a three-paragraph report based on your research.

Apply the Skill
As you read the remaining sections of this chapter, look for subjects that would make good research topics. If necessary, narrow these topics.

BROAD TOPIC	NARROW TOPICS
Advances in Technology	The Bessemer process, electricity, Edison's research laboratory
Advances in Transportation	
Advances in Communications	

II Big Business and Labor Unions

Terms to Know

corporation a large company usually formed by a group of investors

stock a share of ownership in a company

monopoly complete control over a supply, service, or market

collective bargaining talks between a union and an employer about working conditions

Main Ideas

A. The growth of industry created both wealth and poverty.

B. Workers joined labor unions to achieve better wages, hours, and working conditions.

C. In conflicts between union workers and employers, the U.S. government often sided with the employers.

 **Active Reading**

GENERALIZE
A generalization is a broad statement based on several facts or examples. As you read this section, ask yourself the following question: What generalizations can I make about big business and labor unions in the late 1800s?

A. Corporations Become Larger

As technology, transportation, and communications expanded, so did businesses. A growing population, including many immigrants, provided more workers and a larger market for products. By 1900, large businesses controlled American industry, and their owners had made huge fortunes.

Wealth and Poverty

Although business owners were becoming rich, most factory workers remained quite poor. Factory laborers worked in miserable conditions and struggled to feed their families. Aware of this contrast, writers Mark Twain and Dudley Warner called this period the Gilded Age. Gilding refers to the process of laying a thin layer of gold over a worthless metal. To these writers, the rich lifestyle of a few covered up widespread poverty. Business leaders argued that the gap between the wealthy and the poor was natural. Andrew Carnegie, a powerful business leader involved in the steel industry, said,

Andrew Carnegie

ANALYZE PRIMARY SOURCES

DOCUMENT-BASED QUESTION What reason did Andrew Carnegie give for the contrast between wealthy and poor people?

“ The contrast between the palace of the millionaire and the cottage of the laborer with us today measures the change which has come with civilization. This change, however, is not to be deplored [disliked], but welcomed as highly beneficial. ”

Building Businesses

The growth of businesses required money. Business owners needed money to build new factories, buy new equipment, and operate their businesses. To obtain this money, business leaders formed **corporations**. A corporation is a business that is usually made up of many investors. Many corporations sell **stocks**, or shares of ownership, as a way to raise money. The investors who buy the stocks have the right to a share of the profits. Stocks in many different companies can be bought by any private citizen on the New York Stock Exchange and other exchanges.

To organize the sale of stocks, corporations rely on investment bankers. These bankers also provide loans to corporations. In doing so, investment bankers often gain control of large corporations.

One of the most powerful and wealthiest men of the late 1800s was New York investment banker J. P. Morgan. He financed, or obtained money or loans for, railroads, steel mills, silver mines, and many other kinds of corporations.

Business Giants

Two of the largest industries in the late 1800s were the oil and steel industries. At the top of each was a powerful and wealthy person.

John D. Rockefeller controlled almost all of the oil industry in the United States. In 1863, he built an oil refinery in Cleveland, Ohio. Then, he bought other companies. By 1879, his Standard Oil Company controlled more than 90 percent of the country's oil refining. His **monopoly**, or complete control, of the oil industry angered some people. They thought the "oil king" was becoming too powerful. When Rockefeller retired from running his oil business in 1897, he was worth nearly $1 billion.

Another powerful business leader, Andrew Carnegie, was a Scottish immigrant who worked his way up, starting as a telegraph operator, in the railroad industry. Through the buying and selling of stocks, he was worth nearly $500,000 by 1868. He then founded a steel company just outside Pittsburgh.

Carnegie cut costs by owning most of the businesses needed to make steel. He owned iron mines and coal fields that provided the natural resources for the steel. He also owned steamships and railroads that shipped the raw materials and finished products. His lower costs helped him to cut his prices. As a result, Carnegie was able to drive his competitors out of business.

ANALYZE PRIMARY SOURCES

DOCUMENT-BASED QUESTION
According to this cartoon, what did Rockefeller's company have in its grasp?

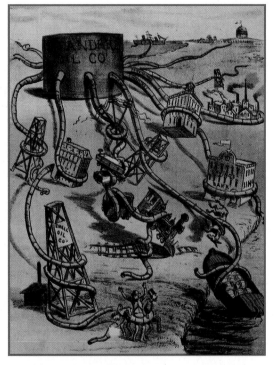

Rockefeller's Standard Oil Company is shown here as a giant octopus.

Investment banker J. P. Morgan helped finance many corporations.

Then & Now

Other wealthy business leaders besides Andrew Carnegie and John D. Rockefeller used their money to fund universities. Leland Stanford and Cornelius Vanderbilt made millions on railroads. These men founded Stanford and Vanderbilt Universities. Today, these schools are considered to be among the finest in the country.

Carnegie sold his company to business leader and banker J. P. Morgan in 1901. Morgan combined the company with his own steel mill to create the United States Steel Corporation. This company was the largest in the nation. It employed 168,000 people and brought in more than $1 billion.

Spreading the Wealth

Many of the men who made their fortunes during the Gilded Age also used their money to help others. John D. Rockefeller founded the University of Chicago and the Rockefeller Institute for Medical Research, now called Rockefeller University. He donated more than $500 million to a number of causes during his lifetime.

Andrew Carnegie founded Carnegie Hall, one of the country's leading concert halls, in 1891 and donated nearly $60 million to open 2,500 libraries. In 1900, he founded Carnegie Mellon University. He also helped to improve education by creating the Carnegie Foundation for the Advancement of Teaching.

★ How did John D. Rockefeller gain control of the oil industry?

B. Workers Form Unions

One way that business owners such as Carnegie and Rockefeller cut costs and increased profits was by paying low wages. They also did not spend money to make their workplaces safe. As a result, factory workers endured almost unbearable working conditions.

Working Conditions

Before the Civil War, most people worked as farmers, merchants, or crafts people in small shops. By the late 1800s, many more people found work in factories. Factory jobs were broken down into small tasks. Each person performed just one task over and over as quickly as possible.

The fast pace combined with dangerous machines created unsafe working conditions. For example, people in steel mills worked with burning liquid metal and fast-moving overhead cranes. As a result, accidents were common. People were often killed on the job. Poor lighting, pollution, and loud noise added to the harsh conditions.

Workdays usually stretched to 10 or 12 hours. The normal work week was six days. If workers demanded higher pay or better working conditions, they risked being fired. African Americans and immigrants were the lowest paid workers. In addition, African Americans faced another problem. Even when they were willing to work for low wages, some factory owners would not hire them.

Unions Make Demands

Many people joined labor unions in the late 1800s. Labor unions formed to bargain for higher pay, a shorter workday, and a safer workplace. One tool they used was the strike, or work stoppage, to force company owners to listen to their demands.

One of the largest labor unions was the Knights of Labor. Founded in 1869, this union included both skilled and unskilled workers. During the 1880s, members such as Mary Harris Jones, known as Mother Jones, recruited new union members. By 1886, the Knights of Labor had more than 700,000 members. However, the union was poorly organized and did not make many gains for workers.

In 1886, another, more powerful labor union was founded. The American Federation of Labor (AFL) was led by Samuel Gompers. Unlike the Knights of Labor, the AFL members were mostly skilled workers. Gompers hoped to achieve gains for workers through **collective bargaining**, or talks between an employer and a union. The AFL, however, was willing to use strikes when necessary. The AFL attracted hundreds of thousands of members and gained some improvements in pay, hours, and working conditions.

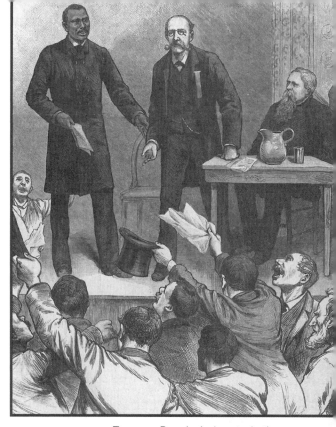

Terence Powderly (center), the leader of the Knights of Labor, organized thousands of workers in one of the country's largest labor unions.

 Why were accidents in factories common in the late 1800s?

C. The U.S. Government Becomes Involved

Leaders of big business kept union organizers out of their factories. If workers went on strike, business owners quickly hired replacements. They posted armies of private guards at factories to keep striking workers from entering. Corporations usually had the U.S. government on their side as well.

Labor Strikes

As employers ignored workers' demands, strikes became more common. Only a few resulted in violence, but those strikes attracted attention. Most strikes were not successful.

On May 4, 1886, a crowd of union workers in Chicago gathered in Haymarket Square. They demanded an eight-hour workday. Police ordered the crowd to leave. Then, someone threw a bomb. Many people were injured, and seven police officers were killed. The incident scared many Americans and turned public opinion against the unions.

The Government Steps In

In 1877, a 10-percent wage cut caused a major railway strike. The strike completely shut down train service in the East. When strikers began destroying railroad cars in Pennsylvania, President Rutherford B. Hayes sent in federal troops. Over several weeks, more than 100 workers were killed before the strike ended.

Another major strike occurred in Homestead, Pennsylvania, in 1892. Employers at Carnegie Steel wanted to cut workers' wages. The company tried to crush the strike by bringing in armed guards. Fighting broke out between the two sides. In response, the governor sent in the Pennsylvania National Guard. The strike was broken, and the union was defeated.

Two years later, another railroad strike stopped rail traffic across the country. To protest a wage cut at the company run by George Pullman, the inventor of the Pullman cars, workers decided to strike. Pullman shut down the company in a lockout to keep out the workers. Eugene Debs, founder of the American Railroad Union, asked thousands of railroad workers to join the Pullman workers by striking, which they did. This strike was crushed after President Grover Cleveland sent in federal troops.

These incidents set an example for future strikes. For the next 30 years, the government often sided with business. Workers continued to be controlled by the large corporations in the United States.

 What role did the federal government play in the railway strikes?

II Review

Review History
A. How did the growth of industry result in a greater separation between wealthy people and poor people?
B. What goals did labor unions have?
C. Why were most labor strikes in the late 1800s unsuccessful?

Define Terms to Know
Provide a definition for each of the following terms.
corporation, stock, monopoly, collective bargaining

Critical Thinking
What effects would granting higher wages to workers have had, both on the workers and the companies?

Write About Economics
Write a paragraph giving your opinion about employee strikes. For what reasons would workers risk their jobs to go on strike?

Get Organized
SQR CHART
Complete the SQR chart you began while reading this section. Write the answers to your questions based on the information in the section.

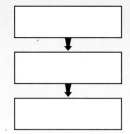

Ⅲ Immigration

Main Ideas

A. Beginning in the 1890s, most immigrants to the United States came from eastern and southern Europe.

B. Immigrants settled in cities in their own cultural neighborhoods.

C. Opposition to immigrants, especially those from China, became widespread.

Active Reading

FACT AND OPINION
A fact is a statement that can be proven or observed. An opinion is a judgment that reflects a person's ideas and attitudes. As you read this section, be sure to separate facts and opinions.

A. The New Immigrants

Since its founding, the United States has been a nation of immigrants. Before 1890, most newcomers had come from countries in northern and western Europe, such as Great Britain, Ireland, and Germany. From 1890 to 1920, immigrants from those countries continued to come to the United States, but many immigrants from other parts of the world also entered the United States. They came mostly from southern and eastern Europe, from countries such as Italy, Poland, Russia, Greece, and Hungary.

Two Waves of Immigrants

Immigrants entered the country in two waves. Before 1890, most came from northern and western Europe. They included large numbers from Ireland, Germany, and the Scandinavian countries of Sweden, Denmark, and Norway. Most immigrants in the first wave were Protestant, and many had some education and experience living under a representative government. For these reasons, they adapted to life in the United States without much difficulty. Many became farmers in the Midwest. Others settled in small towns or in cities such as Cincinnati, Ohio, and Milwaukee, Wisconsin.

Around 1890, this trend began to change. For the next 30 years, Italians, Greeks, Poles, Hungarians, Russians, Armenians, and other immigrants from southern and eastern Europe outnumbered immigrants from other parts of Europe. This second wave of immigrants was called the new immigrants.

Immigrant children arrived in the United States with their families.

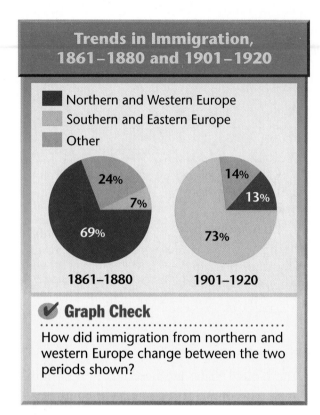

Trends in Immigration, 1861–1880 and 1901–1920

- ◼ Northern and Western Europe
- ◼ Southern and Eastern Europe
- ◼ Other

1861–1880
24%
7%
69%

1901–1920
14%
13%
73%

✔ Graph Check

How did immigration from northern and western Europe change between the two periods shown?

ANALYZE PRIMARY SOURCES

DOCUMENT-BASED QUESTION What picture of the United States is painted by this statement?

This second wave included people of many different religions, including Roman Catholics, Jews, and Eastern Orthodox Christians. Many were poor and could not read or write. Also, many of them came from countries that were not democratic. Their religions, customs, and languages made them stand out from other Americans.

Reasons for Immigration

Like earlier immigrants, the new immigrants came to the United States for many reasons. One was overpopulation in their home countries. In the 1800s, Europe was experiencing a growth in industry. Many people looked for jobs in their homeland but found that there was too much competition. Hungry and unemployed, they hoped to find a better life in the United States.

Many immigrants were drawn by advertisements for free land and plentiful jobs. Others were inspired by letters from relatives who had already moved to the United States. One Polish immigrant wrote to a family member back home:

 We eat here every day what we get only for Easter in our [native] country. 🟰🟰

Some European immigrants left their homelands because of religious or political persecution. In Russia, Jews were victims of prejudice—the unfair judgment of a person or group of people based on race, religion, or nationality. The Russian government organized attacks against Jews. Fearing for their lives, nearly one third of all Jews in Russia and eastern Europe left the region. Many hoped to find freedom in the United States.

⭐ **What attracted immigrants to the United States?**

B. Adjusting to a New Land

For many immigrants, dreams of free land and rich soil never came true. By the late 1800s, much of the farmland on the Great Plains was already claimed. Most newcomers did not have the money to buy land. As a result, many immigrants settled in port cities on the eastern coast. A large number also traveled inland to industrial centers such as Cleveland, Ohio; Detroit, Michigan; and Chicago, Illinois.

Arriving in the United States

Many immigrants traveled to the United States on steamships. For an amount between $15 and $40, they could travel in **steerage**—the large, open area beneath the ship's deck. The cost of the trip was about one month's wages for some people.

Beginning in 1892, the first stop for most newcomers from Europe was the immigration station at Ellis Island in New York Harbor. As the immigrants entered the harbor, they were welcomed by the Statue of Liberty, located on nearby Liberty Island. In 1903, a poem written by Emma Lazarus was placed in the base of the statue. The poem reads:

> "Give me your tired, your poor,
> Your huddled masses yearning to breathe free,
> The wretched refuse of your teeming shore.
> Send these, the homeless, tempest-tost to me,
> I lift my lamp beside the golden door! "

Once the ships arrived, the immigrants filed into the station at Ellis Island. There, officials checked each person's health. Those with serious diseases were often sent back to their homelands.

Settling Into Cities

Most immigrants in the late 1800s were poor farming people who found it hard to adjust to city life. They often lived in apartments that had no plumbing, heating, or windows. Because they spoke little English, the jobs offered to them often involved physical labor. In eastern cities, men paved streets and built bridges. Women often sewed clothes, either at home or in garment factories. All of these jobs paid very little.

Settling into a neighborhood with people of similar background made it easier to survive in a new country. There, people ate the same foods and observed the same customs. While often crowded, these tight-knit **ethnic** communities eased the pain of separation from a person's native land.

Gradually, through newspapers, work settings, and their children's schools, immigrants learned more about American culture. They also began to learn English. Many began to assimilate, or adapt, to the larger American society and wanted their children to embrace American ways.

Then & Now

The Statue of Liberty was given to the United States in 1886 as a gift from France. Today, it continues to be one of the most popular landmarks in the country and a symbol of freedom and opportunity.

ANALYZE PRIMARY SOURCES

DOCUMENT-BASED QUESTION To whom does this poem refer?

Immigrants arrived at Ellis Island carrying their belongings in suitcases, trunks, and bundles.

Reactions to the New Immigrants

Like immigrants in the early 1800s, these new immigrants faced discrimination in many parts of the United States. The growing population of immigrants and the separate communities created by them made many native-born Americans uneasy. They wanted all newcomers to blend in. Some also had a deep prejudice against people with a different appearance or unfamiliar customs. Nativism again spread among native-born Americans.

Nativists formed organizations to stop immigration. In the Midwest and Northwest, the American Protective Association had about 1 million members by 1896. Another nativist group, the Immigration Restriction League, demanded a literacy test to separate "desirable" from "undesirable" immigrants.

 Why did many Americans oppose immigration?

C. Immigrants From Asia and Latin America

While immigrants from Europe were pouring into the northeastern United States, others were arriving from Asia, the Caribbean, and Mexico. Many of these immigrants settled in the West and Southwest.

From Asia to the United States

Most immigrants from Asia entered the United States at Angel Island near San Francisco, California. From 1910 to 1940, about 175,000 immigrants came to Angel Island.

San Francisco had one of the largest Chinese communities in the United States. By the 1870s, thousands of Chinese people lived there in a distinct neighborhood known as Chinatown. Many Chinese people worked in wool mills and cigar-making factories. Others worked on farms in the surrounding area.

Japanese immigrants also settled in California. They took jobs in agriculture, construction, and food-canning factories. Many became fruit or vegetable growers.

Asian immigrants were also the victims of racial insults and discrimination. Nativists in the West feared they would lose their jobs to Asian workers because Asians were willing to work for very low pay. In the 1870s, violent anti-Chinese riots broke out throughout California.

Chinese adults and children stop by a street vendor's stand in San Francisco's Chinatown.

In 1882, Congress passed the Chinese Exclusion Act. **Exclusion** is the act of keeping a person or group out. This act and other restrictions banned the immigration of certain groups of Asians—mostly the Chinese. However, some government officials opposed limiting immigration. They felt the cheap and plentiful labor supply provided by immigrants was helping to spur the nation's economic growth. As a result, some Chinese and other Asian immigrants were allowed to continue entering the United States to live.

Latin American Immigration

In the late 1800s, immigrants arrived from Latin America, or countries south of the United States. Most of them came from Mexico. Between 1910 and 1919, during the Mexican Revolution, about 185,000 Mexicans fled to the United States.

Cuba was trying to achieve independence from Spain in the late 1800s. Many Cubans came to the United States to escape the fighting and disorder. Beginning around 1898, people from the island of Puerto Rico, which the United States controlled, began moving to the United States as well in search of jobs.

Chinese immigrants were beaten and their property was destroyed in riots such as this one in Denver, Colorado, in 1880.

★ **What were the reasons for Latin American immigration to the United States in the late 1800s?**

III Review

Review History

A. How did the first wave of immigrants differ from the second wave?

B. Why did immigrants settle in cities in their own ethnic communities?

C. How did some nativists in the West show their opposition to Chinese immigration?

Define Terms to Know
Provide a definition for each of the following terms.
steerage, ethnic, exclusion

Critical Thinking
How did immigrants in the late 1800s become an essential part of the American economy?

Write About Culture
You are an immigrant who has just entered the United States. Write a letter to a friend in your homeland about your new life in the United States.

Get Organized
SQR CHART
Complete the SQR chart you began while reading this section. Write the answers to your questions based on the information in this section.

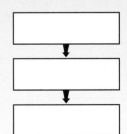

PAST to PRESENT

Working Conditions for Women and Children

In the late 1800s, both women and children worked long hours under conditions that were often unhealthy and dangerous. Women worked in factories sewing clothes, tending spinning machines, and canning meat or fish. Many also served as maids, cooks, and laundry workers. Children as young as six or seven years old worked in cotton mills, canning factories, and coal mines.

Working conditions for women and children began to improve in the early 1900s. Today, U.S. laws have made working conditions safer and cleaner for all workers, and child labor laws are stricter.

Workers who were bent over sewing machines could develop permanently curved spines.

Boys called breaker boys sat hunched over all day to pick out useless rocks mixed in with coal. Breaker bosses would jab the boys with a stick if they talked or did not pay attention to their work.

You Have a Right to a Safe and Healthful Workplace.

IT'S THE LAW!

U.S. Department of Labor · Occupational Safety and Health Administration · OSHA 3165

Government agencies such as the Occupational Safety and Health Administration (OSHA) strive to protect workers from unsafe working conditions.

Today, unions help workers organize and fight for fair working conditions. Some workers go on strike to demand higher wages, better benefits, or shorter workdays.

Events Related To Child Labor	
1886	A New York law bars children under 14 from working in factories in rural areas, but it is poorly enforced.
1901	The first organization to end child labor is formed in Alabama.
1907–1918	Lewis Hine's photographs raise awareness of child labor across the country.
1911–1913	Thirty-nine states pass child labor laws.
1933	Several children's strikes occur in Pennsylvania.
1938	The Fair Labor Standards Act sets a minimum wage and 40-hour work week and outlaws much child labor.
1991	A study by the International Labor Organization points to child labor as a worldwide problem.

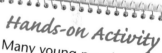

Hands-on Activity

Many young people today work under guidelines set by the government. Other young people are forced to work in conditions that do not meet these guidelines. Find out more about working conditions for people age 16 years and younger. Create a "Did You Know?" list of at least six important facts. To get started, you can go to: www.gfamericanhistory.com.

This chart shows some major events in the development of child labor laws.

Chapter Summary

In your notebook, complete the following outline. Then, use your outline to write a brief summary of the chapter.

The Rise of Industry

I. Technology, Transportation, and Communication

    A. Industrial Technologies
    B.
    C.

II. Big Business and Labor Unions

    A.
    B.
    C.

III. Immigration

    A.
    B.
    C.

Interpret the Timeline

Use the timeline on pages 474–475 to answer the following questions.

1. How long after Bell's introduction of the telephone was London's first telephone exchange established?

2. **Critical Thinking** Which events in the United States and the world show an expanding transportation network?

Use Terms to Know

Select the term that best completes each sentence.

collective bargaining   ethnic   patent
corporation   monopoly

1. Inventors received a _____ to protect the rights to their inventions.

2. The American Federation of Labor wanted to achieve gains for workers through _____, or talks with employers.

3. Most immigrants in cities lived in _____ communities with others of a similar cultural background.

4. Standard Oil, the large oil company owned by Rockefeller, had a _____, or complete control of the oil industry.

5. A _____ formed by business leaders usually included many investors.

Check Your Understanding

1. **Discuss** three inventions or technical developments that made industry more efficient during the late 1800s.

2. **Discuss** developments in the railroad industry in the late 1800s.

3. **Explain** how Andrew Carnegie made huge profits in the steel industry.

4. **Summarize** the main differences between the Knights of Labor and the American Federation of Labor.

5. **Identify** some of the countries from which most immigrants in the 1890s came.

6. **Identify** two reasons why immigrants came to the United States.

Critical Thinking

1. **Analyze Primary Sources** How might Andrew Carnegie, quoted on page 482, respond to people today who feel that millionaires should be taxed heavily because of their huge incomes?

2. **Analyze Primary Sources** How do you think the person who drew the political cartoon on page 483 was asked to portray the oil monopoly? Explain.

3. **Draw Conclusions** What positive effects did a large number of immigrants have on American society?

Put Your Skills to Work
CHOOSE A RESEARCH TOPIC

You have learned that you must think carefully before choosing a research topic. Narrowing the topic is important for producing a high-quality research report.

Copy the following chart. In the second column, add two narrow topics for each broad topic listed.

BROAD TOPIC	NARROW TOPICS
Business Leaders	
Labor Unions	
Immigration in the Late 1800s	

In Your Own Words
JOURNAL WRITING

Many inventions were created during the late 1800s and early 1900s. Often, these inventions changed the way people lived. Think of your own invention that would improve the way people live today. In your journal, write a description of your invention and how it could help people.

Net Work
INTERNET ACTIVITY

Working with a partner, conduct research on the Internet to learn more about American inventions from the mid-1800s to the early 1900s. You may wish to work from the chart on page 477. Use the information you gather to create an album of inventions. The album should include at least five inventions. For each one, include a description of the invention and an explanation of how it changed the way people worked or lived.

For help in starting this activity, visit the following Web site: www.gfamericanhistory.com.

Look Ahead
In the next chapter, learn how problems in industry were addressed by reformers and government leaders.

CHAPTER 21

The Progressive Era 1880–1933

I. **A Troubled Society**
II. **The Progressive Movement**
III. **Political Reforms**

*I*n 1872, Susan B. Anthony broke the law. She, along with 15 other women, voted in the U.S. presidential election. Anthony argued that the Fourteenth Amendment gave all citizens—including women—the right to vote. Anthony was arrested and eventually fined $100, which she refused to pay. Later in the century, people began to listen to Anthony's point of view. They also listened to Elizabeth Cady Stanton, another leader for women's rights. In 1892, Stanton wrote,

> **"** If we are to consider [a woman] as a citizen, as a member of a great nation, she must have the same rights as all other members. **"**

A woman's right to vote was just one issue that many Americans fought for in the early 1900s, in the hopes of making the United States a better place to live.

A stamp supporting women's right to vote

U.S. Events	1880		1890		1900

1883 Civil Service Act becomes law.

1887 Interstate Commerce Act becomes law.

1889 Jane Addams founds Hull House in Chicago.

Presidential Term Begins	1881 James A. Garfield 1881 Chester A. Arthur	1885 Grover Cleveland	1889 Benjamin Harrison	1893 Grover Cleveland	1897 William McKinley

World Events	1880		1890		1900

1883 Germany introduces health insurance.

1893 Women in New Zealand win the right to vote.

1897 Worker's compensation law is passed in Great Britain.

VIEW HISTORY This photograph shows women rallying for voting rights in the early twentieth century. Such rallies were held throughout the United States as people demanded voting rights for women. Women would also use stamps (left) to gain support.

★ What is the significance of the building in the background of the stamp?

Get Organized

MAIN IDEA/SUPPORTING DETAILS CHART

Connecting main ideas and supporting details can help you to organize what you learn. Use a chart like the one below as you read Chapter 21. In the large box, list the main idea. In the small boxes, fill in details that support this idea. Here is an example from this chapter.

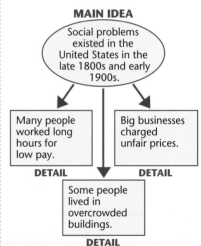

MAIN IDEA

Social problems existed in the United States in the late 1800s and early 1900s.

Many people worked long hours for low pay.
DETAIL

Big businesses charged unfair prices.
DETAIL

Some people lived in overcrowded buildings.
DETAIL

1905
Niagara Movement founded to secure civil rights for African Americans.

1911
Fire at Triangle Shirtwaist Company kills workers.

1912
Roosevelt runs for President as a Progressive.

1913
Federal income tax becomes law.

1920
Women win the right to vote throughout the United States.

1910 **1920** **1930**

1901 Theodore Roosevelt   1909 William H. Taft   1913 Woodrow Wilson

1910 **1920** **1930**

1905
Workers and peasants demand civil rights in Russia.

1911
Sun Yat-sen becomes president of Chinese Republic.

1914
World War I begins.

CHAPTER 21 ★ The Progressive Era **497**

I ★ A Troubled Society

Terms to Know

tenement a run-down apartment building

sweatshop an unhealthy workplace where people are overworked

racism feelings against people because of their ethnic background or skin color

Main Ideas

A. Many people in cities lived and worked in unsafe conditions.

B. Much corruption existed in business and government during the late 1800s.

C. Discrimination and laws in the South separated African Americans and whites.

Active Reading

PREDICT
Predicting is a way to prepare yourself to read. Before you start reading, look at the photographs and read the headings. Ask yourself the following question: Based on this information, what might this section be about?

A. Problems in the Cities

Cities faced many problems at the beginning of the twentieth century. Two widespread problems were poverty and unsafe working conditions in city factories and businesses.

Living in Slums

After the Civil War, industry boomed. People flocked to growing cities to find work. While some city dwellers were well off, others lived in poverty. Workers, often immigrants, could afford to live only in **tenements**. These crowded apartment buildings were dark and dirty and usually lacked running water.

Poverty was widespread in the cities. Immigrants often had no other choice but to live in crowded and unhealthy conditions.

These conditions led to a number of problems. Diseases such as smallpox and typhoid fever raged through working-class neighborhoods. Young children in particular died from these diseases. Violent crime was also high. Robbery, murder, and gang activity made many neighborhoods unsafe.

Working in Sweatshops

The factories where workers spent their days were also unhealthy. These overcrowded and dirty workplaces were often called **sweatshops**. Many people were required to work long hours for very little pay. Even children worked twelve-hour days. The machinery in sweatshop factories could be dangerous, and workers were often forced to work quickly. One worker in a pickle factory wrote:

> “I have stood ten hours. I have fitted 1,300 corks; I have hauled over 4,000 jars of pickles. My pay is 70 cents. ”

Factories were often unsafe places to work. One Sunday morning in 1911, the front page of the *New York Times* announced a terrible disaster. A fire at the Triangle Shirtwaist Factory had killed 146 people. Most were young women. Investigators found that fire exits had been locked, trapping many women inside. The factory owners claimed that the doors needed to be locked to prevent employee theft. Investigators also discovered the building had broken fire escapes. The owners had ignored safety standards to save money. This event opened people's eyes to the unsafe conditions in factories.

Making Some Improvements

Some people tried to improve life in the cities. They were called reformers. One of the most famous reformers, Jane Addams, wanted to help disadvantaged immigrants. In 1889, she bought a large house in a poor section of Chicago. She turned the house into a settlement house, or community center.

The center, called Hull House, provided services for the poor people of the neighborhood. It provided a nursery, classes in English and citizenship, and hot meals. At Hull House, people learned to cook and keep their houses clean to prevent the spread of disease. Families came to see plays, listen to music, or hear speeches.

Hull House was an immediate success. It became a model for settlement houses in other cities. By 1900, settlement houses had opened in cities across the United States, helping Latin Americans, African Americans, and other groups.

★ **How did settlement houses improve life for people in cities?**

ANALYZE PRIMARY SOURCES

DOCUMENT-BASED QUESTION
How do you think the worker who wrote this felt at the end of the day?

Jane Addams founded Hull House in Chicago to help people in need.

B. Problems in Business and Government

While many workers in the cities lived under poor conditions, some big business owners were growing wealthier. Many of these business leaders tried to influence government for their own gain.

The Power of the Railroads

The new business leaders after the Civil War owned factories, steel mills, and railroads. Expansion of transportation and communication systems helped these businesses grow rapidly, making their owners rich. Some critics called the owners of these industries "robber barons" for charging the public unnecessarily high prices. Their admirers called them "captains of industry," praising them for their contributions to society and their leadership in business.

One powerful business owner was Cornelius Vanderbilt. He built his fortune by investing in railroads. Railroads were quickly becoming the main shipping lines in the country. Railroad companies took advantage of this situation by charging shippers and passengers very high prices. Some railroad owners bribed, or paid money and gifts, to officials in order to gain advantages.

To control the railroads, Congress passed the Interstate Commerce Act in 1887. This act required railroads that traveled through more than one state to set "reasonable and just" rates. It also set up a group to deal with complaints against the railroads.

Wrongdoing in Government

Corruption, or dishonest and illegal dealings, was common at all levels of government. Many leaders in city, state, and national government were willing to take bribes from wealthy business owners. One of the worst examples of a corrupt leader was Boss William Marcy Tweed in New York City.

Tweed was a local leader, called a boss. He controlled elections by giving gifts and favors to voters in exchange for their support. Boss Tweed was then paid by the people who benefited from the election. He also made money illegally by padding, or adding to, city bills. Residents paid extra for city services, and Boss Tweed and his supporters kept the extra money for themselves. Tweed also gave jobs to people who would help him, even if those people were not qualified for the jobs.

Congress tried to solve the problems in government. In 1883, it passed the Pendleton Civil Service Act. This law set up a system for filling some government jobs based on ability. People applying for certain jobs now had to pass a test before they could be hired.

Boss Tweed controlled the New York City political machine.

★ **How did Congress respond to corruption in business?**

C. Problems Between People

Many African Americans continued to live in the South after the Civil War. Others moved to the big cities of the North. Regardless of where they lived, they encountered **racism**, a feeling of hatred based on a person's heritage and skin color. Other Americans—including people of Latin American, Asian, and Native American backgrounds—also suffered from discrimination in the late 1800s.

Discrimination Against African Americans

After Reconstruction, African Americans faced particular difficulties in the South. Unfair laws, known as Jim Crow laws, limited the rights of African Americans. These laws were named after an African American character in a song. This character never made any trouble. Eventually, the name came to stand for segregation and inequality.

Some Jim Crow laws kept African Americans from voting. Other laws enforced segregation, or separation of racial groups. African Americans had to sit in separate seats on trains and streetcars. They were barred from restaurants that served white customers. In addition, they had to attend separate schools. African Americans who broke Jim Crow laws were ridiculed, beaten, and sometimes killed.

The U.S. Supreme Court made rulings that weakened African American rights. In 1876, the Court ruled that the Fifteenth Amendment did not guarantee the right to vote to anyone. As a result, laws requiring voters to own property and pay poll taxes were allowed to stand.

Do You Remember?
In Chapter 18, you learned that during Reconstruction, the federal government helped African Americans in the South to rebuild their lives.

THE POLITICAL PINKERTONS.

ANALYZE PRIMARY SOURCES

DOCUMENT-BASED QUESTION Based on this cartoon, what challenges to their rights did African Americans face?

This cartoon shows an African American man facing a polling facility. A group of men blocks the entrance.

The Dawes Act of 1887 divided up reservations and forced Native Americans to adopt white farming practices. However, many could not afford to farm their land and sold it to land-hungry, white settlers. It was not until 1934 that the U.S. government began to give land back to Native Americans.

Jim Crow laws were challenged in 1896 in the case of *Plessy* v. *Ferguson*. In this case, Homer Plessy, an African American, was arrested for attempting to sit in a railroad car that was designated for whites. He eventually pleaded his case before the Supreme Court. The Court ruled that public facilities for white people and African Americans could be separate as long as they were equal in quality. However, the *Plessy* decision was difficult to enforce, and facilities were rarely equal. This decision remained in effect well into the twentieth century.

Discrimination Against Other Groups

In the North, segregation was often the result of custom rather than law. African Americans usually were not welcome in schools, restaurants, or hotels attended by white people. In many parts of the country, Asian Americans, Native Americans, and people from Latin America often faced the same situation.

In some cases, laws limited these groups' rights. Racist attitudes continued against Chinese Americans. In 1882, the Chinese Exclusion Act stopped most Chinese immigration into the United States. Native Americans were under attack as well. Many people believed that Native Americans needed to become "civilized" and adopt white farming practices and customs.

 What was the effect of the Chinese Exclusion Act of 1882?

 **Review**

Review History
A. Why were some areas in cities unhealthy?
B. What type of corruption existed in many city governments?
C. How did *Plessy* v. *Ferguson* affect the rights of African Americans?

Define Terms to Know
Provide a definition for each of the following terms.
tenement, sweatshop, racism

Critical Thinking
Why do you think some business owners were called robber barons?

Write About Citizenship
Reformers wanted to change society in the late 1800s and early 1900s. Write a paragraph considering aspects of society you would want reformed today.

Get Organized
MAIN IDEA/SUPPORTING DETAILS CHART
Use a chart like the one below to record details that support this main idea: Leaders of big business sometimes ignored the law.

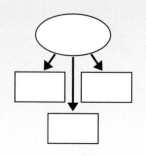

Build Your Skills

MAKE GENERALIZATIONS

Have you ever heard people make statements such as "Most people like sunny days" or "All teenagers love music"? These are examples of generalizations. A generalization is a broad statement based on many facts or details. Valid generalizations usually use words such as *many, most, often, some,* and *few.* Incorrect generalizations often use words such as *all, none, always,* or *never.*

In history, you can make a valid generalization by "adding up" the facts to make a general statement. You can do this by looking for patterns among the facts. Making generalizations can help you when you read, study for a test, or prepare to write a paper.

Here's How

Follow these steps to make a valid generalization.

1. Pick one topic and list facts about it.
2. Study the facts to find something similar about all or most of them.
3. Make a general statement based on all of the facts.

Here's Why

You have just read about problems in cities in the late 1800s and early 1900s. Suppose you had to write an essay on the topic of government during this period. Making generalizations could help you plan and write your essay.

Practice the Skill

Copy the chart and read Section I again. Then add facts to the second and third boxes on the left of the chart. Study the facts and write the generalization in the box on the right.

Extend the Skill

Gather facts about the students in your class, such as what kind of music they listen to and what sports they like. Make generalizations and compare them with another student's. Do both of you agree? Why?

Apply the Skill

As you read the remaining sections of this chapter, examine the facts and then make a generalization about the information you

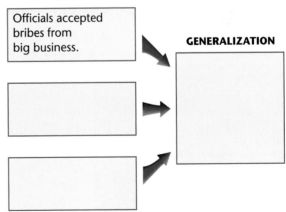

have read. For example, as you read Section II, you might make a chart listing facts and a generalization about Theodore Roosevelt's presidency.

II

The Progressive Movement

Terms to Know

muckraker a writer who brings attention to problems in society

Progressive a person who believes in social progress through reform

Prohibition the ban on the making and sale of alcoholic drinks

direct primary an election in which members of a political party vote to choose their candidates

suffrage the right to vote

Main Ideas

A. Americans learned about problems in the nation and worked to find solutions to them.

B. Local and state governments became more responsible and democratic through reformers' efforts.

C. Some reformers worked toward equality for women and African Americans.

Active Reading

CAUSE AND EFFECT
A cause is something that triggers, or leads to, another event. That event is the effect. As you read this section, look for examples of cause and effect.

A. Highlighting and Solving Problems

By 1900, many people were aware of the serious social problems in the nation, such as poverty, crime, racism, and the inequality of women. During the next two decades, reformers took action to address these and other problems.

Journalists Open Eyes

Journalists played an important role in helping the public see the need for reform. They reported on child labor, tenement life, and factory conditions. They investigated and wrote about crime and wrongdoing in American business and politics. President Theodore Roosevelt called these journalists **muckrakers** because they raked up society's "muck," or dirt.

One muckraker, Lincoln Steffens, investigated government in many American cities. He found corruption in Philadelphia, St. Louis, New York, and other cities. Steffens wrote a series of articles in which he described how political bosses took bribes from businesses. His articles were collected in a book called *The Shame of the Cities*, published in 1904.

Another muckraker was Jacob Riis. He photographed life in the tenements and factories in New York City. These pictures appeared in his book *How the Other Half Lives*. This book showed the poverty in which many working-class immigrants lived. Its realistic look into the lives of the working poor influenced the opinions of many Americans.

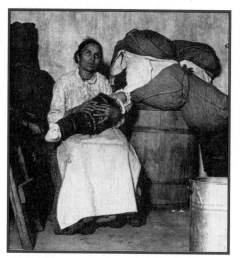

Jacob Riis recorded scenes of poverty in American cities through his photographs.

Some muckrakers wrote about specific industries. Journalist Ida Tarbell wrote articles about the unfair business practices of large oil trusts, such as John D. Rockefeller's Standard Oil Company. In a 1906 novel, *The Jungle*, Upton Sinclair described unclean conditions in factories that processed meat:

> 66 There would be meat stored in great piles in rooms; and the water from leaky roofs would drip over it, and thousands of rats would race about on it. 99

ANALYZE PRIMARY SOURCES

DOCUMENT-BASED QUESTION
What reaction do you think Upton Sinclair is trying to get from his readers?

In 1901, Frank Norris wrote *The Octopus*, which depicted the railroads as strangling the economic life of farmers. Jack London's novels warned that workers might revolt against poor wages and factory conditions.

Reformers Seek Progress

While individuals and small groups of reformers tackled the nation's social problems in the late 1800s and early 1900s, they also believed that the government should be involved in making widespread social reforms. People who shared these goals were called **Progressives**.

They Made History

Ida Tarbell 1857–1944

When Ida Tarbell graduated from college in 1880, she was the only woman graduate of her class. After teaching, she began to edit and write. She became an editor for the literary and political publication *McClure's Magazine* in 1894 and wrote a series of articles about corruption at Standard Oil. Her articles led to a federal investigation of the company. As a result, Standard Oil of New Jersey was broken up in 1911. Tarbell was not only a muckraker, but also a writer of history. She wrote nine books about Abraham Lincoln.

Ida Tarbell uncovered corruption in the oil industry in the United States.

Critical Thinking Would Ida Tarbell be considered a Progressive? Why or why not?

Progressives worked together to reform society. Their efforts were so important that this period is often called the Progressive Era.

Women took an active part in the progressive movement. One issue they focused on was the use of alcohol. Some people felt that alcohol led to poverty and crime. The Women's Christian Temperance Union (WCTU) worked to stop the use of alcohol.

WCTU members wanted the sale and transport of alcohol within the United States to be illegal. They got their wish in 1919 when the Eighteenth Amendment was ratified and a period known as **Prohibition** began. However, this amendment was repealed in 1933.

★ What was the goal of the WCTU?

B. Improving Government

Progressives wanted to make government at all levels work better for the people. Many of their reforms helped to fight against corruption in government.

Reforming City Government

In cities, Progressives worked to limit the power of political bosses. Some cities did this by introducing commissions. A commission is a group of experts who have the power to make decisions for the government. Galveston, Texas, was the first city to use this idea. When a deadly hurricane destroyed the city in 1900, a commission was appointed to take charge of rebuilding the city.

A commission was created in Galveston to rebuild the city and help protect it against future hurricanes.

Some cities began to use a city-manager system. The city manager was a professional hired to handle the day-to-day activities of government. Other experts were hired to run city departments. These experts focused on the job instead of political power.

Reforming State Government

Progressives also had an impact at the state level of government. Many states set up commissions to set rules for making factories safer places to work. States also passed progressive laws. Maryland passed the first workers' compensation laws. These laws guaranteed that workers who were injured on the job would receive some pay while they were unable to work. Other states passed laws to limit working hours. Such reforms helped to improve the quality of life for many working people.

Other progressive reforms made the democratic process work better. These reforms included the use of referendum and initiative which gave citizens the power to propose new laws. Another reform, recall, gave voters the ability to remove officials from office.

Wisconsin became a state known for its progressive government. It was the first state to require a **direct primary**. In a direct primary, members of each political party vote to choose their candidates.

In another reform, people gained the right to elect U.S. senators directly. Under the Constitution, members of the state legislature had elected senators. In 1913, the Seventeenth Amendment provided for the direct election of senators by voters in all states. The amendment gave people the chance to select their own representatives.

★ How did the Progressives change local governments?

C. Working for Equality

Progressives fought to improve life for many Americans. However, progressive reforms did not change the basic situation of African Americans, who continued to struggle for equality.

African Americans Organize

W.E.B. Du Bois, a historian and editor, was determined to change things. In 1905, he and other reformers met at Niagara Falls, Canada, to come up with a plan for ending racism. They demanded access to jobs and equality for African Americans.

Progressive Political Reforms

NAME OF REFORM	WHAT IT DOES
Initiative	Citizens can put an issue onto a state ballot.
Referendum	Citizens can vote directly on whether or not to accept a proposed law.
Recall	Citizens are able to remove elected officials from their jobs if they are doing poorly.

✔ **Chart Check**
....
Which reform allows people to directly vote on measures?

The Niagara Movement, as it was called, led to the creation of the National Association for the Advancement of Colored People (NAACP). Its objective was to secure "equal rights and opportunities for all." This association would become one of the most important civil rights organizations in the United States.

Other African American reformers tackled specific problems. In the South, Ida B. Wells fought against lynching. A lynching is a killing by a mob. In the South, hundreds of African Americans were illegally lynched by racist groups. Wells formed clubs of African American women to oppose lynching. These clubs then joined with white women to form the Association of Southern Women for the Prevention of Lynching.

Women Push for the Vote

Women also struggled for equality. Elizabeth Cady Stanton and Susan B. Anthony were pioneers in the fight for women's **suffrage**, or the right to vote. In the 1890s, both women helped organize the National American Woman Suffrage Association (NAWSA).

In 1900, Carrie Chapman Catt became the head of NAWSA. Catt and other leaders developed a strategy. They decided to work at both the state and federal levels to build support for women's suffrage. Their goal was to get a constitutional amendment passed.

 In what ways did African Americans and women seek equality?

Symbols such as this bird were used to rally people to the cause of women's suffrage.

 **II Review**

Review History

A. How did the muckrakers bring about social reform?

B. What improvements were made in local and state governments?

C. What were African Americans and women fighting for?

Define Terms to Know

Provide a definition for each of the following terms. **muckraker, Progressive, Prohibition, direct primary, suffrage**

Critical Thinking

Why might city managers and commissions be less corrupt than political bosses?

Write About Citizenship

During the Progressive Era, citizens in some states gained the right to propose, or suggest, new laws. Write a paragraph explaining why people would want this right.

Get Organized

MAIN IDEA/SUPPORTING DETAILS CHART

Record one main idea from this section. Then, list details that support it. For example, what details support this main idea: African Americans worked for reforms.

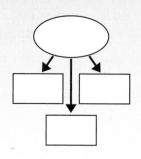

III ★ Political Reforms

Terms to Know

trust a giant corporation made up of a group of companies

conservation protection of natural resources

★ ★ ★ ★ ★ ★ ★

Meet
the President

★ ★ ★ ★ ★ ★ ★ ★ ★ ★ ★ ★ ★ ★ ★

Theodore Roosevelt
1858–1919

Years in office 1901–1909

Political Party Republican

Birthplace New York

Assumed office at age
43, succeeded William McKinley

Age when elected 46

Occupations Assistant Secretary of the Navy, Commander of the Rough Riders, politician

Nickname Teddy

Did you know?
Toy-makers named the "Teddy" bear after Roosevelt.

Quote "Most of us enjoy preaching, and I've got such a bully pulpit!"

Main Ideas

A. Theodore Roosevelt implemented reforms in new laws and policies.

B. William Taft was not as strong a reformer as Roosevelt, but he did accomplish some reforms.

C. Woodrow Wilson focused on reforms to regulate business and banking but did not strongly support civil rights.

 **Active Reading**

POINT OF VIEW
The three Presidents of the Progressive Era had different points of view. As you read this section, ask yourself the following question: What did each President think about the role of government?

A. Roosevelt the Reformer

Theodore Roosevelt became President in 1901 after President McKinley was assassinated. Roosevelt had achieved success as a writer and a cowhand. He had also achieved fame as a war hero. He now quickly showed that he was a leader with a new vision of government. He believed that government should be active in making people's lives better. His actions showed his commitment to Progressive ideas.

A Square Deal for the Miners

Soon after Roosevelt became President coal miners went on strike in Pennsylvania. They had not received a pay raise in 20 years, and they often worked long hours. The miners wanted higher wages and an eight-hour workday. The owners of the coal mine refused to talk to them or to their union, the United Mine Workers.

After several months, the President stepped in. He threatened to have U.S. troops take over the mines. This threat forced the mine owners to talk with union leaders. With the help of a White House commission, the miners won most of their demands and went back to work. President Roosevelt declared he had given the miners and owners a "square deal." This term became his slogan.

To settle problems between workers and business owners, Roosevelt asked Congress to create a Department of Commerce and Labor. It did so in 1903. One part of this department had the power to investigate businesses involved in interstate commerce, or commerce between two or more states.

Teddy Roosevelt was a strong and emotional supporter of Progressive causes.

ANALYZE PRIMARY SOURCES

DOCUMENT-BASED QUESTION
Why does Roosevelt think that places such as the Teton mountain range should be preserved?

Breaking Up Big Businesses

Many wealthy Americans in the late 1800s believed that government should stay out of business activities. Roosevelt did not agree with this idea. He was concerned about the power of the giant **trusts**. A trust is one large business that owns several smaller companies. Some trusts were so large that they were able to lower their prices until all of their competitors went out of business. Then the trusts could raise their prices because there was nowhere else customers could go to buy their goods or services.

Roosevelt used the Sherman Anti-Trust Act as a way to control the trusts. This act was passed in 1890 to regulate organizations that limited free trade. Using the law, Roosevelt was determined to break up what he called "bad" trusts. Roosevelt's most famous target was the Northern Securities Trust Company. This company controlled railroads in the Pacific Northwest. At Roosevelt's urging, the government successfully sued the company, breaking it up into smaller companies. Other lawsuits followed and Roosevelt earned the nickname "trustbuster."

Further Reforms

Roosevelt's trustbusting and support of a "square deal" for all Americans made him very popular. He won the 1904 election easily.

At Roosevelt's urging, Congress passed laws to improve housing, make factories safer, and regulate industries. After reading Upton Sinclair's *The Jungle*, Roosevelt ordered an investigation of meat-packing practices, which in turn led Congress to pass the Meat Inspection Act in 1906. This law set rules to ensure that meat was processed in a clean way. It allowed government inspectors to examine all meat products sold to the public.

A Champion of Conservation

Teddy Roosevelt loved the outdoors and natural beauty. Some of his greatest accomplishments were in the field of **conservation**, or protection of the natural environment. Roosevelt set aside almost 200 million acres of land for protection. He declared:

> ❝There can be nothing in the world more beautiful than the Yosemite . . . the Three Tetons; and our people should see to it that they are preserved for their children and their children's children forever with majestic beauty all unmarred. ❞

⭐ **What was Theodore Roosevelt's vision of government?**

B. Taft in Office

William Howard Taft became President in 1909. Taft had been Theodore Roosevelt's Secretary of War, but he was not as aggressive about reform as Roosevelt was. Reforms during Taft's presidency were limited.

Reforms Under Taft

Taft was not as popular with the Progressives as Roosevelt had been. However, he did achieve some reforms. In fact, his Attorney General filed more lawsuits against trusts than had been filed during the Roosevelt administration. Taft created more national parks and forestland than Roosevelt had. He also signed the Sixteenth Amendment into law. This law gave Congress the power to collect income taxes, or a portion of what individuals, families, and businesses earn. Before 1913, most federal revenue came from tariffs, or taxes on foreign goods.

Despite his accomplishments Taft's reputation was hurt by scandal. His Secretary of the Interior had sold public lands to private investors. While not illegal, it was considered inappropriate. The scandal divided the Republican Party.

The Election of 1912

Despite Taft's efforts at continuing reforms, some people were unhappy with his progress. One such person was Theodore Roosevelt. In the presidential election of 1912, Roosevelt ran against Taft. However, Taft had already won the Republican nomination. Therefore, Roosevelt had to run as a third-party candidate. He and his supporters formed the Progressive Party. This party was nicknamed the Bull Moose Party because when Roosevelt accepted the party's nomination he said that he felt "fit as a bull moose."

Republican voters were split between Taft and Roosevelt. This disagreement helped the Democratic candidate, Thomas Woodrow Wilson, win the election. Wilson, a former governor of New Jersey and president of Princeton University, had an excellent record as a Progressive.

★ **Why did Roosevelt want to defeat Taft in the election of 1912?**

ANALYZE PRIMARY SOURCES

DOCUMENT-BASED QUESTION Based on this cartoon, what do you think Roosevelt's opinion of Taft was?

This political cartoon shows President Taft trying to untangle his problems while Roosevelt watches.

C. Wilson as President

Woodrow Wilson came into office with a plan called the New Freedom. This plan called for a smaller role for government. Would Wilson's plan satisfy the Progressives, however?

The Nineteenth Amendment

President Wilson did not support the women's suffrage movement until 1918. The massive campaign led by Carrie Chapman Catt and NAWSA influenced individual states to grant women the right to vote. By 1919, a little more than half of the states granted women either partial or full suffrage. On August 18, 1920, the Nineteenth Amendment was ratified. It gave women the right to vote in all federal and state elections in the United States.

New Laws for Business and Banking

Wilson worked with Congress to pass laws to control monopolies. The Underwood-Simmons Tariff Act (1913) lowered tariffs, making goods cheaper for American buyers. The same law made income tax rates higher for wealthy people than for the poor. The Federal Reserve Act (1913) reformed the U.S. banking system. The Federal Reserve Act allowed the government to supervise banks.

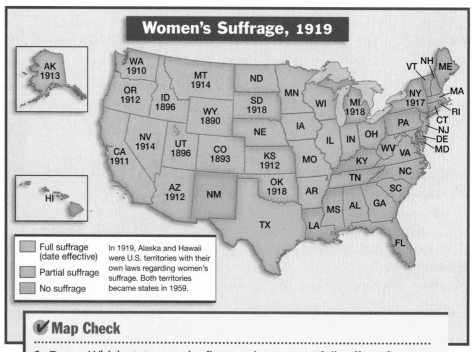

Women's Suffrage, 1919

AK 1913

WA 1910
OR 1912
ID 1896
MT 1914
ND
MN
WI
MI 1918
VT NH ME
NY 1917
MA
RI

CA 1911
NV 1914
UT 1896
WY 1890
SD 1918
IA
IL IN OH
PA
CT
NJ
DE
MD

AZ 1912
NM
CO 1893
KS 1912
MO
WV VA
NE

OK 1918
AR
TN
KY
NC

TX
LA
MS AL GA
SC

HI

FL

■ Full suffrage (date effective)
■ Partial suffrage
■ No suffrage

In 1919, Alaska and Hawaii were U.S. territories with their own laws regarding women's suffrage. Both territories became states in 1959.

✔ **Map Check**

1. **PLACE** Which state was the first to give women full suffrage?

2. **REGION** Which states granted women only partial suffrage?

The Clayton Anti-Trust Act (1914) outlawed unfair trade practices and protected unions. Congress also set up a Federal Trade Commission to oversee business. This group could investigate businesses and order them to follow federal laws.

Wilson did not actively support racial equality. During his campaign, he had promised to appoint a commission to study race relations, but he never followed through on this promise. He also allowed segregated facilities in the offices of the federal government. However, Wilson appointed Louis D. Brandeis to the Supreme Court. Brandeis was the first Jewish person to serve as a Supreme Court Justice.

Two laws were passed during Wilson's presidency that addressed social problems. The Adamson Act helped interstate railway workers by limiting their workday to eight hours. It also gave the federal government powers to regulate industry. The Keating-Owen Act prohibited the shipment of goods made by child labor across state lines.

In 1918, the Keating-Owen Act was declared unconstitutional by the U.S. Supreme Court. It was not until 1938 that laws changed child labor. Today, children who work must be paid a minimum wage. In addition, most jobs require workers to be at least 16 years old, or 18 if the job is hazardous.

 Why was the Federal Reserve Act important?

III Review

Review History
A. How did President Roosevelt show his support for the Progressive movement?
B. What were three Progressive reforms during Taft's presidency?
C. What reforms were made during President Wilson's administration?

Define Terms to Know
Provide a definition for each of the following terms.
trust, conservation

Critical Thinking
Why do you think Roosevelt's promise of a "square deal" was appealing? Explain your answer.

Write About History
Presidents Roosevelt and Taft set aside millions of acres of land for preservation. Write a paragraph explaining why conservation of resources is such an important issue today.

Get Organized
MAIN IDEA/SUPPORTING DETAILS CHART
Use a chart like the one below to record main ideas and supporting details from this section. For example, consider this main idea: Theodore Roosevelt accomplished important reforms. What details support it?

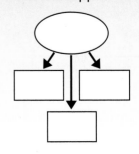

CHAPTER 21 Review

Chapter Summary

In your notebook, complete the following outline. Then, use your outline to write a brief summary of the chapter.

The Progressive Era

I. A Troubled Society

    A. Problems in the Cities

    B.

    C.

II. The Progressive Movement

    A.

    B.

    C.

III. Political Reforms

    A.

    B.

    C.

Interpret the Timeline

Use the timeline on pages 496–497 to answer the following questions.

1. Who was President when the Civil Service Act became law?

2. **Critical Thinking** Which world events show people's concern about individual rights?

Use Terms to Know

Select the term that best completes each sentence.

| muckraker | racism | tenement |
| Progressive | reformer | trust |

1. Upton Sinclair was a _____ who wrote about problems in the meat industry.

2. A _____ is a giant corporation made up of smaller companies.

3. If you lived in a _____, you might not have had running water.

4. A _____ believes that government can help improve individuals' lives.

5. Jane Addams, a _____, started a settlement house in Chicago.

6. African Americans were subjected to _____ or hatred based on one's background or skin color.

Check Your Understanding

1. **Describe** the problems in many factories in the late 1800s to early 1900s.

2. **Evaluate** the effect of the progressive movement on African Americans and Chinese Americans.

3. **Discuss** the history of Prohibition.

4. **Identify** two ways that Progressives fought against corruption in state and local government.

5. **Identify** two examples of Theodore Roosevelt's regulation of big business.

6. **Summarize** President Wilson's record on individual rights.

Critical Thinking

1. Analyze Primary Sources How might a reformer use the information in the quotation from the pickle-factory worker on page 499 to justify changes in labor laws?

2. Draw Conclusions How did the progressive movement fail in some areas?

3. Analyze Primary Sources Do you think most Americans today would agree with Roosevelt's statement on page 510 about preserving wilderness areas? Why or why not?

Put Your Skills to Work

MAKE GENERALIZATIONS

You have learned that some facts can be connected in support of a generalization.

Copy the chart below. In the boxes on the left, write two facts about women from Chapter 21. Look for similarities among these facts. In the box on the right, make a generalization about women during the Progressive Era.

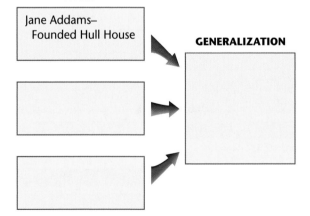

FACTS

Jane Addams–
Founded Hull House

GENERALIZATION

In Your Own Words

JOURNAL WRITING

Think about the different reforms that people worked for during the Progressive Era. What reforms do you think are needed today in business and government? What social problems need to be solved? Write a journal entry describing one or more reforms you think are needed. Offer some suggestions for achieving these reforms. What could you do personally to help solve the problem?

Net Work

INTERNET ACTIVITY

With a partner, research one of the U.S. national parks. Collect information such as the location, sites of interest, and activities available in the park. Write a brief report describing the history and features of the park. Include photos of the major attractions. Then, as a class, compile your reports to create a directory of the national parks.

For help in starting this activity, visit the following Web site: www.gfamericanhistory.com.

Look Ahead
In the next chapter, learn about American foreign policy in the early 1900s.

CHAPTER 22

Expansion Overseas 1853–1919

I. **American Expansion in the Pacific**
II. **The Spanish-American War**
III. **A New Role in Latin America**

At the dawn of the twentieth century, a new spirit was taking hold in the United States. Americans were beginning to look abroad and sensed a bright future. One historian, Brooks Adams, the grandson of John Quincy Adams, wrote about this in a 1902 book called *The New Empire*:

> [Soon], all Central America will become part of our system. We have expanded into Asia. . . . We are penetrating into Europe. . . . [T]he United States will outweigh any single empire, if not all empires combined. The whole world will pay her tribute. Commerce will flow to her both from east and west, and the order which has existed from the dawn of time will be reversed.

Was the United States about to change the part it played on the world's stage? Many Americans thought the time had come for the country to take a more powerful role.

Panama Canal keepsake plate

U.S. Events	1850	1865	1880
		1853 American ships steam into Tokyo harbor under Commodore Matthew Perry.	**1867** William Seward signs treaty to buy Alaska.	**1883** American government expands the U.S. Navy.
Presidential Term Begins		1857 James Buchanan · 1861 Abraham Lincoln · 1869 Ulysses S. Grant	1877 R. Hayes · 1881 James Garfield
World Events	1850	1865	1880
	1855 Japan is reopened to the West.	**1864** International Red Cross is established.	**1876** Korea becomes independent. · **1878** Samoa grants trading rights to the United States.

A generalization is a broad statement based on many facts or details. Use a detail/generalization chart as you read Chapter 22. List details in the top boxes. Then, based on those details, write a generalization in the bottom box. Here is an example from this chapter.

DETAIL	DETAIL
Trade with other countries increased.	Other countries established colonies.

GENERALIZATION

Americans began to look outward.

VIEW HISTORY This modern photograph shows ships passing through the Panama Canal in Central America. The canal is an important waterway that allows ships to travel from the Atlantic Ocean to the Pacific Ocean. The canal's completion is celebrated in keepsakes, such as the decorative plate (left).

 Judging from the photograph, what geographic features might have made it difficult to construct the Panama Canal?

1898
USS *Maine* explodes in Cuba.
Spanish-American War takes place.
Hawaii is annexed to the United States.

1899
United States, Britain, and Germany gain control in Samoa.

1901
President McKinley is assassinated.

1917
United States enters World War I.

1895	1910	1925
1885 G. Cleveland · 1889 B. Harrison · 1893 G. Cleveland · 1897 W. McKinley · 1901 Theodore Roosevelt	1909 W. Taft · 1913 Woodrow Wilson	1921 Warren G. Harding
1895	1910	1925

1895
War of independence from Spain begins in Cuba.

1899
Open Door policy is proposed for China.

1914
World War I begins.
Panama Canal opens.

1919
Women over 20 years of age are given the right to vote in Germany.

1917
Puerto Ricans are granted U.S. citizenship.

I American Expansion in the Pacific

Terms to Know

imperialism the practice of one nation controlling other nations through conquest and colonization

isolationism the policy of staying out of the political affairs of other countries

sphere of influence a region in which one nation has influence or control over other nations

Do You Remember?

In Chapter 15, you learned that Americans believed they had a Manifest Destiny to expand to the Pacific Ocean.

Main Ideas

A. The United States decided to expand beyond its continental boundaries.

B. The United States annexed the Hawaiian Islands, gained power in Samoa, and declared an Open Door Policy in China.

Active Reading

SEQUENCE OF EVENTS
Understanding the sequence of events, or the order in which events happened, can help you understand how they are connected. As you read this section, ask yourself: In which order did the important events occur?

A. Toward Empire

In his Farewell Address in 1796, President George Washington cautioned the American people against becoming involved with foreign nations and their problems. For many years, the United States usually followed this advice.

Different Views of Foreign Affairs

Throughout most of the 1800s, the United States did not become involved in many foreign conflicts. Rather, Americans chose to follow the idea of Manifest Destiny. They were more concerned about expanding American power in North America than expanding overseas.

However, as the 1800s drew to a close, Americans began to debate ideas about overseas expansion. Other nations—such as Britain, Germany, and France—were engaged in **imperialism**, or extending their power to build large empires. Many Americans wanted to see the United States build an overseas empire as well. One reason they sought expansion was to encourage economic growth. American industry and agriculture were producing more goods than the U.S. population could use. Some business owners and farmers wanted to sell these goods abroad. In addition, some Americans felt that it was the duty of the United States to colonize and impose its culture upon the people with which it traded. They believed that the people in foreign territories would benefit from American contact.

Not all Americans believed that the United States should have an overseas empire. Some Americans believed it was wiser for the United States to follow a policy of **isolationism** and stay out of the affairs of other countries. This policy was established by George Washington during his administration.

Japan and Alaska

In the middle of the 1800s, two important events occurred. One was the opening of Japan to U.S. trade. For many centuries, Japan did not welcome foreigners. However, on July 8, 1853, American ships under the command of Commodore Matthew Perry steamed into Tokyo harbor. Under the direction of President Millard Fillmore, Perry was to demand that the Japanese emperor open trade relations with the United States. Perry's impressive fleet forced the emperor to agree to a trade treaty.

Another event was the purchase of Alaska. In 1867, Russia offered to sell Alaska to the United States. Secretary of State William H. Seward offered $7.2 million for the territory. Many Americans thought buying what they considered to be a large, cold wasteland was not a good idea. Alaska became a U.S. territory in 1912, enlarging the United States by more than 580,000 square miles. In 1959, Alaska became the country's largest state.

Spotlight on

Geography

Many people laughed at Seward's purchase of Alaska. Newspapers called the territory "Seward's Folly" and "Seward's Icebox." No one knew how much oil, gold, copper, and other natural resources the Alaska Territory would have. The purchase looked better to many people when large amounts of gold were discovered there during the 1890s.

This 1867 cartoon shows a politician trying to find voters in Alaska.

ANALYZE PRIMARY SOURCES

DOCUMENT-BASED QUESTION What did the person who drew this cartoon think about the Alaska Purchase?

During the 1880s and 1890s, the United States increased its military strength by building more warships.

Expanding the Navy

As overseas trade increased, it became clear that American trading vessels would need the protection of the U.S. Navy, as well as ports in which to safely harbor its vessels. Islands such as Samoa and Hawaii in the Pacific Ocean made excellent places to harbor American ships and replenish coal supplies during long overseas voyages. Some Americans now saw the need to acquire colonies, not only as potential trading partners, but also to provide refueling stations for ships.

For these reasons, Congress decided that it was necessary to expand the Navy. In 1883, the U.S. government agreed to build more than 30 steel battleships. U.S. Admiral Alfred Thayer Mahan also wanted to see American power expand. In his book, *The Influence of Sea Power Upon History*, Mahan argued that it was important to the nation's future to gain new markets overseas. Therefore, a powerful navy was needed to protect American trade interests. He also thought the United States should build a canal in Central America to make it easier for ships to travel from the Atlantic Ocean to the Pacific Ocean.

★ In what ways did the United States begin to expand?

B. Expansion Overseas

Americans soon became interested in the Pacific islands. The U.S. Navy saw the Pacific islands as places to create naval bases in order to expand trade with Asia.

"Hawaii for the Hawaiians"

Americans first saw the Hawaiian Islands when traders and whalers stopped there for supplies in the late 1700s. Missionaries went to Hawaii to convert its people to Christianity in the 1820s. Later, American business owners began buying land in Hawaii to grow sugar cane. These wealthy Americans gained a good deal of power over the Hawaiian government.

In 1891, Queen Liliuokalani came to the throne of the Hawaiian Islands. She wanted to regain economic control of the islands and take power away from the American sugar planters. The queen's slogan was "Hawaii for the Hawaiians." The Americans saw her as a threat to their power.

Two years later, American business owners revolted against Queen Liliuokalani's policy of trying to reduce the power of American planters. They asked the U.S. government for help. Marines stationed on a ship in a Hawaiian harbor came ashore and forced the queen to step down. To avoid any loss of life, the queen and the Hawaiians surrendered. The United States now controlled Hawaii.

Queen Liliuokalani of Hawaii fought against U.S. control of the Hawaiian Islands.

Annexing Hawaii

What was to be done about Hawaii? Some Americans supported annexation, or taking over the smaller country. They feared other nations might annex the islands if the United States did not. However, others felt that Hawaii could never become a part of the United States because it was so far away from the mainland. These people worried that the United States would create a colony it could not govern. Others believed that the United States should not take over people of another nation.

The U.S. government, however, needed a safe harbor for its ships sailing in the Pacific Ocean. In addition, Hawaii was an important trade market for the United States. Therefore, President William McKinley and Congress agreed to annex Hawaii on July 7, 1898. In 1959, Hawaii became the fiftieth state.

Gaining Power in Samoa

The Samoan Islands lie in the southern Pacific Ocean east of Australia. The United States, Great Britain, and Germany all wanted to have influence in Samoa. In 1878 the government of Samoa granted the United States special trading rights and permission to establish a naval station at Pago Pago harbor. However, Great Britain and Germany soon gained the same rights. After tensions rose among the three countries, an agreement was reached in 1899. It gave all three countries control over parts of the Samoan Islands.

U.S. soldiers march through Beijing, China, after helping to end the Boxer Rebellion.

Open Door Policy

By the late 1800s, China's government had become weak. European nations, as well as Japan, took advantage of this situation in order to open trade relations with China. These nations divided China into **spheres of influence**. A sphere of influence is an area of a country in which another nation has gained trading privileges solely for itself—as well as political power.

The U.S. government took the stand that spheres of influence were unfair to trade. In 1899 Secretary of State John M. Hay sent messages to all the countries with spheres of influence in China and asked for an Open Door policy. This policy would allow any nation to trade in China—even in another country's sphere of influence.

Then, in 1900 a secret society called the Boxers led a rebellion to rid China of all foreigners. In the violence that followed, at least 230 foreigners were killed. The United States, along with other countries, sent forces into China where they crushed the rebellion. During this time, Hay sent another set of messages to European nations in an attempt to prevent China from being divided. These messages also reinforced the Open Door policy.

 What was the Open Door policy in China?

I Review

Review History
A. Why did Americans begin looking outward during the late 1800s?
B. What role did business owners play in the annexation of Hawaii?

Define Terms to Know
Provide a definition for each of the following terms.
imperialism, isolationism, sphere of influence

Critical Thinking
In what ways did the annexation of Hawaii benefit the United States?

Write About Geography
Write an editorial for a newspaper explaining what kinds of problems the United States may encounter when establishing distant colonies.

Get Organized
DETAIL/GENERALIZATION CHART
Think about the main events in this section. Use this chart to list details and make generalizations about these main events. Use this main event as an example: U.S. actions in the Pacific.

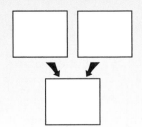

Build Your Skills

USE A LIBRARY

Your school or community library is a great resource for information. However, using the library can sometimes be confusing. Use the steps on this page to help you find the information you are looking for.

Libraries have a great deal of information on the subjects you have read about in this textbook. Use a library to find information about a topic that interests you. For example, to find out more about the history of Hawaii, you can look at reference books such as encyclopedias, state almanacs, and books about U.S. history.

Here's How

Follow these directions to find library resources.

1. Use a computer catalog to find books, CD-ROMs, and other resources.

2. Look up the topic in an encyclopedia to get clues about other specific sources for information.

3. Check the *Readers' Guide to Periodical Literature.* This is a reference that lists magazine articles by topic.

4. Ask the librarian if the library has any primary sources for your topic, such as maps or newspapers.

Here's Why

Your textbook provides you with information about many different people, places, and events in history. To learn more about a particular topic, visit a library to focus your search by using periodicals, primary source material, and research books.

Practice the Skill

Copy the chart on the right. Read Section I again to review the three topics listed on the chart. Then, visit a library to find three sources you could use to prepare a report on each topic. List the sources in the second column.

TOPIC	SOURCES
Admiral Mahan	Biographical Dictionary *World Book Encyclopedia* *Handbook of American History*, D. Cole
Boxer Rebellion	
Queen Liliuokalani	

Extend the Skill

Choose one of the topics on the chart and write a one-page report. Share the report with the class and explain your sources.

Apply the Skill

As you read the remaining sections of this chapter, make notes on people, places, or events mentioned. Then, go to a library to learn more about them.

II ★ The Spanish-American War

Terms to Know

yellow journalism publishing exaggerated or made-up news stories to attract readers and influence their ideas

protectorate a small country protected and controlled by a larger one

Main Ideas

A. Cuban revolts against Spain led to the beginning of the Spanish-American War.

B. The United States defeated Spanish forces in the Philippine Islands, Cuba, and Puerto Rico.

C. Victory in the Spanish-American War led to the building of an American Empire overseas.

 Active Reading

FACT AND OPINION Understanding the difference between facts (statements that can be proven) and opinions (people's beliefs) is an important skill. As you read this section, ask yourself: Which statements are facts and which are opinions?

A. Fanning the Flames of War

In the 1890s, the United States became involved in a conflict between Spain and its island colonies. Before long, war erupted between the two nations.

Yellow Journalism and Interest in Cuba

By the late 1800s, Spain's once-great empire was much reduced. Puerto Rico, Guam, the Philippines, and Cuba were almost all that remained. Cubans had fought against Spain from 1868 to 1878 to gain independence. One of the Cuban rebel leaders, José Martí, a poet, wrote about Cuba's fight against Spain and stirred interest among Americans. He also organized Cuban people living in the United States to fight another rebellion against Spain in Cuba in 1895.

U.S. newspapers used stories about the uprising to boost sales. Two of the country's important publishers, Joseph Pulitzer of the *New York World* and William Randolph Hearst of the *New York Journal*, published emotional stories of Spanish cruelty. These stories were exaggerated and often untrue. Such writing came to be known as **yellow journalism**.

Yellow journalism reached its peak in 1896. The Spanish government sent General Valeriano Weyler to bring order to Cuba. Weyler forced people into prisonlike camps. In two years, more than 200,000 people had died. Angry headlines in U.S. newspapers called for war with Spain. These newspaper stories influenced many people.

The cause of the explosion of the battleship *Maine* is still unknown, but at the time yellow journalists and the American public blamed Spain.

"Remember the *Maine*!"

As interest in Cuba increased in the United States, President William McKinley warned Spain that it must fight the Cuban rebels without so much cruelty. In response, the Spanish government brought General Weyler home. However, tensions in Cuba continued to rise. In the United States, cries to help the rebels grew even louder. McKinley sent the battleship USS *Maine* to Havana, the capital of Cuba, to help protect Americans there.

Then, on February 15, 1898, the *Maine* exploded in Havana harbor. The explosion killed about 260 American sailors. Captain Sigsbee, onboard the *Maine*, described the incident:

❝ I was enclosing my letter in its envelope when the explosion came. It was a bursting . . . and crashing roar of immense volume, largely metallic in character. . . . The electric lights went out. Then there was intense blackness and smoke. **❞**

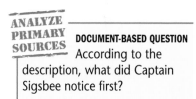

ANALYZE PRIMARY SOURCES

DOCUMENT-BASED QUESTION According to the description, what did Captain Sigsbee notice first?

The cause of the blast was unknown. Today, many historians believe it may have been caused by an accident. In 1898, however, Americans blamed Spain for the disaster.

The headline "Remember the *Maine*!" echoed across the United States. In an effort to avoid war, President McKinley asked Spain to stop fighting and to grant Cuba its independence. Spanish officials refused. McKinley finally responded to American anger, and on April 25, 1898, the United States went to war with Spain.

★ **What events led to war with Spain?**

B. "A Splendid Little War"

One American politician called the Spanish-American War "a splendid little war." It was a little war because it lasted less than four months. It was called splendid because relatively few Americans were killed, and the United States suffered no defeats.

War in the Pacific

The first battle of the Spanish-American War did not take place in Cuba but in the distant Philippine Islands. The United States saw an opportunity to seize those Spanish-controlled islands.

On April 25, the day the United States declared war on Spain, Theodore Roosevelt, who was Assistant Secretary of the Navy at the time, ordered an attack on the Spanish navy at Manila Bay. Success came on May 1, 1898, when U.S. Commodore George Dewey and his fleet defeated the Spanish navy at Manila Bay. Dewey then attacked Manila, the capital of the Philippine Islands. Soon after, President McKinley sent U.S. troops to fight alongside the Filipinos. Together, they defeated Spanish forces.

Volunteers Head to Cuba

In the United States, volunteers were organizing to fight in Cuba. Wishing to become part of the fighting force himself, Theodore Roosevelt resigned his position in the Navy Department. He then became an officer in the U.S. Army and helped organize the First Volunteer Cavalry in the Spanish-American War. This special regiment, known as the Rough Riders, included cowboys, athletes, police officers, and Native Americans who had a spirit of adventure.

African Americans also volunteered to fight, and four African American regiments were sent to Cuba. Many of these soldiers were veterans from wars in the American West. However, their experience did not prevent them from meeting discrimination in training camps and segregation on troop ships. Still, they fought bravely in the war. African American soldiers won numerous certificates of merit and a total of six Congressional Medals of Honor.

Into the Guns

On June 22, 1898, about 17,000 American troops landed at Daiquiri on the southeast coast of Cuba. There, they were joined by

African American troops fought bravely in the Spanish-American War.

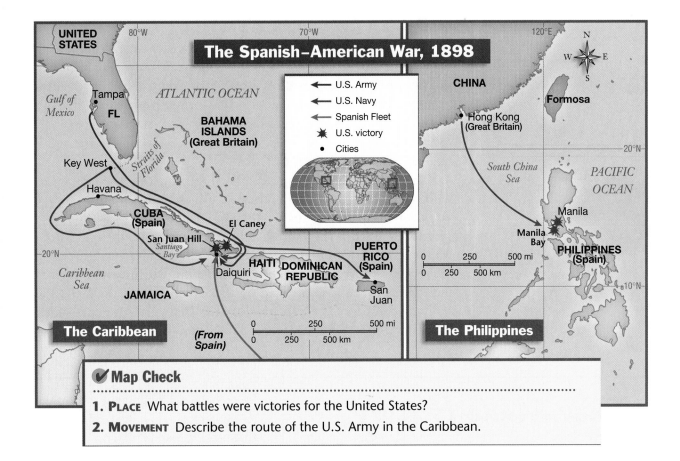

The Spanish-American War, 1898

The Caribbean

The Philippines

Legend:
- ← U.S. Army
- ← U.S. Navy
- ← Spanish Fleet
- ✳ U.S. victory
- • Cities

✔ Map Check

1. PLACE What battles were victories for the United States?

2. MOVEMENT Describe the route of the U.S. Army in the Caribbean.

Cuban troops who fought alongside the U.S. Army. The Spanish positions at El Caney and San Juan Hill were strongly defended even though they had only a small fighting force.

Roosevelt and his Rough Riders forged into battle near San Juan Hill and El Caney. They captured both sites. U.S. forces also held the cliffs overlooking Santiago Bay. When the Spanish navy tried to escape, the U.S. fleet destroyed all of the Spanish ships. The Spaniards surrendered on July 17.

On to Puerto Rico

American troops also invaded Puerto Rico, Spain's other important colony in the Caribbean. The spirit of independence was strong on the island. As early as 1868, Lola Rodríguez de Tió had written a freedom song, "La Borinqueña." Another version of Tió's song later became the national anthem of Puerto Rico. Now in 1898, Puerto Rico was occupied by American forces.

★ **How did the United States conduct the war in Cuba?**

C. Debate Over Imperialism

The United States and Spain signed a treaty on December 10, 1898, officially ending the Spanish-American War. As a result of the treaty, Spain lost most of its empire. Many Americans questioned what should be done with the former Spanish colonies of Cuba, Puerto Rico, Guam, and the Philippine Islands.

United States Control of Cuba

When the Spanish-American War began, the United States had adopted the Teller Amendment. This stated that after the war was over, control of Cuba would be given to Cubans without any interference from the United States. However, by the end of the war the U.S. government changed its policy. Cuba would become a U.S. **protectorate**, an independent nation which would be protected and partially controlled by the United States. In 1901, the United States forced Cuba to adopt the Platt Amendment, which gave the United States the right to interfere in Cuban affairs.

They Made History

Luis Muñoz Rivera 1859–1916

Luis Muñoz Rivera was a journalist and politician who fought against Spain for Puerto Rican independence during most of his adult life. He also founded the newspaper, *La Democracia,* in 1889 to push for independence for his country. When Spain granted Puerto Rico self-government in 1897, he was elected to lead the new administration. Shortly after he took office, the United States took possession of Puerto Rico. Under control of the American government, Puerto Rico was allowed to have a seat in the U.S. Congress, but could not vote. In 1910, Muñoz Rivera represented Puerto Rico in Congress. He continued to work for independence until his death in 1916. Later, the U.S. Congress granted American citizenship to Puerto Ricans.

Luis Muñoz Rivera worked for Puerto Rico's independence.

Critical Thinking How were the goals of Luis Muñoz Rivera similar to the goals of the writers of the Declaration of Independence?

Other Territories Gained

Some people felt that independence should also be granted to the Philippine Islands. Many Filipinos agreed, and Filipino rebels fought for independence. However, President McKinley felt that the Filipinos were not ready to govern themselves. As a result, an American government was set up in the Philippines. The Philippine Government Act of 1902 gave the islands limited self-government.

In the Pacific, Guam became a territory administered by the U.S. Navy. In the Caribbean, Puerto Rico became a U.S. territory, but the Puerto Ricans wanted greater self-government. Puerto Rico's congressional representative, Luis Muñoz Rivera, worked toward this goal. At last in 1917, the Jones Act, which granted U.S. citizenship to Puerto Ricans, was passed. They could now elect their own representatives, but the governor of Puerto Rico was appointed by the U.S. President.

At the end of the Spanish-American War, the United States had become a world power. The United States now controlled areas in both the Caribbean Sea and the Pacific Ocean.

★ **Which former Spanish colony became an American protectorate?**

Then & Now

The question of Puerto Rico's government is still undecided. Today, Puerto Ricans live in a common-wealth, or special territory, of the United States. Many Puerto Ricans support this arrangement. Others want the island to become the fifty-first state in the United States. A small group hopes Puerto Rico will become an independent nation.

II Review

Review History

A. How did newspapers influence the way Americans regarded Cuba?

B. Where was the Spanish-American War fought?

C. How did the Spanish-American War help make the United States a major world power?

Define Terms to Know

Provide a definition for each of the following terms.
yellow journalism, protectorate

Critical Thinking

Do you think the United States made the right decision in going to war with Spain in 1898? Explain.

Write About History

Write an article in the style of yellow journalism about the explosion of the battle-ship USS *Maine*. Include an attention-getting headline and specific details.

Get Organized

DETAIL/GENERALIZATION CHART
Think about the main events in this section. Use this chart to list details and make a generalization. For example, what details and generalization can you provide about how the United States moved toward war with Spain?

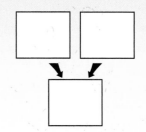

III A New Role in Latin America

Main Ideas

A. Theodore Roosevelt used his "Big Stick" policy to gain land to build the Panama Canal.

B. Both Roosevelt's and Taft's foreign policies led to increased U.S. influence and tensions in Latin America.

C. Woodrow Wilson intervened in Mexican affairs.

 Active Reading

COMPARE
Comparing items can make their differences and similarities clearer. As you read this section, compare the views of the foreign policy of three Presidents.

A. Building the Panama Canal

With the Spanish-American War behind him, President Roosevelt set his sights on a goal many had long dreamed about. That goal was to build a canal connecting the Atlantic and the Pacific Oceans.

The Big Stick Policy

In September 1901, President William McKinley was assassinated. His Vice President, Theodore Roosevelt, then became President. Roosevelt promoted progressive ideas. Looking abroad, he wanted the United States to become a world power. He wanted to defend U.S. business and political interests around the world.

Roosevelt was fond of an African saying: "Speak softly and carry a big stick." He used it to mean that the United States should use force, or the threat of force—especially naval power—to achieve its goals in dealing with other countries.

One of Roosevelt's primary concerns involved finding a site in Central America for a canal that would link the Atlantic Ocean and the Pacific Ocean. People had long dreamed of building a canal across the **isthmus**, or narrow strip of land, that connects North and South America. In particular, many people wanted to build a canal across Panama, where the isthmus was the narrowest. A canal across the isthmus would cut about 9,000 miles off of a trip from New York City to San Francisco.

Planning a Canal

The need for a canal became even clearer during the Spanish-American War. The battleship USS *Oregon* was stationed in the Pacific. When the fighting began in Cuba, the ship was ordered to the Caribbean. The trip took about two months—almost too late to take part in the fighting.

In the early 1900s, Panama was a part of Colombia, in South America. When Roosevelt asked to build a canal across Panama, the Colombian government refused. Roosevelt then helped the people of Panama organize a rebellion against Colombia in 1903. The United States sent a warship into the area and immediately recognized Panama's independence. The revolt was successful, and the new government of Panama agreed to give the United States a ten-mile wide and forty-mile long stretch of land across the country in which to build the canal. In return, the United States agreed to pay Panama $10 million for the land and $250,000 a year in rent.

Digging the Canal

Although the chosen area was a great place for a canal, it was not a healthy place for workers. Yellow fever and malaria were widespread. Both of these deadly diseases are carried by mosquitoes that live in the swampy lands of this area. William Gorgas, an army doctor, improved conditions by draining swamps and having screens placed on windows. As a result, the number of mosquitoes and their bites were reduced, and the diseases declined.

The hard work on the "big ditch" began in 1907. Dynamite was needed to blast through mountains. Thousands of workers operated steam shovels 24 hours a day to move tons of rock and earth through dense jungle and over hills and mountains. When completed, the digging had created the world's largest artificial lake of that time as well as a complex system of locks that would raise and lower ships as they passed between the continents.

In 1914, the canal was finally completed, and the first ship passed through it. The total cost of the project was more than $365 million. The United States controlled the canal until the end of 1999, when it transferred control to Panama.

★ **What major challenges were overcome in building the Panama Canal?**

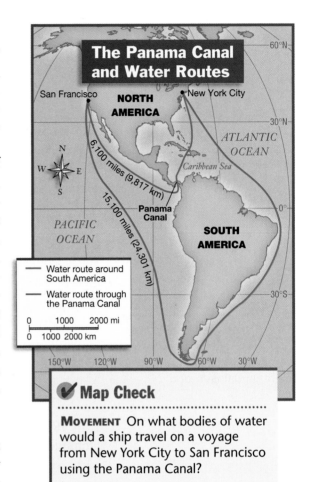

The Panama Canal and Water Routes

- Water route around South America
- Water route through the Panama Canal

0   1000   2000 mi
0   1000 2000 km

✔ Map Check

MOVEMENT On what bodies of water would a ship travel on a voyage from New York City to San Francisco using the Panama Canal?

B. The Roosevelt Principle and Dollar Diplomacy

President Roosevelt and his successor, William Howard Taft, had different ideas about dealing with Latin America. These differing ideas led to two very different American overseas policies.

The Roosevelt Principle

President Roosevelt believed that European nations should not interfere in Latin America because their interference violated the Monroe Doctrine of 1823. That doctrine stated that foreign countries could not intervene in the countries of the Western Hemisphere. Roosevelt announced a **corollary**, or follow-up, to the Monroe Doctrine as a part of his foreign policy. It stated that only the United States could intervene in the affairs of countries in the Western Hemisphere. Roosevelt explained his policy the following way:

> " Any country whose people conduct themselves well can count upon our hearty friendship. . . . Chronic wrong doing. . . may force the United States, however. . . to exercise an international police power. "

In 1905, the United States took over the financial affairs of the Dominican Republic when that country failed to pay its debts. During his presidency, Roosevelt also sent troops to Nicaragua and Cuba.

ANALYZE PRIMARY SOURCES

DOCUMENT-BASED QUESTION According to Roosevelt, who would judge events in Latin America?

This cartoon shows Teddy Roosevelt wielding his "Big Stick" foreign policy.

Taft's Policy

President Taft, who followed Roosevelt, used a different approach in Latin America. Taft believed that the United States should use its economic power to influence countries in that region and around the world. He felt that American businesses could help keep the economies of Latin American countries sound. Taft's policy became known as dollar **diplomacy**. Diplomacy is the peaceful negotiations between governments. U.S. companies bought land in Latin America and put local people to work. However, dollar diplomacy also increased tensions between the United States and Latin American countries. Some Latin American countries were not happy with U.S. actions. U.S. troops were sometimes used to protect American businesses.

President Taft introduced the policy of dollar diplomacy.

⭐ **How did President Roosevelt add to the Monroe Doctrine?**

C. Wilson's Foreign Policy

Beginning in 1913, President Woodrow Wilson hoped to use a U.S. policy of cooperation instead of power in Latin America. However, he soon changed his mind.

A Different Diplomacy

Wilson opposed the Big-Stick policy as well as dollar diplomacy. He said that the United States should respect the interests and rights of small nations. He took steps to allow the Philippine Islands to govern themselves. However, Wilson intervened in Latin American countries when he thought guidance was needed. Wilson's biggest challenge in Latin America was Mexico.

The Mexican Revolution

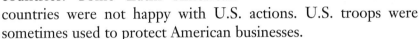

Mexico had a long history of harsh rule. Mexicans suffered under the rule of president Porfirio Diaz. Then, in 1911, Diaz was overthrown and Francisco Madero became Mexico's president. Two years later, General Victorianio Huerta took power. He had Madero thrown in jail and murdered.

Francisco "Pancho" Villa had hoped to control Mexico after the fall of Porfirio Díaz.

President Wilson was shocked by these actions and refused to recognize Huerta's government. Tensions continued to rise. Then, in 1914 Wilson discovered that a German ship was sending weapons to the Huerta government. He sent American warships to bomb the port of Veracruz. Huerta stepped down. Wilson then recognized the new Mexican government under Venustiano Carranza.

Pancho Villa's Mexican Revolt

Fighting in Mexico continued, however. In 1916, Francisco "Pancho" Villa, an opponent of Carranza, led a revolt. He hoped that the United States would take action and that he could become the leader of Mexico. He raided border towns between Texas and Mexico. Then, Villa stopped a Mexican train and killed approximately 16 of the American passengers. He also invaded Columbus, New Mexico, burning the town and killing more than 16 Americans.

Wilson ordered General John J. Pershing to Mexico. His orders were clear: Find Villa and capture him. Pershing and his 10,000 troops marched deep into Mexico. They pursued Villa, but the rebel leader and his men disappeared into the mountains. Finally, Wilson ordered Pershing back to the United States. The President had concerns about another crisis that was brewing across the Atlantic Ocean.

 Who was Pancho Villa?

 **Review**

Review History

A. How did the building of the Panama Canal show Theodore Roosevelt's Big-Stick policy in action?

B. How was President Taft's foreign policy different from President Roosevelt's?

C. Why did conflicts arise between Mexico and the United States?

Define Terms to Know

Provide a definition for each of the following terms. **isthmus, corollary, diplomacy**

Critical Thinking

Do you think U.S. foreign policy toward Latin America during this period was helpful or harmful in establishing long-term relations? Explain your answer.

Write About History

In a letter to President Wilson, explain your opinion of his foreign policy toward Latin America.

Get Organized

DETAIL/GENERALIZATION CHART
Think about the main events in this section. Use this chart to list details and make a generalization. For example, what details and generalization can you provide about the foreign policy of Theodore Roosevelt?

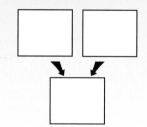

Points of View

United States and Imperialism

As a result of the Spanish-American War, the United States gained an overseas empire. However, Americans continued to debate whether the country should pursue a course of imperialism, by expanding overseas, or remain isolationist, by confining its interests to existing boundaries.

Supporters of imperialism argued that the United States was duty-bound to bring law, good government, and American culture to the peoples of countries in the Caribbean and the Pacific. Those supporting isolationism often argued that a U.S. empire was against the American ideals of equality and democracy. Critics of imperialism labeled U.S. actions as greedy and unhealthy.

Below are two cartoons that illustrate the debate about imperialism. The cartoon on the left focuses on the U.S. acquisition of a new overseas empire during the early 1900s. The cartoon on the right shows the intervention of U.S. forces in Veracruz, Mexico, in 1914.

Regions in the Western Hemisphere

A bloated Uncle Sam is tailored by William McKinley.

Uncle Sam intervenes in Veracruz, Mexico.

ANALYZE PRIMARY SOURCES

DOCUMENT-BASED QUESTIONS

1. In the cartoon on the left, why do you think William McKinley is portrayed as a tailor?

2. Do you think the cartoon on the right supports imperialism? Why?

3. **Critical Thinking** How is Uncle Sam different in the two cartoons?

CHAPTER 22 Review

Chapter Summary

In your notebook, complete the following outline. Then, use your outline to write a brief summary of the chapter.

Expansion Overseas

I. American Expansion in the Pacific

    A. Toward Empire

    B.

II. The Spanish-American War

    A.

    B.

    C.

III. A New Role in Latin America

    A.

    B.

    C.

Interpret the Timeline

Use the timeline on pages 516–517 to answer the following questions.

1. Who was President when the Open Door Policy was proposed?

2. **Critical Thinking** Which world events show people's desire for self-government and independence?

Use Terms to Know

Select the term that best completes each sentence.

corollary   protectorate
isolationism   spheres of influence
isthmus

1. European nations and Japan controlled _____ in China.

2. Believers in _____ felt the United States should stay out of other countries' affairs.

3. Roosevelt issued a _____ to the Monroe Doctrine of 1823.

4. After the Spanish-American War, Cuba became a _____ of the United States.

5. A narrow _____ separates North America from South America.

Check Your Understanding

1. **Explain** what Secretary Hay hoped to gain by the Open Door policy in China.

2. **Identify** three factors that led to the United States becoming more active as a world power.

3. **Discuss** the effect of yellow journalism on American foreign policy at the end of the 1800s.

4. **Summarize** the results of the U.S. victory in the Spanish-American War.

5. **Describe** Theodore Roosevelt's approach to foreign policy.

6. **Explain** how relations between the United States and Mexico were affected by President Woodrow Wilson's action during the Mexican Revolution.

Critical Thinking

1. **Synthesize Information** In what ways did the United States expand its power in the late 1800s?

2. **Analyze Primary Sources** Reread the quotation from Theodore Roosevelt on page 532. How do you think the governments of foreign nations would react to Roosevelt's statement?

3. **Draw Conclusions** How do you think American imperialism influenced relations between the United States and Latin America in the long run?

Put Your Skills to Work

USE A LIBRARY

You have learned that a library is a great resource for learning more about history.

Copy the chart below on a separate sheet of paper. In the first column, list three people, places, or events covered in this chapter about which you would like to know more. Then, in the second column, list three library sources in which you could find more information.

TOPIC	SOURCES
Panama Canal	*The Panama Canal*, K. Moore *History of the United States*, J.F. Rhodes *Encyclopedia Britannica*

In Your Own Words

JOURNAL WRITING

The Panama Canal is a construction marvel that helped speed trade worldwide. Can you think of other kinds of large-scale construction projects that would have a similar impact? Write a journal entry describing a construction project you have seen. Explain how the project affected people when it was completed.

Net Work

INTERNET ACTIVITY

Work with a group of classmates. Use the Internet as a resource to create an exhibit called "Sights and Sounds of the Spanish-American War." In your exhibit, use information you find at different Web sites that portray the events of the war. You may want to include speeches by leaders from the United States and other countries, plus words, pictures, songs, and other material from those who took part in the war. Set up your exhibit, and share it with the class.

For help in starting this activity, visit the following Web site: www.gfamericanhistory.com.

Look Ahead

In the next chapter, learn how a world war brought the United States deeper into world affairs.

Unit 7 Portfolio Project

Voices of Immigration Audiocassette

YOUR ASSIGNMENT

Oral history is a special kind of history. Oral historians record the exact words of people who have taken part in historical events. Sometimes, the people whom oral historians study are famous. Mostly, though, they are ordinary people who have lived through important or unusual experiences. As a class, research the topic of immigration to the United States from the 1840s to the 1920s. Then, turn your research into an oral history project by recording an audiocassette based on your research.

FINDING MATERIALS

Assign Duties Create teams that focus on different periods and sources of immigration. Teams can research immigration from northern and western Europe, southern Europe, eastern Europe, Asia, or Latin America.

Research Accounts Next, find quotes and first-person accounts from immigrants. Start with your school or community library. You can also search the Internet using key words such as *immigration*, *immigrants*, *Ellis Island*, and *Angel Island*. Refer to this Web site for ideas: www.gfamericanhistory.com.

CREATING YOUR ORAL HISTORY AUDIOCASSETTE

Choosing Selections As a team, decide on six accounts to include on your tape. Make sure your choices cover different experiences. Choose sources that show the different aspects of immigrants' journeys to the United States.

Recording Your Tape Practice reading your selections. Then, record them on an audiocassette. Combine all teams' selections, and make copies of the final audiocassette. Finally, play the recording in class, and discuss the different experiences described.

Multimedia Presentation

If you have access to videotaping equipment, turn your audio documentary into a video program. Make costumes to represent the immigrants whose stories you are reading. Display pictures, objects, or other props as you read the historical accounts for the videotape. Then, show the videotape.

A Troubled Nation

"I couldn't find a job. . . . I ended up selling apples. . . . In New York City there was nothing that struck the imagination more than seeing a soup line of 500 people. . . . And it kept on growing and growing."

—Bill Bailey, a New York City resident who lived through the Great Depression

LINK PAST TO PRESENT The figures in this photograph are part of the memorial to President Franklin Roosevelt in Washington, D.C. They represent men standing in a food line during the Great Depression.

★ What do the quotation and the photograph tell you about life during the Great Depression?

539

CHAPTER **23**

World War I 1914–1918

I. **War in Europe**
II. **The United States Enters the War**
III. **Fighting the War**

*T*he Great War, which became known as World War I, engulfed the world. New weapons such as machine guns, hand grenades, and airplanes that dropped bombs made this war more destructive than wars in the past. American soldier Eugene Kennedy described a World War I battle that took place in France:

> **66** A real war and we are walking right into the zone, ducking shells all the way. The artillery is nerve racking and we don't know from which angle [the Germans] will fire next. Halted behind shelter of railroad track . . . after being forced back off main road by shell fire. Trees splintered like toothpicks. **99**

Although the United States at first stayed out of the war, it later joined in the fight overseas. American troops contributed greatly to the outcome of the war.

McClure's magazine cover, March 1918

1913 Sixteenth Amendment allows income taxes to be imposed.	**1914** United States decides not to enter World War I.	**1915** United States begins to prepare for the possibility of entering World War I.	**1916** Jeannette Rankin of Montana becomes the first woman member of Congress.
U.S. Events 1913	1914	1915	1916
Presidential Term Begins 1913 Woodrow Wilson			
World Events 1913	1914	1915	1916
1912 Balkan Wars begin in southeastern Europe.	**1914** Austrian Archduke Franz Ferdinand is assassinated. World War I begins.	**1915** German U-boat sinks the passenger ship *Lusitania*.	

Get Organized

CAUSE/EFFECT CHART

Historical events often have more than one cause. Use a cause/effect chart as you read Chapter 23. List causes in the top oval. Write the event—which is the effect—in the bottom oval. Here is an example from this chapter.

CAUSES
- Expanding empires
- Nationalism
- Alliances

↓

EFFECT
Outbreak of war in Europe

VIEW HISTORY The photo above shows a World War I fighter plane, called a Sopwith Camel, that was made in Great Britain. The magazine cover (left) shows an American soldier during World War I.

★ **How would you describe the fighter plane?**

1917
United States declares war on Germany.
First U.S. troops arrive in France.

1918
President Wilson develops a peace plan called the Fourteen Points.

1919
President Wilson receives the Nobel Peace Prize.

1920
U.S. Senate rejects the Treaty of Versailles for a second time.

1917	1918	1919	1920

1917	1918	1919	1920

1917
Russian Revolution brings communism to Russia.
Balfour Declaration supports a homeland in Palestine for Jews.

1918
Armistice ending World War I is signed.

1918–1919
Worldwide flu epidemic kills about 30 million people.

1919
Paris Peace Conference meets.
Gandhi uses passive resistance to protest British rule in India.

I War in Europe

Terms to Know

arms race a competition to build weapons

pacifist a person who opposes war under any circumstance

mobilize to organize or prepare, as for war

Main Ideas

A. When war broke out in Europe in 1914, President Wilson wanted to keep the United States neutral.

B. Fighting between the Central Powers and the Allies nearly destroyed Europe.

C. New weapons made World War I the deadliest war up to that time.

 Active Reading

PROBLEMS AND SOLUTIONS
You will read about problems in Europe. Some nations tried to solve these problems with war. As you read this section, ask yourself what other solutions might have been possible.

A. Europe on the Eve of War

In 1914, Sir Edward Grey, the British minister to France, looked out over Paris, which is called the City of Lights. He said, "The lamps are going out all over Europe; we shall not see them lit again in our lifetime." Sir Edward believed that the world, as he knew it, was going to change. Europe would be involved in World War I.

The Stage Is Set

Tensions had been high in Europe for years. To expand their empires, stronger nations fought over colonies. In addition, industries were growing, including those that produced military equipment and weapons. An **arms race** among countries was underway. In Germany, Kaiser Wilhelm II built up his nation's army until it was the largest in Europe. Great Britain, which already had a strong navy, began to increase its army.

Many European countries were also experiencing a time of great nationalism as people supported their own nations. Countries with shared languages were uniting. Some countries, such as Germany and Italy, had recently formed from culturally similar states. Groups of people in other countries were trying to win their independence.

By the early twentieth century, Germany, Austria-Hungary, and Italy had signed a treaty that formed the Triple Alliance. Great Britain, France, and Russia made an agreement and formed the Triple Entente. Under both agreements, the member nations promised to support one another. Later, after war broke out, Italy left the Triple Alliance and joined forces with the Triple Entente.

An Assassination in Sarajevo

Tensions were quite high in the Balkans—an area in southeastern Europe that includes the countries of Albania, Bulgaria, Greece, Romania, Turkey, and Serbia—due to fighting over land rights. Serbians, or people from the country of Serbia, made up a large part of Bosnia. Bosnia was part of Austria-Hungary. However, Serbia considered Bosnia part of its territory. On June 28, 1914, a Serbian named Gavrilo Princip assassinated, or killed, Austrian Archduke Franz Ferdinand and his wife, Sophie, the Duchess von Hohenberg, in Sarajevo. Princip was a member of a nationalist society known as the Black Hand. This group wanted the Austro-Hungarians out of Bosnia. The Black Hand society believed that the assassination of Franz Ferdinand would help its cause.

War between Austria-Hungary and Serbia started after Franz Ferdinand's death and soon threatened all of Europe. Because of the system of alliances, members of one side declared war on members of the other side. Great Britain, France, and Russia became the leaders of the Allied Powers, or the Allies. Italy and other nations would join the Allies after the war broke out.

Germany, Austria-Hungary, and the Ottoman Empire were the major Central Powers that the Allies were fighting against. Many people believed that the war would be short. Both sides believed that they would win.

The assassination of Archduke Franz Ferdinand and his wife Sophie triggered the beginning of World War I.

Keeping the United States Out of the War

Many Americans either had been born in Europe or had parents who were. Americans of English descent often sided with the Allies. Some Americans of German descent had ties to Germany. Most Americans, however, did not want to go to war. Some were **pacifists**, or people who rejected war on principle. Others were isolationists, or people who believed the United States should stay out of Europe's problems.

President Woodrow Wilson was not an isolationist. He did, however, announce that the United States would remain neutral and not support either side. The war, he said, is one "with which we have nothing to do, whose causes cannot touch us."

★ How did various groups in the United States view the war?

Do You Remember?

In Chapter 22, you learned that many Americans supported isolationism, hoping to keep the United States out of the affairs of other countries.

Europe During World War I

Allied nations
Central Powers
Neutral nations
• Cities

0 250 500 mi
0 250 500 km

✔ **Map Check**

1. **PLACE** Which countries belonged to the Central Powers?
2. **HUMAN INTERACTION** Why might Germany face battles on both its eastern and western borders?

B. Fighting in Europe

While the United States remained neutral, war spread across Europe. European countries declared war on each other and **mobilized**, or assembled and trained, thousands of troops.

Two Fronts

The conflict between the Central Powers and the Allies focused on two fronts, or major areas of battle. On the eastern front, Russian troops fought against troops from Austria-Hungary and Germany. Troops from the countries involved also clashed in the Ottoman Empire, Serbia, Africa, and on islands in the Pacific Ocean. In an attempt to gain colonies, Japan attacked German colonies in China.

On the western front, German troops tried to invade France. They pushed through Belgium, which had been neutral until the German attack, on their way to Paris, France. The Belgians resisted, but they were defeated by the German forces. Germany's actions against Belgium convinced some Americans that the United States had to enter the war.

"They Shall Not Pass"

By September 1914, the German army was within 20 miles of Paris. Both defending French troops and attacking German troops dug trenches, or ditches, for protection. They strung barbed wire in front of their defenses. The area between opposing trenches became known as no man's land.

This no man's land became a barren plain. No trees stood; no grass grew. One army would attack and gain ground one day. The opposing army would take it back the next.

At the First Battle of the Marne, on the Marne River, French and British troops stopped the German advance on Paris. Then, in 1916, the Germans attacked French forces at the French town of Verdun. They planned to break through the French lines. The French commander at Verdun and his troops stopped the German troops from advancing. His words, "They shall not pass," became a rallying cry as the French were determined to hold their land at all costs.

The Allied forces from the west struck the Germans along the Somme River. The Russians attacked in the east along the Russian border. Both sides suffered many casualties. However, in three years of fighting, neither side gained much ground.

★ What is trench warfare?

C. New Technology Changes War

World War I, or the Great War as it was known, was the first war to involve nations from all areas of the world. Battles were fought in many countries, on every ocean, and in the skies. New and deadlier weapons changed the nature of warfare.

Fighting on the Sea

Germany developed a new class of Unterseeboot (undersea boat), or U-boat. Armed with torpedoes, or self-propelled bombs, U-boats moved underwater and could sink ships on any ocean or sea. In 1915, a German U-boat sank the British passenger ship *Lusitania* without warning. Almost 1,200 people died, including 128 Americans. President Wilson protested, and Germany agreed to stop targeting passenger ships without warning.

Soldiers dug trenches to defend their positions and shield themselves from gunfire.

Spotlight on *Culture*

It is said that poppies were the first plants to grow in the ruined land of northern France and Belgium.

After the war, an American YMCA worker named Moina Michael promoted the wearing of a red poppy in memory of the dead. She also began to sell poppies to raise money for veterans who had been disabled during the war. To this day, red poppies are widely worn on Veterans Day.

Fighting on Land and in the Air

On land, armored tanks carrying weapons could roll toward trenches and launch deadly attacks. Machine guns and hand grenades killed and wounded many soldiers on both sides. Poison gas was also used to fight enemy forces. The gas choked and blinded those who came in contact with it. Soldiers on both sides suffered serious illness and disability from poison gas. Gas masks became standard issue for the troops.

Fighting also took place in the air. Hydrogen-filled airships called zeppelins carried weapons and were used on spy missions. However, because they were so big, zeppelins were easy targets.

Airplanes were another new weapon of World War I. From planes, pilots could locate enemy lines and drop bombs. Many airplanes were also equipped with machine guns. Fleets of fighter planes battled each other in the sky. Pilots who shot down five or more planes were known as aces. The most famous German ace was Baron Manfred von Richthofen—the Red Baron. Before his death in 1918, he shot down 80 Allied planes. Richthofen spoke about the reality of war:

❝I think of this war as it really is, not as the people at home imagine, with a hoorah! . . . It is very serious, very grim. **❞**

ANALYZE PRIMARY SOURCES

DOCUMENT-BASED QUESTION Which words does von Richthofen use to describe World War I?

★ **Why could World War I be described as total war?**

I ★ Review

Review History
A. What were some of the causes of World War I?
B. What were the two major fronts of the war?
C. What forms of technology changed how World War I was fought compared to previous wars?

Define Terms to Know
Provide a definition for each of the following terms.
arms race, pacifist, mobilize

Critical Thinking
How did European alliances lead to a war involving many nations?

Write About Citizenship
Write a brief essay describing how Americans with relatives living in Europe may have felt about Wilson's policy of neutrality.

Get Organized
CAUSE/EFFECT CHART
Think about the main events in this section. Use a cause/effect chart to show causes of an event, which is the effect. For example, what were some of the factors that caused World War I to be so deadly?

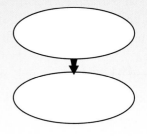

Build Your Skills

CONDUCT RESEARCH ON THE INTERNET

Libraries have been sources of information since ancient times, but people today also have access to an electronic library—the Internet.

When you read about history, you can find additional information on the Internet. Many historical documents and primary sources are available on the Internet. Much of the information is useful, but you need to examine it carefully to determine whether it is reliable, or based on facts.

Here's How
Follow these steps for researching information on the Internet.

1. Go to the search engine provided, or type in the address of another search engine. A search engine is a computer program for finding information on the World Wide Web.

2. Type in the topic you are researching. Be as specific as possible. For example, you might type the keywords *Triple Entente* rather than the word *alliances* to find information about World War I.

3. Check some of the sites the search engine lists. Is the content useful? Is the information based on facts? Education and government Web sites are examples of reliable Web sites.

4. Many of the sites will include links to additional sites. You may check these sites too.

Here's Why
You have just read about the new technology used during World War I. Suppose you have to create a report about one type of technology used during the war. You could research sources on the Internet to find information for your report.

Practice the Skill
Use the Internet to find out about the airships called zeppelins. Use a computer note-taking program or copy the chart on a sheet of paper. Take notes as shown in the chart. Include at least two Web sites that contain information about zeppelins.

Extend the Skill
Use the information you found on the Internet to write a brief report about zeppelins. Include specific facts and details. List your sources at the bottom of your report.

TOPIC: ZEPPELINS	
Web Address	www.gfamericanhistory.com
Content	history, pictures, links
Reliability	good, intended for education

Apply the Skill
As you read the rest of the chapter, be alert to topics you might want to explore further. Search the Internet to find sources of information about the topics.

II ★ The United States Enters the War

Terms to Know

communism a theory in which the economy is controlled by the government, and property is owned by everyone equally

victory garden a garden in which people grow their own food during a war

war bond a loan from U.S. citizens to the government meant to be paid back with interest in several years

propaganda the promotion of certain ideas to influence people's opinions

Main Ideas

A. President Woodrow Wilson began to prepare for war as he campaigned for and won re-election.

B. The United States declared war on Germany.

C. To support the war effort, Americans worked in war industries, bought bonds, and accepted limits on civil liberties.

 **Active Reading**

DRAW CONCLUSIONS
When you read about history, you can draw conclusions about events in the past and about how they affect the present. As you read this section, draw conclusions about America's role in the world during World War I.

A. Wilson Wins Re-election

The war dragged on through 1915 and 1916. President Wilson's attempts to get both sides to accept "peace without victory" were unsuccessful. Meanwhile, the number of dead and wounded continued to rise, while the United States tried to remain neutral.

The Issue of Preparedness

Americans remained divided. Some still wanted to stay out of war. Others, however, wanted the country to prepare for war. Many Americans favored the Allied nations. The United States had strong ties of language and culture to Great Britain. Americans were also aware that during the Revolutionary War, France had helped the colonies win their independence from Great Britain. However, there was also strong support among other Americans for the Central Powers. Millions of Americans who had immigrated to the United States were from Germany, Austria-Hungary, and other countries of the Central Powers. Many American Jews who had fled Russian persecution supported Germany against Russia.

President Wilson wanted to keep the United States from entering the war. However, by late 1915, he was speaking in favor of preparedness, or being ready to go to war. Wilson asked the War Department to increase military spending. He supported a huge increase in the budget for the army and navy. Progressives and the Women's Peace Party—a political organization that wanted to end the fighting in Europe—were alarmed. Some business leaders protested.

During the election of 1916, Americans showed their support of Wilson's policy to keep the United States out of war.

He Kept Us Out of War

Wilson campaigned for re-election in 1916. In the months before the election, U.S. relations with Germany were relatively calm. Thus, Wilson's slogan—He kept us out of war—was a strong argument for his re-election. Republicans thought that Wilson had been too slow to respond to the threat of war. However, Wilson won a narrow victory.

Early in 1917, the Germans announced they would sink all ships sailing toward Great Britain or France. German U-boats sank five American ships within one month. Also, the British government discovered and shared with Wilson a telegram written by Arthur Zimmermann, the German foreign minister. In it, Zimmermann urged Mexico to join the German effort. In return, Germany would help Mexico regain its territory in New Mexico, Texas, and Arizona. Americans were outraged.

 How did the election reflect Americans' attitudes about the war?

B. Americans at War

The sinking of American ships and the Zimmermann telegram changed how many Americans viewed the war. By 1917, President Wilson had come to feel that the United States had to go to war.

On April 2, 1917, Wilson asked Congress for a declaration of war. Many members of Congress opposed war. However, a majority supported it. On April 6, Congress declared war on Germany.

Spotlight on
Government

Wilson told Congress that "The world must be made safe for democracy." Members of Congress debated for four days about entering World War I. Six senators and 50 representatives—including Jeannette Rankin, the first woman elected to Congress—voted against going to war.

In 1917, American men lined up to register for the draft. By 1918, nearly 3 million men had been drafted into military service.

Readying for Battle

In its war with Spain, the United States had depended on a volunteer army. Now, however, Wilson favored conscription as fairer and more effective. In May 1917, Congress passed the Selective Service Act. Men between the ages of 21 and 30 were required to register for the draft. The following year, the law was changed to apply to men between the ages of 18 and 45.

In 1917, only 200,000 people served in the armed services. Over the next two years, almost 4 million more joined. Training and supplying the new soldiers was an immense task. About 400,000 African Americans joined the armed services. In the military as well as at home, they faced discrimination. Two separate combat divisions were created for African American soldiers.

Women could not register for the draft, but more than 30,000 joined the military. They served in military offices and as nurses. Others joined the American Red Cross to work both at home and overseas.

President Wilson called on General John J. Pershing to lead the American Expeditionary Force, the name for U.S. forces in Europe. American soldiers, called doughboys, boarded ships headed for France. By July 1917, 15,000 troops had arrived in France. Many believed they would be home by Christmas. Before the war's end, 2 million American men made the trip to France. They proved to be invaluable to the Allied efforts.

The Russian Revolution

The United States and the other Allied nations had more than fighting in France to worry about. In March 1917, a revolution broke out in Russia. Czar Nicholas II was forced to step down from the throne. He and his family were later taken prisoners and killed.

The Bolsheviks, a group led by Vladimir Ilich Lenin, gained control of the government. The Bolsheviks signed an agreement with Germany that removed Russia from World War I. That meant the Germans no longer had to worry about the eastern front. The U.S. government watched as Russia turned to **communism**, a theory in which the economy is controlled by the government, and property is owned by everyone equally.

 How did the United States prepare to go to war?

C. The Home Front

American troops in Europe would face the horrors of war. Americans at home had to do their part to support them. Posters urged citizens to have "Wheatless Wednesdays," "Meatless Tuesdays," thereby saving food for the troops overseas.

Changes at Home

Because so many men were overseas in the war, women in the workforce found better jobs, many in factories and industries that aided the war effort. The War Labor Board ordered that women be paid as much as men for work done in war industries.

Since the end of the Civil War, many African Americans had hoped to escape the prejudice and unfair treatment that they faced in the South. In the early 1900s, they moved north to find jobs in war industries and factories. Between 1910 and 1930, about 1 million African Americans migrated to northern states. This movement became known as the Great Migration.

In the Southwest, many Mexicans crossed the U.S. border to find jobs. Some worked in new wartime industries. Others worked planting and harvesting vegetables and fruits. Their efforts helped meet the need for huge supplies of food for the Allied armed forces.

Much of the food that farmers produced went to feed the troops. American families did not eat meat or wheat products on certain days of the week to save food for the soldiers. Some families grew their own food in **victory gardens** as another way of supporting the war effort.

Funding the War

Wilson used the Sixteenth Amendment, passed in 1913, to raise income taxes. These new funds would pay for only part of the war, so Americans were encouraged to buy Liberty Bonds, or **war bonds**. These bonds were loans from Americans to the government that would be paid back later. War bonds helped support the war effort—in fact, they paid for two thirds of the cost of the war.

The President set up agencies to conduct the war effort. Some of these agencies gave the government more control over the economy. The War Industries Board oversaw factory work and set prices for goods and services. The Food Administration insured the supply of food to the armed forces. The Fuel Administration supported daylight saving time to conserve energy.

Many women worked in factories during World War I. They assembled gas masks and manufactured other war supplies for soldiers.

Spotlight on *Government*

During World War I, Congress passed a law requiring the United States to observe daylight saving time. Daylight saving time allows people to conserve energy by giving them an "extra" hour of sunlight in the evening.

In 1918, people tended to go to bed earlier than they do today. As a result, the law was very unpopular and was repealed in 1919. Daylight saving time was not observed again until the 1940s.

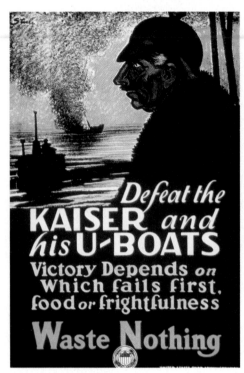

Defeat the
KAISER and
his U-BOATS
Victory Depends on
Which fails first,
food or frightfulness
Waste Nothing

Posters such as this one encouraged Americans to support the war.

War Feelings at Home

Wilson formed the Committee on Public Information (CPI), which sent speakers across the nation to explain why Americans were fighting overseas. They also spoke about the meaning of democracy. Films and posters put out by the CPI pictured German soldiers as blood-thirsty "Huns" and Kaiser Wilhelm II of Germany as "The Beast of Berlin." These films and posters used **propaganda**, or the spreading of certain ideas, to boost Americans' support of the war.

Anti-German feeling grew strong. Americans ate "liberty cabbage" instead of sauerkraut. German newspapers were closed. Many schools stopped teaching the German language. Often orchestras did not play the works of German composers such as Bach, Brahms, or Beethoven. President Wilson and other government leaders felt that German immigrants living in the United States were a threat to the war effort. As a result, many Germans were placed in jail.

Limits were put on civil rights. Under the Espionage Act of 1917 and the Sedition Act of 1918, people were fined or jailed for speaking or writing against the government. Eugene Debs, leader for railroad workers in the 1800s, was sentenced to ten years in prison for opposing the limits on people's civil rights.

★ **What changes did World War I bring to the United States?**

II Review

Review History
A. What measures did President Wilson take to prepare for war?
B. Why did Wilson shift from a policy of neutrality to a declaration of war?
C. How did Americans at home aid the war effort?

Define Terms to Know
Provide a definition for each of the following terms.
communism, victory garden, war bond, propaganda

Critical Thinking
What effect did the events in Russia in 1917 have on the war in Europe?

Write About Citizenship
It is 1917, and the United States has entered World War I. What do you think is the most difficult adjustment for citizens at home to make?

Get Organized
CAUSE/EFFECT CHART
Create a cause/effect chart to show causes of an event —which is the effect—from this section. For example, what were the causes of the U.S. entry into World War I?

CONNECT
History & Media

Radio in War and Peace

In 1898, during the Spanish-American War, it took three days for word of the U.S. victory at Manila Bay to reach New York newspapers. In 1914, it took less than one day for people to learn of the assassination in Sarajevo that would spark World War I.

RADIO GOES TO WAR Radio changed communication greatly because it did not need wires. Messages could travel through the air from a transmitter to a receiver. The first transatlantic radio message was sent by Guglielmo Marconi in 1901. During the early twentieth century, many other inventors, most notably Edwin H. Armstrong, experimented with radio and improved it.

After entering the war in 1917, the U.S. government took over all the transmitters in the country. It ordered thousands of radios for use on ships and in trenches. Woodrow Wilson gave the first presidential radio address to U.S. troops from a ship in 1919.

RADIO FOLLOWING WORLD WAR I The first commercial radio stations—KDKA in Pittsburgh, Pennsylvania, and WWJ in Detroit, Michigan—opened in 1920. By the end of the decade, radio had become important to American life.

Radio produced a new kind of family entertainment. In the afternoons, people listened to dramas, called soap operas, because they were sponsored by soap companies. In the evenings, they listened to comedies like *Fibber McGee and Molly* and adventures like *The Shadow*. They also listened to the jazz of Duke Ellington and Benny Goodman. Radio became a big part of American culture.

Critical Thinking

Answer the questions below. Then, complete the activity.

1. How did radio change communications?
2. Today, radio competes with television and the Internet. Do you think it still plays an important role in society? Explain your answer.

Write About It

Suppose you are a reviewer at the time an early broadcast first aired. Choose one to listen to and write a brief commentary on it. Go to the following Web site to hear old broadcasts: **www.gfamericanhistory.com**.

Edwin H. Armstrong's invention of FM radio and his other inventions greatly improved radio transmission and reception. He is pictured here with a portable radio.

III Fighting the War

Terms to Know

armistice an agreement to stop warfare

self-determination the right of people to decide on their own form of government

reparation the payment for damages

Main Ideas

A. American troops fought in France and helped the Allies defeat the Central Powers.

B. President Wilson and European leaders of the Allied nations met to draft a peace treaty.

C. The U.S. Senate rejected the Treaty of Versailles and the League of Nations.

Active Reading

MAKE JUDGMENTS
When you make judgments, you evaluate something and form an opinion about it. As you read this section, judge whether the U.S. decision not to join the League of Nations was a good one.

Spotlight on

History

In 1905, French psychologists worked out an intelligence scale by determining what things most children can do at different ages. In 1916, the test was improved. The test result was called an intelligence quotient, or IQ.

In 1918, American army psychologists gave IQ tests to soldiers and used the results to choose men for officer training.

A. Fighting in the Trenches

General Pershing led the first troops to France in June 1917. Additional troops landed in 1918. By the end of the war, 2 million Americans were fighting in Europe. American troops marched off their ships to the cheers of the French people. The Allies were losing the war, and the Americans were needed to achieve victory.

U.S. Troops Join in the Battles

The Germans had just launched another attack on France. They hoped to gain control of Paris before the Americans arrived. In May 1918, the Germans drove the Allies back to the Marne River. The Germans were very close to Paris—only 50 miles away.

Then, American soldiers joined the Allies to stop the Germans at the town of Château-Thierry. Soon after, American soldiers fought in battles at Belleau Wood in France. American soldiers quickly discovered what life was like in the trenches. They often stood in water up to their knees. Rats scurried from one trench to another. The pounding of German guns echoed in their ears. Often, the troops had to leave the protection of the trenches to attack enemy lines. Squatting low, they advanced straight into German guns.

After two weeks the Allies finally defeated the German forces and took the woods. There were almost 10,000 American casualties—soldiers who were killed or injured.

The Germans struck again in July, but the Allies, including American troops, drove them back in the Second Battle of the Marne. Fighting was fierce, and many lives were lost on both sides. This battle marked the beginning of Germany's retreat. In September, U.S. troops drove the German forces even farther back by pushing them out of Saint Mihiel.

American and French soldiers then joined together to fight the Germans between the Meuse River and the Argonne Forest. After 47 days of fighting, 120,000 Americans were dead or wounded; but the Germans were retreating. In addition, German supply lines had been cut off. This combat was the last major battle of the war.

Victory!

The German military leaders began to face the fact that they were losing the war. Each of the other Central Powers had already signed an **armistice**, or an agreement to stop fighting. Finally, Germany decided it would agree to sign an armistice and sent word that it would surrender. During this time, Kaiser Wilhelm II was removed from power and forced to leave Germany. At 11:00 A.M. on November 11, 1918—the eleventh hour of the eleventh day of the eleventh month—Germany surrendered. World War I was over.

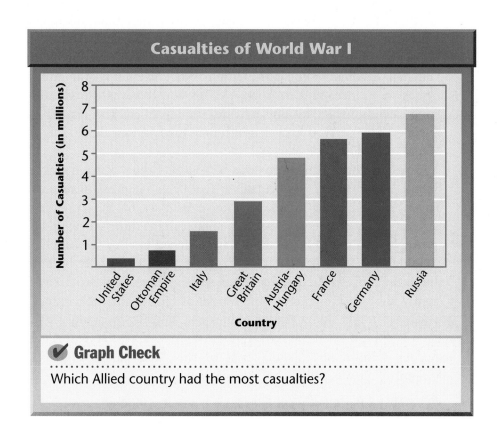

Casualties of World War I

Graph Check

Which Allied country had the most casualties?

African American troops stand in line for an inspection by General Pershing (center) during World War I.

U.S. Contributions to the War

U.S. troops had fought only in a small number of major battles. These battles occurred in the last months of a war that had lasted four years. It was not the supreme fighting skills of the American troops that won the war. Instead, it was the idea of an endless stream of new soldiers entering the war that discouraged the Germans.

The United States had aided the war effort in other ways as well. Supplies of food, weapons, and oil for war machinery helped the Allies greatly. These contributions, along with the millions of soldiers who arrived in Europe, helped defeat Germany.

Military Heroes

Millions of Americans had fought bravely on French soil. The French awarded U.S. soldiers many medals. For example, the African American soldiers of the 369th infantry won the Croix de Guerre (Cross of War) for bravery in the battle of the Argonne Forest.

One hero in the war was Sergeant Alvin York. As a member of the 82nd Infantry Division, he won more medals than any other American soldier. At the battle of the Argonne Forest, he destroyed 35 machine guns and captured 132 prisoners almost single-handedly. Marshall Ferdinand Foch, the commander in chief of the Allied armies in France, said to York, "What you did was the greatest thing accomplished by any private soldier of all the armies of Europe." He received French and Italian medals, as well as the U.S. Medal of Honor.

Another American hero was Captain Eddie Rickenbacker. Before World War I, Rickenbacker had been a successful race car driver. In 1917, he sailed to France as part of the American Expeditionary Force and became General Pershing's driver. He transferred to the U.S. Air Force and learned how to fly. In 1918, he joined the 94th Aero Pursuit Squadron and eventually became the commanding officer. During the war, he shot down a total of 26 enemy aircraft. He received the Medal of Honor for a dogfight in which he fought seven enemy planes and shot down two of them. He was also awarded the Distinguished Service Cross and a French medal. Because he was the best of the American flying aces, Rickenbacker was called the "Ace of Aces."

★ **Why did the Allies need help from the United States?**

Then & Now

After World War I, most of the Allies set aside November 11 as a day of remembrance called Armistice Day. In 1954, the United States changed the name to Veterans Day to honor those who had served in all American wars. Today, Veterans Day is a holiday often observed with parades and speeches.

B. Winning the Peace

Waging war had been hard. President Wilson, however, found that winning the peace was equally difficult.

Wilson's Peace Plan

In 1918, Wilson developed a peace plan called the Fourteen Points. The plan included freedom of the seas and free trade. It called for an end to secret alliances and a cutback on weapons. It called on all nations to return to their original boundaries, and it supported **self-determination** so that people could decide what type of government they wanted.

You can read the Fourteen Points on page R8.

Wilson believed the fourteenth point of his plan was the most important. It proposed an organization—what would become the League of Nations—to keep world peace. This organization could use force against any nation that refused to follow its rules. Wilson received the 1919 Nobel Peace Prize for his efforts in making peace.

Wilson met with the leaders of Great Britain, France, and Italy in Paris, in 1919, to draft a formal peace treaty. The treaty would be called the Treaty of Versailles, because the meeting was held at the Palace of Versailles.

The Paris Peace Conference

Wilson had promised a "peace without victory." He soon found that he could not obtain it. The other Allies insisted that Germany accept "war guilt" and pay damages for its part in the war.

According to the terms of the treaty, Germany was required to make $33 billion in **reparations**, or money to pay for the cost of war damages. That was more than Germany could possibly afford. Germany also had to give up most of its weapons and some of its territories, including lands in Europe and some overseas colonies. The treaty granted self-determination to several European nations but not to the German colonies. These colonies were taken over by Allied nations. The Allied leaders did adopt Wilson's plan for the League of Nations. However, neither Germany nor Russia joined it.

Many people, including Wilson, had hoped that the Great War would be the "war to end all wars." However, the Treaty of Versailles and the League of Nations would not be enough to prevent another world war.

★ **How was Germany punished under the treaty?**

The Allied leaders at Versailles included (left to right) David Lloyd George of Great Britain, Vittorio Orlando of Italy, Georges Clemenceau of France, and Woodrow Wilson of the United States.

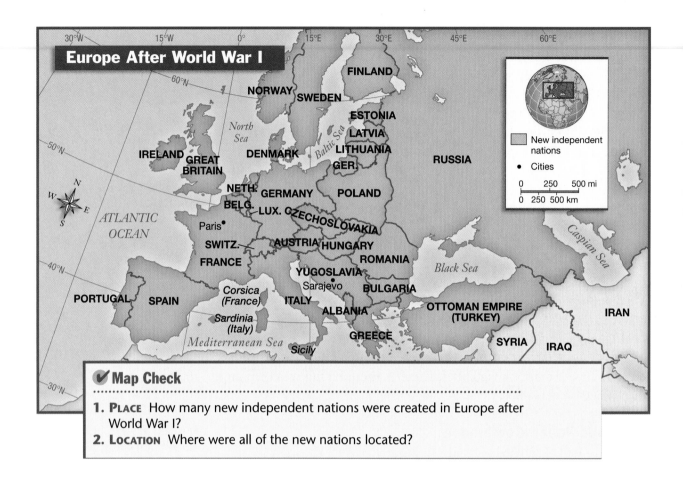

Europe After World War I

FINLAND

NORWAY
SWEDEN

ESTONIA

North Sea

LATVIA

LITHUANIA

IRELAND
GREAT BRITAIN

DENMARK

GER.

RUSSIA

NETH.
BELG.
GERMANY
LUX.
POLAND

ATLANTIC OCEAN

Paris•

CZECHOSLOVAKIA

SWITZ.
AUSTRIA
HUNGARY

FRANCE

ROMANIA

Black Sea

YUGOSLAVIA

Caspian Sea

PORTUGAL
SPAIN

Corsica (France)

Sarajevo•

BULGARIA

ITALY
ALBANIA

OTTOMAN EMPIRE (TURKEY)

IRAN

Sardinia (Italy)

GREECE

SYRIA
IRAQ

Mediterranean Sea
Sicily

New independent nations

• Cities

0   250   500 mi
0 250 500 km

✔ Map Check

1. **PLACE** How many new independent nations were created in Europe after World War I?
2. **LOCATION** Where were all of the new nations located?

C. Defeat of the Treaty

President Wilson was proud of the League of Nations. He was anxious for the United States to become a member. Politics, however, would keep that dream from becoming a reality.

Enemies in the Congress

According to the U.S. Constitution, the Senate must approve all treaties made by the U.S. government. Wilson brought the Treaty of Versailles back to the Senate to be approved. However, he had made many Republican enemies by not including them in his administration or in the peace conference.

In the 1918 election, Republicans won the majority in both the House of Representatives and the Senate. Republicans in the Senate wanted to defeat Wilson's peace treaty. Many thought the League of Nations would limit U.S. independence of action in world affairs.

Senator Henry Cabot Lodge of Massachusetts was determined to defeat the League of Nations. He led the fight in the Senate. President Wilson was just as determined that the peace treaty and the League would pass with no changes.

A Fateful Campaign

Wilson decided to tour the country by train. Everywhere he went, he spoke about the treaty and the League of Nations. Across the country, he explained the need for the League:

> The League of Nations . . . [is] the only possible guarantee against war. . . . Is it an absolute guarantee? No; there is no absolute guarantee against human passion. . . . I can predict with absolute certainty that within another generation there will be another world war if the nations of the world do not [arrange] a method by which to prevent it. 🙳

ANALYZE PRIMARY SOURCES

DOCUMENT-BASED QUESTION
How does this quotation relate to Wilson's hope that World War I would be a "war to end all wars"?

During the tour, Wilson became ill. He was rushed back to Washington, D.C. There, he suffered a stroke, which is a severe medical condition caused by a sudden failure of the blood supply to the brain. He could not meet with the Cabinet. He could not work to get support for the League. He told his supporters not to vote for the peace treaty if changes were made. They followed his orders. The Senate rejected the treaty in 1919 and again in March 1920. The United States made a separate treaty with Germany and never joined the League of Nations.

★ Why did Wilson believe so strongly in the League of Nations?

III Review

Review History
A. How did the United States help the Allies win World War I?
B. How did Wilson hope to keep the world at peace after the war?
C. In the United States, what happened to the proposal to join the League of Nations?

Define Terms to Know
Provide a definition for each of the following terms.
**armistice,
self-determination,
reparation**

Critical Thinking
Do you think the Treaty of Versailles was too hard on Germany? Explain.

Write About History
It is March 1920. Write a brief speech supporting or opposing the United States joining the League of Nations.

Get Organized
CAUSE/EFFECT CHART
One event can have many causes. Use a cause/effect chart to show causes of an event—which is the effect—from this section. For example, what caused the U.S. Senate to reject the Treaty of Versailles and the League of Nations?

Chapter Summary

In your notebook, complete the following outline. Then, use your outline to write a brief summary of the chapter.

World War I

I. War in Europe

   A. Europe on the Eve of War

   B.

   C.

II. The United States Enters the War

   A.

   B.

   C.

III. Fighting the War

   A.

   B.

   C.

Interpret the Timeline

Use the timeline on pages 540–541 to answer the following questions.

1. How long after the Balkan Wars began did World War I start?

2. **Critical Thinking** Which U.S. event do you think had the most significant effects? Explain your answer.

Use Terms to Know

Select the term that best completes each sentence.

armistice   communism   reparation
arms race   propaganda   war bond

1. A U.S. citizen could buy a _____ to help pay for the war.

2. After an _____ was signed, fighting stopped.

3. The United States used _____ to influence people's opinions of the war.

4. An _____ occurs when countries compete to build up military power.

5. The payment for damages is called _____.

6. In _____, property is owned by everyone equally.

Check Your Understanding

1. **Explain** how European alliances in the early 1900s made a war more likely.

2. **Summarize** the ways that World War I was different from earlier wars.

3. **Explain** why Wilson's 1916 campaign slogan soon became untrue.

4. **Discuss** the effects of World War I on Americans at home.

5. **Identify** the main ideas of Wilson's Fourteen Points.

6. **Describe** the political battle that defeated the Treaty of Versailles in the United States.

Critical Thinking

1. **Draw Conclusions** What advantages can membership in an alliance give a country? What disadvantages might it pose?

2. **Analyze Primary Sources** Why might a soldier's view of war, as expressed in the quotation on page 546, be different from that of people at home?

3. **Analyze Primary Sources** What role does Wilson see for the League of Nations in the quotation on page 559?

Put Your Skills to Work

CONDUCT RESEARCH ON THE INTERNET

You learned that you can find a great deal of information on the Internet. You also learned that it is important to keep track of the Web sites you find and to judge their reliability.

Copy the chart on a sheet of paper for each topic that you research. In the first row, write the name of the person, event, or item from this chapter. Use the Internet to research and find one reliable source for each topic. Then, complete the rest of the chart.

TOPIC:	
Web Address	
Content	
Reliability	

In Your Own Words

JOURNAL WRITING

Democracy allows people to express different opinions, as Americans did about whether or not to enter World War I. Think of an issue in the news today about which you have a strong opinion. Write a journal entry about this issue. Why do you believe as you do? What are others' reasons for believing differently?

Net Work

INTERNET ACTIVITY

Working with a group of classmates, use the Internet as a resource to analyze propaganda posters from World War I. Find and print two or three posters that interest you. Then, discuss them among your group members. To whom is the poster talking? What is its message? Is the poster effective? Summarize your answers on index cards. Then, share your posters and responses with the class.

For help in starting this activity, visit the following Web site: www.gfamericanhistory.com.

Look Ahead
In the next chapter, learn how American business and culture changed during the 1920s.

CHAPTER 24
Life in the 1920s 1920–1929

I. Business Booms
II. The Roaring Twenties
III. A Time of Unrest

In the 1920s, the United States was recovering from World War I. As the economy bounced back, life in the United States began to change. There were automobiles to buy, radios to listen to, and movies to see. There were new music forms, a strong interest in sports, and heroes to be found in many areas of American culture. The 1920s are often referred to as the Roaring Twenties. One reporter, named Robert L. Duffus, observed in 1924,

" Our own age may take its place in the historical pageant as the age of the Great War . . . as the age of cities, or as the age of man's victory over nature. . . . But, undoubtedly, the best title for this particular segment of eternity . . . is the Age of Play. "

Gas pump from the 1920s

1920
Nineteenth Amendment gives women the right to vote.

1921
Congress passes the Emergency Quota Act.

Sacco and Vanzetti Trial is held.

1924
Congress passes the National Origins Act.

1919
Eighteenth Amendment begins Prohibition.

1923
Teapot Dome Scandal is revealed.

U.S. Events	1919	1921	1923
Presidential Term Begins		1921 Warren G. Harding	1923 Calvin Coolidge
World Events	1919	1921	1923

1920
First meeting of the League of Nations takes place.

1922
Union of Soviet Socialist Republics (USSR) is formed.

1924
Vladimir Lenin dies.

VIEW HISTORY In this photo taken in the 1920s, hundreds of automobiles were parked at a beach in Massachusetts as people celebrated the Fourth of July along the shore. A gas pump (left) like this one from the 1920s kept Americans moving on the roads.

★ How did the automobile change the ways people had fun in the 1920s?

Get Organized

SPIDER DIAGRAM

A spider diagram is a way of recognizing main ideas and supporting details. Use a spider diagram as you read Chapter 24. Write a main idea in the center circle. Then, write the important events or ideas on the lines that extend from the circle. Here is an example from this chapter.

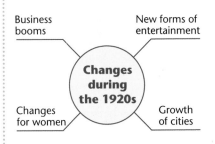

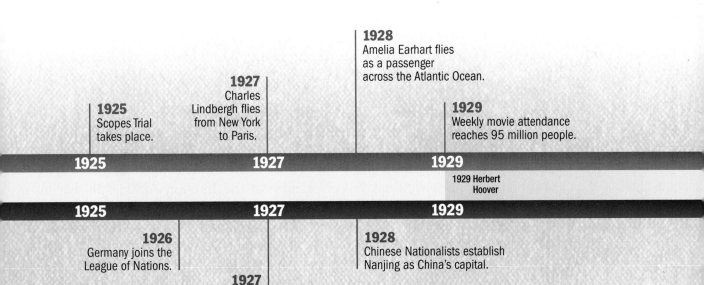

1925
Scopes Trial takes place.

1927
Charles Lindbergh flies from New York to Paris.

1928
Amelia Earhart flies as a passenger across the Atlantic Ocean.

1929
Weekly movie attendance reaches 95 million people.

1925   1927   1929

1929 Herbert Hoover

1925   1927   1929

1926
Germany joins the League of Nations.

1927
Joseph Stalin gains complete control of the Communist Party in the USSR.

1928
Chinese Nationalists establish Nanjing as China's capital.

I ★ Business Booms

Terms to Know

assembly line a row of factory workers who put together a product, part by part, as it passes by on a conveyor belt

installment plan the payment for an item in small, regular amounts over a period of time

Main Ideas

A. Under the Republicans, business and government became partners in aiding the U.S. economy.

B. The automobile industry boomed and changed the way Americans lived.

C. The United States became a nation of consumers, but not everyone enjoyed the same level of wealth.

 Active Reading

GENERALIZE
When you generalize, you make a broad statement based on facts you have heard or read. As you read this section, generalize by making a broad statement about economic conditions in the 1920s.

A. Republicans Regain the White House

President Wilson's illness, which would lead to his death in 1924, and the fight over the peace treaty made Republicans believe that they could regain the White House in 1920. They were right.

The Election of 1920

The Republicans nominated Warren Gamaliel Harding as their candidate for President. He promised a return to "normalcy." In other words, he wanted to return to the life that Americans had enjoyed before World War I.

Warren Harding won the election, beating the Democratic candidate James Cox. Once in the White House, the Republicans shifted the government's attention from foreign affairs to business.

Scandals in the Harding White House

Harding was a popular President. However, Americans eventually learned—in 1923—that many scandals, or illegal activities, had been going on in the White House. The most famous was the Teapot Dome Scandal. As Secretary of the Interior, Albert Fall was in charge of most government lands. In 1922, he gave oil that was reserved for the navy to private oil companies. The oil reserves were in Elk Hills, California, and Teapot Dome, Wyoming. In return, Fall received money from the companies. Fall's actions were illegal, and he was found guilty by a court of law. He was the first Cabinet member ever to be sent to prison.

Harding campaign button

ANALYZE PRIMARY SOURCES

DOCUMENT-BASED QUESTION What are the Washington officials trying to run away from?

This political cartoon shows Washington officials running on an oil-slicked road toward the White House.

There were other scandals as well. The Attorney General, Harry Daugherty, was involved in scandals, and the head of the Veterans Bureau was responsible for the loss of millions of dollars from federal programs. Harding died in 1923 before the full story of these scandals was known. The Vice President, John Calvin Coolidge, became President of the United States.

Government and Business

Coolidge believed that the country's best hope for a strong economy lay in strong businesses. He said, "The chief business of the American people is business." As a result of the government policy, business boomed. The Republicans lowered taxes, and the demand for factory labor kept workers employed. Coolidge was re-elected President in 1924 and continued to strengthen the economy.

In 1928, Coolidge decided not to run for President again. The Republicans chose Herbert Clark Hoover as their candidate. He defeated the Democratic candidate Al Smith. Hoover believed that government and business should work as partners. Together, they could bring prosperity, or economic well-being, to Americans.

One of President Hoover's goals was to create more government departments, which he did. The number of government employees almost doubled. Government and business were working together to improve the American economy.

★ **Why did Hoover believe in American industry and government working together?**

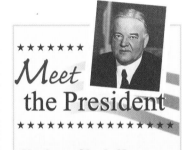

★★★★★★
Meet
the President
★★★★★★★★★★★★★★

Herbert Clark Hoover
1874–1964

Years in office 1929–1933

Political Party Republican

Birthplace Iowa

Age when elected 54

Occupations Mining engineer, Head of the U.S. Food Administration, Secretary of Commerce

Nickname Chief

Did you know? Hoover's first job after college was pushing a cart in a mine.

Quote "We in America today are nearer to the final triumph over poverty than ever before in the history of any land."

B. A Revolution in Industry

In 1920, American workers were the highest paid in history. People wanted new automobiles, clothing, furniture, and appliances. The demand for consumer goods grew, and American industry expanded to supply them. The United States entered a second industrial revolution.

The Automobile Industry

The automobile industry was booming. In 1920, there were 10 million cars in the United States. By 1929, there were 26 million cars. The automobile industry became the nation's largest industry.

Henry Ford wanted to make cars less expensive so that more people could afford one. He was able to achieve that goal with his Model T. By the mid-1920s, the cost of a Model T dropped from a high of $950 to just under $300. The secret was mass production and **assembly lines**. Assembly lines allowed workers to put a product together part by part. Workers stood along a moving conveyor belt. Each person on the assembly line performed one task. By the end of the line, an automobile had been assembled. In 1913, it took about 13 hours to produce one automobile. By 1925, cars were rolling off the assembly line as quickly as every 10 seconds. Ford could make more cars, so he was able to drop the price.

Ford also kept costs down by keeping his cars simple and offering them in only one color. He is said to have joked that you could have a car in any color you wanted, as long as it was black. Other companies soon adopted Ford's assembly line techniques.

Automobile–Related Industries

Americans found jobs building, selling, servicing, parking, and driving all of these new cars. Other industries connected to automobiles also grew. The rubber industry grew to produce tires, hoses, and belts. The petroleum industry expanded. States like Texas and Oklahoma experienced oil booms. Gasoline stations opened to service the new cars. Workers constructed thousands of miles of new roads. These new roads made it possible for people to live farther away from their jobs. Many new homes were built. Small roadside businesses such as motels and diners sprang up as drivers took to the roads. The automobile changed how people worked, lived, and played. Americans became a people on the move.

★ **How did the automobile affect other industries?**

This 1920s advertisement for the Pierce-Arrow car emphasizes its fine quality to prospective buyers.

THE PIERCE-ARROW CAR takes a just credit and no more than a just credit for the quality of it's engine, but it has added to that engine conveniences, refinements and luxuries which, together with perfect service and easy control, give the luxury that is expressed by the words "Pierce-Arrow Car"

The Pierce-Arrow Motor Car Company, Buffalo, New York

C. Building a Consumer Economy

As the economy grew and people became serious consumers, Americans had to change the way they did business. Many of the trends in marketing and business today began in the 1920s.

The Advertising Industry

The advertising industry grew to take advantage of Americans' desire to buy goods. U.S. citizens had more material goods than ever. It was the job of advertisers, however, to convince them that they needed more. Americans were told that they needed new appliances, as well as new cars. Increases in sales certainly helped the economy grow.

In the past, newspaper and magazine advertisements had provided basic information about products. Now, advertisers began focusing on the needs, wants, and concerns of consumers. Advertising became a bigger business in the United States. In addition to placing ads in newspapers and magazines, businesses could now advertise on billboards along roadways and in commercials on the radio.

Changing the Way Americans Shop

New appliances such as vacuum cleaners, washing machines, and electric refrigerators made life easier. Before refrigerators, people could keep meat in the icebox for only a few days. Fresh produce, or fruits and vegetables, spoiled easily. With the electric refrigerator, people did not have to shop as often.

New chain stores changed the way people shopped by offering household items, produce, and meat in one place and often at lower prices. Separate trips to the butcher, baker, and green grocer, or someone who sells fruits and vegetables, were no longer necessary. Five-and-ten-cent and department stores became popular. People no longer had to shop within walking distance of their homes. They could drive to a store and buy everything they needed. The same products that were available in cities were now available in many towns in the United States. Thanks to advertising, Americans recognized the names of the major product brands.

For families wishing to buy expensive items, such as appliances and furniture—also called durable goods—the **installment plan** provided a solution. People could buy a refrigerator or washing machine for a small down payment. Then, they would continue to make regular payments until they had paid the total. Enjoy now, pay later became the American way of purchasing consumer goods.

Then & Now

In the 1920s, people walked or drove their cars to stores and shopping centers. Today, people still shop at these places, as well as at malls. In addition, if people do not want to travel to shop, they can shop from home by phone or on the computer and have the items delivered directly to them.

Corporations Versus Labor

After World War I, the economy helped upper-class Americans become wealthier. Heads of large corporations gained both wealth and power. The increase in spending by Americans caused businesses to continue making more products. More Americans invested more money in the stock market, and the value of stocks rose tremendously. Investors who were lucky enough or smart enough to invest wisely in growing companies became rich.

Most people did not become wealthy. Income for the average American worker remained about the same as before the economic boom. Labor unions worked to get better wages for their members. However, the American Federation of Labor (AFL), a powerful labor union, did not organize unskilled workers. Many companies did not want their workers to join unions. They gave their workers pension or retirement plans and paid vacations in an effort to keep them out of the unions. Others offered workers "yellow-dog contracts," which stated that workers could not join unions.

Many American workers across the country decided to go on strike. They felt it was necessary to strike after employers had refused to meet their demands for higher pay. Workers in the telegraph and telephone industries did win higher pay. Unions in other industries were less successful.

 How did advertising help to strengthen the economy in the 1920s?

Do You Remember?

In Chapter 20, you learned that the Knights of Labor was a large labor union. You also learned that Samuel Gompers led the American Federation of Labor.

Review

Review History
A. What was the main concern of the three men who were elected President in the 1920s?
B. How did Henry Ford change the way Americans lived?
C. How did the business boom affect the average American?

Define Terms to Know
Provide a definition for each of the following terms. **assembly line, installment plan**

Critical Thinking
What effects did the boom in the auto industry have on the American economy?

Write About Culture
Create an advertisement for an automobile in the 1920s. Explain all the ways in which having a car could change a person's life, and why every person should have one.

Get Organized
SPIDER DIAGRAM
Think about what you have learned in this section. Use a spider diagram to help you organize the information. For example, start with the main idea of business. Then, write important ideas and events on the lines.

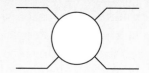

Build Your Skills

ANALYZE VISUALS

Visuals include photographs, paintings, sculptures, posters, advertisements, and even maps and charts. Visuals can give you different information from written words. Visuals can show how people dress, how they live, and what places look like. They can give a better sense of "being there" than a written description. It is important to remember, though, that a visual can give the artist's point of view. The artist can choose what to show and what not to show. Therefore, a visual may be biased, or slanted.

Examine the visuals in a history book carefully. Observe what information you obtain that you could not get from the text. Decide if there is any information you can infer from the visuals.

Here's How

Follow these steps to analyze a visual.

1. Determine the subject of the visual.
2. Carefully examine all the details of the visual.
3. Describe the details of the visual.
4. Decide what information obtained from looking at the visual is not in the text.
5. Think about inferences you can make from the information in the visual.

Here's Why

You have just read about the booming business era of the 1920s. There are many photographs from that era. Analyzing them could reveal new information about the period.

Practice the Skill

Look at the visual on this page. Use the steps above to analyze the visual. Then, answer the following questions.

1. Which item in the visual represents life in the 1920s?
2. How does the visual show the impact of the automobile in the 1920s?

Extend the Skill

Find a visual that interests you in a current newspaper or magazine. Analyze the information in the visual. What message does it portray? Bring your visual to class, and explain what it shows.

A line of automobiles outside Detroit, Michigan, in the 1920s

Apply the Skill

As you read the remaining sections of the chapter, study the visuals carefully. Tell what different information they offer from the text.

II The Roaring Twenties

Terms to Know

Jazz Age the name given to the 1920s because of the new popularity of jazz music

Harlem Renaissance a cultural movement of African American writers, painters, and musicians, many of whom lived in the Harlem area of New York City

Main Ideas

A. New forms of music, literature, and entertainment emerged during the 1920s.

B. Americans found heroes in aviation and sports.

C. Women gained the right to vote and made their mark in sports and politics.

Active Reading

ANALYZE
When you analyze, you determine why something happened. As you read this section, consider what has happened and ask why. For example, why was this period called the Roaring Twenties?

A. The Jazz Age

During the 1920s, new forms of entertainment became popular American activities. Americans listened to the radio and went to the movies. They also read more books and magazines than ever before.

Jazz and the Blues Go North

Thousands of American families had radios in the 1920s. Americans listened to comedy shows and different types of music. Two new music forms, jazz and blues, were brought north from New Orleans and St. Louis by African American musicians.

Louis Armstrong made jazz famous around the world. Bessie Smith sang the blues, telling of the suffering of African Americans. People flocked to the Cotton Club, in New York City's Harlem section, to hear great artists such as Duke Ellington and Ethel Waters. Jazz became so popular that the decade became known as the **Jazz Age**.

The Harlem Renaissance

Music was not the only art form that blossomed during this time. Harlem became the center of African American culture and politics. James Weldon Johnson and Langston Hughes wrote poetry that told of the black experience. Zora Neale Hurston wrote novels based on African American folklore. The works of African American writers, painters, and musicians became part of American culture. This cultural movement during the 1920s is known as the **Harlem Renaissance**.

Blues singer Bessie Smith earned the title Empress of the Blues for her powerful singing.

Jacobia Hotel by artist William H. Johnson is an example of a Harlem Renaissance painting.

Harlem was also home to scholars such as W. E. B. Du Bois—one of the founders of a new organization called the National Association for the Advancement of Colored People (NAACP). The NAACP was created to help African Americans in their fight for equal rights. It was in Harlem that the NAACP published its magazine, *The Crisis*. Du Bois edited the magazine, which addressed issues affecting African Americans, such as racism. *The Crisis* also featured the work of many writers during the Harlem Renaissance.

Changes in American Literature

Shorter workdays and new timesaving appliances such as electric refrigerators, washing machines, and vacuum cleaners meant that people had more leisure time. With more free time, Americans were reading more newspapers and magazines. By 1926, people were able to buy books each month from the Book of the Month Club.

Many American writers wrote about the changes in American society. They felt that World War I had taken away the promise of the United States. Many left the country to live overseas. The poet T. S. Eliot lived in England. Ernest Hemingway and F. Scott Fitzgerald were among the writers who lived in France.

These writers wrote about life as it really was. Sinclair Lewis captured life in American small towns in a book called *Main Street*. Edith Wharton wrote stories that portrayed American life from a woman's rather than a man's point of view. In F. Scott Fitzgerald's book *The Great Gatsby*, he wrote about what can happen when people are too interested in becoming rich. This book, more than any other book of the time, reflected life in the 1920s.

Movies—The Great American Escape

Advances in film and camera technology made movies available to people across the country. Americans went to the movies in order to escape their daily lives. Through the movies, they experienced action, adventure, romance, and comedy.

The first moving pictures were silent. A piano or organ was played in a theater during a movie, but there was no sound on the film itself. People had to read words on the screen to follow the story. Still, movies had adventure and glamour. The first movie stars came out of these early films—Gloria Swanson, Mary Pickford, Lillian Gish, Harold Lloyd, Charlie Chaplin, Douglas Fairbanks, John Barrymore, and Rudolph Valentino.

The first "talkie," or movie with spoken words, was *The Jazz Singer*, starring Al Jolson. It was released in 1927. Movie producers at the time thought that "talkies" were a passing fad. When weekly movie attendance reached 95 million in 1929, they realized that "talkie" movies were here to stay.

 What was the Harlem Renaissance?

B. National Heroes

After World War I, Americans began searching for heroes. They were fascinated with humans' new ability to fly. Two of Americans' greatest heroes were aviators, or pilots. Americans also had many sports heroes, as fans went to sporting events in record numbers.

Baseball legend Babe Ruth (right) poses with Yankee mascot Ray Kelly.

The Golden Age of Sports

Many Americans used their time off from work to attend sporting events. They cheered boxing champs like Jack Dempsey and stood quietly by to watch golf pros like Bobby Jones. Thousands attended tennis matches to see Bill Tilden, and swimming became popular because of record-breaking stars like Johnny Weismuller.

The greatest sports hero in the 1920s was George Herman "Babe" Ruth, who played for the New York Yankees. This legendary baseball player thrilled Americans simply with the swing of his bat. In 1927, Ruth hit 60 home runs in one season. It was a record that would remain for more than 30 years.

While all sports had their fans, baseball was Americans' favorite. The giants of the game—Babe Ruth, Ty Cobb, and Lou Gehrig— packed stadiums like never before. Fans crowded into the stadiums for both regular season games and the World Series. Americans loved their baseball heroes. As Lou Gehrig, who also played for the Yankees, said to a crowd after learning that he had a serious disease,

 Fans, for the past two weeks you have been reading about the bad break I got. Yet today I consider myself the luckiest man on the face of the earth. . . . I have an awful lot to live for. "

ANALYZE PRIMARY SOURCES

DOCUMENT-BASED QUESTION Why do you think that Lou Gehrig considered himself lucky even though he had a serious disease?

Heroes in Flight

In the field of aviation, Charles Lindbergh became an American hero when he flew nonstop from New York to Paris in 1927. He was the first person to fly across the Atlantic Ocean alone. The flight took 33 hours in his single-engine plane, the *Spirit of St. Louis*. When he arrived back in New York, Americans greeted him with a huge parade.

A year later, Amelia Earhart became the first woman to fly as a passenger across the Atlantic Ocean. Like Lindbergh, Earhart was welcomed back as a hero, complete with a parade. In 1932, she flew across the Atlantic, this time as the first woman pilot to make that journey.

★ Where did Americans find their heroes in the 1920s?

They Made History

Amelia Earhart 1897–1937

Amelia Earhart was born in Atchison, Kansas. She became interested in flight after her first airplane ride in 1920. Despite her family's objections, Earhart signed up for flying lessons. As a passenger, she became the first woman to fly across the Atlantic Ocean. In May of 1932, she became the first woman to fly a plane across the Atlantic. Then in 1937, she set out to fly around the world. After completing more than two-thirds of the flight, her plane disappeared over the central Pacific Ocean. Neither Earhart nor her plane has ever been found.

Amelia Earhart was one of Americans' greatest heroes. Her courage to fly around the world is still admired today.

Critical Thinking Why do you think that Earhart's family objected to her becoming a pilot?

C. Women in the 1920s

As the world changed, women and their role in American society changed as well. One symbol of the 1920s was the "flapper." Women bobbed their hair, or cut their hair short; shortened their skirts; and danced the Charleston.

Women in Sports

In the 1920s, women proved they could be world-class athletes too. Swimming legend Gertrude Ederle was the first woman to swim across the English Channel from France to England. Another woman who made sports news was Helen Wills. She won the U.S. women's tennis championship when she was 17.

Women in Politics

In 1920, the Nineteenth Amendment was ratified. The amendment guaranteed that women could not be denied the right to vote.

In 1924, Nellie Tayloe Ross was elected governor of Wyoming after her husband, who had been governor, died. On the same day, Miriam Amanda Ferguson was elected the first woman governor of Texas. Like Ross's husband, Ferguson's husband had been governor before her. Miriam Ferguson served two terms as governor of Texas.

Miriam Amanda Ferguson was the first woman governor of Texas.

★ **How did women show that their role in society had changed?**

II Review

Review History
A. What were some of the changes in American literature?
B. Who were some of the heroes of the 1920s?
C. What gains did women make in politics in the 1920s?

Define Terms to Know
Provide a definition for each of the following terms.
Jazz Age, Harlem Renaissance

Critical Thinking
How did the invention of timesaving appliances affect the popularity and growth of movies and sports?

Write About History
Write a short essay comparing women of the 1920s to women today. Use facts to support your conclusions.

Get Organized
SPIDER DIAGRAM
Think about what you have learned in this section. Use a spider diagram to help you organize what you learned. For example, use music as the main idea. Write ideas and events about music on the lines.

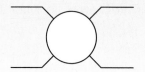

III A Time of Unrest

Terms to Know

bootlegger a person who made or transported alcohol illegally

deport to force someone to leave a country

quota a fixed number of a certain group of immigrants admitted to a country

fundamentalist a person who believes in a strict interpretation of the Bible or another religious book

Main Ideas

A. During the 1920s, there was an increase in organized crime.

B. A time of distrust of people who were different existed in the United States.

C. The United States became a place where residents in urban areas and rural areas often held different beliefs.

Active Reading

POINTS OF VIEW
When you contrast points of view, you consider the different opinions about an issue. As you read this section, contrast points of view about Prohibition, nativism, and fundamentalism.

A. The Rise of Organized Crime

In 1919, the United States ratified, or approved, the Eighteenth Amendment. This amendment started an era of Prohibition, making it illegal to manufacture, sell, or buy alcoholic beverages.

Reaction to Prohibition

Millions of churchgoers saw Prohibition as a moral victory. However, people continued to drink alcoholic beverages, and overall, consumption did not go down.

Because there was still a large demand for alcohol, **bootleggers**, or people who made or distributed alcohol illegally, continued to provide it. Illegal stills, or equipment for making bootleg whiskey, operated around the nation. Trucks traveling at night carried alcohol to speakeasies, or secret clubs. Some people even made gin at home in their bathtubs.

Organized Crime

Outlaws known as gangsters saw Prohibition as an opportunity for making money. These gangsters, such as Al Capone, transported and sold alcohol illegally. Organized crime controlled many businesses in Chicago and New York City. Competition between gangs was fierce, and arguments were usually settled with guns. Chicago alone had hundreds of gangland murders between 1920 and 1930.

The word *bootlegger* was also used in the 1920s to describe people, such as this woman, who hid bottles of alcohol inside their boots.

Lawmakers could not ignore the fact that Prohibition had led to a huge increase in crime. They also accepted the fact that it was almost impossible to enforce Prohibition. In 1933, the Twenty-first Amendment, which repealed the Eighteenth Amendment, was passed. Prohibition ended.

★ **How did Prohibition lead to an increase in organized crime?**

B. A Time of Distrust

Other problems emerged in the United States by the 1920s. An increase in crimes targeted at immigrants occurred. A movement aimed at limiting the number of immigrants entering the country gained support.

Racial tensions also ran high. African Americans and white people often competed for jobs and housing. In addition, African American soldiers who fought bravely in the war were angered by the unequal conditions they faced after the war. These tensions erupted in race riots across the United States.

The Ku Klux Klan

The 1920s saw a revival of the Ku Klux Klan. However, African Americans were not the only targets of Klan activities. This new Klan was anti-Catholic and anti-Jewish as well. Klan members saw all foreigners as a threat to the United States. In the South, Klan members lynched, or illegally hung, African Americans. The Klan also spread to other parts of the country. It was active in the Southwest and the Midwest.

In 1925, members of the Ku Klux Klan marched along Pennsylvania Avenue in Washington, D.C.

The Red Scare

Many Americans feared foreigners and thought they might be Communists. People were afraid that Communists planned to take over the United States. They thought "reds," or Communists, were part of the labor movement and were making workers go on strike.

Many people who were suspected of being Communists were jailed. Others were **deported**, or sent out of the country.

The Trial of Sacco and Vanzetti

In May of 1920, two Italian immigrants were arrested in Massachusetts. Nicola Sacco and Bartolomeo Vanzetti were charged with a payroll robbery and the murder of a paymaster and his guard. At the trial, in 1921, they were found guilty. Even before the verdict, the judge had spoken out against the two men. Many people believed that Sacco and Vanzetti were innocent but had been convicted because they were foreigners with radical ideas to change the government.

Bartolomeo Vanzetti (left) and Nicola Sacco sit in the courtroom waiting for the jury's decision.

After their convictions, protests were held. A national debate in the newspapers showed that people were divided about the case. A committee reviewed the evidence, but the two men were still found guilty. Both were executed on August 23, 1927.

Limiting Immigration

A feeling of nativism, or the view that favors people born in a country over immigrants to that country, grew in the 1920s. Some people blamed immigrants for the presence of Communists in the United States. Others blamed them for taking jobs away from people who were born here.

In 1921, Congress passed the Emergency Quota Act. It limited the number of people coming to the United States from Europe by setting a **quota**, or a fixed number of immigrants who could enter the country during a specific period. Still, more than 350,000 European immigrants were allowed into the country every year.

In 1924, Congress passed the National Origins Act, which was designed to keep out certain groups, such as Jews and Catholics. Immigration levels were still considered too high by many Americans. In 1929, the number of European immigrants was limited to 150,000 per year. This number was a radical decrease from the high of more than 1 million per year in the early 1900s.

★ **Why did some people think Sacco and Vanzetti had been wrongly convicted?**

U.S. Rural and Urban Populations, 1890–1920		
YEAR	PERCENTAGE RURAL	PERCENTAGE URBAN
1890	64.9	35.1
1900	60.4	39.6
1910	54.4	45.6
1920	48.8	51.2

✔ **Chart Check**

What percentage of people lived in urban areas in 1920?

C. Religious Thought in the 1920s

Some people saw the mass immigration of Catholics and Jews as a threat. These immigrants—mostly from southern and eastern Europe—brought with them cultural practices and ideas that often differed from those of Americans whose ancestors were from western Europe. Religious groups rose to challenge the new ideas that immigrants brought with them.

Some Urban and Rural Differences

In 1920, cities across the nation experienced a population boom as the number of people in the United States climbed to about 106 million. Many new immigrants arrived from around the world and settled in the larger cities where they could find work. Also, many Americans left farms to take factory jobs. For the first time in U.S. history, the number of people living in cities was greater than the number of people living in rural areas.

Since many new immigrants tended to settle together, a variety of immigrant neighborhoods developed in the cities. In rural areas and small towns, churches were an important part of people's lives. They were social and cultural centers as well as religious centers. Some people came to be **fundamentalists**, or people who believe in strict obedience to religious laws. They rejected any idea that went against their beliefs.

New fundamentalist churches grew, especially in the South and West. Evangelist Aimee Semple McPherson built a large church in downtown Los Angeles that appealed to people who had recently moved to the city. There, thousands of worshipers heard her dramatic sermons.

Charles Darwin and Evolution

In 1859, Charles Darwin had published his theory of evolution. He believed that humans and apes may have had a common ancestor. Many scientists accepted the theory, but some religious groups were opposed to it. Fundamentalists, in particular, spoke out against the theory. They believed that humans were created directly by God.

Fundamentalist legislators worked to prevent the teaching of evolution in schools across the country, and some succeeded. William Jennings Bryan, who believed that the Bible was absolute truth, toured the country speaking out against Darwin's ideas.

The Scopes Trial

In 1925, Tennessee passed a law stating that no teacher could teach any theory that denied God had created the world. The American Civil Liberties Union (ACLU) disagreed with the law. They offered to defend any teacher who would teach Darwin's theory. A young biology teacher, John T. Scopes, accepted their challenge. He taught Darwin's theory and was arrested and put in jail.

The ACLU hired Clarence Darrow, the most famous trial lawyer in the country, to defend Scopes. William Jennings Bryan represented the state of Tennessee. The judge was a fundamentalist. A sign in his courtroom stated, Read Your Bible Daily. Newspapers and radio stations covered the "Monkey Trial," as it was called. It was the first trial ever to be broadcast. The trial drew tremendous attention. It was one of the most famous and controversial cases in the nation's history.

The judge did not allow any discussion of evolution. He was interested only in whether or not Scopes had broken the law. Even Scopes admitted that he had. Scopes was convicted and fined $100. The Tennessee Supreme Court later reversed the decision.

Clarence Darrow, the defense lawyer in the Scopes Trial, wanted to argue that teaching Darwin's theory of evolution should be allowed in the classroom.

★ **What was the outcome of the Scopes Trial?**

 **Review**

Review History

A. How did Prohibition lead to an increase in organized crime?

B. What were two reasons people wanted to limit immigration?

C. What was one way religion and science seemed to differ in the 1920s?

Define Terms to Know
Provide a definition for each of the following terms. **bootlegger, deport, quota, fundamentalist**

Critical Thinking
What connection can you make between World War I and the changing attitudes about immigration and communism?

Write About Government
Write an account of how the Scopes Trial might have been different if it had taken place in New York City.

Get Organized
SPIDER DIAGRAM
Think about what you have learned in this section. Use a spider diagram to help organize the information. For example, you might choose Prohibition as your main idea. Then, write important events and ideas on the lines.

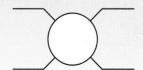

PAST to PRESENT

Movie Technology and Attendance

During the 1920s, the movie industry became big business. An average of nearly 40 million Americans went to the movies every week. Often, an organist would play music that fit the mood of each scene in a silent movie. After *The Jazz Singer* was introduced, audiences began to demand more new "talkies." Theater owners rushed to install sound equipment, and attendance skyrocketed.

Today, many movies feature digital sound and special effects created with computers. Although sound and picture technology have improved since the 1920s, movie attendance has dropped. By the end of the 1990s, only about 20 million people per week went to the movies. Today, many Americans prefer to buy or rent movies or watch them on television.

In the 1920s, audiences were often treated to a short animated film before the main feature. Felix the Cat was a popular cartoon character during the silent film era.

Moviegoers in 1926 flocked to the New York opening of *Don Juan*—the first movie that used a soundtrack for music and sound effects.

Today, many movies feature digital sound and computer-generated special effects.

While movie attendance has dropped since the 1920s, many people, including young people, still enjoy going to the movies today.

MOVIE FACTS

	1920s	Today
Cost of a movie ticket	10¢ – $2.00	$7.00 – $10.00
Average cost of making a movie	$30,000	$40 million
Types of movies	Love stories, Westerns, War films, Gangster movies, Comedies	Love stories, Comedies, Horror movies, Action/adventure movies, Science fiction
Top annual salaries of major movie stars	$40,000	$20 million+

The chart above compares movies of the 1920s with today's movies.

Hands-on Activity

Create a silent movie of your own. Write several scenes. Then, using props and costumes, act out the scenes. Record your movie using video equipment. Use the Internet and other resources to learn more about silent movies. To get started, go to www.gfamericanhistory.com.

CHAPTER 24 Review

Chapter Summary

In your notebook, complete the following outline. Then, use your outline to write a brief summary of the chapter.

Life in the 1920s

I. Business Booms

    A. Republicans Regain the White House

    B.

    C.

II. The Roaring Twenties

    A.

    B.

    C.

III. A Time of Unrest

    A.

    B.

    C.

Interpret the Timeline

Use the timeline on pages 562–563 to answer the following questions.

1. Which constitutional amendments were passed?

2. **Critical Thinking** Which events on the U.S. timeline would have been supported by people who feared foreign influences? Explain your answer.

Use Terms to Know

Match each term with its definition.

a. assembly line   d. Harlem Renaissance

b. bootlegger   e. installment plan

c. deport   f. Jazz Age

1. a cultural movement of African American writers, painters, and musicians, many of whom lived in the Harlem area of New York City

2. to force someone to leave a country

3. a person who made or transported alcohol illegally

4. a row of factory workers who put together a product, part by part, as it passes by on a conveyor belt

5. the payment for an item in small, regular amounts over a period of time

6. the name given to the 1920s because of the new popularity of jazz music

Check Your Understanding

1. **Identify** the three men who held the office of President during the 1920s.

2. **Describe** how an assembly line in the 1920s worked.

3. **Summarize** what Americans did with their leisure time in the 1920s.

4. **Discuss** African American contributions to the United States during the 1920s.

5. **Describe** how the United States limited immigration after World War I.

6. **Explain** what the "Red Scare" was.

Critical Thinking

1. **Analyze Primary Sources** What images in the political cartoon on page 565 indicate that the cartoon is about the Teapot Dome Scandal?

2. **Analyze Primary Sources** What makes Lou Gehrig's quote on page 573 inspirational to people even today?

3. **Draw Conclusions** Do you think that Prohibition had its intended effect?

Put Your Skills to Work

ANALYZE VISUALS

You have learned that visuals can give a better sense of life during a period in history. Analyzing visuals can help you understand information beyond what you have read.

Look at this visual. It appeared on the cover of *Life* magazine on February 18, 1926. Analyze the information that is conveyed by the visual. Then, answer the following questions.

1. What is the subject of this visual?

2. What elements of life in the 1920s are shown in this picture?

Life magazine cover, 1926

Net Work

INTERNET ACTIVITY

Working with a partner, use the Internet as a resource to find out more about the trial of John Scopes in 1925. Find actual quotes from the trial. Have one person research Clarence Darrow's arguments and the other person research William Jennings Bryan's arguments. Write the quotes on a divided piece of poster board: one side for the prosecution, one side for the defense. Illustrate the poster board with photographs or drawings of the courtroom scene. Share your project with the class.

For help in starting this activity, visit the following Web site: www.gfamericanhistory.com.

Look Ahead

In the next chapter, learn about the Great Depression of the 1930s.

CHAPTER 25

The Great Depression and the New Deal 1929–1940

I. The Stock Market Crash
II. Hard Times at Home
III. The New Deal

*I*t seemed to happen almost overnight and without warning. The prosperity of the 1920s turned into the Great Depression and the misery of the 1930s. Most people could not understand what had happened to the strong American economy. People could not believe things had changed so fast.

This verse from a Great Depression song by Maurice Sugar expresses people's sense of disbelief. It is sung to the tune of "My Bonnie Lies Over the Ocean."

> " I spent 15 years in the factory
> I did everything I was told
> They said I was faithful and loyal
> Now why am I out in the cold?
> Soup, soup, they gave me a bowl of soup. "

A bushel of apples for sale

1933
New Deal begins.
Frances Perkins becomes
Secretary of Labor.

1929
Stock market crashes and
the Great Depression begins.

1932
Bonus Army marches
on Washington.

U.S. Events	1929	1931	1933
Presidential Term Begins	1929 Herbert Hoover		1933 Franklin D. Roosevelt
World Events	1929	1931	1933

1929
Airship *Graf Zeppelin* flies
around the world in 21 days.

1930
The planet Pluto
is discovered.

1931
British
Commonwealth
of Nations
is established.

1933
Adolf Hitler rises
to power in
Germany.

VIEW HISTORY During the Great Depression, people waited in soup or bread lines to receive food from charities. About one-fourth of all American workers were jobless. Some desperate Americans sold apples (left) in order to survive.

★ **How do you think these men felt standing in a line to receive free food?**

Get Organized

FIVE Ws CHART

Do you know what the Five Ws are? They are questions—*Who? What? Where? When?* and *Why?*—that news writers ask themselves when they write a story. When you read about history, ask yourself the same questions. Make a Five Ws chart, and fill in the answers as you read. Here is an example from this chapter.

Who?	U.S. farmers
What?	The Great Depression, the drought, and the Dust Bowl cause economic disaster.
Where?	The Great Plains
When?	The 1930s
Why?	Farmers cannot grow crops and repay loans.

1935
Congress passes the Social Security Act and the Wagner Act.

1936
Mary McLeod Bethune is appointed to the National Youth Administration as a director.

1939
John Steinbeck's *The Grapes of Wrath* is published.
Marian Anderson sings on the steps of the Lincoln Memorial.

1935   1937   1939

1935   1937   1939

1936
Francisco Franco starts the Spanish Civil War.

1937
Japan invades China.

1939
World War II begins in Europe.

1940
Winston Churchill becomes prime minister of Great Britain.

I The Stock Market Crash

Main Ideas

A. The stock market crash and underlying economic problems caused many Americans to lose their jobs and savings.

B. President Hoover asked local governments to help people.

C. Many farmers were forced to leave their land and move westward in search of jobs.

 **Active Reading**

PREDICT
When you predict, you look for clues that tell you about future events. As you read this section, ask yourself the following question: Based on what I have learned about the Great Depression, will Hoover's plans succeed?

This headline announced the crash of the stock market in 1929.

A. The Beginning of the Great Depression

The Roaring Twenties came to a screeching halt in 1929. It was the end of the decade, and the end of an era. The good times of the 1920s were replaced with hardship and despair in the 1930s.

Buying Into the Stock Market

Through most of the 1920s, the prices of stocks had risen higher and higher. Many Americans bought stocks in the hope of getting rich quickly. They expected the stock market to continue its upward climb.

Many investors began to borrow money from their stockbrokers to pay for their stock purchases. This borrowing was called buying on margin. Margin buyers paid only a small part of the stock's cost. They borrowed the rest of the money from their stockbrokers, or the actual sellers. Then, if the value of the stocks rose, the buyer would sell the stocks and pay back what he or she owed. Through margin buying, buyers could make a **profit**, or earnings from their investments. However, if the value of the stocks fell rather than rose, the buyer then owed the seller what was borrowed.

In September 1929, some investors realized that prices could not rise forever. They began selling their stocks, which caused stock prices to fall. Many stockbrokers asked margin buyers to pay in full for their stocks. Those who could not pay were forced to sell their stocks. This sell off caused prices to drop even more.

Many Americans were forced to sell luxury items, like this car, that had been purchased during the 1920s boom.

The Market Crashes

On October 29, 1929, the stock market crashed as investors tried to sell as much stock as possible before prices fell even lower. As more people sold their stocks, prices kept falling. This day has become known as Black Tuesday. Prices continued to tumble through November.

Fortunes were lost. The lifetime savings of many Americans were gone. People who had savings deposited in banks withdrew their money. This caused many banks to close. As more banks failed, many Americans lost all of their savings. People lost their jobs. Some even lost their homes. The nation had entered a **depression**. A depression is a long economic downturn. The Great Depression lasted for ten years. For many Americans, it lasted even longer.

Underlying Problems

Even before the stock market crash, there were signs of a coming depression in the United States. American industries were making more consumer goods than they could sell. When companies do this, it is called overproduction. These goods, such as washing machines and wristwatches, were bought for convenience and pleasure, rather than for need.

In the 1920s, times were hard for many people outside the United States. World War I had left many countries in ruins. Germany could not pay its war debt. Many people overseas could no longer afford to buy American goods. Because American businesses were selling fewer products overseas, production of those goods decreased. As a result, fewer factory workers were needed. Some people were laid off, and unemployment increased.

★ What were two causes of the Great Depression?

Do You Remember?

There have been other depressions in U.S. history. In Chapter 9, you learned about a downturn that followed the Revolutionary War. In Chapter 12, you learned about the Panic of 1837.

B. Hoover Responds

Many people looked to their local governments and to service agencies such as the Red Cross for help. However, there was not enough state and local money to help everyone, so the states asked the federal government for aid.

Efforts to Improve the Economy

President Hoover told Americans, "Prosperity is just around the corner." He asked Congress to cut taxes. He also asked for more **public works,** or government-financed projects for public use. He wanted to put people to work building dams, roads, and public buildings. Employing people would help the economy. If people had jobs, they could buy more goods.

Hoover also signed the Hawley-Smoot Tariff Act, which placed high tariffs on foreign goods. Backers of the tariff hoped it would protect U.S. manufacturers. However, the move backfired when European countries also raised their tariffs. As a result, trade between the United States and Europe dropped sharply.

To restore confidence in the economy, Hoover tried to help banks and insurance companies. In 1932, Congress formed the Reconstruction Finance Corporation. It loaned government money to banks and insurance companies so that they would not go bankrupt.

Searching for Help

President Hoover believed that it was the duty of states and local governments, not the federal government, to take care of citizens. However, cities and states could not take care of everyone. Volunteer and charity groups tried to help, but they soon ran out of money. Still, the President refused to send surplus food products and money to the states. He believed that handouts would weaken Americans' self-confidence.

Hoover's loans to banks and businesses were too limited to be very effective. Banks continued to fail. Some businesses closed their doors and laid off workers. People roamed the nation looking for work. Some of these unemployed people sneaked onto empty railroad boxcars to travel to other parts of the country in the hope of finding a job. One man told of "riding the rails":

> **"** Twenty-five or thirty would be out on the side of the rail. . . . they didn't have no home . . . they didn't have no food, they didn't have nothing. **"**

★ **Why did the Hawley-Smoot Tariff Act backfire?**

ANALYZE PRIMARY SOURCES

DOCUMENT-BASED QUESTION How would you describe the lives of the people the man is talking about?

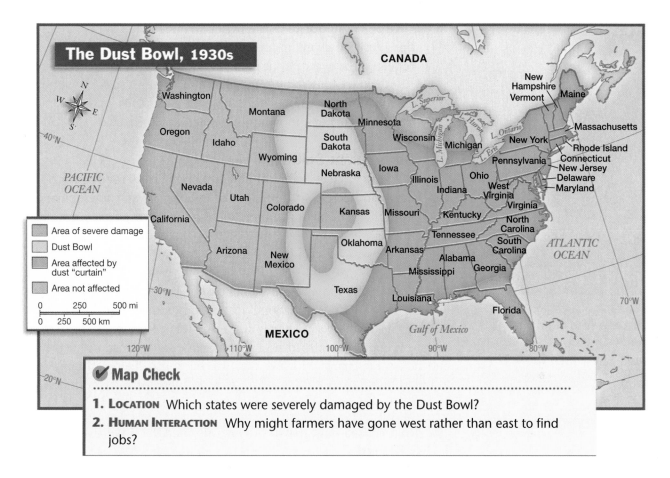

The Dust Bowl, 1930s

CANADA

Legend:
- Area of severe damage
- Dust Bowl
- Area affected by dust "curtain"
- Area not affected

0   250   500 mi
0   250   500 km

✔ **Map Check**

1. **LOCATION** Which states were severely damaged by the Dust Bowl?
2. **HUMAN INTERACTION** Why might farmers have gone west rather than east to find jobs?

C. Farm Problems

Business owners and factory workers were not the only ones who suffered during the Depression. Farmers were hit especially hard. Like many other Americans, they often lost both their money and their homes.

The Dust Bowl

Between 1931 and 1940, parts of U.S. farmland in the Great Plains experienced a drought. Clouds of dust swirled through towns and into homes. Thousands of farm animals died from lack of water. Dust clouded the sky throughout the Great Plains states. This area became known as the Dust Bowl. Winds were so strong that they blew a "curtain" of dust all the way to the east coast.

Farmers' crops were ruined. With no income, they could not repay their bank loans. As a result, banks foreclosed, or seized farmers' land. As many as 3 million people were forced off their land. The land they counted on to make their living had blown away.

Dorothea Lange took many photographs of farm families during the Great Depression. This one is called "Migrant Mother."

In 1939, author John Steinbeck wrote about a family fleeing the Dust Bowl in his novel *The Grapes of Wrath*. His book reflected the situation of many real families who traveled U.S. Route 66 looking for a better life in California. Like the family in the novel, many people reached California and became **migrant workers**, moving from place to place to harvest crops.

Government Solutions

Farmers faced still another problem. Prices for farm products had been falling because of oversupply and low demand for American farm products in Europe. Often, farmers could not sell the crops they raised. President Hoover asked farmers to grow fewer crops so that prices would rise. He also asked them to form cooperatives to sell their crops.

In 1929, Congress established the Federal Farm Board. It loaned money to farm cooperatives and bought surplus crops. Hoover asked banks to lower interest rates on loans to farmers. Farmers could not afford high loan payments because they could not sell their crops. However, banks were also losing money, so some refused to cut rates. Also, the problem of overproduction remained, so farm prices stayed low.

★ **What caused farm families to migrate from the Great Plains to California?**

I Review

Review History
A. What part did consumer goods play in causing the Great Depression?
B. What steps did President Hoover take to help the economy?
C. What caused the Dust Bowl?

Define Terms to Know
Provide a definition for each of the following terms.
profit, depression, public works, migrant worker

Critical Thinking
Do you think President Hoover should have done more to end the Great Depression? Why?

Write About History
During the 1930s, many farmers had to leave their homes. Write a poem describing how you would feel if you had to leave your home.

Get Organized
FIVE Ws CHART
Fill in this Five Ws chart with information about stock investors at the beginning of the Great Depression.

Who?	
What?	
Where?	
When?	
Why?	

Build Your Skills

USE A LINE GRAPH

Graphs are drawings that present information containing numbers. One type of graph is a line graph. Numbers are usually shown along the left side of a line graph. Time is often shown across the bottom. A line shows the pattern of numbers going up or down over time. Most often, line graphs are used to show a change over time.

When you read about history, you will often see information presented in line graphs. A line graph lets you see the trend, or the general direction, that something takes. For example, if the population of a city is growing, a line graph will very clearly show the increase. The trend, or general direction of the line, will go up.

Here's How
Follow these steps to use a line graph.
1. Read the title of the graph.
2. Identify the horizontal axis (the line across the bottom of the graph) and the vertical axis (the line up the left side). Read the labels of these axes.
3. Study the graph to find trends.

Here's Why
You have just read about the beginnings of the Great Depression. Suppose you needed to read a graph that showed the number of people who were unemployed at different times during the Depression.

Practice the Skill
Look at the graph on this page. Then, answer the following questions.
1. What does the graph show?
2. How many people were unemployed in 1929? in 1933?
3. What trend do you see reflected?

Extend the Skill
Write a paragraph explaining why so many people lost their jobs during the Great Depression.

Apply the Skill
Identify topics in Section II that would be clarified by showing information on a line graph.

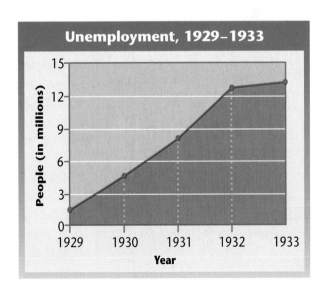

II Hard Times at Home

Terms to Know

relief a direct money payment to the unemployed

tenant farmer a person who pays for the right to farm someone else's land

barrio a community in which mostly Spanish-speaking people live

Main Ideas

A. Americans of many backgrounds lost their jobs and their homes, and African Americans and Mexican Americans faced increased discrimination.

B. President Hoover's failure to end the Great Depression led to the election of Franklin Delano Roosevelt in 1932.

 Active Reading

GENERALIZE
When you generalize, you collect details, examine them, and make a general statement about them. As you read this section, make a generalization about the situation of Mexican Americans during the Great Depression.

A. Surviving the Great Depression

From farms to cities, Americans felt the effects of the Great Depression. Some people stood in lines for bread or soup. Others sold apples or pencils on street corners. They hoped to make money to buy food.

A Severely Troubled Economy

By the summer of 1932, the American economy had almost totally collapsed. Factories cut production, and new construction had almost ceased. Tens of thousands of businesses went bankrupt, and millions of Americans lost their jobs. Out-of-work men drifted from place to place looking for jobs. Many lived in shantytowns, or temporary communities, set up in large cities. Their homes were shacks made of scrap wood, old tin, and other materials they found. The residents, who often blamed their problems on President Hoover, called their new communities "Hoovervilles." Poor people wanted Hoover to send **relief**, or money to assist the unemployed.

Many students had to leave college and return home to find jobs. Families could not afford to keep students in school. Millions of children had to work to help their families survive. Children as young as seven years old sold newspapers, delivered groceries, and took on any task that would earn a few cents.

Looking for work during the Depression could be discouraging, as this scene from a 1933 movie shows.

JOBLESS MEN
KEEP GOING
WE CAN'T TAKE CARE OF OUR OWN
CHAMBER OF COMMERCE

Some Americans who lost their jobs and their homes during the Great Depression were forced to live in flimsy shacks.

African Americans Out of Work

African Americans, Mexican immigrants, and Mexican Americans had always known hard times. To many of these people, the Great Depression meant just more of the same. Poet Maya Angelou remembered the time:

> ❝I think that [African Americans] thought the Depression, like everything else, was for the white folks. ❞

In the 1920s and earlier, many African Americans had left the South for jobs in northern cities. After the Depression began, they found they were the first to be laid off. By 1932, about 50 percent of African Americans in some northern cities were out of work. At the same time, a smaller percentage of white people were unemployed. Some African Americans drifted back to the South. Others became homeless.

African Americans protested their job losses. Some organized a campaign to boycott products and businesses called "Don't Buy Where You Can't Work." The boycott was used in New York, Chicago, and 23 other cities. Though protests were popular, they did not solve the problems created by the Depression.

ANALYZE PRIMARY SOURCES **DOCUMENT-BASED QUESTION** Why do you think the people Maya Angelou knew felt that white people had "everything"?

African American tenant farmers worked long hours in the fields.

African Americans in the South suffered greatly. Many still worked in the fields as sharecroppers or **tenant farmers**. Tenant farmers paid landowners for the use of their farmland. Women joined men in the fields, making little money for picking crops such as cotton. Often, groups of workers piled into trucks, moving from one field to another in search of work.

As the Depression continued, segregation and discrimination against African Americans increased. Violence broke out in many communities, and lynchings, or illegal hangings, increased. In 1935, a riot broke out in Harlem. African Americans, angry about unemployment as white workers took jobs they had traditionally held, protested in the city streets. Hundreds of police officers had to be sent to Harlem to end the riot. At least three African Americans were killed.

Mexican Americans Face a Hard Choice

Immigrants from Mexico also suffered during the Great Depression. Many had entered the United States between 1910 and 1920 during the Mexican Revolution. Others answered the call for workers during World War I.

Now, they faced increased discrimination. Some Americans felt that they were taking jobs away from people who had lived in the United States for many years. As a result, many Mexican immigrants lost their jobs and had to return to Mexico. Families were torn apart. Those who stayed in the United States often clustered in **barrios**, or communities of Spanish-speaking people. Some barrios had no sidewalks or running water. There, men and women managed to raise their children and keep their Mexican culture alive.

Mexican immigrants and Mexican Americans living in cities often worked in factories. Men worked in steel mills, meatpacking plants, and oil refineries. Some women worked as dressmakers, often in sweatshops. Others worked canning fruits and vegetables. Both men and women were paid low wages. Often, women's pay was even lower than men's pay. Mexicans and Mexican Americans worked long hours, and conditions in factories were poor. Like many other workers, they joined unions and became part of the labor movement.

★ **Why did some immigrants return to Mexico during the Great Depression?**

B. Americans Look for Help

As time wore on, Americans sank deeper into the Great Depression. They asked themselves, Isn't there anything we can do to battle our way out of these hard times?

The Bonus Army

In the summer of 1932, a group of about 20,000 unemployed World War I veterans, called the Bonus Army, decided to march to Washington, D.C. The veterans wanted a bonus, or sum of extra money, which Congress had agreed to pay them by 1945. Veterans and their families were suffering so they asked to receive the bonus early. The Bonus Army settled into tents and old buildings in Washington, D.C. They said they would stay until they received their bonuses.

Veterans of World War I formed the Bonus Army and demanded to be paid the extra money they had been promised for their service in the military.

Some members of Congress wanted to give the bonus to the veterans. However, President Hoover disagreed. He sent troops, led by General Douglas MacArthur, to force the veterans out. Fighting erupted between the troops and the veterans. Bonus marchers threw bricks. The troops used tear gas and tanks. Tear gas, which causes irritation of the eyes, is sometimes used to control crowds. The troops also burned the veterans' tents.

The army's attack on the veterans became known as the Battle of Washington. Many people were injured, and two veterans were killed. One family tried to hide from the fighting in a house, but soldiers threw a tear gas bomb into the front yard. The mother of the family told her story:

> " The house was filled with gas, and we all began to cry. We got wet towels and put them over the faces of the children. About half an hour later my baby began to vomit. . . . Next day she began to turn black and blue and we took her to the hospital. "

ANALYZE PRIMARY SOURCES

DOCUMENT-BASED QUESTION
Why would this story upset other Americans so much?

The soldiers were able to chase the marchers from Washington. However, the sight of American soldiers attacking veterans shocked the country. Americans became even more upset the next day when they learned that the baby who had been taken to the hospital had died.

"Happy Days Are Here Again"

Many Americans blamed President Hoover for their hardship. They felt he had failed to solve the problems of the Great Depression. He had sent in troops against the Bonus Army. He had been unsuccessful at putting Americans back to work.

By the time of the presidential election of 1932, people were ready for a change. The Democrats knew that they had a good chance to win the election. The Democratic candidate for President was the popular governor of New York, Franklin Delano Roosevelt, known by his initials, FDR. He was a cousin of former President Theodore Roosevelt.

FDR was a powerful speaker. His cheerfulness and confidence made Americans feel that the Depression could be beaten. He promised Americans a "New Deal." Contrary to Hoover's beliefs, FDR thought that "the national government has a positive duty to see that no citizen shall starve." His hopeful theme song, "Happy Days Are Here Again," was heard throughout the country. In November 1932, Roosevelt received 57 percent of the vote. He and the Democrats won the election with strong support from African Americans, labor unions, and others. Then, it was up to FDR to end the Great Depression.

★ **Why did Americans support Franklin Roosevelt in 1932?**

II Review

Review History
A. Why did African Americans, Mexican immigrants, and Mexican Americans face especially hard times during the 1930s?

B. How did the Bonus Army events help turn the nation against President Hoover?

Define Terms to Know
Provide a definition for each of the following terms.
relief, tenant farmer, barrio

Critical Thinking
How did FDR help the country's mood in 1932?

Write About Culture
During the Great Depression, some children had jobs or did tasks to earn money. Write a short paragraph about something that you would do to earn money if you lived during the Great Depression.

Get Organized
FIVE Ws CHART
Fill in the following Five Ws chart with information about the Bonus Army and the Battle of Washington.

Who?	
What?	
Where?	
When?	
Why?	

Points of View

The Role of Government in the Economy

What role should the federal government play in the economy? At the time of the Great Depression, the answer to this question became tremendously important. The financial health of the country was at risk. People disagreed about whether or not the government should control some activities of businesses.

President Herbert Hoover, a Republican, expressed one set of ideas. His successor in the White House, Democrat Franklin Roosevelt, expressed another. Ever since, the two ideas have remained important principles of the Republican and Democratic parties.

Hoover (left) and
Roosevelt (right)

> ❝The Republican Party . . . restored the Government to its position as an umpire instead of a player in the economic game. . . . our opponents propose that we must thrust government a long way into the businesses. . . . You cannot extend the mastery of the government over the daily working life of a people without at the same time making it the master of the people's souls and thoughts.❞
>
> —Herbert Hoover, campaign speech, 1928

> ❝Our greatest primary task is to put people to work. . . . It can be accomplished in part by direct recruiting by the Government itself, treating the task as we would treat the emergency of a war, but at the same time, through this employment, accomplishing greatly needed projects to stimulate and reorganize the use of our natural resources. . . . Through this program of action we address ourselves to putting our own national house in order.❞
>
> —Franklin Roosevelt, inaugural address, 1933

ANALYZE PRIMARY SOURCES

DOCUMENT-BASED QUESTIONS

1. How would you describe Hoover's point of view?

2. How does Roosevelt think the United States can put its "national house in order"?

3. **Critical Thinking** Do you think a government should be an "umpire" rather than a "player" in the "economic game"? Explain your answer.

III The New Deal

Main Ideas

A. President Roosevelt's New Deal programs lifted Americans' spirits as they provided relief, recovery, and reform.

B. The Second New Deal brought more programs but also some opposition.

C. The New Deal led to an expanded federal government, but it did not end the Great Depression.

 Active Reading

COMPARE AND CONTRAST
Comparing and contrasting two items can help you understand them more clearly. As you read this section, compare and contrast Hoover's and Roosevelt's plans for fighting the Great Depression.

Then & Now

In the 1930s, polio was a dreaded disease that caused paralysis. Children were especially prone to the disease. Today, there is a vaccine to prevent polio.

A. Roosevelt Tackles the Great Depression

Franklin D. Roosevelt offered new hope to the American people. Eleven years before he was elected President, he was struck with polio and his legs were paralyzed. However, he did not let this challenge stop him. As a presidential candidate, he told Americans, "I pledge you, I pledge myself, to a new deal for the American people." The words *new deal* became the name for the programs initiated by FDR.

The Three *R*s

When he took office, Roosevelt had several goals to battle the Depression. He called them the three *R*s: relief, recovery, and reform. He aimed to do the following:

1. Provide relief to suffering people.
2. Bring economic recovery.
3. Produce reforms so that a depression would not happen again.

One of the first things FDR did was declare a "bank holiday." He ordered all banks closed to protect savings while Congress passed new banking laws. Then, he asked Congress to work especially hard to solve the country's most pressing problems. During the first three months of FDR's presidency, Congress passed 15 major laws and created many programs to bring relief, recovery, and reform. This period from March 9 to June 16 is known as The Hundred Days.

New Deal Programs

Roosevelt's programs focused on many different problems. One was created to better control the stock market. Another loaned people money so they could keep making their house payments.

One of the most important programs created by the New Deal was the Tennessee Valley Authority (TVA). Through this program, dams were built along the Tennessee River to stop flooding and to prevent topsoil from washing away. The dams also produced electricity for people in that region.

Most of the programs were known by the first letter of each word in the program's name. Many people called them the "alphabet soup" agencies. Some of them are listed in the chart on this page.

New Deal Programs and Agencies

PROGRAM OR AGENCY	DATE	PURPOSE OF PROGRAM OR AGENCY
Civilian Conservation Corps (CCC)	1933	Provided jobs, such as planting trees and building small dams, for young men from needy families
Agricultural Adjustment Administration (AAA)	1933	Paid farmers not to grow crops so that farm prices would rise
Federal Emergency Relief Administration (FERA)	1933	Helped families needing food, housing, clothing, and other necessary items
Tennessee Valley Authority (TVA)	1933	Built dams on the Tennessee River to control flooding and to help produce hydroelectricity, or electricity produced by the power of quickly moving water
Public Works Administration (PWA)	1933	Created jobs in public works to stimulate the economy
Federal Deposit Insurance Corporation (FDIC)	1933	Protected people's savings in banks
Home Owners Loan Corporation (HOLC)	1933	Gave loans at low cost to homeowners so they could continue making their house payments
Federal Communications Commission (FCC)	1934	Set rules for radio, telephone, and telegraph systems
Securities and Exchange Commission (SEC)	1934	Regulated stocks and gave stock information

✔ Chart Check

Which programs and agencies helped get people back to work?

Americans gathered around their radios to listen to FDR's weekly radio address.

Roosevelt's Fireside Chats

Roosevelt's New Deal programs convinced Americans that the federal government was finally doing something to pull the nation out of the Great Depression. Another way Roosevelt lifted the spirits of the country was by talking directly to the people. Often, he described his policies over the radio from a chair near a White House fireplace. Some of Roosevelt's talks, including his Sunday evening radio broadcasts, became known as fireside chats. These radio talks often calmed Americans' fears.

★ What were the three *R*s?

B. The Second New Deal

By 1935, most Americans supported the President's efforts. However, the Great Depression was not over—nine million people were still out of work. Some Americans felt that the President had not gone far enough. Roosevelt proposed new bills to Congress in 1935. These bills became known as the Second New Deal.

Social Security

One of the programs of the Second New Deal focused on providing money for retired people. Roosevelt got the idea from  Francis Townsend, a California doctor who saw that many older people had lost their savings in the stock market crash and bank failures. Townsend wanted the federal government to give $200 each month to every citizen over age 60. He thought that the government could pay for this **pension**, or retirement income, with a sales tax.

Both Congress and the President disagreed with some of the ways Townsend's plan worked. In 1935, Congress, with Roosevelt's support, passed the Social Security Act. The act provided monthly pensions for retired people older than age 65. Unlike Townsend's plan, government pensions were funded by a tax on workers and employers. The Social Security Act also assisted unemployed workers, blind people, children with physical disabilities, and poor families with dependent children. For the first time, the federal government took responsibility for helping these people.

Labor Relations and Opposition to the New Deal

Roosevelt also wanted to improve conditions for workers. Two people who helped him were Senator Robert Wagner of New York and Frances Perkins, the Secretary of Labor. In 1935, Congress passed the National Labor Relations, or Wagner, Act. This act protected workers from unfair practices and guaranteed the rights of workers to join unions and negotiate with their employers.

Some people felt that Roosevelt's programs had gone too far. **Conservatives**, or those who wanted fewer government controls, feared the President's actions would allow the government too much involvement in their lives. They also feared that government regulation of business would harm the American economy.

Other critics believed that the New Deal reforms were only a temporary solution. **Liberals** were in favor of increased government action to bring about social and economic change. They felt that a new system of government and economy was needed.

One of FDR's challengers was Huey Long, a senator from Louisiana. He promised every American an income of $5,000 a year—enough to buy a home, an automobile, and a radio. To pay for this program, he would tax the wealthy. With this money, he also hoped to build roads, schools, and hospitals.

Roosevelt and the Supreme Court

Roosevelt faced opposition in the Supreme Court as well. In 1935 and 1936, the Court had declared some New Deal programs unconstitutional. Roosevelt won re-election in 1936, and early the next year he suggested that six more judges be added to the existing nine on the Court. Many people thought that he was trying to "pack" the Court with judges who supported his programs.

The American people disagreed with Roosevelt's idea of adding judges, and Congress rejected the plan. However, the Supreme Court did begin to approve more New Deal programs.

 What was the Second New Deal?

Frances Perkins was the first woman to serve in a President's Cabinet. She became the Secretary of Labor in 1933.

C. Effects of the New Deal

The New Deal did not end the Great Depression. However, Roosevelt's programs changed the United States in many ways.

Greater Power for Many Americans

New Deal programs led to more power for many groups. The Wagner Act gave workers more power to improve their lives. Many large land-owning farmers found their lives improved as well. They were able to keep their farms because of New Deal reforms.

Some African Americans, Mexican Americans, and immigrants from Mexico found jobs through New Deal programs. Others gained the help of labor unions to find and keep work. Roosevelt also appointed some African Americans, such as educator Mary McLeod Bethune, to positions in government agencies.

Women played a part in the New Deal. In addition to Frances Perkins, FDR appointed a few other women to government posts. However, no woman was more important to the President's success than his wife and closest advisor, First Lady Eleanor Roosevelt.

They Made History

Mary McLeod Bethune 1875–1955

Mary McLeod Bethune was one of 17 children. Her parents had been enslaved, and they wanted her to be educated. She finished her schooling at Moody Bible Institute in 1895, and nine years later she started her own school for African American girls. Her first students sat on boxes and wrote with splinters of wood dipped in berry juice. Eventually, the school merged with Cookman Institute for Men to become Bethune-Cookman College. Bethune was president of the school for a total of 40 years. In 1924, Bethune became president of the National Association of Colored Women, and in 1936, President Roosevelt appointed her director of the National Youth Administration's Division of Negro Affairs. She was the first African American woman to serve as the head of a federal agency.

President Roosevelt said of Mary McLeod Bethune, "I believe in her because she has her feet on the ground." Bethune (left) is shown here with Eleanor Roosevelt.

Critical Thinking What experiences in Bethune's life made her a good choice to advise Roosevelt on education and youth issues?

Before Eleanor Roosevelt, Presidents' wives had quietly supported their husbands. Eleanor Roosevelt shattered this role, becoming an active reformer. Roosevelt depended on his wife to meet Americans and report to him about their lives.

Eleanor Roosevelt traveled thousands of miles to meet people in all kinds of jobs—factory workers, coal miners, farmers, newspaper editors, and many others. She spoke up loudly for African Americans, poor people, and other forgotten Americans through radio broadcasts, newspaper columns, and speeches. She became an especially powerful opponent of racial discrimination.

Expanding the Role of the Federal Government

The expansion of the federal government into almost every aspect of people's lives was one of the major results of the New Deal. The federal government took responsibility for the well-being of all U.S. citizens. It made relief payments and ran a pension plan. FDR made it clear that the federal government, not the state governments, needed to protect the welfare of Americans.

FDR also proved that democracy was a political system that could reform itself. The government had to make major changes in order to reshape the economy and society. Yet these changes were done in a peaceful and democratic way.

★ **How did the New Deal help many American groups?**

III Review

Review History
A. What was the overall effect on the country of Roosevelt's first New Deal programs?
B. Why did some people oppose Roosevelt's programs?
C. What role did women play during Roosevelt's presidency?

Define Terms to Know
Provide a definition for each of the following terms.
pension, conservative, liberal

Critical Thinking
Do you think the federal government gained greater power over people's lives during the New Deal? Explain.

Write About Citizenship
You are a young person listening to one of Roosevelt's fireside chats. Write a letter to the President giving your opinion about the purpose and value of his radio broadcasts.

Get Organized
FIVE Ws CHART
Fill in this Five Ws chart with information about New Deal programs and agencies.

Who?	
What?	
Where?	
When?	
Why?	

CHAPTER 25 Review

Chapter Summary

In your notebook, complete the following outline. Then, use your outline to write a brief summary of the chapter.

The Great Depression and the New Deal

I. The Stock Market Crash

   A. The Beginning of the Great Depression

   B.

   C.

II. Hard Times at Home

   A.

   B.

III. The New Deal

   A.

   B.

   C.

Interpret the Timeline

Use the timeline on pages 584–585 to answer the following questions.

1. How long after the stock market crashed was the Social Security Act passed?

2. **Critical Thinking** Who was President when the Social Security Act was passed?

Use Terms to Know

Match each term with its definition.

a. conservative
b. depression
c. liberal
d. pension
e. profit
f. relief
g. tenant farmer

1. a long period of economic decline

2. money gained from a business or an investment after expenses have been paid

3. an income for retired workers

4. a person who favors using government resources to bring about social and economic change

5. a person who pays for the right to farm someone else's land

6. a person who believes in limited government involvement in the economy

7. a direct money payment to the unemployed

Check Your Understanding

1. **Summarize** the effects of the stock market crash of 1929.

2. **Explain** how the Dust Bowl affected farmers in the United States.

3. **Describe** the Bonus Army and its effect on other Americans.

4. **Discuss** the differences in Hoover's and Roosevelt's approaches to ending the Great Depression.

5. **Identify** three New Deal programs, acts, or agencies and tell what they did.

6. **Summarize** different reasons that some people opposed the New Deal.

Critical Thinking

1. **Make Inferences** Why do you think that President Hoover told Americans "prosperity is just around the corner"?

2. **Analyze Primary Sources** Reread Maya Angelou's quotation on page 593. Why might discrimination and violence against minority groups increase during hard economic times?

3. **Make Judgments** Franklin Roosevelt had excellent communication skills. Do you think it is important for every President to be able to communicate as well as Roosevelt? Explain your answer.

Put Your Skills to Work

USE A LINE GRAPH

You have learned that line graphs are excellent tools for showing trends. Study the following line graph. Then, answer the following questions.

1. What does this graph show?

2. How many banks closed in 1933?

3. What trend is reflected in this graph?

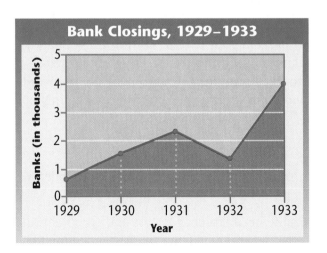

Bank Closings, 1929–1933

Banks (in thousands) / Year

Net Work

INTERNET ACTIVITY

Many of the greatest U.S. photographers took part in a government program to photograph people and places during the Great Depression. The Farm Securities Administration funded photographic studies of the movement of farmers to California to escape the Dust Bowl. One of the most famous of these photos appears on page 590. You can find many more photos of the Great Depression online. Working with a group of classmates, research and prepare an exhibit of photographs of the Great Depression.

For help in starting this activity, visit the following Web site: www.gfamericanhistory.com.

Look Ahead
In the next chapter, learn how war inflamed the world.

Unit 8 Portfolio Project

Debate: The Role of Government

YOUR ASSIGNMENT

The draft during World War I, Prohibition in the 1920s, and the New Deal programs showed a trend in government. The federal government gained power and began to affect different aspects of people's lives. Some people, like President Hoover, believed that the government should stay out of people's affairs. Others, like President Roosevelt, believed that it was the government's job to help solve problems for Americans. As a class, conduct a debate on the role of the federal government.

PREPARING FOR THE DEBATE

Agree on a Debate Topic First, write a statement about the issue that each team can either support or oppose. This statement is called the proposition. For example, you might write, "Government involvement in people's lives should be limited." One team will gather evidence and use it to argue in favor of the proposition. The other team will look for evidence to use to argue against it.

Choose Teams Select two debate teams, one for the affirmative (in favor of the statement) and one for the negative (against the statement).

Research Your Position Research your team's position at the school or community library and on the Internet. Meet with your teammates to decide how you will present your argument. Be prepared to respond to your opponents' argument. You may refer to this Web site to help you: www.gfamericanhistory.com.

STAGING THE DEBATE

Debate the Proposition Present your argument based on the evidence you have researched.

Vote on a Winner Have audience members discuss and comment on the debate. Who won the debate by making the better argument?

Multimedia Presentation

Now, use the information you have collected for the debate to write a newspaper editorial. For example, support your suggestions for social security benefits with evidence you used in the debate. Display your editorial in the classroom. If your school has a Web site, you can post your editorial there.

America Becomes a World Leader

"Missions came and went. In time I was lead or deputy lead of several great air battles. . . . These missions were hours of horrifying screaming in our headphones, mixed with sounds of voices calling 'bombs away,' 'fighters at two o'clock high, coming in.'"

—from *Bomber Pilot: A Memoir of World War II*
by Philip Ardery, a World War II pilot

LINK PAST TO PRESENT The fighter planes shown in this photograph were just one of many kinds of weapons used in World War II. Some of these planes are now displayed in museums throughout the United States.

★ Judging from the quotation, what do you think the experience of war was like for fighter pilots?

CHAPTER 26

World War II 1939–1945

I. **The Road to War**
II. **The World at War**
III. **Winning the War**

*W*hen war broke out in Europe in 1939, most Americans did not want to become involved. The memory of the horror of World War I, coupled with the struggle to survive the hard times of the Great Depression, made Americans more concerned with problems at home than abroad. This attitude was to change on one fateful day in December 1941, when Japanese forces attacked Pearl Harbor, Hawaii. The day after the attack, President Franklin D. Roosevelt said,

> "Yesterday, December 7, 1941, a date which will live in infamy—the United States was suddenly and deliberately attacked by . . . the Empire of Japan. . . . With the unbounding determination of our people—we will . . . triumph."

After the bombing of Pearl Harbor, Americans once again found themselves in the middle of a world war, fighting not only in Europe but also in the Pacific and in Africa.

A Pearl Harbor poster

1941
Congress passes the Lend-Lease Act.
Roosevelt and Churchill agree to the Atlantic Charter.
United States enters World War II.

1940
Franklin D. Roosevelt re-elected for a third term.

1942
Manhattan Project begins.

U.S. Events	1939	1940	1941	1942
Presidential Term Begins	Franklin D. Roosevelt (first elected in 1932)			
World Events	1939	1940	1941	1942

1939
Soviet Union and Germany sign a nonaggression pact.
Germany invades Poland.
World War II begins in Europe.

1940
Germany conquers France.
Japan, Italy, and Germany form the Axis alliance.

1941
German submarines sink a U.S. destroyer.
Japan bombs Pearl Harbor, Hawaii.

VIEW HISTORY This photo was taken immediately after the attack on Pearl Harbor. More than 2,300 Americans were killed. Posters like the one on the left were used to rally the war effort.

★ How do you think the attack on Pearl Harbor affected Americans?

Get Organized
FLOWCHART

Using a flowchart can help you to connect events and understand the relation-ships between those events. Use a flowchart as you read Chapter 26. Begin by listing an event in the top box. Then in the boxes below, list other events in the order in which they occurred.

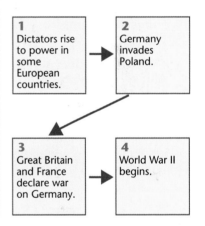

1 Dictators rise to power in some European countries. → **2** Germany invades Poland.

3 Great Britain and France declare war on Germany. → **4** World War II begins.

1944
U.S. troops arrive in France during D-day invasion.
Roosevelt re-elected for a fourth term.

1945
Franklin Roosevelt dies.
First atomic bomb tested in New Mexico.
U.S. Marines take control of Iwo Jima.
United States drops two atomic bombs on Japan.
World War II ends.

1943	1944	1945	1946

1945 Harry S Truman

1943	1944	1945	1946

1945
Roosevelt, Churchill, and Stalin meet at Yalta.
Adolf Hitler commits suicide.
Germany and Japan surrender, ending World War II.

I The Road to War

Terms to Know

dictator a ruler who has complete power

fascism a political system that emphasizes nationalism and is ruled by a dictator

totalitarian state a country in which one person or group has complete control

appeasement an attempt to keep peace with an enemy by giving in to its demands

Main Ideas

A. After World War I, many European countries were in economic disorder.

B. In the 1920s and 1930s, strong rulers replaced existing governments in Italy, Germany, and the Soviet Union.

C. Several countries used military force to expand their power.

Active Reading

PREDICT
When you predict, you use information in order to guess what will happen next. As you read this section, use the information that you learn to predict how the events discussed changed the world.

A. Economic Trouble in Europe

While Americans were suffering through the Great Depression, Europeans also were dealing with economic problems. Some countries still had not recovered from World War I. Many people had lost their homes as well as their jobs.

Depression in Europe

World War I had left both the Allies and the Central Powers in debt. With the devastation left by the war, many European nations had to rebuild factories, houses, and other structures. Even as Europe began to recover, the Great Depression started in the United States and soon spread to the rest of the world, including Europe. Most people were concerned about survival—they had little time to think about their government and politics. In some countries, the depression created an atmosphere of hopelessness that leaders used to their advantage.

Germany After World War I

Germany was one of the countries that suffered the most after World War I. The Treaty of Versailles, which ended the war, put the blame on Germany for causing it. The treaty required Germany to make reparations, or payments, of more than $33 billion for the cost of war damages to the Allies in Europe. In order to pay reparations, the German government began to print more money. This made the currency less valuable.

German currency was worth so little after World War I that these boys used the money to make a kite.

By 1923, German money became so worthless that it took a bag full of paper bills just to buy a loaf of bread. It was cheaper for Germans to burn their money than to purchase kindling to fuel stoves.

Germany also was forced to give up important economic territory to France after World War I. These regions on the border of France had rich ore deposits that were valuable to industry. The loss of these resources further worsened the economic situation in Germany.

★ **How did the payment of reparations affect Germany?**

B. The Rise of European Dictators

People in various European nations, such as Spain, Germany, and Italy, looked for ways to solve their problems. They lost their faith in democratic governments. In these countries, strong leaders came to power. These strong leaders became **dictators**, or single rulers who have absolute power. Not all European nations turned to dictators. In countries that had long traditions of democracy, such as Great Britain, democratic governments remained.

Adolf Hitler (right) and Benito Mussolini set up dictatorships in their countries after World War I.

The Growth of Fascism and Nazism

The people of Italy faced hard times after World War I. With the country in economic trouble, a political leader named Benito Mussolini came to power. Mussolini was the leader of a party called the Fascists. The members of this political party supported **fascism**. Fascism is a political system with a strong leader, who is the chief source of law and order and who encourages feelings of nationalism. In 1922, Mussolini became prime minister. He had enough support to force the king to name him as the head of the government. Then, he assumed the role of dictator and outlawed all other political parties.

In Germany, economic problems during the 1920s helped Adolf Hitler rise to power. Hitler was a leader in the National Socialist Party, also called the Nazi Party.

As unemployment rates rose, so did the Nazi Party's popularity. In 1933, Hitler was appointed chancellor. The Nazi Party quickly eliminated democracy in Germany by outlawing other political parties and by arresting opponents. Hitler set up a dictatorship, and in 1934, men of the armed forces swore an oath of allegiance to him.

Jewish people in Germany were forced for wear yellow stars on their clothes.

Do You Remember?
In Chapter 23, you learned that communism is a political system in which the government plans and runs the economy and there is no private property.

Hitler blamed many of Germany's problems on the Treaty of Versailles. He felt that Germany had been treated unfairly by being forced to make reparations and to give up some of its territory. Hitler also blamed Germany's problems on Jewish people. Hitler believed that German people were a "master race." According to his views, Germans were superior to other ethnic groups.

Hitler's "Master Race"

By 1935, Hitler used his ideas about Germans belonging to a "master race" in order to justify persecuting German Jews and other minority groups. One of the first actions Hitler took was to declare that the Jews were no longer German citizens. In time, their businesses were closed and their homes were taken. In addition, Jews were subject to physical attacks and humiliation at the hands of other Germans. They were forced to sew a yellow star onto their clothing to indicate their religious background. Many Jews fled Germany, giving up all their property.

Hitler began rebuilding the German military in the 1930s, an act that violated the Treaty of Versailles. The other powers in Europe did not take any action against Hitler. Their silence made him even bolder. To strengthen Germany's position, Hitler entered into an alliance with Italy. Later, Japan would enter the alliance as well. These countries became known as the Axis Powers.

Stalin and the Soviet Union

Even before the end of World War I, Russia was going through turmoil. By 1921, Communists under Vladimir Lenin took control of Russia and suppressed all opposition. The Communists changed the name of Russia to the Union of Soviet Socialist Republics, or the Soviet Union. In 1924, Lenin died and Joseph Stalin seized power by eliminating his political enemies. A brutal dictator, Stalin tried to control every aspect of Soviet citizens' lives. He took away many of their rights. He also placed the country's businesses and farms under government control. He turned the Soviet Union into a **totalitarian state**, or a place in which the government has complete control of people's lives.

Anyone who opposed Stalin's policies was punished. Soviet peasants who refused to work on large government-run farms were arrested. Some were shot. Others were sent to labor camps where many prisoners were worked to death. In 1934, Stalin began a campaign of political terror in the Soviet Union by killing those who opposed him.

★ **What dictators rose to power during the 1920s and 1930s?**

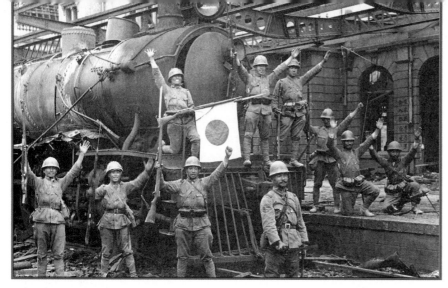

Japanese troops invaded Manchuria, a region rich in resources, in northern China.

C. Military Expansion

The totalitarian governments of Europe focused on developing and using military strength. The same was true for Japan. In the 1930s, Japan's economy was struck hard by the worldwide depression. Japan turned away from a more democratic government and moved toward military leadership.

Japan Invades China

As a small group of islands, Japan had limited natural resources. By the 1930s, Japan was facing shortages of important resources, such as oil, iron, and coal. Determined to expand its territory, Japan looked to mainland China. In 1931, the Japanese army invaded northern China and made it part of Japan. The resources there were used to produce arms and provide fuel for Japan's growing military.

The U.S. government notified Japan that it did not approve of the attacks on China. Yet, many Americans did not want to become involved in the affairs of other countries. Congress took steps to maintain its noninvolvement. For example, in 1935, Congress forbade the selling of weapons to countries at war. In 1936, it ended loans to warring nations. However, these steps had little impact on other countries.

Hitler Makes His Move

In Europe, Adolf Hitler was also expanding German power. On March 12, 1938, German troops marched into Austria and took it over. Next, Hitler demanded possession of the Sudetenland, in northwestern Czechoslovakia. Because 3 million Germans lived in this region, Hitler thought it should be part of Germany. The Czechoslovakian government refused to turn over the Sudetenland and asked Great Britain and France for help.

In September 1938, British and French leaders met with Hitler in Munich, Germany. At Munich, they agreed that Hitler could take the Sudetenland if he promised to seize no other lands. Britain and France did not want a war, so they chose a policy of **appeasement**. They gave in to a demand in order to avoid conflict. The appeasement did not stop Hitler. He seized the rest of Czechoslovakia in 1939.

The Invasion of Poland

Hitler's next goal was an invasion of Poland. However, he was concerned that this might provoke a war with the Soviet Union in the east and France and Britain in the west. Hitler, however, had a plan. He knew that Stalin was interested in territory in eastern Europe.

In August 1939, Nazi Germany and the Soviet Union signed a nonaggression pact in which they agreed not to attack each other. This meant that Hitler would not have to fight on two fronts. The French and British governments warned Germany that if Poland was invaded, they would take action. Hitler ignored them.

The Germans attacked Poland on September 1, 1939. Soon after, the Soviet Union invaded Poland from the east. Within a few months, Germany and the Soviet Union had divided Poland. The invasion convinced France and Great Britain to respond. On September 3, 1939, both countries declared war on Germany.

 What agreement did Germany and the Soviet Union make?

I Review

Review History
A. What effects did the Treaty of Versailles have on Germany?
B. What factors led to the rise of dictators during the 1920s and 1930s?
C. Why did Germany and Japan invade other countries?

Define Terms to Know
Provide a definition for each of the following terms.
dictator, fascism, totalitarian state, appeasement

Critical Thinking
Why did many people in Germany support Adolf Hitler?

Write About Citizenship
Write a journal entry explaining how you would feel if your rights were taken away simply because you belonged to a certain religious or ethnic group.

Get Organized
FLOWCHART
Think about the main events in this section. Use a flowchart to link these events. For example, what events took place in Germany after the end of World War I?

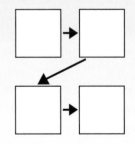

Build Your Skills

RECOGNIZE PROPAGANDA

Propaganda is a method of presenting information. It is designed to influence people's thoughts and actions. Propaganda tools include political cartoons, speeches, posters, and films.

During World War II there were many films and posters that showed victorious Americans fighting the enemy. These examples of propaganda kept up people's spirits and supported the war effort.

It is important to realize that some propaganda will try to sway people to a particular point of view by using only selected facts or distorting information. Being able to recognize and understand propaganda is a very useful skill.

Here's How

Follow these steps in order to recognize propaganda.

1. Identify the purpose of what you are reading or looking at. What is the writer or artist trying to make you think?
2. Identify the techniques used to persuade you. Did the writer or artist exaggerate or use emotional images?
3. Analyze the material. What facts does it contain? What facts are ignored?

Here's Why

It is important to recognize propaganda to be able to form your own ideas. Reaching conclusions based on analyzing propaganda is a valuable skill when studying history.

Practice the Skill

Look at the poster to answer these questions.

1. What is the purpose of this poster?
2. What impression does the poster give about the importance of workers on the home front?

Extend the Skill

Write a paragraph describing how you would have reacted to this poster if you had lived during World War II. Would it have swayed your opinion? Why or why not?

Apply the Skill

As you read the rest of the chapter, apply what you have learned when examining

A poster supporting the American war effort

visuals and reading quotations. Look for ways that both the United States and Germany used propaganda to influence people.

II The World at War

Terms to Know

blitzkrieg the German method of conducting war with speed and force

internment camp a place in which people are confined, especially during a time of war

Main Ideas

A. Germany used quick massive attacks to conquer much of western Europe.

B. Japan's surprise attack on Hawaii drew the United States into the war.

C. U.S. troops joined the Allies to battle Germany and Japan.

 Active Reading

SUMMARIZE
When you summarize, you tell briefly about the main ideas and events of something you have read. As you read this section, summarize the events that led the United States into World War II.

A. War in Europe

Both Great Britain and France expected the fighting in this new war to be very similar to the trench warfare of World War I. They were mistaken. Germany used a new military strategy called **blitzkrieg**, which is German for "lightning war." This strategy used swift land and air attacks to surprise and defeat the enemy.

A March Across Europe

When Britain and France declared war on Germany, Adolf Hitler decided to invade western Europe. His Nazi forces stormed into western Europe by air and land, using bomber planes and powerful tanks. In April 1940, Denmark and Norway were conquered by German troops. Then in May, the Nazi troops seized the Netherlands, Belgium, and Luxembourg as they pushed toward France. The Nazi advance was so fast that an entire British army was trapped at the port of Dunkirk, France. Even though the British army was rescued, it was now obvious that the fighting in this war was very different from that of World War I. By mid-June 1940, German troops occupied most of France.

The Battle of Britain

By July 1940, much of Europe was under the control of the Axis Powers. Hitler's next plan was to weaken Great Britain with air raids, and then launch a land invasion. Night after night in the summer of 1940, the German air force bombed British military and civilian targets. This siege by air lasted five months and is known as the Battle of Britain.

Tanks were an important part of the German blitzkrieg.

Germany used air power to weaken its European enemies.

As a result of a good defense by the Royal Air Force, Hitler canceled the invasion of Britain. Unfortunately, he was successful elsewhere in Europe. During these same months of 1940, his Nazi troops had overtaken Hungary, Romania, Bulgaria, Yugoslavia, and Greece.

Europe Crumbles

Although Germany had been unable to invade Great Britain, it still had conquered most of Europe by 1941. However, Hitler's plan had always been to conquer all of Europe, including the western part of the Soviet Union. Although Germany had signed a non-aggression pact with the Soviet Union in 1939, the agreement was just a way to trick Joseph Stalin, the Soviet dictator.

In June 1941, a German army of 3 million men made a surprise attack on the Soviet Union. By the winter, German tanks had driven deep into the Soviet Union, almost to Moscow. However, the winter weather forced them to stop. The surprise attack led the Soviet Union to join the Allied Powers, led by Great Britain and France, in the war against the Axis Powers.

The End of Neutrality

During the 1940 Battle of Britain, British Prime Minister Winston Churchill asked President Franklin D. Roosevelt to enter the war. Roosevelt believed that the actions of dictators like Hitler could endanger American democratic ideals. However, he knew that most Americans did not want to go to war.

During World War II, American soldiers used V-mail, or victory mail, to write home. Soldiers' letters were reviewed by officials. Any information in the letters that could endanger American forces was censored, or blocked out, before the letters were sent to their destinations.

Today, members of the U.S. armed forces serving in foreign countries use electronic mail, or e-mail, to stay in touch with family and friends. E-mail is the fastest way of corresponding with others.

While Roosevelt was aware of many citizens' reluctance to have the United States enter the war in Europe, he did believe that the country needed to be more involved. He tried to persuade the Congress to give money to Great Britain and its allies by arguing that the United States had a role to play in protecting democracy everywhere.

The Lend-Lease Act

To help the Allied nations, Roosevelt proposed a lend-lease plan. Under this plan, the United States could lend or lease weapons and other goods to nations whose defense was essential to the protection of the United States. Congress passed the Lend-Lease Act in March 1941. This program offered planes, tanks, and other equipment to the Allied nations as a loan. There was no time set for repayment. Over the course of the war, the United States gave more than $50 billion in lend-lease aid to the Allies.

American ships began carrying planes, tanks, and weapons to Britain and later the Soviet Union. Then, in October 1941, the United States found itself at a turning point in its decision to enter the war. German submarines, called U-boats, fired on two U.S. ships, killing more than 100 Americans. Many people in the United States felt that they were now in an undeclared war with Germany.

★ **How did President Roosevelt help Allied nations?**

B. Japanese Expansion

By 1940, Japanese forces controlled much of China. Japan's military leaders soon began to look beyond China for further expansion.

The Attack on Pearl Harbor

With the attacks on China, Japan's industries and military forces depleted important resources, especially oil. Without these resources, Japan could not continue to expand. Japan had been importing oil, steel, and iron from the United States. Roosevelt restricted these exports in 1940 to protest Japan's military expansion in Asia. This embargo, or restriction of trade, made Japanese leaders desperate to find their resources elsewhere. In January 1941, Japanese troops invaded Southeast Asia, an area that was rich in resources.

The United States was concerned that Japan would invade other countries in the Pacific region. Roosevelt froze all remaining trade between the United States and Japan. To prevent such an invasion and persuade the Japanese to leave China, U.S. leaders began negotiating with Japan. As the tensions between the two nations grew, the Japanese struck an unexpected blow.

At 7:55 A.M. on December 7, 1941, Japanese bombers attacked the U.S. Pacific Fleet at Pearl Harbor, Hawaii. More than 2,300 Americans were killed, and 19 ships and more than 180 aircraft were destroyed or damaged. Americans were stunned and angered by the attack. On December 8, Congress declared war on Japan.

Relocating Japanese Americans

After the attack on Pearl Harbor, many people feared that Japanese Americans, even though many were U.S. citizens by birth, might become spies for Japan. The U.S. government acted on this fear. It moved many Japanese Americans from the West Coast to **internment camps**, which they were not allowed to leave. There, Japanese Americans were crowded into temporary housing that gave them little privacy.

Over 100,000 Japanese Americans were sent to internment camps like this one during World War II.

Not all Japanese Americans remained in the camps. Many young men volunteered as soldiers. They fought on the battlefields of Europe during the war and received medals for their bravery.

★ **Why were many Japanese Americans sent to internment camps during the war?**

C. The United States Enters the War in Europe

After the United States declared war on Japan, its ally Germany declared war on the United States. This action brought the United States fully into the European conflict. The United States entered the war as one of the Allied Powers.

Allied Victories

During the war, Franklin Roosevelt, Winston Churchill, and Joseph Stalin, leaders of the "Big Three" allied nations, met several times to discuss military strategy and to plan for peace. The Big Three decided on a "Europe First" policy. Germany, with its huge army and great industrial strength, was a stronger enemy than Japan. After defeating Germany, the Allies thought they could then focus all their might on beating Japan.

The Allies began to carry out their strategy by first driving German troops out of North Africa in 1942. U.S. forces under the command of General Dwight D. Eisenhower landed in North Africa in November 1942. Germany's army was now outnumbered, and its supplies were running low. By May 1943, the German General Erwin Rommel was forced to withdraw his troops from the region.

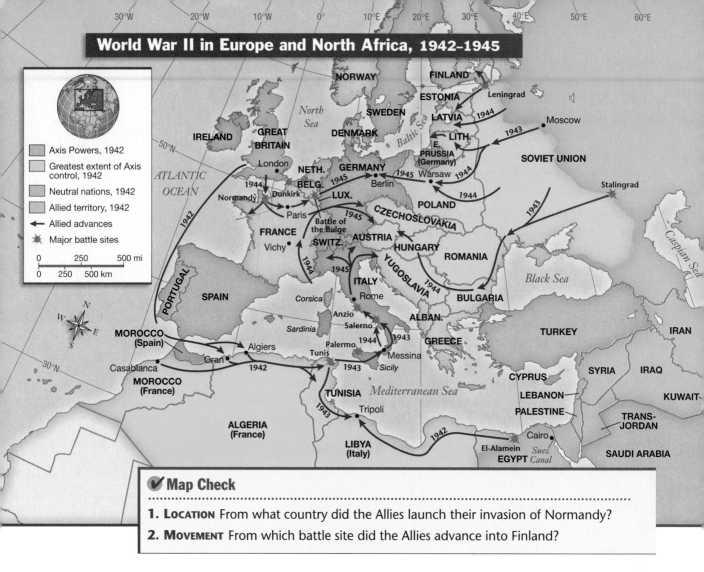

World War II in Europe and North Africa, 1942–1945

Map Check

1. **LOCATION** From what country did the Allies launch their invasion of Normandy?
2. **MOVEMENT** From which battle site did the Allies advance into Finland?

In 1943, U.S. troops, with other allies, invaded Italy. The Americans pushed the Axis forces north. After months of fighting, Allied troops finally controlled Italy. The Italian people overthrew Mussolini and surrendered to the Allied forces in September 1943.

Germany Is Driven Back

Another breakthrough occurred in August 1942, when the German army launched a siege on the Soviet city of Stalingrad. By November 1942, German troops had nearly taken the city. Then, the Soviet army surrounded the city, cutting off German supply lines. The fighting continued until February 1943, when the Germans surrendered.

In western Europe, the Allies, under General Eisenhower, planned an attack on the German army in France. They chose to invade on the coast of Normandy. The day of the invasion, called D-day, was set for June 6, 1944. More than 11,000 airplanes, 600 warships, 1,500 tanks, and 175,000 soldiers were assembled for the invasion.

Allied Invasion

On the morning of D-day, the troops waited for bad weather to clear. Then, they scrambled from ships onto the beaches as Allied planes bombed German defense posts located on the cliffs above them. More than 6,600 American soldiers died on the first day of the invasion, but within a week, the Allies had taken the entire coast. By the end of September 1944, all of France was in Allied hands.

The Allies' next goal was to conquer Germany. Led by General George S. Patton, Allied troops began to push German forces eastward through Belgium. However, Patton advanced too quickly, and he could not keep his troops supplied with enough ammunition and gasoline. This error allowed German forces to plan another attack in Belgium. There, in December 1944, Hitler staged a last, desperate counterattack. This battle is known as the Battle of the Bulge. Outnumbered American soldiers were surrounded by German tanks in the Ardennes Forest in Belgium. However, the German attack was halted by American troops after several weeks of fighting. Nineteen thousand Americans died during the Battle of the Bulge. It was the largest land battle that involved American forces in World War II.

The invasion of Normandy, also called Operation Overlord, was the largest land-and-sea attack in history.

⭐ **Why was D-day important?**

 **II Review**

Review History

A. How and where did Germany extend its conquests in Europe in 1940?

B. What did Congress do after the Japanese bombing of Pearl Harbor?

C. What was the Allies' "Europe First" policy?

Define Terms to Know

Provide a definition for each of the following terms.
blitzkrieg, internment camp

Critical Thinking

President Roosevelt compared lending arms to the Allies with lending a neighbor a hose to put out a fire. Is this argument persuasive? Why or why not?

Write About History

Write an article describing the attack on Pearl Harbor. Include details answering the Five Ws: *Who? What? Where? When?* and *Why?*

Get Organized

FLOWCHART
Use a flowchart to connect the events in this section. For example, what events drew the United States away from neutrality?

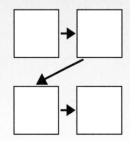

PAST to PRESENT

Women in the Workforce

Many American men went off to war. Women helped the war effort by joining the workforce. More than 6 million women took jobs outside the home during World War II. More than half of them had never worked for wages before. Women worked on assembly lines building airplanes, ships, trucks, and the original jeeps used by the armed forces.

Today, more than half of all women work outside the home. They make up more than 40 percent of the nation's workforce. Employment opportunities for women have expanded greatly over the last few decades. It is very difficult to think of any profession today in which there are no women workers.

SOLDIERS *without guns*

This poster was used during World War II to encourage women to work outside the home.

During the war, women performed jobs that were traditionally men's work. These women are building a B-26 Marauder Medium Bomber.

There are no jobs that women cannot do.

Women of today hold a variety of jobs. They are doctors, lawyers, secretaries, teachers, managers, and in many other professions. Some women, such as these pictured here, work in large corporations.

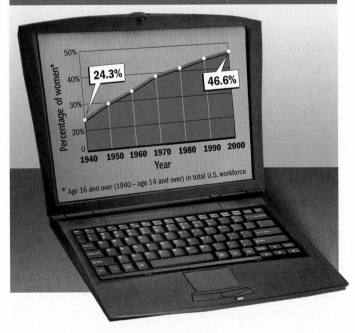

Women in the Workforce, 1940–2000

24.3%

46.6%

50%

40%

30%

20%

0

Percentage of women*

1940 1950 1960 1970 1980 1990 2000

Year

* Age 16 and over (1940 – age 14 and over) in total U.S. workforce

This chart shows how the percentage of women (ages 16 and over) in the workforce has increased steadily since the 1940s.

Hands-on Activity

Today, many women juggle a career and a family. Interview a woman who works outside the home about her typical day. Take notes during the interview. Use your notes to write a short report about the woman you interviewed. Learn more about women in the workforce at www.gfamericanhistory.com.

III Winning the War

Terms to Know

ration to limit to small portions in order to make something last

kamikaze a Japanese pilot who crashes his plane into an enemy ship

concentration camp a place where political prisoners and members of religious and ethnic groups are sent

Holocaust Hitler's policy of killing European Jews and others considered "unfit to live" during World War II

genocide the deliberate destruction of a group of people based on their race, culture, or beliefs

atomic bomb a nuclear weapon that causes large-scale destruction

Main Ideas

A. The U.S. involvement in the war affected life in the United States while it provided important help for the Allies.

B. The United States used a strategy of island hopping to defeat Japan.

C. After the war, the balance of power in the world shifted, and the United States emerged as a world leader.

 Active Reading

IDENTIFY MAIN IDEAS
Sometimes, main ideas are stated in what you read. Sometimes, you must consider the details given in order to come up with the main idea. As you read this section, list at least five details for each main idea.

A. American Involvement in the War

When the United States entered the war, the effects were felt at home and abroad. One of the greatest effects was that the creation of war-related jobs helped to finally end the Great Depression.

The War Effort at Home

During World War II, ordinary factories were changed to produce the machines and weapons needed for war. For example, auto makers began making tanks and warplanes instead of automobiles.

Because most of the nation's raw materials were needed for the war, civilians had to do without many items. Sugar, butter, meat, rubber tires, and gasoline were **rationed**, or limited.

People were also encouraged to buy war bonds. They could be cashed in after the war.

Americans Make Contributions

By 1945, about 15 million Americans were serving in the armed forces. This number included 300,000 women, and 1.8 million African Americans and Latinos, who played critical roles in the war effort. Women served in the armed forces in nonfighting roles, such as typists, clerks, control-tower operators, aviators, and mechanics. Many of the country's nurses served in the war effort. As in World War I, African Americans and Latinos joined the military, serving their country in a variety of ways from fighter pilots to infantry.

 Why were goods rationed during the war?

B. War in the Pacific

As the war in Europe intensified during 1942 and 1943 so too did the fighting in the Pacific region. In the Pacific, General Douglas MacArthur led U.S. forces in the struggle against Japan.

Battles in the Pacific

A key battle in the Pacific occurred at Midway Island, about 1,000 miles west of Hawaii. The Americans had only a small force in this U.S. territory, but they had broken the Japanese code and learned of a planned attack ahead of time. During the Battle of Midway, which lasted from June 3 to June 6, 1942, the Japanese navy suffered heavy losses.

In order to eventually invade Japan, the Allies had to win control of Japanese-held islands in the Pacific Ocean. Because there were so many islands to conquer, Allied commanders decided to use a strategy of island hopping. In this strategy, Allied forces would capture some islands and bypass others. Once an island was taken, it could be used to attack still other islands. The islands skipped over would be cut off from supplies, making them useless to Japan's war effort.

Spotlight on Government

One of the most important contributions during the war in the Pacific was made by Navajo "code-talkers." Using their own language as the basis for military code, they baffled Japanese code-breakers.

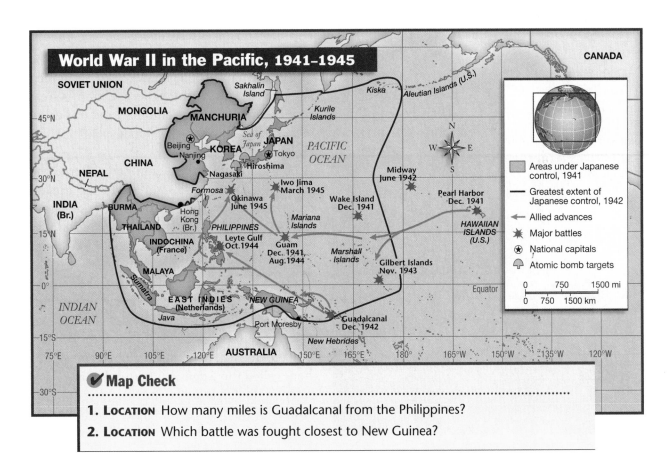

World War II in the Pacific, 1941–1945

Areas under Japanese control, 1941
Greatest extent of Japanese control, 1942
Allied advances
Major battles
National capitals
Atomic bomb targets

✔ **Map Check**

1. **LOCATION** How many miles is Guadalcanal from the Philippines?

2. **LOCATION** Which battle was fought closest to New Guinea?

Preparing to Invade

With the island hopping strategy, the Allies staged offensive attacks from 1942 to 1944. Allied forces took Guadalcanal in the Solomon Islands and then jumped to the Philippines. From there, they launched an attack on the tiny Japanese islands of Iwo Jima and Okinawa in 1945. At Okinawa, the desperate Japanese military leaders used **kamikazes**, or suicide pilots, who crashed their bomb-loaded airplanes into U.S. ships. Casualties were high on both sides, but Japan suffered more losses. By June 1945, the Allies were in a position to invade Japan.

★ **What strategy did the United States use to defeat Japan?**

C. The Last Days of the War

During the war, Allied leaders met to make plans for the end of the war. By 1943, the Allies agreed to form a world peace organization known as the United Nations. This organization would replace the League of Nations. In February 1945, Franklin Roosevelt, Winston Churchill, and Joseph Stalin, held a conference at Yalta, in southern Russia.

The Meeting at Yalta

The decisions made at Yalta by the Big Three helped to shape what the world would be like after the war. First, the Allies agreed that after the war the United States, the Soviet Union, Great Britain, and France would divide Germany and its capital, Berlin, into four parts, or zones. The Allies also developed plans for the United Nations.

Churchill, Roosevelt, and Stalin (from left to right) made plans for the end of the war.

Because the Soviet Union had suffered the greatest loss of life and material during the war, Stalin wanted Germany to make reparations to the Allies, most of which would be given to the Soviet Union. In addition, Stalin wanted to expand Soviet influence in eastern Europe. He wanted Poland to have a pro-Soviet government. Roosevelt and Churchill disagreed. They feared Soviet control of Eastern Europe. In 1941, the United States and Great Britain secretly signed an agreement called the Atlantic Charter. It stated that every nation that was controlled by the Axis Powers should have the right to choose its own government through free elections.

Death of a Leader

President Roosevelt, who had arrived at Yalta very ill, died in April 1945. Vice President Harry S Truman became the President of the United States and assumed the role as leader of the strongest of the Allied Powers. By the end of April, the war in Europe was almost over. Soviet forces met other Allied forces on the outskirts of Berlin. With his defeat almost certain, Hitler took his own life on April 30. On May 8, known as V-E Day, or Victory in Europe Day, Germany formally surrendered. The war in Europe was over.

The Holocaust

After victory in Germany, Allied soldiers throughout Europe began to free people held in large prison camps in Germany and Poland, called **concentration camps**. The Allied soldiers soon learned about the horrors of the **Holocaust**, or the murder of millions of people by the Nazis. The victims of the Holocaust were mostly Jewish people. Other victims included people of Eastern European countries and Gypsies, as well as people with disabilities. Hitler thought of all of these people as "unfit to live."

Hitler had issued orders to begin killing Jews soon after the invasion of Poland in 1939. Those who were not killed were sent to concentration camps. There, they lived in horrible conditions and were forced to work as slaves. With only scraps of bread to eat and water to drink, many people starved to death. Others died of disease or maltreatment.

Before long, Hitler decided to take even harsher action. In a policy called the "final solution," all Jews were to be killed in an act of **genocide**, or mass murder of a people. The Nazis built death camps in which thousands of people were killed each day. Most died in gas chambers and were then burned to ashes in huge ovens. Judith Jaegerman, a survivor of the Holocaust, described one of the death camps:

> **"** The very first sight of this ghastly camp, was a huge hill of . . . dead people, who were practically only skeletons. Such a terrible and frightening sight . . . and right away I was thinking, that within only a few short days we would be looking the same, stacked like these ones. **"**

As Allied troops liberated, or freed, the people in the camps, even the toughest soldiers were shocked by what they saw. General George Patton became sick when he walked through the concentration camp at Ohrdruf, Germany.

ANALYZE PRIMARY SOURCES **DOCUMENT-BASED QUESTION** This quote describes a terrible scene. Why do you think it is important to learn about such things?

General Eisenhower, who also toured the death camp at Ohrdruf, ordered that all nearby American units be brought to the camp. Eisenhower felt it was necessary to show the American troops so that they would "know what they are fighting against." He urged representatives from around the world, including journalists, to come to witness the horror so that it would not be forgotten.

To prevent such terrible crimes from happening again, the Allies decided that the Nazi leaders had to take responsibility for what they had done. In November 1945, in Nuremberg, Germany, the Allies held war crimes trials. Twenty-four Nazi leaders were tried in the first of these trials. Twelve were sentenced to death.

After being starved and tortured by the Nazis, these people were freed from a concentration camp at the end of the war.

Dropping the Atomic Bomb

As the truth of the Holocaust was revealed in Europe, the war in the Pacific was coming to a close. After the United States declared victory at Okinawa, the Japanese had almost no ships or planes left with which to fight. Yet Japanese leaders refused to surrender. President Truman wondered what he should do next. One choice was to invade Japan. Truman estimated that an invasion would cost up to 1 million American lives. The other choice was to use the **atomic bomb**.

The atomic bomb was a new weapon with a huge, destructive power generated from nuclear energy. One bomb could destroy a large city. Throughout the war, scientists had been working to build such a bomb. In the United States, this secret research and design effort was known as the Manhattan Project.

In July 1945, the atomic bomb was tested in the United States in an unpopulated area of New Mexico. Scientists were able to build a bomb that had a force equal to 20,000 tons of dynamite. Truman became convinced that using the bomb would end the war quickly.

On August 6, 1945, the United States dropped an atomic bomb on Hiroshima, Japan, a city with a population of 250,000 people. The city was destroyed, and 100,000 people died from the blast. Many thousands more died slowly from radiation sickness. Three days later, a second bomb was dropped on Nagasaki, an equally large city. At last, the Japanese decided to surrender. On August 15, 1945, Japanese officials accepted the Allied terms of surrender in what became known as V-J Day, or Victory Over Japan Day. The official articles of surrender were overseen by General MacArthur on September 2, 1945. World War II was over at last.

The Cost of War

By the war's end in 1945, much of the world was in economic and social ruin. Cities had been bombed into dust. Transportation networks such as roads, bridges, and railroads had been destroyed in Europe, Asia, and Africa. Millions of people were now refugees without homes.

Many people died of hunger and disease after the fighting stopped. Governments could not help these people much because almost all of their resources had been used to fight the war. Some governments, like those in Italy and Germany, collapsed.

The greatest price of all was the human cost of the war. More than 60 million people around the world had perished. Almost 300,000 Americans died in the war.

The war also changed the position of the United States in the world. The United States emerged stronger than it had been before the war. Other than Pearl Harbor, no American cities had been bombed. The Great Depression was over. The United States had become a center of political and economic power.

 What was Truman's reason for using the atomic bomb?

Casualties of World War II

COUNTRY	WOUNDED	TOTAL DEATHS
China	1,752,951	2,200,000
France	400,000	563,000
Germany	5,000,000	4,200,000
Great Britain	277,077	357,000
Italy	66,000	395,000
Japan	4,000,000	1,972,000
Poland	236,606	5,798,178
United States	671,801	298,000
USSR	5,000,000	18,000,000

Total deaths are both civilian and military fatalities.
Wounded are military casualties only.

✔ **Chart Check**

Which two countries had the greatest number of wounded during World War II?

 **III Review**

Review History
A. What effect did the war have on the U.S. economy?
B. What happened at the Battle of Midway?
C. What major event led to the surrender of the Japanese forces?

Define Terms to Know
Provide a definition for each of the following terms.
ration, kamikaze, concentration camp, Holocaust, genocide, atomic bomb

Critical Thinking
What events at Yalta showed that world tensions would probably continue after the war?

Write About History
Write a letter to the President explaining why the horrors of the Holocaust should not be forgotten.

Get Organized
FLOWCHART
Use a flowchart to connect the events in this section. For example, what were the events that led to the defeat of Japan?

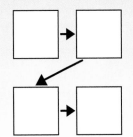

CHAPTER 26 Review

Chapter Summary

Copy the following outline in your note-book. Complete the outline to create a summary of Chapter 26.

World War II

I. The Road to War

    A. Economic Trouble in Europe

    B.

    C.

II. The World at War

    A.

    B.

    C.

III. Winning the War

    A.

    B.

    C.

Interpret the Timeline

Use the timeline on pages 608–609 to answer the following questions.

1. How long had the Allies been at war with Germany before the United States entered the war?

2. **Critical Thinking** Which events show that the United States supported the Allies before it entered World War II?

Use Terms to Know

Select the term that best completes each sentence.

appeasement   Holocaust
atomic bomb   internment camps
fascism   ration

1. During World War II, many Japanese Americans were sent to _____.

2. Americans had to _____ certain items that were in short supply during the war.

3. Six million Jews were killed during the _____.

4. Japan surrendered after the United States dropped an _____ on two Japanese cities.

5. Italian dictator Benito Mussolini called his type of government _____.

6. In Munich, British and French leaders followed a policy of _____ by giving in to Hitler's demands.

Check Your Understanding

1. **Describe** Hitler's idea of a "master race" and how it influenced his actions.

2. **Explain** why Japan expanded in the 1930s and 1940s.

3. **Summarize** Roosevelt's lend-lease program and why he promoted it.

4. **Explain** D-day and why it was important.

5. **Explain** why the Allies did not invade Japan.

6. **Identify** Stalin's concerns at the Yalta conference.

Critical Thinking

1. **Evaluate** How did events at the end of World War I lead to World War II?

2. **Compare and Contrast** How were Japanese American internment camps different from Nazi concentration camps? How were they the same?

3. **Draw Conclusions** Why was the United States able to become the major Allied power during and after World War II?

Put Your Skills to Work

RECOGNIZE PROPAGANDA

You have learned that recognizing propaganda can help you to better understand history material. Look at this poster from World War II. It says, "Leader, We Follow You!" Then, answer the following questions.

1. What is the purpose of the poster?

2. Does this poster show a one-sided view of Hitler? Explain your answer.

German World War II poster

In Your Own Words

JOURNAL WRITING

At Yalta, Allied leaders made key decisions that shaped history for years to come. Write a journal entry about a decision you made that had lasting consequences.

Net Work

INTERNET ACTIVITY

Working with a partner, use the Internet as a resource to create an oral presentation about the Holocaust. Research the names of concentration camps and the estimated number of people who died at each one. Find interviews of people who survived the concentration camps. Use photos as visual aids during your presentation. Share your presentation with the class.

For help in starting this activity, visit the following Web site: www.gfamericanhistory.com.

Look Ahead

In the next chapter, learn about how the Cold War developed between World War II allies.

CHAPTER 27

The Cold War 1945–1960

I. **The Cold War Begins**
II. **The Korean War and the Red Scare**
III. **The Changing Nation**
IV. **Life in the Fifties**

After World War II, a division began between the Communist and democratic countries of the world. Winston Churchill, the former prime minister of Great Britain, was alarmed at the growth of Soviet influence in Eastern Europe. He warned Americans in 1946, saying,

> " . . . an iron curtain has descended across the Continent of Europe. Behind that line lie all the capitals of the ancient states of Central and Eastern Europe . . . all these famous cities and the populations around them lie in . . . the Soviet sphere, and all are subject . . . to a very high and . . . increasing measure of control from Moscow. "

Churchill's speech marked the beginning of a new type of war that would be waged between the United States and the Soviet Union.

Fallout shelter sign

1950
Joseph McCarthy claims many U.S. government workers are Communists.

1951
President Truman fires General MacArthur.

1947
Jackie Robinson signs with Brooklyn Dodgers.

1949
NATO is formed.

U.S. Events	**1945**			**1950**
Presidential Term Begins	1945 Harry S Truman			
World Events	**1945**			**1950**

1945
World War II ends.

1948
The modern state of Israel is declared.

1950
Korean War begins.

1949
Communists take control in China.

VIEW HISTORY Increased tensions between the Soviet Union and the United States led to the threat of nuclear war. Many Americans built fallout shelters to protect themselves from nuclear bombs. Signs (left) were used to indicate the location of fallout shelters.

★ **What do the sign and the photograph tell about the mood of the nation during this period?**

Get Organized

SPIDER DIAGRAM

A spider diagram helps you better understand an important idea by adding descriptive words and phrases. Use a spider diagram as you read Chapter 27. List a topic in the center circle. Then, add descriptions on the lines surrounding the circle. Here is an example from this chapter.

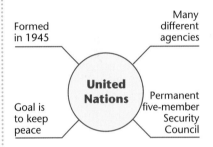

- Formed in 1945
- Many different agencies
- Goal is to keep peace
- **United Nations**
- Permanent five-member Security Council

1954
Jonas Salk tests a polio vaccine successfully.
Supreme Court orders desegregation of schools in *Brown v. Board of Education of Topeka* decision.

1955
Montgomery, Alabama, bus boycott begins.

1958
Congress establishes NASA.

1955 — 1960

1953 Dwight D. Eisenhower

1955 — 1960

1955
Warsaw Pact is formed.

1957
Ghana gains independence.
Soviet Union launches *Sputnik*.

1959
Fidel Castro comes to power in Cuba.

I ★ The Cold War Begins

Terms to Know

Cold War a conflict between countries, with no actual fighting

iron curtain a barrier of secrecy that kept Soviet-controlled nations apart from the rest of Europe

satellite a nation controlled by another country

containment a policy of preventing a country from expanding its power

refugee a person who flees to a foreign country

Main Ideas

A. The United Nations was formed to promote world peace as tensions between the Soviet Union and the United States increased.

B. Truman's foreign policy helped rebuild Western Europe.

C. The spread of communism after World War II increased existing tensions in Asia and the Middle East.

Active Reading

SUPPORTING DETAILS
When you identify supporting details, you look for facts and examples that relate to the main idea. As you read this section, look for details that support the main ideas listed on this page.

A. A Plan for Peace

The United States and the Soviet Union had been allies in World War II. However, distrust arose between the two nations as the war ended. They did not fight a war against each other, but political tensions grew between them. This period of increased tensions would last for nearly 50 years. It was known as the **Cold War**.

The United Nations

During World War II, national leaders worked to create an organization that would replace the League of Nations. In 1945, delegates from countries around the world met in San Francisco, California, to set up the United Nations, or UN. In the charter, the delegates outlined the organization's main goal, which was to promote peace among nations. In the aftermath of World War II, members wanted to prevent wars and to bring an end to wars that did erupt. Members promised to work together to find peaceful solutions to international disputes.

The main agencies of the new organization were the Security Council and the General Assembly. The United States, Great Britain, the Soviet Union, France, and China were the permanent members of the Security Council. Each of the five members had the power to veto any UN action. The chart on the next page shows how the United Nations, presently headquartered in New York City, is organized.

The United Nations has grown from 51 member nations in 1945 to 189 member nations in 2001.

The Soviets and the Spread of Communism

Even as the UN charter was being signed, disagreements were arising between wartime allies. As part of the agreement at Yalta, the Big Three leaders divided Germany into four zones of control—one each for France, Britain, the United States, and the Soviet Union.

The German capital of Berlin, located inside the Soviet zone, was also divided into four zones. The Soviet government then set up Communist governments throughout eastern and central Europe. As tensions grew between the United States and the Soviet Union, Germany was divided into two separate nations—The Federal Republic of Germany in the west, and the German Democratic Republic in the east. West Germany was democratic and consisted of the combined zones of the United States, Britain, and France. In East Germany, a Soviet-backed, Communist government was in charge. Leaders in Western nations referred to the **iron curtain** that separated the Soviet nations from the rest of Europe. President Harry Truman and other Western leaders feared that more nations would become Soviet **satellites**, or controlled nations. The alliance between the United States and the Soviet Union ended. The two countries came to view each other as enemies.

★ **What was the Cold War?**

The United Nations	
Security Council	• Investigates situations that threaten peace • Sets UN policies • Works for peaceful settlement of disputes
General Assembly	• Discusses world problems • Votes on actions • Controls UN budget
Secretariat	• Coordinates work of all UN agencies • Is headed by Secretary General
Economic and Social Council	• Works for improved economic and social conditions • Cooperates with member nations to improve standards of living
Trusteeship Council	• Administers territories that were not self-governing when the UN was established
International Court of Justice	• Helps settle legal disputes between nations • Gives legal opinions to General Assembly

✔ **Chart Check**

Which UN agency would most likely help to settle legal disputes between nations?

B. Rising Tensions

After World War II, the world quickly became deeply divided. On one side were the United States, Western Europe, and their allies. On the other were the Soviet Union and its satellites.

The Truman Doctrine

President Truman asked Congress to help Greece and Turkey defend themselves against Communists who were trying to take over their countries. Congress agreed, and a new policy, called the Truman Doctrine, was established.

The Truman Doctrine pledged that the United States would help any country threatened by communism. This doctrine was part of an overall policy of **containment**, which meant that the United States would try to contain, or stop, the spread of communism.

Another important part of Truman's foreign policy was the Marshall Plan. President Truman had asked his Secretary of State, George C. Marshall, to create a plan to bring economic recovery to the battered countries of Europe. The war had left millions of people homeless and hungry. The Marshall Plan gave or lent about $13 billion to 17 countries. The money was used to rebuild bridges, factories, railroads, hospitals, and schools. It helped restore the economies of several Western European countries, including Britain, France, and West Germany. It also helped democracy grow in Western Europe, while preventing future Communist takeovers. The Soviet Union did not allow its satellite countries to take part in the Marshall Plan. As a result, they did not recover from the war as quickly as did countries in Western Europe.

The Berlin Blockade

The Marshall Plan aided some people in Germany. The Soviets were afraid that Germany would ally itself with the West. The United States, Great Britain, and France had combined their zones in Germany into one nation. The Soviet Union responded with a blockade. It closed all routes connecting Berlin and West Germany and prevented goods from entering or leaving. The Soviet government hoped to force the Western powers out of Berlin.

President Truman responded quickly. He ordered U.S. pilots to deliver food, fuel, and medical supplies to West Berlin. The Berlin airlift was successful. Eventually, the Soviets lifted the blockade.

NATO and the Warsaw Pact

President Truman believed that the best way to contain the Soviet Union was to stand together with other nations. The United States, Canada, and ten Western European countries founded the North Atlantic Treaty Organization (NATO) in 1949. The organization promised that if one nation was attacked, the others would come to its aid. Forming NATO meant the United States gave up its old policy of isolationism. U.S. troops, ships, and aircraft were sent to military bases throughout Europe.

The Soviet government saw NATO as a threat. In response, in 1955, the Soviet Union organized the Warsaw Pact, a military alliance with its Eastern European satellites.

★ **How did NATO and the Warsaw Pact divide Europe?**

Then & Now

When NATO was formed, it was designed to protect Western Europe from Soviet attacks. After the fall of communism in 1989, three former members of the Warsaw Pact joined their old enemies. Hungary, Poland, and the Czech Republic became members of NATO.

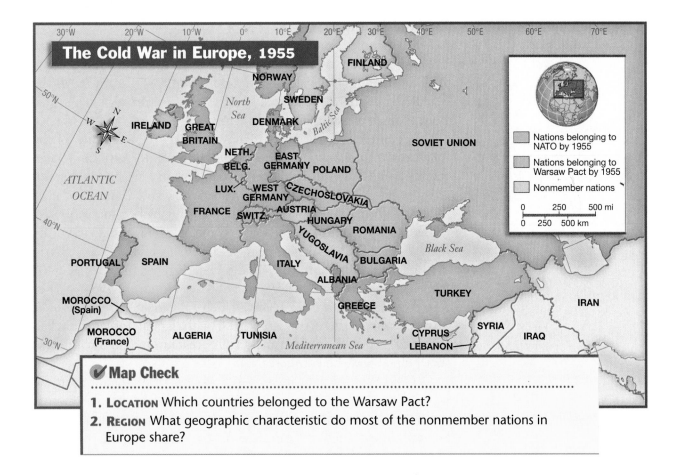

The Cold War in Europe, 1955

Nations belonging to NATO by 1955

Nations belonging to Warsaw Pact by 1955

Nonmember nations

0   250   500 mi
0   250   500 km

✔ Map Check

1. **LOCATION** Which countries belonged to the Warsaw Pact?
2. **REGION** What geographic characteristic do most of the nonmember nations in Europe share?

C. Communism and Nationalism Around the World

Some areas that experienced great changes after World War II were in Asia and the Middle East.

Successes and Failures in Asia

A civil war had raged in China since the 1920s. Communists, under Mao Zedong, and Nationalists, led by Chiang Kai-shek, fought for control of the Chinese government. The United States supported the Nationalists. An increasing number of people in China supported Mao, who promised to return land to the peasants. In 1949, the Communists defeated the Nationalist forces and established a government called the People's Republic of China. The Nationalists fled to the island of Taiwan, where they formed their own government called the Republic of China. The United States insisted that Taiwan was still the legal government of China. The United States kept Communist China from taking China's seat at the UN.

Changes followed World War II in other Asian countries. For example, Japan was occupied by the U.S. military until 1952. India and Pakistan gained independence in 1947.

Spotlight on

Government

General Douglas MacArthur, who was in charge of U.S. forces in Japan, actually governed the country for several years. Under his leadership, Japan adopted democracy.

The Middle East

Jewish people from Europe had been settling in Palestine since the late 1800s. After World War II, many Jewish survivors of the Holocaust moved to Palestine, a British-controlled territory in the Middle East. This move alarmed Arabs who were already in Palestine. Both groups wanted their own independent nations.

The United Nations divided Palestine into two states: one for the Palestinians and one for the Jews. On May 14, 1948, Jews announced the creation of the state of Israel in their part of Palestine. However, the announcement angered Palestinians, who wanted control of all of Palestine. War broke out, and many Palestinians became **refugees**, or people who fled to neighboring countries. This war marked the first of many clashes between Israelis and Palestinians.

Other crises flared in the Middle East. Egypt's president Gamal Abdel Nasser accepted aid from the Soviet Union. In 1956, Nasser seized control of the Suez Canal, which France and Britain used as a trade route. These two countries, with Israeli forces, attacked Egypt to regain use of the canal. A UN resolution and Soviet pressure helped end the conflict.

As Cold War tensions increased, many developing nations in the world did not want to be aligned with either the United States or the Soviet Union. Nevertheless, both the United States and the Soviet Union tried to gain the favor of developing countries through economic and political means.

 What changes occurred in Asia after World War II?

The state of Israel was created in 1948.

 **Review**

Review History
A. What was the main goal of the United Nations?
B. In what ways did the Marshall Plan encourage European recovery?
C. What changes occurred in the Middle East after World War II?

Define Terms to Know
Provide a definition for each of the following terms.
Cold War, iron curtain, satellite, containment, refugee

Critical Thinking
Why did the United States help European countries recover after the war?

Write About History
Write a newspaper article in which you explain the political situation in Germany that led to the Berlin Blockade.

Get Organized
SPIDER DIAGRAM
A spider diagram can help you to organize supporting details. Use a spider diagram to describe the Marshall Plan.

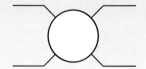

Build Your Skills

READA TIME-ZONE MAP

The world is divided into 24 time zones. When it is noon in one city, it can be a different time or day in another. Time zones are measured according to the distance from the Prime Meridian, or 0° longitude. To find out where the time zones change, you can use a time-zone map.

Here's How

Follow these steps in order to read the time-zone map.

1. Locate two places on the map.
2. Count the number of time zones between places.
3. As you move east, add an hour for each time zone you counted. As you move west, subtract an hour for each.

Here's Why

Knowing what time it is in different places is important when you travel or communicate with people in different regions.

Practice the Skill

Use the map to answer these questions.

1. Through what city does the Prime Meridian run?
2. If it is 3:00 P.M. in Washington, D.C., what time is it in Moscow?

Extend the Skill

Use the map to write a short quiz.

Apply the Skill

As you read, use the map to find time differences between places named in the text.

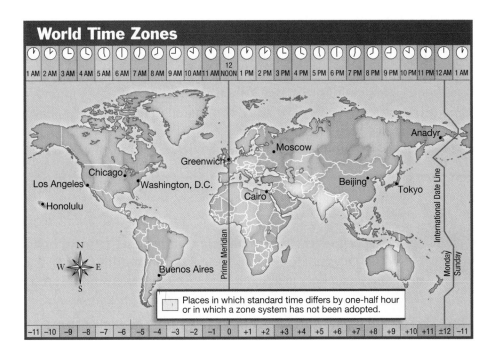

World Time Zones

Places in which standard time differs by one-half hour or in which a zone system has not been adopted.

II The Korean War and the Red Scare

Terms to Know

superpower one of the most powerful nations in the world

demilitarized zone an area that military forces cannot enter

perjury telling a lie under oath

McCarthyism named after Senator Joseph McCarthy, the practice of publicly accusing people of political disloyalty without regard for evidence

Main Ideas

A. The presidential race of 1948 produced a great surprise in U.S. election history.

B. The political struggle between the United States and the Soviet Union led to a war in Korea.

C. Americans' fears of communism led to Congressional investigations.

Active Reading

PREDICT
When you predict, you look for clues and other information about future events. As you read this section, ask yourself the following question: Based on the information, what is the likely outcome?

A. The 1948 Campaign

While Americans were fighting communism around the world, they faced other problems at home. Prices were rising quickly, but wages were not. Strikes were held in many industries. Members of the Republican Party thought that with such a troubled situation at home, they would be able to defeat President Harry Truman in the 1948 election. They nominated the popular governor of New York, Thomas E. Dewey, to challenge Truman.

A Surprising Election

The President also had trouble within his own party. Conservative Democrats nominated their own candidate, Strom Thurmond of South Carolina. Liberal Democrats felt Truman had not done enough to defend Roosevelt's New Deal. They founded the Progressive Party and nominated Henry A. Wallace, Roosevelt's Vice President from 1941 to 1945.

With Democratic loyalties divided, Truman would have a hard time winning. He campaigned tirelessly, however, blaming the country's problems on the "Do-Nothing" Republican Congress.

When Americans went to bed on election night in 1948, most pollsters were predicting that the next President would be Dewey. However, the experts had not discovered that Truman was catching up. When all the votes were counted, Truman and the Democrats had won a shocking upset.

⭐ **Who were the candidates for President in 1948?**

Harry Truman held up a copy of a newspaper announcing his loss to Thomas Dewey. The famous headline error shows how close the race was.

The Korean War was the first major conflict in which African American and white soldiers fought in the same battalions.

B. War in Korea

During Truman's second term, the Cold War was heating up. The United States and the Soviet Union had become **superpowers**, the most powerful countries in the world. Neither country wanted the other to gain more influence. Their struggle led to a war in Korea. This former Japanese colony had been divided into two parts after World War II. U.S. soldiers occupied South Korea, and Soviet troops occupied North Korea. The dividing line was 38 degrees north latitude, or what was called the 38th parallel.

Conduct of the War

On June 25, 1950, the North Koreans surged across the 38th parallel and invaded South Korea. The North Koreans wanted to unify Korea under a Communist government. The United Nations sent troops, mostly Americans, to Korea in order to push the North Korean army back. President Truman never asked Congress for a declaration of war. Therefore, government officials referred to the Korean War as a "police action."

Truman wanted to reunite Korea under a democratic government, and he chose General Douglas MacArthur to command forces in Korea. At first, the North Koreans had the upper hand. Their army marched almost all the way to the southeastern tip of South Korea. Then, MacArthur made a daring landing behind North Korean lines at Inchon. The UN army, led by MacArthur, forced the invaders all the way back to the Chinese border. This success gave Truman hopes of uniting Korea.

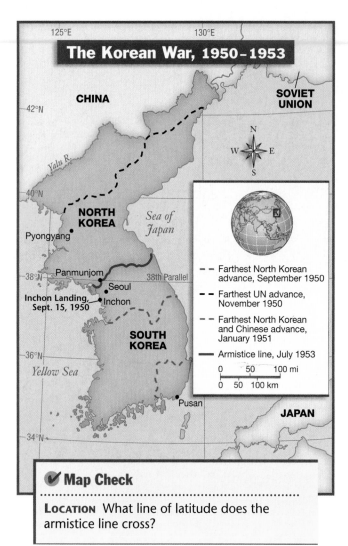

The Korean War, 1950–1953

CHINA

SOVIET UNION

Yalu R.

NORTH KOREA

Sea of Japan

Pyongyang

Panmunjom

38th Parallel

Seoul

Inchon Landing, Sept. 15, 1950

Inchon

SOUTH KOREA

Yellow Sea

Pusan

JAPAN

– – Farthest North Korean advance, September 1950

– – Farthest UN advance, November 1950

– – Farthest North Korean and Chinese advance, January 1951

— Armistice line, July 1953

0   50   100 mi
0 50 100 km

✔ Map Check

LOCATION What line of latitude does the armistice line cross?

China Enters the War

The Chinese government became concerned about the fact that American troops were advancing toward the Chinese border. China warned MacArthur not to go farther, but he ignored the warning. As a result, China entered the war to help the North Korean forces. A Chinese army of 300,000 soldiers poured across the border and drove the UN forces back to the 38th parallel. At this point in the war, a disagreement developed. MacArthur wanted to attack China, but President Truman did not want to widen the war. He feared that an attack on China would draw the Soviet Union into the war, which might lead to a larger war and the use of atomic weapons.

General MacArthur did not agree with the President, his commander in chief. He wrote a letter attacking the Truman administration. In response, Truman fired him for insubordination, or disobedience. Many Americans were angry with Truman's decision because they wanted the Communists out of Korea and China.

MacArthur returned to the United States to a hero's welcome. He made one last appearance before Congress and made a very famous speech in which he gave an emotional farewell, saying that "old soldiers never die; they just fade away."

The Final Settlement

The Korean War continued until July 1953. At that time, neither side had won a victory. The two sides decided to quit fighting. The armistice agreement created a **demilitarized zone**, or DMZ, at the 38th parallel. A demilitarized zone is a territory from which the military is excluded. This DMZ became the border between the countries of North Korea and South Korea. North Korea became a Soviet satellite. South Korea signed a defense treaty with the United States. Many Americans blamed President Truman for the war and the deaths of 54,000 U.S. soldiers.

★ **Why did President Truman oppose an attack on China?**

C. The Red Scare

The frustrations of the Korean War increased Americans' fear of communism and the Soviet Union. These fears led to a period known as the Red Scare. Communists were called Reds because the color red was considered the symbol of communism. Some Americans turned against one another in fear of communism.

Investigating Communism

Many Americans were afraid that Communist spies were working secretly inside the U.S. government. Members of Congress, who were especially worried about Communists in the government, began investigations. The House of Representatives Un-American Activities Committee, known as HUAC, was the most active group. This committee investigated Communist influence in the U.S. government, labor unions, movie industry, and other areas.

One of the best known cases during the Red Scare involved Julius and Ethel Rosenberg. The married couple was accused of passing atomic secrets that made it possible for the Soviets to build an atomic bomb. Although the Rosenbergs claimed innocence, they were found guilty of spying and were executed.

Another case involved Alger Hiss. Hiss worked in the State Department during the 1930s. HUAC charged him with passing top-secret material to Soviet agents. A young congressman from California named Richard Nixon played an important role in the investigation of Hiss. Hiss was sent to jail for **perjury**, or lying under oath.

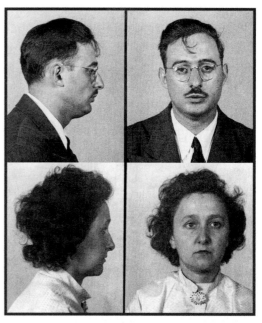

On March 29, 1951, Julius and Ethel Rosenberg were convicted of giving the Soviet Union information about the atomic bomb.

The Rise and Fall of Joseph McCarthy

The Hiss trial convinced many people that more government workers might be Communists. One believer was Republican Senator Joseph McCarthy of Wisconsin. At a speech in Wheeling, West Virginia, McCarthy said,

“ I have here in my hand a list of the names of 205 men that were known to the Secretary of State as being members of the Communist Party. ”

ANALYZE PRIMARY SOURCES

DOCUMENT-BASED QUESTION
What do you think the purpose of McCarthy's speech was?

During the Red Scare, Congress investigated charges of Communist influence in the government.

McCarthy did not show his list to anyone. Some people believed he was making up the charges. However, others believed his accusations. Soon, the country was in the grip of "**McCarthyism**." McCarthyism is the practice of publicly accusing people of political disloyalty without regard for evidence. For many, the accusations led to ruined lives or careers.

While many Americans believed McCarthy's charges, others felt that he was trampling on people's civil rights. Reputations were ruined by charges that were not proven. Workers were blacklisted, or put on a list of people who were not to be employed. When McCarthy announced that even the U.S. Army was filled with Communists, many people decided he had gone too far. The Senate agreed and censured, or condemned, McCarthy in 1954. McCarthyism faded, but fears of communism remained strong.

★ **What factors led to the Red Scare and McCarthyism in the 1950s?**

II Review

Review History
A. Why did pollsters expect President Truman to lose the election in 1948?
B. How did the Korean War end?
C. What events in the early 1950s showed Americans' concern about Communist influence in the United States?

Define Terms to Know
Provide a definition for each of the following terms.
superpower, demilitarized zone, perjury, McCarthyism

Critical Thinking
Do you think McCarthyism could be revived today? Why or why not?

Write About History
Writing as a U.S. Army historian, create a timeline of the events in the Korean War.

Get Organized
SPIDER DIAGRAM
A spider diagram can help you organize supporting details. Use a spider diagram to describe the Red Scare.

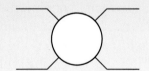

III The Changing Nation

Terms to Know

space race the competition among countries to be the first in exploring space

summit meeting a meeting between important leaders of nations

Main Ideas

A. In 1952, Republicans took control of the White House.

B. The struggle for civil rights gained momentum, helped by court decisions and protests.

C. Foreign affairs dominated Eisenhower's second term.

Active Reading

GENERALIZE
When you generalize, you gather details. Then, you analyze them and write a general statement that includes the information from the details. As you read this section, generalize about the civil rights movement.

A. A New President for a New Era

Even though Harry Truman was re-elected in 1948's great upset, his popularity fell. However, he was able to pass some of his programs, known as the Fair Deal. The minimum wage was raised, social security benefits were expanded, and low-income housing was built. As Americans worried about Communists and Korea, many other programs were blocked by Congress. By the 1952 election, most Americans felt that after 20 years of Democrats in the White House, it was time for a change.

"I Like Ike"

With change in mind, Americans looked to a tall, friendly war hero with a big smile. Americans called him Ike.

Dwight David Eisenhower had led U.S. and Allied forces to victory in Africa and Europe during World War II. He was Supreme Commander of Allied forces during the D-day invasion of France in 1944. In 1948, both the Democrats and the Republicans wanted Eisenhower to run as their party's candidate. He refused at the time. However, in 1952 he changed his mind and ran for President as a Republican. To many people, Eisenhower represented firmness, friendliness, and honesty. He won the presidency in 1952 by a landslide, defeating Governor Adlai Stevenson of Illinois. Americans were ready to enjoy peacetime prosperity and calm, steady government. Ike seemed to be just the man for the job.

Do You Remember?
In Chapter 26, you read about Eisenhower's role in World War II. Many other military heroes also became President, beginning with George Washington.

Campaign button during the 1952 election

The Eisenhower Years

Eisenhower wanted to slow the growth of the federal government, limit government spending, and allow the economy to function with less government involvement. He supported social programs, however, by creating the Department of Health, Education, and Welfare. This government agency oversaw federal food, drug, health, and educational programs, as well as social security benefits. In addition, Eisenhower proposed the Federal Aid Highway Act of 1956, under which most of today's interstate highway system was built.

During Eisenhower's presidency, the National Aeronautics and Space Administration (NASA) was created in 1958. Its job was to develop and oversee the nation's space program. The creation of NASA was in response to the 1957 launching of *Sputnik* by the Soviets. *Sputnik* was the first space satellite. Americans worried that the United States had fallen behind the Soviet Union in developing space technology. The worries led to a competition for dominance in space. The competition became known as the **space race**.

To ensure that Americans did not fall behind the Soviets, Eisenhower supported programs that would improve education. The National Defense Education Act promoted the study of science and foreign languages and provided low interest loans to college students.

★ **Why did Americans vote overwhelmingly for Eisenhower?**

B. The Fight for Civil Rights

During the 1950s, civil rights issues began to capture headlines in the nation's newspapers. Two of the first targets for civil rights groups were the public educational system and transportation system.

Brown v. Board of Education of Topeka

Many African American children attended overcrowded, segregated public schools miles from their homes. White children often walked to schools that were larger, newer, and better equipped. Schools for African American students were clearly separate, but they were usually far from equal to those of white students. The National Association for the Advancement of Colored People, or NAACP, led the fight against segregated schools.

In 1952, the NAACP began to present its case to the Supreme Court. In Topeka, Kansas, the parents of an African American third-grade student named Linda Brown wanted her to attend a neighborhood school. However, the school was for white students only, and Linda was not allowed to attend.

A lawyer named Thurgood Marshall represented the Brown family before the Supreme Court. He argued that segregation in the schools was unconstitutional and damaging to African American students. On May 17, 1954, the Supreme Court agreed. The Court issued a unanimous decision stating that separate schools were unequal and that schools should move to desegregate, or end segregation, with all "deliberate speed."

Trouble in Little Rock

The Supreme Court had spoken, but President Eisenhower did little to enforce the Supreme Court's ruling until a crisis occurred in 1957. This crisis was brought about by the attempt of nine African American students to enroll in a high school in Little Rock, Arkansas.

The governor of Arkansas, a strong segregationist, ordered the state national guard to block the students from entering the school. White students and adults hurled insults and threats at the nine African American students. Television viewers across the country saw the threatening crowds and the terrified students.

Like many other Americans, President Eisenhower was disturbed by the events in Little Rock. He also believed that the governor of Arkansas was defying the federal government. Finally, Eisenhower sent federal troops to protect the African American students and enforce desegregation.

Do You Remember?

In Chapter 21, you read about *Plessy v. Ferguson.* This 1896 Supreme Court decision ruled that segregation was constitutional.

African American students walked to class at Little Rock Central High School in 1957 while being heckled by a white crowd.

Bus Boycott in Montgomery

Many civil rights leaders felt that nonviolent protests were needed to advance civil rights. In December 1955, an African American woman named Rosa Parks was asked by a bus driver in Montgomery, Alabama, to give up her seat to a white man. She refused, was removed from the bus, and was promptly arrested.

In response, the local African American community organized a boycott of city buses. African Americans in Montgomery began walking or carpooling to work. A young Montgomery minister named Dr. Martin Luther King Jr. was asked to help with the boycott.

The boycott lasted over one year. Some white people turned to violence against the protesters. A bomb exploded on King's front porch. However, the attacks did not change King's belief that nonviolence was the best way to fight injustice. In November 1956, the Supreme Court ruled that segregation on Alabama buses was unconstitutional. King and his followers founded the Southern Christian Leadership Conference (SCLC) in 1957. It was dedicated to gaining full equality for African Americans.

★ **What did the Supreme Court rule in _Brown_ v. _Board of Education of Topeka_?**

They Made History

Rosa Parks Born 1913

Rosa Parks worked as a seamstress at a Montgomery department store in 1955. At that time, buses in many southern cities were segregated by law. White people sat in front. African Americans sat in the back. By refusing to give up her seat near the front of a bus to a white man, Parks became a symbol of the civil rights movement. She lost her job, and suffered harassment by angry white Southerners. Her actions began a year-long boycott that would ultimately win the right for African Americans to sit in any seat on the bus.

Years later, Parks toured the country frequently, giving lectures on civil rights. In 1999, Congress awarded her the Congressional Gold Medal of Honor for bravery in the face of discrimination.

Rosa Parks was arrested for refusing to give up her seat on a bus to a white man.

Critical Thinking In what way was Parks a symbol of the civil rights movement?

C. Foreign Affairs Under Eisenhower

The Korean War ended in 1953. However, the Cold War continued, and Americans continued to worry about the spread of communism. Still, President Eisenhower hoped to ease tensions with the Soviet Union. After Joseph Stalin's death, the new Soviet leader Nikita Khrushchev expressed a similar hope.

The Arms Race

Eisenhower's Secretary of State, John Foster Dulles, feared the Soviets. He argued for a tougher response to communism. He urged people in satellite nations to revolt against their Communist rulers.

Dulles's urging, along with the fear Americans and Soviets felt about each other, led to an arms race. Each side developed more powerful weapons. During the Eisenhower administration, more funding was spent on the development of nuclear weapons than on other kinds of weaponry. The new technology included satellites and rockets as well as huge missiles and deadly submarines that could carry nuclear, or atomic, weapons to enemies around the world. Americans hoped that the ability to strike the Soviet Union with nuclear weapons would protect them from any possible Soviet aggression in the future.

At the same time, however, Eisenhower wanted to create a test-ban treaty to stop the testing of nuclear weapons. Many Americans hoped it would also lead to the elimination of such terrible weapons. However, efforts to write a treaty were unsuccessful.

The U-2 Incident

Late in his presidency, Eisenhower planned to meet with Soviet leader Nikita Khrushchev in Paris. Meetings between important heads of state are called **summit meetings**. Both sides hoped that talking about issues would lessen the tensions between the two countries.

Just before the summit was scheduled to start, the Soviets shot down a U.S. U-2 spy plane. At first, the United States claimed that the plane was on a weather mission. The pilot, Gary Francis Powers, was actually taking photographs over Soviet territory. After he was captured, the pilot confessed to spying. Unknown to most Americans, U.S. spy planes had been photographing Soviet military sites since 1956. The Soviets were furious and boycotted the summit meeting. Hopes for improved relations were crushed.

Then & Now

In 1960, Soviets shot down a U-2 spy plane and captured the pilot, Francis Gary Powers. The incident caused Soviet leader Nikita Khrushchev to boycott the Paris summit meeting.

In 2001, an American spy plane and a Chinese F-8 fighter plane collided in the air near China. The Chinese plane and pilot were lost. The Chinese held twenty-four Americans captive for almost two weeks.

Created in 1947 by President Truman, the CIA is one of the chief sources of foreign intelligence to the United States.

Continuing Tensions in Developing Nations

A government organization, the Central Intelligence Agency, or CIA, worked to help foreign nations resist Communist takeover. The CIA was active in Iran, Guatemala, Indonesia, and other countries.

The CIA also helped the United States keep watch on emerging nations in Africa and Asia. Following the end of World War II, nationalism increased in these areas. People wanted to be free from colonial rule and form their own independent nations. Starting with Ghana in 1957, more than 30 African nations would become independent by 1970.

The same trend was followed in Asia, where many countries broke free from their colonial pasts. One Southeast Asian country, Vietnam, fought for and gained its independence from France. In 1954, Vietnam was divided into a northern part and a southern part. The northern part was controlled by Communists, led by Ho Chi Minh. When the French left South Vietnam, Eisenhower sent military advisors to help the South Vietnamese fight communism. This action was the beginning of U.S. involvement in Vietnam.

 In what ways did the Cold War intensify during Eisenhower's administration?

III Review

Review History

A. What were some achievements of the Eisenhower administration?

B. What were two important events in the fight for civil rights?

C. What was the arms race?

Define Terms to Know

Provide a definition for each of the following terms.
space race, summit meeting

Critical Thinking

Could the United States and the Soviet Union have avoided the arms race that began in the 1950s? Why or why not?

Write About Government

You are a TV reporter covering the Supreme Court's decision in the *Brown* v. *Board of Education of Topeka* case. Write a script for a TV report covering the decision.

Get Organized

SPIDER DIAGRAM

A spider diagram can help you organize supporting details. Use a spider diagram to describe the civil rights movement following World War II.

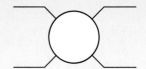

CONNECT
History & Medicine

Jonas Salk and the Polio Vaccine

The 1950s was a time of many great advances in the field of medicine. Perhaps the one that had the widest impact was the vaccine against poliomyelitis, or polio. This dreaded disease had caused the paralysis or death of millions of people. One of the most famous victims was Franklin D. Roosevelt, whose legs were permanently paralyzed.

THE DISEASE Polio, also called infantile paralysis, is caused by a virus. The virus is thought to enter the body through the throat. It then enters the blood stream and is carried to different parts of the body. Four out of five people who contract the disease suffer only mild symptoms, such as fever, sore throat, and headache. Most recover within a few days.

However, in some victims, the virus destroys the nerves in the spinal cord. When this happens, people may lose the use of their arms and legs. Sometimes, the disease destroys the nerves and muscles that control breathing. In 1950, more than 33,000 cases of polio were reported in the United States alone. Many victims became paralyzed.

THE VACCINE Some diseases that are caused by viruses can be prevented by the use of a vaccine. Vaccines are dead or weakened forms of the virus. In 1954, Dr. Jonas Salk and his team successfully tested a polio vaccine. Another vaccine was developed by Albert Sabin in 1959. Vaccines quickly came into wide use, and the feared disease of polio was brought under control.

Critical Thinking
Answer the questions below. Then, complete the activity.

1. How would advances in medicine, such as the polio vaccine, affect society?

2. Which disease do you think presents the greatest challenge to today's doctors and health experts? Why?

Write About It
Examine Jonas Salk's research on the polio virus, as well as his other achievements. Then, write a short biography of Salk and share it with the class. You can learn more about Salk at: www.gfamericanhistory.com.

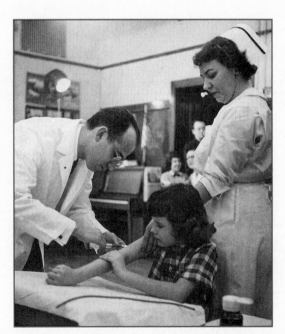

Jonas Salk's discovery of a polio vaccine wiped out the disease in the United States.

IV Life in the Fifties

Terms to Know

suburb a community at the edge of a city

baby boom the increase in the birthrate after World War II

generation gap a difference in tastes and values between young people and their parents

Main Ideas

A. In the 1950s, many Americans moved to communities outside of cities.

B. Television became a powerful influence on Americans, and rock-and-roll music attracted young people.

 **Active Reading**

COMPARE AND CONTRAST When you compare and contrast, use critical thinking skills to find differences and similarities. As you read this section, relate the way some people rejected U.S. society in the 1950s to the way some people reject it today.

A. Lifestyle Changes

During the 1950s, several important changes to American lifestyles, or patterns of living, occurred. One of the most important was that many families moved to **suburbs**, which are communities located just outside of cities.

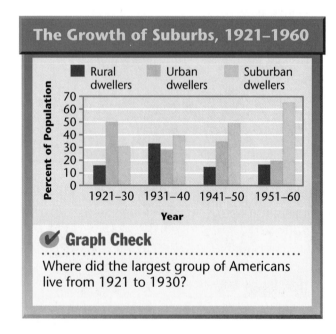

The Growth of Suburbs, 1921–1960

Rural dwellers | Urban dwellers | Suburban dwellers

Percent of Population

70 60 50 40 30 20 10 0

1921–30   1931–40   1941–50   1951–60

Year

✔ **Graph Check**

Where did the largest group of Americans live from 1921 to 1930?

Growth of the Suburbs

At the end of World War II, the U.S. population began to grow rapidly. Married couples felt that the hard times of the 1930s and 1940s were over. They were confident enough to start families. This large increase in the population became known as the **baby boom**. It lasted from 1946 to 1964.

Many young couples during this period also wanted to own their own homes. To meet this demand, homebuilders created new suburbs on the outskirts of most American cities.

The first planned community was developed by William Levitt on Long Island, New York, and was named Levittown. Many developers followed Levitt's example and created communities of affordable homes that were built quickly in an assembly-line method.

By 1960, one third of the U.S. population lived in suburbs. This shift in the population meant big business for many people. New shopping centers, schools, office buildings, roads, and hospitals sprang up. Cars quickly choked the new roads as people living in the suburbs began to drive longer distances to work.

To build houses quickly, one or two designs were used for all the houses. As a result, many communities included homes that looked almost exactly alike.

Women in the Workforce

During World War II, women had entered the workforce in record numbers. However, when the war was over, men returned to their jobs, and many women had to return to working at home. They were under pressure from business and government to leave their jobs. Although some women preferred to work at home, one survey reported that 75 percent wished to keep their jobs outside the home. After the war, many women continued to hold part-time jobs.

As the decade continued, more and more women went back into the workforce. By the end of the 1950s, women held one third of all jobs. However, their career choices were very limited, and they were still paid less, on average, than men. In fact, women earned only about 60 percent as much as men in 1960.

 Why did many Americans move to the suburbs in the 1950s?

B. Culture in the 1950s

During the 1950s, American culture reflected the desire for a comfortable life after years of struggle. New forms of popular culture, such as television and rock-and-roll music, shaped the decade of the 1950s.

The Influence of Television

Television had a great impact on American society in the 1950s. Families spent less time in the evening reading, listening to the radio, or talking about the day's events. Instead, they gathered around the screens to watch the black-and-white images. Newscasts, sports events, situation comedies, and dramatic programs captured the attention of people across the country. In 1955, the average American family watched television four to five hours a day.

Television began to influence families in the 1950s.

Children grew up on programs like *The Mickey Mouse Club* and *Howdy Doody Time*. Some watched situation comedies such as *I Love Lucy* and *Leave it to Beaver*.

To many people in the 1950s, the good life they wanted was represented on television. Advertisers used this idea to sell their products to all members of the family. Viewers wanted what they saw on TV, and many had the money to buy it.

Advertisers found new markets among teenagers. Young people who grew up in the 1950s are often called the first "TV generation." Many product advertisements were directed at teens—from soft drinks to clothing to films.

The Youth Culture

Another powerful influence on young people of the 1950s was popular music. A new kind of music, rhythm and blues, jazz, country, and other styles, began to fill the nation's radio airwaves. Soon, it came to be known as rock-and-roll.

Chuck Berry, Little Richard, and other African Americans had the first rock-and-roll hit songs. Then, a truck driver from Mississippi named Elvis Presley became a major national rock-and-roll star. Many other rock stars followed.

Many adults found the music hard to understand and appreciate. However, its messages spoke to millions of American teens in the mid-1950s. A difference in clothing, attitude, and values also separated the younger generation from the older generation. This difference between teens and their parents became known as the **generation gap.**

African American Achievements

After World War II, the works of African American artists, writers, and musicians gained national recognition. Jazz music became popular nationwide. African American actors were now recognized for their important roles in movies. Sidney Poitier was the first African American to win the Best Actor award at the Academy Awards (Oscars) 1963.

One of the best known achievements by African Americans in the years following World War II came in sports. At that time, African Americans were not allowed to play baseball in the Major Leagues. In 1947, Branch Rickey, president of the Brooklyn Dodgers, broke this racial barrier by signing a player named Jackie Robinson to a contract. Robinson had been a star athlete in college and in the Negro National League, the African American baseball league.

Robinson faced taunts by baseball fans and was ignored by his fellow players during his first few months. Soon, however, his talent won him large numbers of white and African American fans. In his first season, Robinson was named Rookie of the Year. More important, he paved the way for players of all backgrounds to compete in professional sports.

 What contribution did Jackie Robinson make toward equality in the United States?

IV Review

Review History
A. How did many Americans change their ways of living in the 1950s?
B. What is one way television influenced Americans?

Define Terms to Know
Provide a definition for each of the following terms.
suburb, baby boom, generation gap

Critical Thinking
How do you think the large population of children born during the baby boom affected education?

Write About Culture
Baseball is often considered the national pastime. Write an essay explaining why Jackie Robinson's accomplishments were important.

Get Organized
SPIDER DIAGRAM
A spider diagram can help you organize supporting details. Use a spider diagram to describe suburbs in the 1950s.

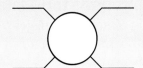

Chapter Summary

In your notebook, complete the following outline. Then, use your outline to write a brief summary of the chapter.

The Cold War

I. The Cold War Begins

    A. A Plan for Peace

    B.

    C.

II. The Korean War and the Red Scare

    A.

    B.

    C.

III. The Changing Nation

    A.

    B.

    C.

IV. Life in the Fifties

    A.

    B.

Interpret the Timeline

Use the timeline on pages 632–633 to answer the following questions.

1. Which U.S. events led to increased rights for African Americans?

2. **Critical Thinking** Which world events raised tensions during the Cold War?

Use Terms to Know

Match each term with the correct definition.

a. baby boom c. space race e. superpower
b. Cold War   d. suburb

1. one of the most powerful nations

2. a conflict between countries without actual fighting

3. a community at the edge of a city

4. the competition among countries to be the first in exploring space

5. the increase in the birthrate after World War II

Check Your Understanding

1. **Summarize** the Truman Doctrine.

2. **Discuss** the ways in which the United States responded to the growth of communism in Europe.

3. **Identify** the nations that were involved in the Korean War.

4. **Describe** how Senator Joseph McCarthy increased fears of communism.

5. **Explain** the importance of the Supreme Court's decision in *Brown* v. *Board of Education of Topeka*.

6. **Describe** how the U-2 incident increased Cold War tensions.

7. **Identify** two ways in which the baby boom affected life in the 1950s.

8. **Discuss** the influence of television on American culture in the 1950s.

Critical Thinking

1. **Analyze** In what ways did the formation of NATO both unite and divide the nations of Europe?

2. **Analyze Primary Sources** Why was Senator McCarthy's statement on page 643 alarming to Americans?

3. **Make Inferences** President Truman worried that attacking China during the Korean War would bring the Soviet Union into the war. Why was the Soviet Union likely to support China at that time?

4. **Recognize Relationships** Do you believe that peaceful protests, such as the Montgomery bus boycott, can bring about changes in the way people feel about important issues? Explain your answer.

Put Your Skills to Work
READ A TIME-ZONE MAP

You have learned that the world is divided into 24 time zones, one for each hour of the day. Using the map on page 639, answer the question below.

The Marshall Plan delivered billions of dollars of goods to Europe following the end of World War II. A plane leaves Washington, D.C. at noon to deliver supplies to Greenwich, England. The flight takes 8 hours. What time will it be in Greenwich when the plane lands?

In Your Own Words
JOURNAL WRITING

During the Red Scare, many people who were not Communists were accused unjustly. Write a journal entry about a time when you were blamed for something you did not do. How did you feel? How was the situation resolved?

Net Work
INTERNET ACTIVITY

Many of the early pioneers of rock-and-roll have been elected to the Rock-and-Roll Hall of Fame in Cleveland, Ohio. Work with a partner to prepare a short multimedia biography of one early rock-and-roll star. You may want to include text, photos, music selections, or videos. Share your biography with the class.

For help in starting this activity, visit the following Web site: www.gfamericanhistory.com.

Look Ahead
In the next chapter, learn how a dynamic young President energized the country.

CHAPTER 28

The Kennedy Years 1961–1963

I. The Communist Threat
II. The New Frontier
III. The Civil Rights Movement

During the 1960s, African Americans across the South raised their voices. They demanded justice, equal rights, and an end to segregation. One of the most bitter demonstrations occurred in Birmingham, Alabama. There, in the spring of 1963, Dr. Martin Luther King Jr. led thousands of people, many of them children, on a march. One of the children who took part in the demonstration described it the following way:

Some of the times we marched, some people would be out there and they would throw rocks and cans and different things at us. I was afraid of getting hurt, but still I was willing to march on to have justice done.

Equal rights for all Americans was just one of the challenges facing the United States as a new President took office in 1961. Many wondered whether John Fitzgerald Kennedy could lead the nation through difficult times.

Civil rights poster

U.S. Events	1961		1962

May 1961
Freedom Riders travel through the South.

April 1961
Bay of Pigs invasion fails.

February 1962
John Glenn becomes the first American to orbit Earth.

Presidential Term Begins — 1961 John F. Kennedy

World Events	1961		1962

April 1961
Russian cosmonaut Yuri Gagarin becomes the first human in space.

August 1961
Construction of the Berlin Wall in Germany begins.

August 1962
African National Congress leader Nelson Mandela is imprisoned.

VIEW HISTORY Martin Luther King Jr. was a leader in the 1963 March on Washington to protest the lack of civil rights for African Americans. Civil rights supporters often carried signs such as this one (left) at demonstrations.

★ What do these pictures tell you about the rights that people in the civil rights movement wanted?

Get Organized

FACT/CONSEQUENCE CHART

When you read about history, you learn that the facts often lead to consequences, or outcomes. Use this chart to determine a consequence that results from connected facts. Write two related facts in the top two boxes and a consequence in the bottom box. Here is an example from this chapter.

FACT

East Germans did not want to live under communism.

FACT

Millions of people fled from East Berlin to West Berlin.

The Soviets built a wall to prevent escape.

CONSEQUENCE

September 1962
James Meredith enrolls at the University of Mississippi.

October 1962
Cuban Missile Crisis occurs.

April 1963
Martin Luther King Jr. is arrested during a civil rights demonstration in Birmingham, Alabama.

August 1963
March on Washington is held.

November 1963
John F. Kennedy is assassinated.
Lyndon B. Johnson becomes President.

1963

1963 Lyndon B. Johnson

1964

1963

August 1963
Limited Test Ban Treaty is signed.

1964

November 1963
South Vietnamese leader Ngo Dinh Diem is assassinated.

I ★ The Communist Threat

Terms to Know

exile a person who is forced to live away from his or her home country

guerrilla war fighting involving surprise raids

quarantine to isolate

Main Ideas

A. John F. Kennedy won the 1960 presidential election, the first one in which television played an important role.

B. Kennedy continued most of Eisenhower's Cold War policies of dealing with the Soviets.

C. The Cuban Missile Crisis brought the world to the brink of nuclear war.

Active Reading

SEQUENCE OF EVENTS
The sequence of events is the order in which events occur. As you read this section, make a timeline of the important events, starting with the presidential election of 1960.

A. The Election of 1960

As the election of 1960 drew nearer, Americans seemed to be in a mood for a change. Two men challenged each other for the presidency. One was Republican Richard Milhous Nixon, Eisenhower's Vice President. The other was a young senator from Massachusetts, Democrat John Fitzgerald Kennedy.

Debating the Issues

John Kennedy came from a powerful Irish American family from Boston, Massachusetts. During World War II, Kennedy became a war hero when he helped his crew to safety after his navy torpedo boat was attacked and sunk by a Japanese destroyer. He received the Purple Heart for his injuries and the Navy and Marine Corps Medal for his daring actions. Kennedy appealed to many people because he was young and energetic. He promised a bright future for the United States.

The Democrats called for civil rights laws, healthcare for elderly Americans, funds for education, and help for poor people. Republican candidate Nixon stressed his government experience and opposition to communism.

For the first time ever, the two candidates debated on national television. To millions of viewers, Kennedy looked fit and self-confident. Nixon, who was recovering from an illness, looked tired and uncomfortable. Voters' impressions of the candidates had an effect on the election results.

The first presidential debate on television occurred between candidates Nixon and Kennedy in 1960.

The Election Results

During much of the campaign, Nixon was ahead of Kennedy according to surveys and questionnaires, called polls. One reason for Nixon's lead was that Kennedy was young—only 43 years old. Also, he was a Roman Catholic. No Catholic had ever been elected President. Some Americans were worried that as President he might be influenced by the Pope and the Catholic Church. Kennedy assured voters that he would uphold the Constitution as the nation's highest authority and represent all the people of the United States.

After a total of four televised debates, the polls swung in Kennedy's favor. In one of the closest elections in U.S. history, John F. Kennedy and his running mate, Lyndon Baines Johnson, defeated the Republicans. Kennedy received 49.9 percent of the votes. Vice President Nixon received 49.7 percent.

At his inauguration in January 1961, President Kennedy gave a speech in which he offered hope to the nation. He ended the speech by saying,

> In the long history of the world, only a few generations have been granted the role of defending freedom in its hour of maximum danger. . . . The energy, the faith, the devotion which we bring to this endeavor will light our country and all who serve it—and the glow from that fire can truly light the world. And so, my fellow Americans, ask not what your country can do for you—ask what you can do for your country.

★ **How did televised debates affect the presidential election of 1960?**

B. The Cold War Heats Up

Foreign policy was President Kennedy's top priority. He warned other countries that he would do anything to guarantee the "survival and success of liberty."

The Bay of Pigs Invasion

One foreign policy challenge involved Cuba. In 1959, Fidel Castro took power in Cuba. He asked for military and economic aid from the Soviet Union. Americans felt threatened because Cuba was located only 90 miles south of Florida. Tensions grew as Castro placed private businesses, including many U.S. companies in Cuba, under government control. The United States responded by cutting off all diplomatic relations with Cuba.

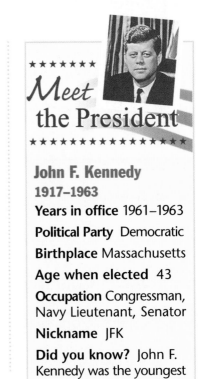

★★★★★★★
Meet **the President**
★★★★★★★★★★★★★★

John F. Kennedy
1917–1963

Years in office 1961–1963

Political Party Democratic

Birthplace Massachusetts

Age when elected 43

Occupation Congressman, Navy Lieutenant, Senator

Nickname JFK

Did you know? John F. Kennedy was the youngest President ever elected.

ANALYZE PRIMARY SOURCES
DOCUMENT-BASED QUESTION What dangers might Kennedy have meant when he spoke of the "maximum danger"?

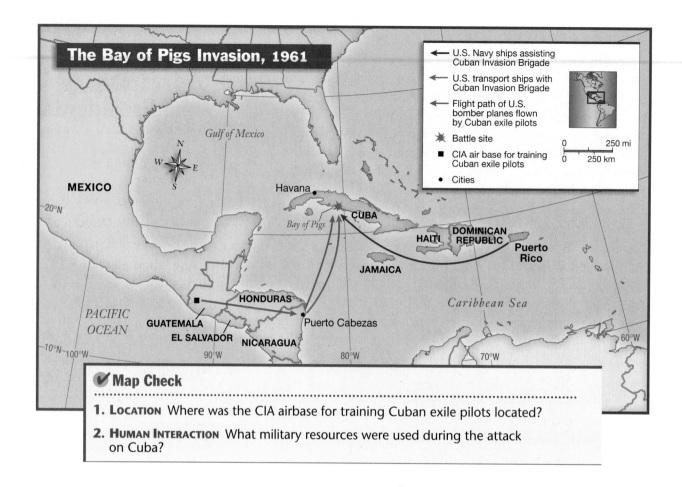

The Bay of Pigs Invasion, 1961

← U.S. Navy ships assisting Cuban Invasion Brigade

← U.S. transport ships with Cuban Invasion Brigade

← Flight path of U.S. bomber planes flown by Cuban exile pilots

✳ Battle site

■ CIA air base for training Cuban exile pilots

• Cities

0   250 mi
0   250 km

MEXICO

Gulf of Mexico

Havana

CUBA

Bay of Pigs

HAITI DOMINICAN REPUBLIC

Puerto Rico

JAMAICA

PACIFIC OCEAN

HONDURAS

GUATEMALA

EL SALVADOR NICARAGUA

Puerto Cabezas

Caribbean Sea

20°N   10°N   100°W   90°W   80°W   70°W   60°W

✔ Map Check

1. **LOCATION** Where was the CIA airbase for training Cuban exile pilots located?

2. **HUMAN INTERACTION** What military resources were used during the attack on Cuba?

During Eisenhower's last year in office, a group of Cuban **exiles**, people who had been forced to leave their country, began training in Guatemala. The American Central Intelligence Agency, or CIA, helped them prepare to invade Cuba and overthrow Castro.

After Kennedy became President, he allowed the plan to go forward. On April 17, 1961, about 1,500 Cuban exiles, called the Cuban Invasion Brigade, landed at the Bay of Pigs in Cuba. The Cuban people supported Castro, and the invasion was quickly defeated.

The failed invasion had several effects. Many Americans felt that Kennedy had acted too aggressively. People in Cuba and Latin America saw the invasion as an attempt to overtake a smaller country. Cubans and other Latin Americans lost trust in the United States.

The Berlin Wall

Another early foreign policy challenge to President Kennedy's administration occurred in Berlin, Germany, which was located within Communist East Germany. At the end of World War II, Berlin was divided. West Berlin was supported by the Western nations, whereas East Berlin became the capital of East Germany.

The United States offered West Berlin strong support. Americans believed that the city served as a symbol of freedom behind the iron curtain. However, the escape of almost 3 million Germans from Communist East Berlin shamed Soviet leader Nikita Khrushchev. In 1961, Khrushchev ordered that the escapes be stopped. Workers built a 103-mile long, 12-foot high wall that divided the two parts of the city. The wall, topped with barbed wire and armed guard towers, stopped many of the escapes from East Berlin. However, it was a symbol of the failure of communism to provide a decent life for its people.

Containing Communism

Competition between the United States and the Soviet Union continued. Like Presidents Truman and Eisenhower, Kennedy believed in containing communism. Southeast Asia proved to be a major test.

In Vietnam, a civil war was flaring. A communist leader from North Vietnam, Ho Chi Minh, was leading a **guerrilla war** against U.S.-supported troops from South Vietnam. In guerrilla war, small bands of fighters make surprise attacks. Kennedy continued supporting South Vietnam by sending more economic aid and military advisors. By the end of 1963, more than 16,000 U.S. military personnel had been sent to South Vietnam.

★ **Where did the United States confront communism?**

C. The Cuban Missile Crisis

After the failed Bay of Pigs invasion, many Cubans felt threatened by the United States. Cuba began to receive military aid and support from the Soviet Union.

A Shocking Discovery

In the summer of 1962, the Soviet Union secretly sent 60 guided missiles and their nuclear warheads to Cuba. President Kennedy ordered U-2 spy planes to find out what was happening in Cuba. He was shocked to learn that the Soviet Union had installed nuclear missiles that could destroy much of the U.S. east coast.

For six tense days, the President and his advisors discussed what to do. One choice was an immediate air attack on Cuba, which might lead to war. Instead, the President decided to **quarantine**, or cut off, Cuba. U.S. warships created a blockade to prevent the delivery of any more missiles to Cuba. Kennedy also demanded that the Soviet Union remove the missiles already there.

A construction worker helps to build the Berlin Wall in 1961. The wall divided East and West Berlin.

Do You Remember?
In Chapter 27, you learned that the Soviet Union shot down a U-2 spy plane in 1960. The pilot, Francis Gary Powers, confessed to spying. The event led Soviet leader Nikita Khrushchev to boycott a summit meeting with President Dwight Eisenhower.

"Eyeball to Eyeball"

Soviet ships were on their way to Cuba. The world was on the brink of nuclear war. Then, on October 24, 1962, the Soviet ships turned around. Secretary of State Dean Rusk described the standoff:

 We were eyeball to eyeball, and I think the other fellow just blinked. "

Several days later, Khrushchev agreed to withdraw the Soviet missiles from Cuba and to stop construction of missile sites there. In return, the United States promised not to invade Cuba and to remove its own missiles from Turkey, on the Soviet Union's southern border.

The near-disaster led Kennedy and Khrushchev to take steps to ease tensions. In 1963, the United States, Great Britain, and the Soviet Union signed the Limited Test Ban Treaty, which banned aboveground and underwater testing of nuclear weapons. The treaty did not prohibit underground testing. The United States and the Soviet Union also set up an emergency telephone system. If another crisis occurred, the two leaders could speak directly with each other. The war of words between the United States and the Soviet Union slowed down, but the Cold War continued.

★ **What discovery set off the Cuban Missile Crisis in 1962?**

ANALYZE PRIMARY SOURCES

DOCUMENT-BASED QUESTION
What did Secretary of State Rusk mean by this statement?

Review

Review History
A. How did the 1960 election differ from earlier elections?
B. Why did the Soviet Union order the building of the Berlin Wall?
C. What did Khrushchev and Kennedy agree to do to settle the Cuban Missile Crisis?

Define Terms to Know
Provide a definition for each of the following terms.
exile, guerrilla war, quarantine

Critical Thinking
Did President Kennedy and his advisors make the right decision during the Cuban Missile Crisis? Why or why not?

Write About History
Write a paragraph describing how you might have felt if you had lived during the Cuban Missile Crisis.

Get Organized
FACT/CONSEQUENCE CHART
In the top two boxes, write two facts about the Cuban Missile Crisis. In the bottom box, write a consequence that resulted from them.

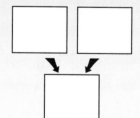

Build Your Skills

Social Studies Skill

ANALYZE PUBLIC OPINION POLLS

Political parties and other organizations often poll people with surveys or questionnaires. Parties want to find out how people feel about their candidates or about party positions on certain issues. A poll is given to a relatively small group of people, called a sample, as representative of the entire country. Analysts then use the answers to conclude what the U.S. population feels or thinks.

Public opinion polls can help you discover the mood of the country during periods in the past. For example, you might want to know how Americans felt about the Bay of Pigs invasion. To find out, you could research public opinion polls taken at the time.

Here's How
Follow these steps to analyze and understand public opinion polls.

1. Identify the kind of information presented in the poll.

2. Find out how many people took part in the poll. If the number is too small, the results may not be accurate.

3. Analyze the poll results. What conclusions can you make? Compare the results to other information on the issue.

Here's Why
You have just read about a close presidential election. Knowing how to analyze a poll can help you understand how people feel about particular issues in politics today.

Practice the Skill
Look at the chart on this page. Identify what information the chart shows. Draw a conclusion based on this information.

Extend the Skill
Make a similar chart for a female or an African American presidential candidate. You can find information from public opinion polls at the library or on the Internet.

Apply the Skill
As you read the remaining sections of this chapter, think about other questions that might be asked in a public opinion poll. For example, after reading Section II, you might ask about people's attitudes toward space exploration.

Would you vote for a Roman Catholic presidential candidate?	Yes	No	No Opinion
February 1999	94%	4%	2%
April–May 1983	92	5	3
July 1978	91	4	5
July 1965	87	10	3
August 1961	82	13	5
July–August 1958	69	24	7
February 1937	60	30	10

II ★ The New Frontier

A. Kennedy's Plan for the Future

President Kennedy proposed many new programs during his administration. He called his plan the **New Frontier**. He stressed his vision for the future in his inaugural address, delivered on January 20, 1961, when he said,

> 66 Let the word go forth from this time and place, to friend and foe alike, that the torch has been passed to a new generation of Americans. 99

ANALYZE PRIMARY SOURCES

DOCUMENT-BASED QUESTION
What did Kennedy mean when he said the torch had been passed?

Beginning the New Frontier

Kennedy gathered around him a group of talented advisors—"the best and brightest" people. His advisors helped him make policy and create programs. This group included his younger brother Robert (Bobby) Kennedy, who became the Attorney General of the United States.

Although President Kennedy and his group of advisors were popular among the American public, many members of Congress opposed Kennedy's programs. Some conservative southern Democrats and most Republicans voted against Kennedy's plans for national health insurance and federal aid for education. They did not want the federal government to become further involved in these issues. They believed these issues should be left to the states.

Kennedy did manage to raise the minimum wage, increase social security benefits, provide aid for cities, and create programs for worker training. In addition, Congress passed antipollution laws and increased defense spending.

The Supreme Court in the Kennedy Years

During the Kennedy administration, the Supreme Court made several important decisions that expanded the rights of individuals. In one case, *Engel* v. *Vitale*, the Court ruled that school officials could not force students to say a prayer. The Court ruled that prayer in schools went against the Constitution's freedom of religion.

Another important case was *Gideon* v. *Wainwright*. The justices decided that any person accused of serious crimes had the right to a lawyer. If the person could not afford a lawyer, the government would pay for one.

A third case, *Baker* v. *Carr*, changed the way states arrange legislative districts. The Court ruled that election districts must have almost equal populations so that each person's vote would have equal importance. This case established the idea of one person, one vote.

Working With Other Nations

Another important part of the New Frontier looked beyond the borders of the United States to grant economic aid to developing nations around the world. In addition to helping these nations, Kennedy also believed that through this aid he could prevent the spread of communism.

President Kennedy proposed sending volunteers to developing countries to build hospitals, roads, schools, and other structures. The volunteers would also teach in schools and share improved farming methods. This idea was carried out through the **Peace Corps**.

Then & Now

President Kennedy thought of Peace Corps volunteers as people who were willing to respond to his ideal of serving the country by helping abroad. In 1961, the first six volunteers worked in six countries. Today, there are more than 7,000 volunteers in 135 countries.

Peace Corps volunteers work to improve living conditions in other countries.

The President explained the value of the Peace Corps as "winning friends and helping people . . . supplying trained and dedicated young men and women, to give these new nations a hand in building a society."

The Peace Corps was one of Kennedy's most successful programs. It helped other countries improve living conditions while fighting the spread of communism. It also helped the foreign relations of the United States by encouraging cooperation between the United States and other countries.

Kennedy also established the Alliance for Progress. This program provided economic aid, assistance in fighting communism, support for health and education, and other assistance to Latin American countries.

★ What was one effect of the Peace Corps?

B. The Space Program

A third part of the New Frontier looked even farther beyond the nation's borders than the Peace Corps did. It was a frontier that had never been explored before and was indeed "new." This frontier was outer space.

The United States developed spacecraft, like *Friendship 7*, to orbit Earth and explore outer space.

ANALYZE PRIMARY SOURCES DOCUMENT-BASED QUESTION How would this proposal motivate Congress to grant more money to the space program?

A Far-Reaching Goal

Back in 1958, Congress had appropriated money to begin the Mercury space program. However, President Kennedy wanted more money for the National Aeronautics and Space Administration, or NASA. He explained his goal to Congress:

❝ I believe that this nation should commit itself to achieving the goal, before this decade is out, of landing a man on the moon and returning him safely to the earth. ❞

Many Americans shared the President's dream of exploring outer space. Like the President, they were worried that the Soviet Union had pushed ahead in the space race. In 1957, it had launched *Sputnik*, the first manufactured satellite in space. Both the United States and the Soviet Union felt that winning the space race would increase their power and win allies. In April 1961, a Soviet cosmonaut, Yuri Gagarin, became the first person to orbit, or travel around, Earth.

In May 1961, President Kennedy announced the Apollo program, promising that the United States would put an American on the moon before 1970.

Putting an American on the moon would cost a huge amount of money—$20 to $40 billion over the next 10 years. Many scientists debated the scientific value of putting a person on the moon, and many citizens pointed to the need for greater spending on public education and social programs. However, government funding began for a U.S. space program, and Kennedy's dream was one step closer to becoming a reality.

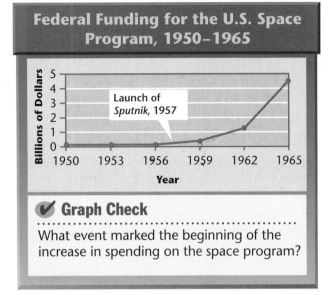

Federal Funding for the U.S. Space Program, 1950–1965

Launch of *Sputnik*, 1957

✔ Graph Check

What event marked the beginning of the increase in spending on the space program?

Orbiting Earth

Nine months later, the United States recognized a new hero. In February 1962, an astronaut named John Glenn became the first American to orbit Earth. His space capsule, the *Friendship* 7, traveled 76,000 miles in less than 5 hours. Glenn's journey in space was the first step by the United States toward reaching the moon.

 What was President Kennedy's goal in funding the space program?

II Review

Review History
A. How did the Supreme Court expand the rights of individuals?
B. How did competition with the Soviet Union affect the U.S. space program?

Define Terms to Know
Provide a definition for each of the following terms.
New Frontier, Peace Corps

Critical Thinking
How did Kennedy's programs relate to his theme of new frontiers?

Write About Government
The space race cost billions of dollars. Write a persuasive essay explaining whether you believe space exploration is a wise way to spend government money.

Get Organized
FACT/CONSEQUENCE CHART
Think about President Kennedy's dream of exploring outer space. In the top two boxes, write two facts about the American-Soviet space race. In the bottom box, write a consequence that resulted from them.

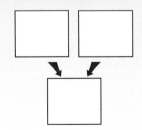

III The Civil Rights Movement

Main Ideas

A. Civil rights protesters demanded equal rights for all Americans.

B. Martin Luther King Jr. led the struggle for civil rights.

C. When President Kennedy was killed in Dallas, Texas, Vice President Lyndon Johnson became President.

 Active Reading

RELATE
When you relate something from history to something in the present, you make comparisons. As you read this section, compare the challenges facing African Americans in the 1960s to challenges some people face today.

Spotlight on
Citizenship

The original four students who quietly sat at the lunch counter to protest segregation were freshmen from North Carolina Agricultural and Technical State University in Greensboro. In the spring of 1960, a conference of students from around the nation formed the Student Nonviolent Coordinating Committee (SNCC). The courage of student protesters inspired other people to become involved in the civil rights movement.

A. The Struggle for Equality

The Montgomery bus boycott of the mid-1950s had shown that nonviolent protests could work. It inspired people to fight other segregation laws. Protests flared in many areas of the South.

Civil Rights Protests

A new kind of nonviolent protest was born in 1960. In most of the South, restaurants and lunch counters were segregated. Many places refused to serve African Americans. In February 1960, four African American students sat at the lunch counter of a local five-and-dime store in Greensboro, North Carolina. When they were refused service, the students remained seated at the counter until the store closed. The next day, an additional 25 students sat with them. These protests, called **sit-ins**, soon attracted crowds of angry people. They insulted the protesters and dumped food on them. However, the protesters remained seated and did not fight back.

Soon, hundreds of sit-ins were taking place at segregated movie theaters, stores, restaurants, libraries, and swimming pools. In all, 70,000 protesters joined the sit-ins. More than 3,500 were arrested. However, by 1961, segregated lunch counters had almost disappeared from many cities.

Out of the sit-in movement arose the Student Nonviolent Coordinating Committee (SNCC), often called "Snick." Founded in 1960, this organization worked to reduce segregation in the South and to register African Americans to vote.

The nonviolent reactions of sit-in protesters sent a powerful message about the injustice of segregated lunch counters.

Another type of protest of the early 1960s was the **Freedom Ride**. These rides were used to break the segregation rules on buses and at bus stations across the South. The Congress of Racial Equality, or CORE, a civil rights group, wanted to make sure that officials upheld a law banning segregation on buses and in bus stations. In May 1961, a group of protesters, both white and African American, boarded two buses in Washington, D.C., that were traveling to New Orleans, Louisiana.

The Freedom Riders met with very little trouble until they reached Alabama. Then, Attorney General Robert Kennedy received this report from a federal official at the scene:

> ❝Now the passengers are coming off. They're standing on a corner of the platform. Oh, there are fists, punching! A bunch of men led by a guy with a bleeding face are beating them. There are no cops. It's terrible. It's terrible! There's not a cop in sight. People are yelling . . . 'Get 'em. Get 'em!' It's awful. ❞

ANALYZE PRIMARY SOURCES
DOCUMENT-BASED QUESTION How would you have felt if you had witnessed this scene yourself?

Upset by the report, Robert Kennedy sent federal marshals to protect the Freedom Riders. The violence shocked many Americans. More people across the country began to support the protesters. Soon after, segregation no longer existed in southern bus and train stations and airports.

James Meredith (right) was stopped from enrolling at the University of Mississippi until federal marshals and troops arrived.

Gaining Ground in Universities

In September 1962, an African American named James Meredith wanted to enter the University of Mississippi. However, the university did not allow African American students. President Kennedy sent federal marshals and troops to make sure Meredith could enroll.

Violence broke out, and two people died. However, the University of Mississippi agreed to enroll Meredith. Federal marshals stayed at the university to protect him until he graduated in 1963.

⭐ **What are some methods that civil rights protesters used to battle segregation?**

B. "I Have a Dream"

Martin Luther King Jr. had become a symbol of resistance to segregation. He led protests and campaigns throughout the South.

Protest in Alabama

In the spring of 1963, King decided to focus on Birmingham, Alabama. He called it the most segregated city in the United States. King felt a victory there would inspire people everywhere to fight against segregation. Demonstrators marched to demand jobs, better housing, and an end to segregation.

Authorities in Birmingham struck back hard at the thousands of marchers, many of them children. The city's police chief, Eugene "Bull" Connor, used fire hoses, clubs, and police dogs—in front of television cameras—to stop the marchers. Connor had promised that "blood would run in the streets" before Birmingham was **integrated**, or open to all racial groups. Hundreds of people were arrested, including Martin Luther King Jr. While in jail, he wrote his famous *Letter from a Birmingham Jail*. You can read a selection of King's *Letter from a Birmingham Jail* on page 675.

Reaching a Settlement in Birmingham

Television showed the cruelty of the police against the unarmed marchers. Americans watched as protesters were sprayed with powerful fire hoses or beaten with clubs. These sights angered many Americans.

Under pressure from the federal government, city leaders in Birmingham agreed to desegregate some public facilities. It was a great victory for the civil rights movement. However, that fall, members of the Ku Klux Klan bombed an African American church in Birmingham. Four young girls were killed.

Martin Luther King Jr. speaks at the March on Washington, D.C., in 1963.

The March on Washington

After their success in Alabama, Martin Luther King Jr. and other civil rights leaders decided to rally in the nation's capital. They would celebrate the one-hundredth anniversary of the Emancipation Proclamation at the Lincoln Memorial.

On August 28, 1963, in front of 250,000 people of all races, King delivered a speech. It is known as the "I Have a Dream" speech. King spoke of his hopes for the country. He wanted the United States to provide true freedom and liberty for all Americans. He said,

> **❝**I have a dream that my four little children will one day live in a nation where they will not be judged by the color of their skin but by the content of their character. **❞**

"Let freedom ring," he said. He hoped that people of all races and religions would "join hands and sing, in the words of the old Negro spiritual, 'Free at last! Free at last!'"

⭐ **What event did the March on Washington celebrate?**

C. The Death of a President

On November 22, 1963, President Kennedy made a trip to Dallas, Texas. He hoped to gain the support of Texans for the 1964 presidential election.

You can read King's "I Have a Dream" speech on page R9.

ANALYZE PRIMARY SOURCES

DOCUMENT-BASED QUESTION
What does Martin Luther King Jr. mean by "the content of their character"?

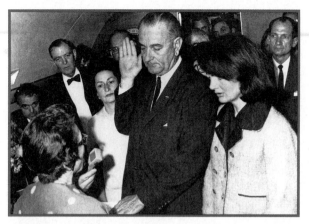

Lyndon B. Johnson is sworn in as President. Jacqueline Kennedy is on Johnson's left, and Johnson's wife, Lady Bird, is on his right.

Shots in Dallas

With his wife Jacqueline, the President rode through Dallas in an open-topped convertible. Suddenly, Kennedy was shot and rushed to a hospital. Attempts to save his life failed. The President was dead. His body was flown back to Washington, D.C. On the plane, Vice President Lyndon Baines Johnson was sworn in as the new President.

Dallas police arrested a suspect, Lee Harvey Oswald. He was charged with shooting the President from a building along the route. The next day, Oswald was killed by a Dallas business owner named Jack Ruby. The President's assassination brought the nation to a standstill. Even those who had opposed Kennedy's policies were shocked and saddened.

The Warren Commission

President Johnson appointed a commission headed by Chief Justice Earl Warren to study the assassination. People wondered if Oswald had acted alone or was part of a larger plan. The Warren Commission determined that Oswald had acted alone. Some people, however, still believed that there had been a plot to kill the President.

 How did Kennedy's assassination affect the country?

III Review

Review History
A. What was the goal of sit-ins and Freedom Rides?
B. How did television affect civil rights protests in Birmingham and other cities?
C. What did the Warren Commission determine?

Define Terms to Know
Provide a definition for each of the following terms.
sit-in, Freedom Ride, integrate

Critical Thinking
Why do you think protesters chose to use nonviolent methods of protest?

Write About Government
You are a newspaper reporter in Dallas on the day that President Kennedy is shot. Write an article describing the event and the nation's reaction. Include an appropriate headline.

Get Organized
FACT/CONSEQUENCE CHART
Think about the events of the civil rights movement described in this section. In the top two boxes, write two facts about one of these events. In the bottom box, write a consequence that resulted from them.

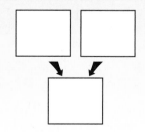

The Early Civil Rights Movement

During the early years of the civil rights movement, many people did not agree on the best way to gain equal rights for all Americans. Some people felt that Martin Luther King Jr.'s demonstrations were rushing the civil rights movement too quickly and causing damage to communities. King and others felt it was important not to wait any longer but to fight for civil rights.

In 1963, King was leading protest marches in Birmingham, Alabama. The selection on the left contains part of a letter written by some religious leaders to the local newspaper. The selection on the right is part of King's reply, *Letter from a Birmingham Jail*.

Martin Luther King Jr. at the time he wrote *Letter from a Birmingham Jail*

> "However, we are now confronted by a series of demonstrations by some of our Negro citizens. . . . But we are convinced that these demonstrations are unwise and untimely. . . . actions as incite to hatred and violence, however . . . peaceful those actions may be, have not contributed to the resolution of our local problems. We do not believe that . . . extreme measures are justified in Birmingham."
>
> —Statement by Alabama clergy, 1963

> "We know through painful experience that freedom is never voluntarily given by the oppressor; it must be demanded by the oppressed. . . . For years now I have heard the word 'Wait!' . . . We have waited for more than 340 years. . . . an individual who breaks a law that . . . is unjust and who willingly accepts the penalty . . . is in reality expressing the highest respect for the law."
>
> —*Letter from a Birmingham Jail*, Martin Luther King Jr., 1963

ANALYZE PRIMARY SOURCES

DOCUMENT-BASED QUESTIONS

1. What charges do the Alabama clergy make against King and the demonstrations?

2. Why does King believe that African Americans cannot wait for equal rights?

3. **Critical Thinking** Do you feel King's reply to the clergy answers their charges and gives a good defense of his actions? Explain your answer.

Chapter Summary

In your notebook, complete the following outline. Then, use your outline to write a brief summary of the chapter.

The Kennedy Years

I. The Communist Threat

   A. The Election of 1960

   B.

   C.

II. The New Frontier

   A.

   B.

III. The Civil Rights Movement

   A.

   B.

   C.

Interpret the Timeline

Use the timeline on pages 658–659 to answer the following questions.

1. Which U.S. events show the growing importance of the civil rights movement?

2. **Critical Thinking** Which events on the timeline reflect the Cold War rivalry between the United States and the Soviet Union?

Use Terms to Know

Select the term that best completes each sentence.

exile   New Frontier   quarantine
guerrilla war   Peace Corps   sit-in

1. A _____ is a protest in which people remain seated and refuse to leave a place.

2. Someone who is forced to live away from his or her home country is an _____.

3. President Kennedy's goals and programs for the future were known as the _____.

4. Kennedy decided to _____ Cuba to prevent more missiles from arriving there.

5. A _____ involves surprise attacks by small bands of fighters.

6. The _____ brought volunteers to other countries to improve living conditions.

Check Your Understanding

1. **Discuss** how television influenced the outcome of the 1960 presidential election.

2. **Identify** conflicts between the United States and the Soviet Union during the early 1960s.

3. **Summarize** the different parts of Kennedy's New Frontier program.

4. **Explain** why the United States committed billions of dollars to space exploration.

5. **Identify** methods used by civil rights protesters to fight against segregation.

6. **Describe** the events surrounding the assassination of President Kennedy in November 1963.

Critical Thinking

1. **Analyze Primary Sources** How did the last line of Kennedy's inaugural speech on page 661 inspire people to work together for the good of the country?

2. **Analyze Primary Sources** President Kennedy outlined a goal for the country regarding the space program. What parts of his statement on page 668 make the goal very specific?

3. **Draw Conclusions** Do you think that Martin Luther King Jr.'s dream that people be judged not "by the color of their skin but by the content of their character" is becoming fulfilled today? Why or why not?

Put Your Skills to Work
ANALYZE PUBLIC OPINION POLLS

You have learned that analyzing public opinion polls can help you understand the thoughts and feelings of people about candidates and issues.

Use the following chart to write several questions for a public opinion poll of your own. Write questions related to an important issue in your school, town, or community. Poll a sample of your classmates to conclude what the whole class might think about the issue. Then, analyze the results.

Question	Yes	No	Not Sure
1. Should our school have a dress code?			
2.			
3.			

In Your Own Words
JOURNAL WRITING

The August 1963 civil rights rally at the Lincoln Memorial in Washington, D.C., had a powerful effect on the 250,000 people who attended and on others across the country. Write a journal entry about a time when you attended an event that had a powerful effect on you.

Net Work
INTERNET ACTIVITY

The Kennedy years included a number of important and dramatic events in the nation's history. Working with a partner, choose one of the events you read about in this chapter. Use the Internet as a resource to create a short "You Are There" presentation. You may want to include photographs and other illustrations, quotations, video or music clips, and other media in your presentation. Share your presentation with the class.

For help in starting this activity, visit the following Web site: www.gfamericanhistory.com.

Look Ahead
In the next chapter, learn how a new President faced the challenges of civil rights issues and a war in Vietnam.

CHAPTER 29
The Johnson Years 1963–1968

I. **The Great Society**
II. **Equal Rights**
III. **Conflict in Vietnam**

After President Kennedy's assassination, Americans hoped that someone would solve the country's problems. President Johnson had a plan for the country. He hoped to improve life for all citizens of the United States. The 1960s, however, turned out to be one of the most troubled decades in U.S. history. War, protests, riots, and assassinations—these events defined the decade. As Craig McNamara, son of the Secretary of Defense, said,

" You know, things were so split in the Sixties. You were either for the Vietnam War or against it, and I was definitely against it. My father knew where I stood, but we didn't discuss it. . . . It just wasn't possible during those years for us to talk about the issues of the war . . . "

President Johnson wanted to fight a war on poverty and on inequality at home. He did not realize how much a faraway war would affect his presidency and the nation.

Vietnam War draft card and dog tag

1964
Race riots erupt in Harlem, in New York City.
Gulf of Tonkin Resolution is passed by Congress.
The 24th Amendment abolishes the poll tax.

1965
Malcolm X is assassinated.

U.S. Events	1963	1964	1965
Presidential Term Begins	1963 Lyndon Baines Johnson		
World Events	1963	1964	1965

1963
The United States, USSR, and Great Britain sign a nuclear testing ban.
Ngo Dinh Diem is assassinated in South Vietnam.

1964
Tokyo hosts the Olympic Games.

1965
Winston Churchill of Great Britain dies.

VIEW HISTORY This photograph shows soldiers waiting in Vietnam while a helicopter delivers supplies. When young men turned 18, they registered for the draft and received draft cards (left). Then, if they became soldiers, they carried dog tags, which identified them.

★ What do the photograph and the images on the left tell you about the lives of young men during the Vietnam War era?

Get Organized

SQR CHART

SQR stands for Survey, Question, and Read. An SQR chart helps you know what to look for as you read. First, survey the material. Look at the headings and visuals. Then, scan the text and write questions you hope to answer as you read. Finally, read and write the answers. Here is an example from this chapter.

SURVEY
Johnson takes office, starts the Great Society programs.

QUESTION
What is the Great Society?

READ
The Great Society is Johnson's goals and programs for the United States.

1966
Black Panther Party is formed.

1967
Kerner Commission begins study of violence in cities.

1968
Martin Luther King Jr. is assassinated.

President Johnson decides not to run for re-election.

1966   **1967**   **1968**

1966   **1967**   **1968**

1966
Indira Gandhi becomes prime minister of India.

1967
Six-Day War between Israel and the Arab nations begins.

1968
Pierre Trudeau becomes prime minister of Canada.

North Vietnam launches the Tet Offensive.

The Great Society

Terms to Know

Great Society President Johnson's goals and programs for the future of the United States

urban renewal a program to rebuild rundown areas of cities

Medicare national health insurance for older Americans and people with certain disabilities

Medicaid public health program that pays medical expenses for low-income people

Main Ideas

A. President Johnson worked to pass Kennedy's tax cuts and civil rights bill.

B. Johnson organized government agencies to fight a war on poverty and to build a Great Society.

C. The federal government worked to protect freedoms and allow more immigrants into the United States.

 Active Reading

PREDICT
When you predict, you make an educated guess about what will happen. As you read this section, use the information provided to predict Johnson's focus in his first years in office.

This cartoon illustrates the policies that Johnson guided through Congress.

A. Working With Congress

After President Kennedy's assassination, Vice President Lyndon Johnson became President of the United States. He worked to calm the nation and to pass some of Kennedy's bills into law.

Continuing Kennedy's Work

Johnson had served in both the House of Representatives and the Senate. He was a master politician. He knew how to work with people, and he had many political connections. Perhaps Johnson's greatest political gift was his ability to persuade people to do things his way. He had the skills to get bills passed.

President Johnson used his experience in politics and his persuasive powers to have President Kennedy's measures passed. He called on Congress to "continue on our course" and to pass civil rights laws. He also worked to get Kennedy's tax cuts passed by giving Kennedy's name to the tax cut bill and guiding it through Congress. He told Congress, ". . . let us here highly resolve that John Fitzgerald Kennedy did not live or die in vain."

The 1964 Election

Johnson had become President through a tragic event. However, in 1964, he had to campaign to remain President. His strongest challenger was a conservative Republican from Arizona, Senator Barry Goldwater.

Goldwater was a strong anti-Communist. He favored an all-out war with North Vietnam. He stated that he was not afraid to use atomic weapons. Many Americans were worried that he would do just that. During the campaign, Johnson aired a television commercial that suggested Goldwater might use the atomic bomb.

Johnson and his running mate Hubert Humphrey won the election by more than 60 percent of the vote. It was the largest margin of victory ever in a presidential election. Many other Democrats won seats in Congress as well. They would vote to help President Johnson put his ideas into action.

★ Who were the candidates in the 1964 presidential election?

B. Improving Life in the United States

Soon after Johnson took office, he outlined his ideas for several new programs. He called his plans the war on poverty and the **Great Society**. His vision of the Great Society included new opportunities for all Americans. His social programs were designed to improve life for everyone. Some of these programs are still in effect today.

The War on Poverty

One focus of Johnson's social programs was a reduction in the number of people living in poverty. Advances in technology had allowed machines to take over unskilled jobs that people had once held. As a result, fewer workers were needed. Many remaining jobs required highly skilled workers. For these reasons, unskilled laborers often had a hard time finding jobs and were paid less for the jobs they did find. African Americans, women, and some other groups were also denied jobs because of discrimination.

Poverty levels rose among young adults, the elderly, and immigrants. Johnson recognized these problems and planned a way for the government to help these people. He told Americans,

> **“**This administration today, here and now, declares unconditional war on poverty in America. **”**

An agency created in 1964 by the Economic Opportunity Act (EOA) to fight poverty was the Office of Economic Opportunity (OEO). It set up programs for low-income people. One of these programs was Project Head Start, which helped prepare children from low-income families for elementary school. The OEO also set up the Job Corps, which provided job training for people who did not finish high school and other disadvantaged youths.

★★★★★★★
Meet
the President
★★★★★★★★★★★★★★★

Lyndon Baines Johnson
1908–1973

Years in office 1963–1969

Political Party Democratic

Birthplace Texas

Assumed office at age 55, succeeded John F. Kennedy

Age when elected 56

Occupations Teacher, Naval commander

Nickname LBJ

Did you know? Mrs. Johnson was known as Lady Bird. The Johnson daughters also had the initials *LBJ*. They were named Lynda Bird and Luci Baines.

Quote "Yesterday is not ours to recover, but tomorrow is ours to win or to lose."

ANALYZE PRIMARY SOURCES DOCUMENT-BASED QUESTION
Why do you think Johnson chose the phrase "war on poverty" to describe his programs to help the poor?

Yet another program overseen by the OEO, Volunteers in Service to America (VISTA), was similar to the Peace Corps, but it worked in the United States. Volunteers brought social services to poor areas. Other programs established under the EOA set up day-care centers, legal-aid services, and classes to help adults learn to read.

Helping Cities and the Environment

Congress also set up the Department of Housing and Urban Development (HUD). The goal of HUD was **urban renewal**, or the improvement of run-down areas of American cities. Federal funds were used to redevelop inner cities, to build low-income housing, and to help people pay their rent. Johnson appointed Robert Weaver as secretary, or head, of the new department. He was the first African American to serve in a President's Cabinet.

President Johnson wanted to protect the environment. In 1964, Congress passed the Wilderness Preservation Act, which preserved 9.1 million acres of land as wilderness. No permanent roads or buildings could be built in these areas. Johnson's other environmental programs included the National Wildlife Refuge System and the Wild and Scenic Rivers Act.

Better Education and Health Care

Johnson made education and healthcare top priorities. He pushed Congress to pass the Elementary and Secondary Education Act. This act gave $1.3 billion to schools to pay for textbooks and special education classes. Congress also passed the Higher Education Act, which provides student loans and gives money to universities for research.

Johnson also focused on the arts. In 1965, Congress established the National Foundation on the Arts and the Humanities. It encouraged the growth of the arts and culture and supported research, education, and public television.

In the area of healthcare, President Johnson supported the Medical Care Act. The programs created by this act are some of the most important of Johnson's Great Society. One is **Medicare**, which provided low-cost health insurance for people age 65 and over and for younger people with certain disabilities. Another is **Medicaid**, which helped states pay for medical care for low-income people.

★ **What were President Johnson's main goals in his war on poverty and Great Society programs?**

Then & Now

While Johnson was in office, his wife Lady Bird worked to improve the environment. She worked to pass the Highway Beautification Act. This act passed Congress in 1965.

Today, Mrs. Johnson heads the Lady Bird Johnson Wildflower Center in Austin, Texas. It promotes the planting of wildflowers along roads and highways. It also restores native wildflowers in other areas of the country.

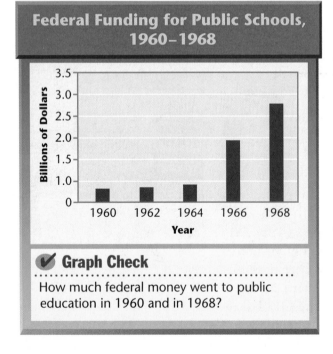

Federal Funding for Public Schools, 1960–1968

Billions of Dollars / Year

✔ **Graph Check**

How much federal money went to public education in 1960 and in 1968?

An elderly woman thanks President Johnson for signing the Medicare bill.

C. Greater Freedoms and Rights for All

In addition to easing poverty, Johnson focused on the rights and freedoms of citizens. Again, some of the changes brought about during Johnson's administration are still in effect today.

The Supreme Court

Johnson appointed two liberal justices to the Supreme Court while he was President. He thought they would rule to protect people's freedoms and support civil rights causes.

One of the justices appointed by Johnson was Thurgood Marshall. A former NAACP lawyer, Marshall was the first African American to serve on the Supreme Court. He had been the lawyer in the 1954 court case *Brown* v. *Board of Education of Topeka*. During that landmark case, he had represented the family of Linda Brown.

In the 1960s, there were several important Supreme Court decisions that protected people's rights. In *Escobado* v. *Illinois* (1964), a murder suspect, Danny Escobado, was not allowed to see his lawyer. Escobado confessed to the crime after hours of police questioning and was convicted. When he appealed the decision, the Supreme Court ruled that the confession could not be used as evidence because Escobado had been denied a lawyer. The conviction was overturned.

Thurgood Marshall

In 1963, Ernesto Miranda was arrested and charged with a crime. Miranda confessed, but he did not know that anything he said could be used against him in court. He also did not know that he had the right to remain silent. The Supreme Court ruled in *Miranda* v. *Arizona* (1966) that all people must be told about their rights after they are arrested or placed in custody.

Since 1966, all people who will be interrogated while in police custody must first be read the Miranda warning. It says, "You have the right to remain silent. Anything you say can and will be used against you in a court of law. You have the right to an attorney."

Immigration

Johnson and Congress changed the nation's immigration policies that had been in effect since 1924. The Immigration and Nationality Act of 1965 altered the quota system, which favored immigrants from countries in northern and western Europe over immigrants from other areas. Beginning in July 1968, a total of 170,000 immigrants from the Eastern Hemisphere and 120,000 immigrants from the Western Hemisphere could enter the country each year.

The Immigration and Nationality Act allowed more people from Asia, Latin America, and Eastern Europe to come to the United States. Many new immigrants came from Asia and settled in California and other parts of the United States. Thousands of immigrants also came from Cuba to escape communism under Fidel Castro.

 Why was Johnson's appointment of Thurgood Marshall to the Supreme Court an important one?

Do You Remember?
In Chapter 24, you learned that quotas had been set in the 1920s to limit the number of immigrants in the United States.

Review

Review History
A. Why was Johnson able to persuade Congress to pass many programs?
B. What programs did Johnson create to help poor people?
C. How does the *Miranda* v. *Arizona* decision protect Americans' rights?

Define Terms to Know
Provide a definition for each of the following terms.
Great Society, urban renewal, Medicare, Medicaid

Critical Thinking
Why did President Johnson support many programs for children and young people?

Write About Government
Write an essay to persuade the government to fight a war against an important problem today.

Get Organized
SQR CHART
You can use an SQR chart to organize information. Complete the chart you began at the beginning of this section. Then, answer the questions you wrote.

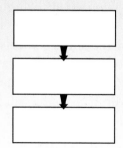

Build Your Skills

PRESENT AN ORAL REPORT

In school, presenting an oral report is a way of sharing information about a topic. An oral report is somewhat like a written report, but the information is spoken. The oral reports you give in school can help you become a better speaker. They may also help you later when you have a job. You may be asked to give oral reports to co-workers or customers.

You can make your oral report more interesting and memorable by varying the tone and loudness of your voice. You can also use your hands and facial expressions to help to make your points. Sometimes using visuals—such as charts, graphs, pictures, or lists—can make an oral report more effective.

Here's How

Follow these steps to present an oral report.

1. Research your topic.
2. Write main ideas, key facts, and details on notecards.
3. Practice your presentation.
4. Refer to your notecards when you give your report. Speak slowly and clearly.

Here's Why

You have just read about President Johnson's appointments to the Supreme Court. You have been asked to give an oral report about Thurgood Marshall. Following the steps above would help you give an interesting and informative report.

Practice the Skill

Copy the information on the right onto a sheet of paper or a note-card. Then, read Section I again. Complete the notecard with information from the section. Prepare a speech using the notecard.

Extend the Skill

Obtain or create a picture or other visual aid to improve your oral report.

Apply the Skill

As you read the remaining sections of this chapter, think about possible topics for an oral report. How would you organize an oral report on the war in Vietnam? Would you cover both sides of the issue? Think about how you could use your voice, facial expressions, and visual aids to make your report interesting.

> Johnson and the Supreme Court
>
> - Thurgood Marshall
>   - First African American on Court
>   - Lawyer for Brown family
>
> - Miranda v. Arizona
>   - _____
>   - _____

II ★ Equal Rights

Terms to Know

filibuster to give a long speech in order to delay the vote on a bill in Congress

Black Power a movement among African Americans to gain political and economic power

feminism the belief that women's rights should be equal to men's rights

Main Ideas

A. President Johnson worked for civil rights for all Americans.

B. Some Americans turned to violence, and the leader of nonviolent protests, Martin Luther King Jr., was assassinated.

C. Women and many minority groups worked for equal rights during the 1960s and 1970s.

 Active Reading

ANALYZE INFORMATION
When you analyze something, you look at each part to better understand the whole. As you read this section, analyze the black separatist movement to better understand why some African Americans supported it.

A. Working for Equal Rights

Before his death, President Kennedy had proposed a civil rights bill that would end segregation. However, during his presidency, Congress did not pass the bill. When Johnson became President, he continued to push for the civil rights bill. He told Congress that he would not fail to get it passed. President Johnson said,

ANALYZE PRIMARY SOURCES **DOCUMENT-BASED QUESTION**
Why is it important that equal rights be written in the "books of law"?

> **❝** We have talked long enough in this country about equal rights. We have talked for a hundred years or more. It is time now to write the next chapter, and to write it in the books of law. **❞**

The Civil Rights Act of 1964

The civil rights bill passed easily in the House of Representatives, but it met opposition in the Senate. Southern senators delayed the vote on the bill by a **filibuster**, or by giving long speeches that kept the senators from voting. The Senate debate continued for 57 days.

Finally, in June 1964, Congress passed the Civil Rights Act. It is considered to be one of the most important pieces of civil rights legislation in U.S. history. It outlawed segregation in public places, such as hotels, restaurants, and stores. It also sped up desegregation of public schools and allowed for the withdrawal of federal funds from programs that practiced discrimination. In addition, the law created the Equal Employment Opportunity Commission (EEOC) to work against discrimination in the workplace.

Freedom Summer

Many southern states prevented African Americans from voting. Often, African Americans who wanted to vote were charged a poll tax even though the Twenty-fourth Amendment, passed in 1964, outlawed such taxes. People registering to vote sometimes had to take literacy tests, which were designed to keep African Americans from passing. Finally, discrimination and threats of violence prevented many African Americans from registering to vote.

While Congress was working on the Civil Rights Act, 1,000 African American and white volunteers went to the South to register African Americans to vote. Their voter registration campaign was called Freedom Summer. As it began in Mississippi, the state enlarged its police force to greet the "invaders." The Ku Klux Klan held meetings to scare the volunteers. However, by the end of the campaign, national attention was focused on the situation, and some African Americans had registered to vote.

Johnson called on Congress to pass the Voting Rights Act. He told Americans that denying the vote to anyone was "deadly wrong." The act was passed in 1965. No longer could states make voters pay a poll tax or take a literacy test. Federal officials also helped oversee elections to make sure that no laws were broken.

 What were two effects of the Voting Rights Act of 1965?

B. African Americans Struggle for Equality

Segregation had been outlawed, but injustice still remained. Some African Americans felt that creating a separate nation within the United States was the only answer. These African Americans were known as black separatists.

African American Leaders

The Nation of Islam, or Black Muslims, was one black separatist group. These groups taught total rejection of white society. Black Muslims supported pride, unity, and self-help for African Americans. Malcolm X became a leader within the Nation of Islam. Unlike Martin Luther King Jr., he believed in using violence to gain rights for African Americans.

In 1964, Malcolm X broke with the Nation of Islam. He went to Mecca, a Muslim holy city, and toured Africa. He began to believe that African Americans and white people could work together. His new ideas angered some people. On February 21, 1965, Malcolm X was assassinated by three members of the Nation of Islam.

Dr. Martin Luther King Jr. (left) and Malcolm X in 1964

Stokely Carmichael was a believer in black separatism who wanted African Americans to take pride in their heritage and work together toward their goals. He began a movement known as **Black Power**.

The Black Panther party was formed by Bobby Seale and Huey Newton in Oakland, California, in 1966. They felt that African Americans should take control of their communities and fight against unfair treatment by the police. They supported armed rebellion if it was necessary to reach their goals.

Violence in the Cities

By the mid-1960s, violence broke out in some cities. In July 1964, riots began in Harlem after New York City police officers shot a young African American man who was suspected of a crime. The violence soon spread to other cities, including Los Angeles, California; Newark, New Jersey; and Detroit, Michigan. African American people and neighborhoods suffered most from the violence.

In July 1967, President Johnson appointed a commission to study the riots. The National Advisory Commission on Civil Disorders, also called the Kerner Commission, stated, "Our nation is moving toward two societies, one black, one white—separate and unequal."

Death of a Leader

While some African American groups were turning to violence, Dr. Martin Luther King Jr. still believed that nonviolence was the best way to gain equality. In April 1968, King went to Memphis, Tennessee. He was supporting a strike by sanitation workers. There, he was killed by an assassin's bullet.

Large crowds gathered to mourn the death of Dr. Martin Luther King Jr.

The civil rights movement had lost its most eloquent voice. King had the power to stir Americans of every race to support civil rights. In 1986, King's birthday was declared a holiday in his honor.

★ **How did Malcolm X's beliefs change?**

C. Others Fight for Equal Rights

African Americans were not the only ones seeking equal rights during the 1960s. Women became a major political force, fighting for equality in the workforce and other areas. Mexican Americans, Native Americans, and others also wanted equal rights.

Women's Rights

In 1963, a new book, *The Feminine Mystique*, expressed the feelings of many women. Its author, Betty Friedan, encouraged women who were housewives and mothers to take on additional responsibilities. Her book led to a revival of **feminism**, or the idea of equal rights for women. In 1966, Friedan and other women formed the National Organization for Women (NOW). NOW works for equal rights for women in the workplace, education, and politics.

In 1963, Congress passed the Equal Pay Act. It required that women be paid the same amount as men for doing the same job. The Civil Rights Act of 1964 also protected women from discrimination.

Women in Politics

In the late 1960s, Shirley Chisholm became the first African American woman to be elected to Congress. She served from 1969 until 1983. Her election opened the door for more women to enter national politics.

Many women supported the Equal Rights Amendment (ERA) to the Constitution. In 1972, the Equal Rights Amendment was passed by Congress. To become law, 38 states had to ratify it within 10 years. Many people did not think the ERA was necessary. By 1982, only 35 states had approved the ERA. So, it never became law.

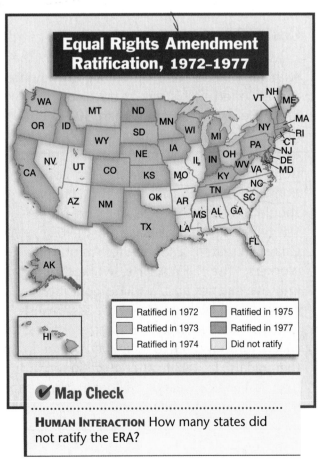

Equal Rights Amendment Ratification, 1972–1977

Ratified in 1972
Ratified in 1973
Ratified in 1974
Ratified in 1975
Ratified in 1977
Did not ratify

✔ **Map Check**

HUMAN INTERACTION How many states did not ratify the ERA?

Latin America includes countries in North and South America that are south of the United States. People from Latin America or of Latin American descent are often called Latinos. In 1960, Latinos were a minority throughout the United States.

The 2000 census showed a large surge in the Latino population. By 2020, one state, New Mexico, may have a Latino majority.

Mexican Americans Organize

Mexican Americans also worked for equal rights. They created the Mexican American Political Association (MAPA). It focused on electing Mexican Americans to political office. Mexican American students worked for bilingual education in schools. Calling themselves Chicano and Chicana to express their cultural background, they demanded Mexican literature and history classes. They also wanted more Chicano teachers.

César Chávez, a leader in the struggle for Latino rights, worked to help migrant farm laborers improve their working conditions. These workers traveled from farm to farm, often working long hours for little pay. In 1962, Chávez founded the National Farm Workers Association (NFWA) in California. Soon people across the country knew about the farmworkers' cause.

They Made History

César Chávez (1927–1993)

As a child, César Chávez worked in the fields with his parents. Like other migrant children, he moved often as his family traveled from farm to farm. He attended more than 30 schools before graduating from eighth grade. Chávez learned early that migrant farmworkers suffered from low wages and poor working conditions. He believed that the farmworkers should join together and demand better working conditions. In 1962, Chávez created a union for migrant workers, the NFWA. He worked to improve salaries and working conditions for farmworkers throughout the Southwest. Chávez marched, fasted, organized strikes, and called for boycotts to help farmworkers achieve their goals. In 1970, after a nationwide boycott that lasted for years, California grape growers finally recognized the union.

Supporters of Chávez wore buttons (left) to show their participation in the grape boycott.

Critical Thinking Why do you think Chávez felt so strongly about the unfair treatment of migrant farmworkers?

Native Americans Fight for Their Rights

Many Native Americans lived in poverty during the 1960s. Life on reservations often meant a lack of good food and water as well as few jobs. Native Americans often held the federal government responsible for their poor living conditions.

Some Native Americans organized to fight for their rights. The American Indian Movement (AIM) worked to change government policy toward Native Americans. In 1969, AIM supported the occupation of the abandoned prison on Alcatraz Island in San Francisco Bay by a group called the Indians of All Tribes (IAT). This event brought national attention to their cause. In 1972, AIM members seized the headquarters of the Federal Bureau of Indian Affairs in Washington, D.C. They felt that this department was a symbol of broken promises made by the U.S. government. AIM also started education, health, and legal programs for Native Americans.

In 1968, Congress passed the Indian Civil Rights Act to protect the constitutional rights of Native Americans. It also stated that Native Americans had the right to make laws on their reservations.

Members of IAT try to claim Alcatraz for Native Americans. They remained on the island until 1971.

 Why did the Equal Rights Amendment die without becoming law?

II Review

Review History
A. How did the Civil Rights Act of 1964 affect civil rights for African Americans?
B. How were the beliefs of Malcolm X and Martin Luther King Jr. different?
C. What groups besides African Americans worked to gain equal rights in the 1960s and 1970s?

Define Terms to Know
Provide a definition for each of the following terms.
filibuster, Black Power, feminism

Critical Thinking
Why do you think cities were the places where race riots occurred in the 1960s?

Write About Citizenship
Write a paragraph explaining what you can do to work for equal rights for all people of the United States today.

Get Organized
SQR CHART
Complete the SQR chart you began at the beginning of this section. Reread the section to find the answers to your questions.

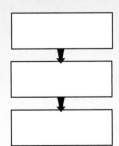

III Conflict in Vietnam

Terms to Know

domino theory the belief that if one country falls to communism, others nearby will fall, one after the other

escalation an increasing involvement

napalm a sticky gasoline jelly used in bombs

deferment a postponement, or a delaying, of having to serve in the armed forces

Main Ideas

A. U.S. involvement in Vietnam expanded.

B. About 2.7 million young Americans served in the Vietnam War.

C. Antiwar feelings spread throughout the United States as the war escalated and American casualties continued.

 **Active Reading**

POINTS OF VIEW
When you compare points of view, you look at an issue from the viewpoint of two or more groups of people. As you read this section, compare points of view toward the Vietnam War.

A. Growing Involvement in Vietnam

As Americans fought a war against poverty and struggled for equal rights at home, the United States became increasingly involved in another war overseas. The conflict in Vietnam turned into an all-out war after 1964.

Origins of American Involvement

Vietnam is one country today. However, at the time of the Vietnam War, the country was divided into two parts: South Vietnam and North Vietnam. For several years the United States had helped South Vietnamese leaders fight communism.

The Communist threat came from North Vietnam, led by Ho Chi Minh. It also came from inside South Vietnam, where many supporters of Ho Chi Minh lived. They were organized as the National Liberation Front (NLF), or Viet Cong. They received supplies from North Vietnam along the Ho Chi Minh Trail.

Many U.S. leaders felt the United States should help the South Vietnamese fight communism. They felt that if one country in Southeast Asia fell to communism, other countries would also fall. This idea was known as the **domino theory**.

In 1957, the Viet Cong launched a war against Ngo Dinh Diem, the leader of South Vietnam. The U.S. government sent aid to help him stay in power. However, as time passed, U.S. leaders realized that Diem was not very popular with the South Vietnamese people. A major problem was that Diem took rights away from people of the Buddhist religion—the most common religion in South Vietnam.

Do You Remember?
In Chapters 27 and 28, you learned that Presidents Eisenhower and Kennedy sent military advisors to aid South Vietnam in its fight against North Vietnam.

On November 1, 1963, Diem was overthrown and killed by South Vietnamese military leaders. The United States had supported the plot, but not Diem's assassination. Three weeks later, President Kennedy was assassinated. President Johnson became responsible for U.S. involvement in Vietnam.

The Gulf of Tonkin Resolution

Johnson sent Secretary of Defense Robert McNamara to Vietnam to investigate the situation. McNamara reported that the South Vietnamese government would not be able to resist the Viet Cong without help. Johnson had doubts, but he decided that the United States should send more troops to help South Vietnam. He said, "I am not going to be the President who saw Southeast Asia go the way China went." China is a Communist country.

On August 2, 1964, a U.S. warship in the Gulf of Tonkin reported that it had been attacked by North Vietnamese patrol boats. Two days later, two U.S. ships reported that they were also attacked by Vietnamese ships. The U.S. commanders stated they had destroyed the ships. These reports were never confirmed, but Congress responded by passing the Gulf of Tonkin Resolution. It gave the President permission to take "all necessary measures" to protect American forces in Vietnam. The President now had the power to wage war without formally declaring war.

Operation Rolling Thunder

Plans for **escalation**, or growing involvement, in the war were already being made. This escalation took two forms: bombing attacks on North Vietnam and the use of American ground troops in South Vietnam. Under Operation Rolling Thunder, the code name for the bombing campaign, the United States began daily air raids over North Vietnam. From 1965 to 1968, planes dropped 640,000 tons of bombs on North Vietnam.

At the same time, U.S. Marines arrived at Da Nang, South Vietnam, to protect air bases. Soon, U.S. forces were also conducting search-and-destroy missions in the fight against the Viet Cong. By 1966, more than 380,000 U.S. troops were stationed in Vietnam.

★ **What power did the Gulf of Tonkin Resolution give the President?**

ANALYZE PRIMARY SOURCES **DOCUMENT-BASED QUESTION** How does the cartoonist picture the mood of Americans?

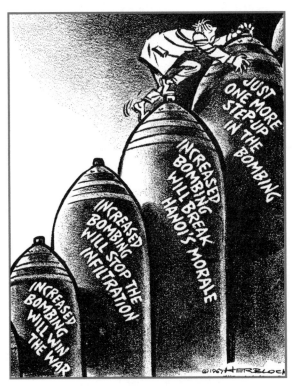

This cartoon highlights the increased bombing and the failed promises of the Johnson administration.

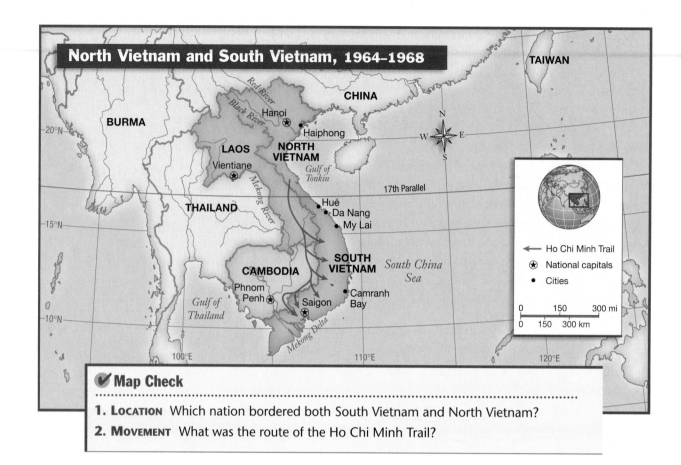

North Vietnam and South Vietnam, 1964–1968

TAIWAN

CHINA

BURMA

Red River

Black River

Hanoi

Haiphong

LAOS

NORTH VIETNAM

Vientiane

Gulf of Tonkin

17th Parallel

Mekong River

THAILAND

Hué
Da Nang
My Lai

CAMBODIA

SOUTH VIETNAM

South China Sea

Phnom Penh

Saigon

Camranh Bay

Gulf of Thailand

Mekong Delta

20°N

15°N

10°N

100°E

110°E

120°E

→ Ho Chi Minh Trail
⊛ National capitals
• Cities

0   150   300 mi
0   150   300 km

✔ Map Check

1. **LOCATION** Which nation bordered both South Vietnam and North Vietnam?
2. **MOVEMENT** What was the route of the Ho Chi Minh Trail?

B. Fighting in Vietnam

Many Americans had expected a short war. However, the war dragged on. American soldiers and Vietnamese soldiers and civilians were killed each day. The North Vietnamese seemed willing to accept a large number of casualties and a long war. They felt that they could win the war by simply outlasting the United States.

The Horrors of War

Few Americans were prepared for the horrors of ground warfare in jungles, rice paddies, and villages. The Viet Cong used guerrilla warfare. They hid among the trees and in underground tunnels. They launched surprise attacks and set booby traps and land mines. The American forces had to deal with unfamiliar territory and areas so dense with trees and other plants that it was hard to see the enemy. Both sides suffered high casualties, yet there were few major victories on either side.

To help U.S. troops see enemy troops in the jungle, airplanes dropped bombs that contained **napalm**, a gel made with gasoline.

Napalm was used to burn the leaves from the trees. It also stuck to human skin. Napalm bombs killed or injured millions of Vietnamese people.

Tour of Duty

The average age of American soldiers in Vietnam was 19. Some people, including about 6,000 women who served as nurses, volunteered for duty in Vietnam. Many soldiers were drafted. Most served a one-year tour of duty. In all, about 2.7 million Americans served during the Vietnam War.

American soldiers in Vietnam often lived in miserable conditions. Besides the threat of being killed or seriously injured, many soldiers experienced heatstroke and other illnesses. Food, water, and sleep were sometimes in short supply. To make matters worse, as the war dragged on, many soldiers began to question the reasons why they were in Vietnam.

 Why were napalm bombs used in Vietnam?

C. Growing Opposition at Home

As the war escalated, so did feelings against it. Many protests took place on college campuses. Students took over university offices and staged sit-ins. They marched through the streets of major cities. Some demonstrations turned violent. Police were called in to use tear gas and pepper gas for crowd control.

A helicopter crew rescues wounded U.S. soldiers.

Draft Protests

Most young people did not protest against the war, but many did. In October 1967, more than 100,000 protesters marched on Washington, D.C. About 50,000 protesters gathered outside the Pentagon to protest the draft, the use of napalm, and the continuation of U.S. participation in the war.

Many antiwar protesters focused on the draft, the system that provided soldiers for the war. These protesters felt that the draft was unfair in several ways. First, middle class white men were more likely to receive a student **deferment**, or a delay in having to serve in the military. Therefore poor whites and minorities were more likely to be drafted. Second, young men could be drafted at age 18 when they could not even vote until age 21. Third, many young people came to believe that the United States did not belong in Vietnam. They did not think they should be forced to take part in a war in which they did not believe.

In 1969, the U.S. government tried to make the draft fairer to all groups of young men. A lottery based on birthdays was started. Deferments were shorter and harder to get. Some young people fled to Canada and other countries. Some burned their draft cards and refused to serve.

Two Versions of the War

Americans saw and heard two versions of the war: one on television and another from their President. On the news, they saw combat in Vietnam and student protests at home. They heard body counts of American soldiers killed each day. According to television reports, the war did not seem to be going very well. In fact, it was hard to know who the enemy was, or even what the South Vietnamese people really wanted. Yet President Johnson kept telling Americans that the United States and South Vietnam were winning the war.

By 1968, many Americans had stopped believing what President Johnson said about the war. Then, at the beginning of Tet, the Vietnamese New Year, the Viet Cong launched a major attack on South Vietnamese cities. The Viet Cong even raided the U.S. embassy in Saigon. Many Americans were convinced that the Tet Offensive would not have happened if the United States was winning a war that was about to end.

A military helicopter flies over a rice paddy where South Vietnamese farmers are working. Paddies are wet lands in which rice is grown.

The Tet Offensive was a turning point. Many U.S. leaders decided the war could not be won. President Johnson decided to de-escalate, or slow down, U.S. involvement in the war.

Vietnam Defeats a President

President Johnson faced a presidential campaign in 1968. He was challenged by Senator Eugene McCarthy of Minnesota. McCarthy spoke out against the war. Then, Senator Robert F. Kennedy entered the presidential race. Democratic support for Johnson weakened.

On March 31, 1968, the President delivered a television address to the nation. In a surprise move, he announced that he would not run again. Instead, he would devote the rest of his time in office to working for peace.

The President called a halt to most of the bombing. In May, peace talks began between the United States and North Vietnam. Johnson would not live to see peace in Vietnam. He died at his Texas ranch on January 22, 1973.

This newspaper headline referred to President Johnson's decision not to run for re-election.

 Why did President Johnson decide not to run for re-election?

III Review

Review History
A. How did the U.S. involvement in the Vietnam War change after 1964?

B. What factors made the war in Vietnam difficult for the United States to win?

C. What effect did the Tet Offensive have on Americans' opinion of the war?

Define Terms to Know
Provide a definition for each of the following terms.
domino theory, escalation, napalm, deferment

Critical Thinking
Do you think people have the right to protest against a war? Why or why not?

Write About Citizenship
Write a journal entry from the point of view of a U.S. soldier fighting in Vietnam. Describe why you might be disappointed about war protests at home.

Get Organized
SQR CHART
You can use an SQR chart to organize information. Complete the chart you began at the beginning of this section. Reread the text to find the answers to your questions.

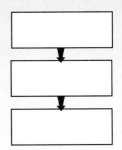

Chapter Summary

In your notebook, complete the following outline. Then, use your outline to write a brief summary of the chapter.

The Johnson Years

I. The Great Society

    A. Working With Congress

    B.

    C.

II. Equal Rights

    A.

    B.

    C.

III. Conflict in Vietnam

    A.

    B.

    C.

 Interpret the Timeline

Use the timeline on pages 678–679 to answer the following questions.

1. What leader was assassinated in 1968?

2. **Critical Thinking** Which events on the U.S. timeline show how important the decade of the 1960s was in the African American struggle for equality?

Use Terms to Know

Select the term that best completes each sentence.

domino theory   feminism   Medicare
escalation   filibuster

1. The Gulf of Tonkin Resolution led to an _____ of the U.S. involvement in the Vietnam War.

2. The _____ stated that if one country fell to communism, others would follow.

3. The government provided health insurance for people age 65 and over with the creation of _____.

4. Politicians _____ by making long speeches to avoid a vote.

5. The idea that women are entitled to equal rights is known as _____.

Check Your Understanding

1. **Identify** the goals of Johnson's Great Society.

2. **Summarize** the major programs Johnson supported for improved healthcare.

3. **Explain** the significance of the Civil Rights Act of 1964 and the Voting Rights Act of 1965.

4. **Discuss** several effects of the feminist movement.

5. **Describe** the escalation of U.S. involvement in Vietnam between 1965 and 1968.

6. **Identify** two reasons many young people protested the war in Vietnam.

Critical Thinking

1. **Draw Conclusions** Do you think the war on poverty has been won today? Explain.

2. **Recognize Relationships** Many groups fought for equal rights during the 1960s. What did these groups have in common?

3. **Analyze Primary Sources** How do you think President Johnson would have felt about the political cartoon on page 693? Explain how you think he might have reacted to it.

Put Your Skills to Work

PRESENT AN ORAL REPORT

You have learned how an oral report is different from a written report. You can use your voice and facial expressions to help you make your points in an oral presentation.

Copy the notecard below. On the first blank line, write a topic from Chapter 29 that would make a good topic for an oral report. On the second and third blank lines, write two facts about that topic.

```
(topic)_____
        - (fact)_____
        - (fact)_____
```

In Your Own Words

JOURNAL WRITING

The Vietnam War divided Americans because the war was so far from home and because it did not directly involve the United States. Do you believe that U.S. troops should be used in faraway conflicts that do not directly involve the United States? Write a journal entry describing how you would feel if you were sent to fight in a faraway country.

Net Work

INTERNET ACTIVITY

Working with a group of classmates, use the Internet as a resource to create a poster of statistics about the Vietnam War. How many people served in the war? How many were drafted? How many Americans were killed, wounded, or captured during the war? Answer these and other questions you may have. Then, create charts and graphs for the statistics you have found.

For help in starting this activity, visit the following Web site: www.gfamericanhistory.com.

Look Ahead

In the next chapter, learn about President Nixon's administration and the end of the Vietnam War.

Unit 9 Portfolio Project

An American Scrapbook

YOUR ASSIGNMENT

Make a scrapbook about the United States from the 1940s through the 1960s. Each decade of that period brought changes in American culture. In your class, form teams to work on a scrapbook. Each team will choose a decade. Team members will collect items from that decade to put in their "chapter" of the scrapbook. When each chapter is completed, it will be put together with the others to make one scrapbook about the United States from the 1940s through the 1960s.

SCRAPBOOK STARTUP

Choose and Review Each team will select one of the following decades: 1940s, 1950s, 1960s.

Plan Your Chapter Discuss with your team what types of things to include in your chapter of the scrapbook. Many of your team-mates will have friends and relatives who were alive during your decade. They may have items to contribute to your scrapbook. You may also find the Internet a useful resource. You may refer to this Web site for ideas: www.gfamericanhistory.com.

SCRAPBOOK ASSEMBLY

Meet and Select Gather all the items your team has collected. As a team, choose the best items to include in the scrapbook.

Mount Your Items When all the items have been collected, mount them neatly in the scrapbook. Label each and explain its use. Be sure to take special care of those you have borrowed. Items that might be damaged by mounting can be arranged in a display box for your decade.

Put it All Together Have a person from each group help assemble the three chapters of the scrapbook.

Multimedia Presentation

Interview someone who lived during the decade you selected. Write questions to ask about life during that period. Also, show the person the items you have collected, and ask for comments or stories related to the items. Record the interview and include a copy of it in your scrapbook or display box.

Modern America

"The sky is not limits but endless possibilities ... and if we do not test the limits of our perception and our abilities and our worlds, we will never know what lies beyond."

—from a speech made by
Jeanne Tessier Barone, in 1996

LINK PAST TO PRESENT Space travel is just one of the ways that people continue to explore. New discoveries in science, medicine, and technology create endless possibilities for the future.

★ How do you think new discoveries within the next 20 years will affect people's lives?

701

CHAPTER 30

Turbulent Times 1968–1979

I. **The End of the Vietnam War**
II. **Nixon's Administration**
III. **Domestic Crises**

*D*uring a campaign stop in 1970, protesters threw rocks at the President of the United States. Later that day, Richard Milhous Nixon spoke about what had happened:

> “This is a great and good country . . . but . . . there is a small group . . . of people that hate this country. . . . The way to answer them [is] . . . for the great silent majority to speak out. ”

The 1970s were a difficult time in the United States. The Vietnam War and economic and political problems at home led many people to lose confidence in the American government. Some people responded to these problems with violence and anger. Others waited silently for the problems to end. Richard Nixon called on this silent majority to come to the aid of the country.

Peace button

1969 First astronauts walk on the moon. Nixon withdraws some troops from Vietnam. Americans learn about My Lai massacre.		**1970** Students are killed at Kent State and Jackson State universities.	

1968
Robert Kennedy is assassinated.

U.S. Events	1968		1972
Presidential Term Begins		1969 Richard Nixon	
World Events	1968		1972

1968
My Lai massacre occurs.

1970
Invasion of Cambodia
takes place.

VIEW HISTORY Police with guns were usually present at antiwar demonstrations in the late 1960s and early 1970s. Some protesters wore buttons or pins that called for peace (left).

★ How does the image of a flower being placed in a gun symbolize the conflict in the United States during this time period?

Get Organized

TIMELINE

A timeline can help you organize facts and events. Use a timeline as you read Chapter 30. List important events that you read about in the correct order on the timeline. Here is an example using some events from this chapter.

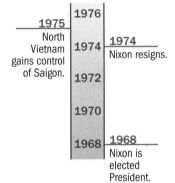

1975 North Vietnam gains control of Saigon.

1976

1974 Nixon resigns.

1972

1970

1968 Nixon is elected President.

1973
Truce is signed with North Vietnam.

1974
Nixon resigns.

1975
U.S. Marines airlift people from Saigon.

1978
Camp David Accords are signed by Egypt and Israel.

1979
Nuclear accident occurs at Three Mile Island.

1976   **1980**

1974 Gerald Ford   1977 Jimmy Carter

1976   **1980**

1973
Arab oil embargo is enforced.

1974
OPEC increases oil prices.

1975
Human rights pact is signed in Helsinki, Finland.
Vietnam War ends.

1979
American hostages are seized in Iran.

I The End of the Vietnam War

Terms to Know

Vietnamization
President Nixon's plan to train the South Vietnamese to fight the Vietnam War

truce a temporary agreement to stop fighting

Main Ideas

A. Social and political issues divided the nation in the late 1960s.

B. Americans lost their lives at home and abroad while politicians struggled to end the Vietnam War.

C. Americans felt the harsh effects of the war after it was over.

 **Active Reading**

PREDICT
When you predict, you use information that you know in order to guess what might happen next. As you read this section, predict the outcome of the 1968 election.

A. Battles at Home

In the 1960s, Americans were bombarded with vivid scenes on the evening news. Each night they saw the raging battles in Vietnam and the faces of wounded soldiers. They also saw the faces of protesters—some opposing the war, some demanding equal rights. At the same time, they heard politicians promising to solve these problems.

Showdown in Chicago

In 1968, Americans faced the task of choosing a new President. President Lyndon Johnson had surprised everyone by deciding not to run for a second term. Who would get the Democratic Party nomination?

Hubert Humphrey, Johnson's Vice President, was one of the top candidates. He was challenged by Eugene McCarthy and Robert Kennedy, who both strongly opposed the war. Kennedy won every state primary that spring except Oregon. Then, on June 6, 1968, Kennedy was assassinated after winning the California primary.

Humphrey won the nomination at the Democratic National Convention in Chicago. While the convention was taking place, rioting broke out in the streets. Antiwar protesters felt that Humphrey would continue Johnson's war policies in the White House. Some protesters turned violent, and police used clubs and tear gas to restore order. Later, eight rioters were indicted along with eight policemen. Seven of the policemen were charged with assaulting protesters.

Do You Remember?
In Chapter 28, you learned that Robert Kennedy, the younger brother of President John F. Kennedy, served as Attorney General of the United States.

The 1968 Election Results

Republican candidate Richard Nixon won support by saying that he wanted to end the war in Vietnam. He said he would bring "peace with honor" to America. Humphrey began to gain support because he promised to stop the bombing of North Vietnam.

Governor George Wallace of Alabama, a supporter of segregation, ran under a third party, the American Independent Party. He showed surprising strength in the polls. He won votes among white Southerners and Democrats who were dissatisfied with their party. However, by election day, Wallace's support had dwindled, and the race between Humphrey and Nixon remained too close to call.

Richard Nixon won the 1968 election by only about half a million popular votes. However, he received 110 more electoral votes than Humphrey. Nixon took his electoral victory to mean that there was a "silent majority" of people who wanted to end the demonstrations of the 1960s. The silent majority, he believed, would calm the country while he worked to end the war.

★ **Which issue was important in the 1968 election?**

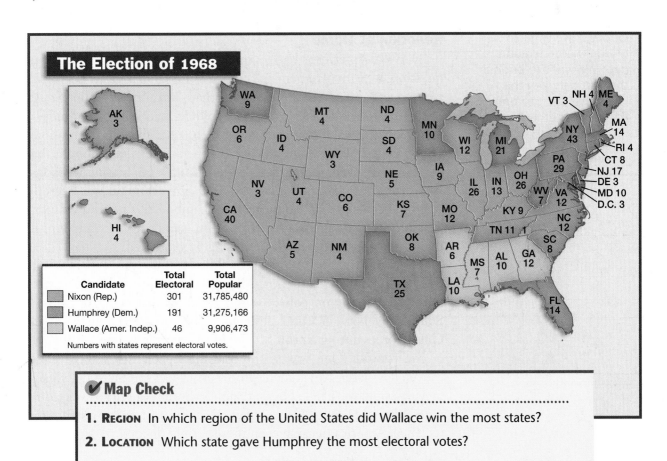

The Election of 1968

Candidate	Total Electoral	Total Popular
Nixon (Rep.)	301	31,785,480
Humphrey (Dem.)	191	31,275,166
Wallace (Amer. Indep.)	46	9,906,473

Numbers with states represent electoral votes.

✔ Map Check

1. REGION In which region of the United States did Wallace win the most states?

2. LOCATION Which state gave Humphrey the most electoral votes?

B. The Deepening Crisis

Richard Nixon inherited the Vietnam War. While Nixon worked to end the war, Americans continued to lose their lives in Vietnam.

Nixon's Plan for Troop Withdrawal

Nixon and his administration could not force the North Vietnamese government to discuss a peaceful ending to the war. Their efforts were turned down by the North Vietnamese. However, Nixon knew Americans would not accept a stronger war effort, even if the goal was to force the enemy into peace talks. As more U.S. soldiers were killed overseas, Americans at home became convinced that the war must end.

Nixon's answer to the growing crisis was called **Vietnamization**. He planned to make it possible for South Vietnamese forces to fight the war themselves. The United States agreed to send supplies, airplanes, and advisors to help in the effort, but responsibility for running the war would shift to South Vietnam. This would allow the United States to begin to withdraw its troops. For a while it appeared that U.S. involvement in the war might be ending.

Reaction at Home

By 1970, Americans had learned two things that caused them to question U.S involvement in Vietnam. First, in November 1969, newspapers reported an incident that had occurred in South Vietnam on March 16, 1968. U.S. soldiers had killed hundreds of unarmed people, many of them women and children, in the small South Vietnamese village of My Lai. The soldiers had thought that the villagers were helping the Viet Cong and hiding weapons. Americans also learned that the U.S. government was secretly bombing the Ho Chi Minh Trail in Cambodia, a neutral country. The North Vietnamese used this trail to send supplies to troops in the South, so Nixon felt the bombing was justified.

Americans were tired of the war. They had been told that the war was ending when it was not. All across America, antiwar protests took place, many on college campuses. On May 4, 1970, at Kent State University in Ohio, four students were killed by National Guard forces during a protest. Two of the victims were not even part of the protest. One was simply passing by on her way to class. Eleven days later, two student protesters at Jackson State University in Mississippi were killed by state police. Some Americans were outraged by these events. Others blamed the protesters for starting the violence. America became even more deeply divided.

★ **What was Vietnamization?**

This cartoon shows Presidents Eisenhower, Kennedy, Johnson, Nixon, and Ford promising a quick end to the Vietnam War.

DOCUMENT-BASED QUESTION What does this political cartoon say about the government's ability to end the Vietnam War?

C. The Final Scene

Americans began to realize that the United States was not going to win the Vietnam War. Failure was difficult to accept after losing more than 58,000 American lives and spending about $150 billion.

Peace at Last

In 1969, Nixon's national security advisor, Henry Kissinger, had begun secret talks with North Vietnamese leaders, but the North Vietnamese were not ready to end the war. In 1972, however, they agreed to discuss ending the war after the United States increased its bombing campaign. A **truce**, or temporary peace agreement, was signed on January 27, 1973. In return for the removal of U.S. troops, North Vietnam would release all American prisoners of war. North Vietnam was allowed to keep troops in South Vietnam, so its attacks there continued. The United States withdrew troops in March 1973 but continued bombing in Cambodia until August.

In November, Congress passed the War Powers Act, declaring that the President should consult with Congress before committing U.S. armed forces to conflicts overseas. This act also stated that to keep troops overseas for more than 60 days, war must be declared or Congress must approve the action. The purpose of the act was to increase legislative control over the nation's military and limit the President's ability to begin a long-term war.

The truce did not end the war. On April 30, 1975, North Vietnamese troops captured Saigon. The remaining Americans were evacuated by helicopter along with thousands of South Vietnamese people who feared for their lives under the new government.

The final scene of the airlift was dramatic. In 18 hours the U.S. military evacuated more than 1,000 American civilians and soldiers and almost 6,000 South Vietnamese people out of Saigon. On that day, the city fell to North Vietnamese forces. Communists controlled both North and South Vietnam, and the war was finally over.

A Sad Homecoming

At the war's end, there was no victory parade. Soldiers came home from the war, but they were not given a hero's welcome. Many found that Americans did not want to hear about the war. As one Vietnam veteran said,

 We did a fine job there. If it had happened in World War II, they still would be telling stories about it. But it happened in Vietnam, so nobody knows about it. 🙶

ANALYZE PRIMARY SOURCES
DOCUMENT-BASED QUESTION
How do you think this veteran felt about the way he was treated when he returned home from the war?

It took nearly ten years for the sacrifices made by Vietnam's veterans to be recognized officially. In November 1982, a memorial for these veterans was dedicated in Washington, D.C. It was designed by Maya Ying Lin, a Chinese American woman. The names of all the dead and missing in action were engraved on a smooth, black granite wall for the world to see.

★ **What is the War Powers Act?**

I Review

Review History
A. What divided the U.S. in the 1960s and 1970s?
B. What happened in the village of My Lai?
C. What step did Congress take to prevent another conflict like the Vietnam War from occurring?

Define Terms to Know
Provide a definition for each of the following terms.
Vietnamization, truce

Critical Thinking
Why did U.S. troops airlift South Vietnamese people out of Saigon?

Write About History
Write a journal entry about how it would feel to be a Vietnam veteran returning to the United States at the end of the war.

Get Organized
TIMELINE
Make a timeline for Section I that shows three related events. Think about the sequence of events in this section. Use a timeline to understand how they are related.

Build Your Skills

EVALUATE INFORMATION

People are often swayed, or convinced to change their mind, by what they read and hear. Some messages, such as newspaper and television advertisements, are created to sway your opinion. Advertisers hope that you will believe the information in their ads and then buy their products. In order to convince you, they use slogans or images that favor their products.

Political campaigns use posters, television commercials, buttons, and ads to sway voters' opinions. Political advertisements, like most other types of ads, contain bias. They provide one-sided information to convince you that one candidate is better than the other. In order to make wise political and purchasing decisions, you must be able to evaluate the information you are given.

Here's How

Follow these steps to evaluate information.

1. Distinguish facts from opinions. Which statements can be proven?

2. Identify words, phrases, or images that are designed to influence your feelings.

3. Examine words that appear unemotional but might somehow affect your feelings about a person or an issue.

Here's Why

You have just read about some of the issues that divided the United States in the 1960s and 1970s. Suppose you had to evaluate campaign buttons from that time period. Separating facts from opinions and identifying emotional words and images would help you evaluate the information.

Practice the Skill

Look at the campaign buttons for Richard Nixon and Hubert Humphrey. List all of the words, phrases, and images used to sway voters. Then, choose the button that you feel is more effective. Explain why in a paragraph.

Extend the Skill

Find an advertisement in a newspaper or magazine. Use two different colored highlighters to identify facts and opinions. Use a colored pen to circle one-sided words, phrases, or images. As a class, discuss your findings.

Apply the Skill

As you read newspapers and other chapters in this textbook, evaluate the information presented in political advertisements or cartoons. Think about the purpose of the ad or cartoon. Is it effective?

PAST *to* PRESENT

Reporting Wars

Americans watched reporters' footage of the Vietnam War every night on the evening news. In the early 1960s, the film from Vietnam was flown by airplane overnight to Los Angeles, California, or to Paris, France. There it was developed and then sent to New York for broadcast on the nightly news. In the late 1960s, the film was flown to Hong Kong or Bangkok for developing. It was then fed to a satellite that would send the signal to New York. Because of the time difference between New York and Vietnam, Americans were able to see the day's news on the same calendar day that it happened.

Today, we see footage in "real-time" on television or the Internet. Fighting in places such as Afghanistan is broadcast live via satellite. As we watch it, the broadcast is recorded on videotape for future use. These live broadcasts allow us to be witnesses to historic events as they happen.

In this photo, Walter Cronkite is shown interviewing soldiers in Vietnam. Reporters were flown to combat areas, often by military transport, and then returned to Saigon to finish their stories.

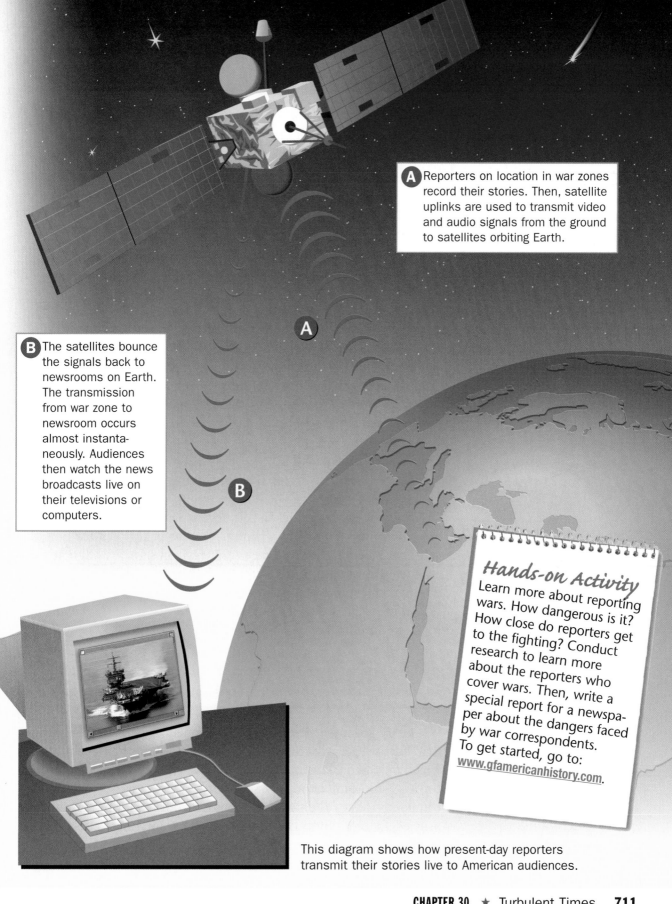

A Reporters on location in war zones record their stories. Then, satellite uplinks are used to transmit video and audio signals from the ground to satellites orbiting Earth.

B The satellites bounce the signals back to newsrooms on Earth. The transmission from war zone to newsroom occurs almost instantaneously. Audiences then watch the news broadcasts live on their televisions or computers.

Hands-on Activity
Learn more about reporting wars. How dangerous is it? How close do reporters get to the fighting? Conduct research to learn more about the reporters who cover wars. Then, write a special report for a newspaper about the dangers faced by war correspondents. To get started, go to: www.gfamericanhistory.com.

This diagram shows how present-day reporters transmit their stories live to American audiences.

II Nixon's Administration

Terms to Know

affirmative action programs for reversing the effects of discrimination

détente easing tensions between unfriendly nations

stagflation the economic condition of higher prices without economic growth

Main Ideas

A. Even with the Vietnam War raging, Nixon had some successes with domestic and foreign policy.

B. Problems with the economy and scandal plagued Nixon's presidency.

 **Active Reading**

SUPPORTING DETAILS
The main ideas in this section tell you what it is about. The supporting details give you more information. As you read this section, identify supporting details for each main idea.

A. Nixon's Accomplishments

Even while Richard Nixon struggled with the war in Vietnam, other issues required his attention. Advances were made in environmental protection, civil rights, and foreign relations. President Kennedy's challenge to land a man on the moon was finally met.

The Environment

One of the many issues that concerned Americans in the late 1960s and 1970s was the environment. President Nixon and Congress worked together to pass several laws aimed at cleaning up the environment. Congress banned the use of DDT, a toxic pesticide that killed wildlife. Then, in 1970 Nixon signed a bill that created the Environmental Protection Agency (EPA). The EPA enforces environmental laws and protects the nation's water and air. Nixon made the following comment about Americans' responsibility to stop pollution:

ANALYZE PRIMARY SOURCES
DOCUMENT-BASED QUESTION
What did Nixon mean by these words?

> **"**We must learn not how to master nature but how to master ourselves, our institutions, and our technology. **"**

The environment became such a popular cause in 1970 that the first Earth Day was celebrated on April 22. The first celebration, which included a large gathering in New York City, called attention to this important national issue. The day's events included environmental fairs on college and high school campuses. Attendees learned about pollution and other environmental issues. Earth Day is still celebrated each year.

Civil Rights

Before Nixon took office, several laws, such as the Civil Rights Act of 1964, had been passed to aid in desegregating schools. In 1971, the Supreme Court ruled that school districts must bus children to schools away from their neighborhoods. The goal of busing was to desegregate schools and create better educational opportunities for African American students. Nixon opposed these busing programs.

Nixon did, however, support **affirmative action** programs which were designed to increase opportunities for African Americans, women, Latinos, and Native Americans. The goal of affirmative action was to allow minorities and women to find jobs in fields that had been closed to them and gain admission to institutions of higher education.

The Space Program

Major advances were also made in the space program during Nixon's administration. On July 20, 1969, *Apollo 11* landed on the moon. For the first time, astronauts walked on the moon's surface. Americans across the country watched this amazing event on television. Between 1969 and 1972, American astronauts would make five more trips to the moon.

Do You Remember?

In Chapter 28 you learned about President Kennedy's space program. The moon landing was the result of Kennedy's emphasis on space exploration.

They Made History

Neil Armstrong Born 1930

Neil Armstrong was fascinated with planes and flight from the age of nine. He became a licensed pilot at age 16 and was a test pilot for several years at Edwards Air Force Base. Armstrong joined NASA in 1962. On July 16, 1969, Armstrong, along with fellow astronauts Edwin "Buzz" Aldrin and Michael Collins, blasted off the launch pad at Cape Kennedy, Florida, in *Apollo 11*. On July 20, 1969, Neil Armstrong became the first man to walk on the moon. As he stepped onto the moon's surface, he uttered these famous words: "That's one small step for man, one giant leap for mankind."

Six hundred million television viewers watched as Neil Armstrong and Buzz Aldrin placed an American flag on the moon's surface on July 20, 1969.

Critical Thinking Why was Armstrong's walk on the moon a "giant leap for mankind"?

In 1972, Nixon gave approval for NASA to develop a space shuttle. A space shuttle is a reusable rocket-launched vehicle that can travel between Earth and an orbiting spacecraft. On its return to Earth, it glides to a landing like a regular jet plane. Nixon announced a plan to spend $5.5 billion over a period of six years to build and test the shuttle.

Foreign Policy

From his earliest days in public office, Nixon had been an anti-Communist. He served on the House Un-American Activities Committee (HUAC) in Congress. In the 1940s and 1950s, HUAC investigated charges of Communist activity among Americans. Nixon later worked to improve relations with Communist countries such as the Soviet Union and the People's Republic of China.

Nixon and his national security advisor, Henry Kissinger, tried to ease the tensions between the United States and the Communist superpowers of the world. This policy was known as **détente**. In February 1972, Nixon and Kissinger visited China. The visit resulted in U.S. support for admitting China into the United Nations. It also opened the door for trade between the two countries.

In May, Nixon and Kissinger traveled to the Soviet Union. They continued negotiations called Strategic Arms Limitation Talks (SALT), which started in 1969. These talks were aimed at limiting certain kinds of nuclear weapons. During this visit Nixon and Soviet leader Leonid Brezhnev signed an agreement known as SALT I.

★ **How did Nixon handle desegregation?**

Nixon was the first U.S. President to visit the People's Republic of China. Here he stands on the Great Wall with Li Shiennian, the Chinese Vice Premier.

B. Troubles for Nixon

Nixon was President after Johnson's war on poverty had begun increasing federal spending for social programs. This increase in spending, plus the high cost of the Vietnam War, strained the federal budget. The government was spending more money than it collected through taxes. Then, an energy crisis began.

OPEC's decision to limit the sale of oil affected the United States. Motorists often found empty pumps or restrictions at gas stations.

The Energy Crisis

The United States and many other nations purchased oil from countries in the Middle East who belonged to the Organization of Petroleum Exporting Countries (OPEC). This group hoped that the need for oil around the world would allow its members to get a higher price for the oil they sold. OPEC member countries also tried to use their power to influence international politics.

In 1973, after two Middle Eastern countries, Egypt and Syria, went to war with Israel, the United States sent military aid to the Israelis. In response, OPEC raised the price of oil and stopped the sale of oil to the United States. The price of a barrel of crude oil rose from $1.80 in 1971 to $11.65 in 1974. Higher oil prices and the embargo hurt the United States and its allies. Because of the oil shortage, many Americans endured long lines at gas stations. In addition, gas prices went up. Energy prices continued to soar even after the shortage ended.

A Changing World Economy

Since the Industrial Revolution, the United States had enjoyed its place as the world leader in manufacturing. However, by the late 1960s, competition increased from Western Europe and Japan. Entire U.S. industries, including automotive, steel, and electronics, had to make changes that would allow them to be more competitive in a global market. Global competition and other factors caused American factories to close. As a result, hundreds of thousands of people lost their jobs. Unemployment rose, prices climbed, and economic activity fell.

Efforts to control the economy failed. The high price of oil and OPEC's embargo contributed to the problem. The United States experienced an unusual economic situation known as **stagflation**, during which prices rose, but the economy was stalled. (The words combined to create this term are *stagnation* and *inflation*.) Americans were disappointed with Nixon's inability to improve the country's economic situation.

Nixon won re-election in 1972, but reporters Bob Woodward and Carl Bernstein continued to investigate Watergate after his re-election.

The Watergate Scandal and Nixon's Resignation

On June 17, 1972, five men were arrested for breaking into the offices of the Democratic National Committee at the Watergate building complex in Washington, D.C. The burglars were looking for documents to help defeat the Democrats in the next election. Two others were later charged with organizing the crime. Investigators learned that these men had once worked for the Committee for the Re-election of the President (CREEP). The ties to CREEP went back to the White House.

Nixon did not plan the break-in. Still, he tried to cover up the connection between people in his administration and the crime. Investigators discovered that after the break-in, Nixon had ordered the CIA to tell the FBI to stop investigating the case. He told his staff to tell investigators nothing. Also, Nixon refused to turn over tapes of conversations recorded in his White House office.

After a Supreme Court decision, Nixon finally did turn over some of the tapes, but sections had been erased. The tapes showed that Nixon knew about the break-in and the cover-up. Based on the evidence, the House Judiciary Committee recommended impeachment. Rather than face impeachment, Nixon resigned on August 9, 1974—a dramatic moment in American history.

★ **How did OPEC impact the U.S. economy?**

 **II Review**

Review History
A. How did Nixon assist the space program?
B. What economic problems did the United States face in the 1970s?

Define Terms to Know
Provide a definition for each of the following terms. **affirmative action, détente, stagflation**

Critical Thinking
Do you think President Nixon's accomplishments outweigh his failures? Why or why not?

Write About Government
Write an editorial about Watergate and Nixon's efforts to cover it up. Explain why you think Nixon should or should not have resigned.

Get Organized
TIMELINE
Think about the main events in this section. Make a timeline listing at least five events in chronological order.

III Domestic Crises

Active Reading

SUMMARIZE
When you summarize information, you restate the main ideas in your own words. As you read this section, summarize the problems that existed in the United States during the 1970s.

A. Ford Takes Over

When President Nixon resigned, he and his family left Washington, D.C., the same day, leaving behind a weakened presidency and a nation that no longer trusted its government. Vice President Gerald Rudolph Ford became President. Ford attempted to resolve the problems that had plagued Nixon. He also wanted to continue the successful programs of the Nixon administration.

Richard Nixon announces his resignation.

Ford Pardons Nixon

Ford's first major act upon taking office was to pardon Nixon. He released the former President from any possible penalty that might result from federal crimes he may have committed in office. Nixon had not been found guilty of any federal crimes, but this action ensured that he would never stand trial.

By pardoning Nixon, Ford hoped to restore confidence in the White House. He reasoned that the United States would then be free to focus on the future. Ford reassured the American people that "our long national nightmare is over." Unfortunately, many people did not agree with the President. They felt that if Nixon had broken the law, he should stand trial like any other citizen.

Gerald Ford was the first person to serve as Vice President and President without ever having been elected to either office.

During Nixon's presidency, Vice President Spiro Agnew resigned. Nixon chose Gerald Ford as Agnew's replacement. Then, Ford took over the office of President after Nixon resigned in 1974.

Problems With the Economy Continue

Ford inherited an ailing economy from Nixon. Unemployment and prices were high. No end to inflation was in sight. Ford explained to the American people that "the State of the Union is not good."

President Ford believed that a balanced budget was the key to bringing down inflation. A balanced budget occurs when government spending is equal to or less than government income. Ford tried to achieve this by cutting spending. The Democratic Congress, however, then increased funding for social programs.

Ford also asked Americans to help stop inflation by holding down prices and wages voluntarily. Though buttons urged people to "WIN" (Whip Inflation Now), Americans did not take the program seriously.

Ford's Foreign Policy

Ford continued Nixon's policy of détente in foreign affairs. Like Nixon, Ford traveled to China and the Soviet Union to improve relations with these Communist countries.

Ford also eased the Cold War slightly. In 1975, Ford met with delegates from Canada, the Soviet Union, and 35 European countries in Helsinki, Finland. Their goal was to discuss arms control and ease tensions between the Soviet Union and other countries in Europe. These talks resulted in the signing of the Helsinki Accords. The provisions of the Helsinki Accords included the following:

1. Each country would respect the post-World War II boundaries in Europe.
2. **Human rights**, or freedoms that all people should have, would be observed in all cooperating countries.

★ **In what two ways did Ford try to improve the economy?**

B. Democrats Win Back the White House

In 1976, the United States celebrated its bicentennial—the two-hundredth anniversary of the adoption of the Declaration of Independence. It also conducted a presidential election.

The Election of 1976

President Ford sought a full term as President in 1976. Some Americans blamed Ford for the poor economy. In the two-and-a-half years he was in office, Ford had made few changes. The economy was in a **recession**, or a period of reduced economic activity. Others felt Ford should not have pardoned Nixon. Nevertheless, he won the Republican nomination for President in 1976.

The Democrats nominated James Earl Carter, Jr. the former governor of Georgia. Jimmy Carter emphasized the fact that he was a Washington outsider. In this way, he hoped to distance himself from America's distrust of government leaders. Some voters viewed being an outsider as an advantage. Others saw it as a drawback.

Carter won the election by a slim margin. Voter turnout was very low, and Americans remained unhappy with the government. Carter hoped to renew Americans' trust in the government. He said,

> **"**We must once again have full faith in our country— and in one another. I believe America can be better. We can be even stronger than before. **"**

ANALYZE PRIMARY SOURCES

DOCUMENT-BASED QUESTION
According to Carter, how can Americans strengthen the country?

The Economy, the Energy Crisis, and the Environment

One of the greatest challenges that President Carter faced was the economic situation. Inflation continued to soar. The rate of inflation rose from 11.3 percent in 1979 to 13.5 percent in 1980. The United States remained dependent on imported oil, and the price of gas continued to rise. Fossil fuels such as coal and oil were being used faster than they could be extracted from their underground sources. This shortage of fuel created an energy crisis. In response, Carter urged Americans to search for alternative energy sources.

Scientists studied wind and solar energy—energy from the power of the sun—as alternatives. Both sources were clean and inexpensive, but they were not practical in most areas of the country. A constant supply of wind or sun was needed to provide enough energy. Also, without a way to store wind or solar power, the systems could not be used all the time.

Another solution to the energy crisis was nuclear power. However, environmentalists were concerned about radioactive waste and the possibility of a nuclear explosion. Their fears were realized in March 1979. An accident at the Three Mile Island nuclear plant in Pennsylvania threatened to spread radioactive fallout to the surrounding area. Thousands of women and children were evacuated from their homes. The problem was eventually solved, but people's fears about nuclear power increased.

The Effects of Inflation

1976		1980
	Gallon of Gasoline	
$0.59		$1.19
	Bicycle	
$74.99		$93.99
	Guitar	
$19.95		$24.95
	Minimum Wage	
$2.30		$3.10

✔ **Chart Check**

If you earned the minimum wage in 1980, how many hours would you have to work to buy a bicycle?

The economy continued to suffer. Government leaders attempted to improve the economy by tightening credit and curbing spending. However, continuing OPEC hikes in the price of oil reversed any gains that the government made.

★ **In what ways did Americans try to solve the energy crisis?**

C. Carter's Foreign Policy

Although he had little experience in foreign policy, President Carter promoted peace and human rights across the globe. However, his policies provoked negative responses from some nations.

The Middle East and the Soviet Union

Carter's greatest success as President was an agreement between the leaders of Egypt and Israel. Conflicts in the Middle East had been occurring for years. However, in 1977, Egyptian President Anwar el-Sadat moved toward establishing peace. Carter invited President Sadat and Israeli Prime Minister Menachem Begin to Camp David, the presidential retreat. At the end of two weeks of discussions, the leaders signed the Camp David Accords. This agreement led to a formal treaty in 1979. Egypt agreed to recognize Israel as a nation. In return, Israel returned the Sinai Peninsula to Egypt.

Carter did not enjoy the same success with the relationship between the United States and the Soviet Union. Carter criticized the Soviet Union's restraint of free speech and other basic human rights. Tensions between the two countries increased, and the Cold War escalated.

President Sadat (left) and Prime Minister Begin (right) are shown here with President Carter.

Americans Held in Iran

Another major setback in foreign policy occurred in 1979. For more than 20 years, the United States had supported the Iranian monarch, known as the shah. However, a revolution in Iran in 1979 removed the shah from power. The Ayatollah Khomeini, a religious leader, took control of Iran. Khomeini encouraged his followers to fight against the Western influence of the United States. When the U.S. government allowed the shah to enter the United States for medical treatment, angry Iranians stormed the U.S. embassy in the capital city of Tehran on November 4, 1979. They took more than 60 Americans **hostage**, or captive, and demanded that the shah be returned to Iran.

Americans were outraged over the hostage crisis. When efforts to negotiate with Khomeini proved unsuccessful, President Carter ordered a rescue mission. However, several of the rescue helicopters were disabled in a sandstorm, and one collided with another aircraft and crashed in the Iranian desert. Eight American soldiers died. The mission's failure caused Americans to question Carter's abilities as a leader. In January 1981, after 444 days of captivity, the hostages were finally released—on the day that Ronald Reagan became President.

American hostages were held captive in Iran for more than a year.

 How was Carter's foreign policy both successful and unsuccessful?

 **III Review**

Review History
A. What was the first major task President Ford felt he needed to accomplish?
B. Why did President Carter encourage Americans to develop alternative sources of energy?
C. What prompted the hostage crisis in Iran?

Define Terms to Know
Provide a definition for each of the following terms.
human rights, recession, hostage

Critical Thinking
Why do you think the economic problems during the 1970s affected Americans' view of the presidency?

Write About Citizenship
Write a letter to President Carter expressing the feelings of Americans during the hostage crisis. What would you ask the President to do?

Get Organized
TIMELINE
Look at the dates given in this section. Place at least five of them on your timeline so you can get a better sense of what happened during the Ford and Carter presidencies.

Chapter Summary

In your notebook, complete the following outline. Then, use your outline to write a brief summary of the chapter.

Turbulent Times

I. The End of the Vietnam War

    A. Battles at Home

    B.

    C.

II. Nixon's Administration

    A.

    B.

III. Domestic Crises

    A.

    B.

    C.

Interpret the Timeline

Use the timeline on pages 702–703 to answer the following questions.

1. How many years passed between the My Lai massacre and the end of the Vietnam War?

2. **Critical Thinking** Which event marked the beginning of the end of the Vietnam War? Explain your answer.

Use Terms to Know

Select the term that best completes each sentence.

affirmative action   **hostage**   **stagflation**
détente   **recession**

1. When economic activity declines, the economy is in a _____.

2. Nixon's policy to ease tensions between the United States and the Soviet Union was known as _____.

3. The goal of _____ was to increase opportunities for minorities and women.

4. A condition of no economic growth and rising prices is known as _____.

5. The Iran _____ crisis outraged many Americans.

Check Your Understanding

1. **Explain** why protesters in Chicago were upset at the nomination of Hubert Humphrey in 1968.

2. **Describe** the process of Vietnamization.

3. **Identify** Nixon's main foreign policy successes.

4. **Explain** why Nixon's actions after the Watergate break-in were considered cause for impeachment.

5. **Identify** Ford's first major act upon becoming President.

6. **Discuss** what many people consider to be Carter's main success.

Critical Thinking

1. **Analyze Primary Sources** Do you think the artist who drew the cartoon on page 707 thought that the Vietnam War would end soon? Explain.

2. **Make Inferences** Why do you think Nixon resigned rather than face an impeachment trial?

3. **Compare and Contrast** What were the same and different about the Ford and Carter administrations?

Put Your Skills to Work
EVALUATE INFORMATION

You have learned that evaluating information can help you make intelligent political decisions. Look at the poster about Jimmy Carter. List the emotional words and images. Explain why they are or are not effective.

Carter campaign poster

In Your Own Words
JOURNAL WRITING

Americans enjoy honoring important events in U.S. history. The bicentennial celebrations in 1976 lasted throughout the year. Festivals, concerts, and parades were held in all 50 states to honor the two-hundredth anniversary of the Declaration of Independence. Each year Americans also celebrate this event with fireworks displays on the Fourth of July. Write a journal entry describing a patriotic celebration you have attended.

Net Work
INTERNET ACTIVITY

Work with one other student in your class. Use the Internet as a resource to research the harmful effects of fossil fuels on the environment. Create a cause/effect chart to illustrate your findings. Then, create a poster suggesting ways that people can reduce the effects of fossil fuels. Include illustrations, photographs, or diagrams to make your poster more persuasive.

For help in starting this activity, visit the following Web site: www.gfamericanhistory.com.

Look Ahead
In the next chapter, learn about issues the United States faced from the 1980s to the present.

CHAPTER 31

New Challenges for the Nation 1980–Present

I. **The Reagan Years** 1981–1989
II. **A Changing World** 1987–1993
III. **Americans Respond to Crises** 1992–Present

On January 20, 1981, Ronald Wilson Reagan's inauguration day, the American hostages were freed in Iran. In his inaugural address, Reagan warned the enemies of the United States:

 " Above all, we must realize that no . . . weapon . . . is so formidable [fearful] as the will and moral courage of free men and women. It is a weapon our adversaries [enemies] in today's world do not have. It is a weapon that we as Americans do have. Let that be understood by those who practice terrorism and prey upon their neighbors. **"**

In the coming decades, however, new challenges at home and abroad would test the "will and moral courage" of Americans and their leaders as never before.

Presidential Seal

U.S. Events	1982	1986	1990
	1981 President Reagan is shot and recovers. Sandra Day O'Connor is first woman appointed to U.S. Supreme Court.	**1986** Iran-Contra scandal is made public.	**1990** Congress passes the Americans with Disabilities Act.

Presidential Term Begins   1981 Ronald Reagan   1989 George Bush

World Events	1982	1986	1990

1981 American hostages are released in Iran.

1985 Mikhail Gorbachev becomes leader of Soviet Union.

1989 Berlin Wall opens. U.S. troops arrive in Panama.

1991 Iraq is defeated in Persian Gulf War.

VIEW HISTORY The White House is the temporary home of the President's family. For most of its history, public areas of the house have been open to visitors. The Presidential Seal (left) appears on official documents and soldiers' buttons.

★ **What are some advantages and disadvantages of allowing tourists to visit the White House?**

Get Organized

SPIDER DIAGRAM

A spider diagram helps you organize information. As you read Chapter 31, use a spider diagram to organize important facts from each section. Write a topic in the circle. Then, list related facts on the lines outside the circle. Here is an example from this chapter.

Cut taxes
Make government smaller
Reduce some government spending
Reagan's economic plan
Increase money for defense

1993
Ruth Bader Ginsburg is appointed to U.S. Supreme Court.

1994
North American Free Trade Agreement (NAFTA) takes effect.

1995
Federal building in Oklahoma City is bombed.

1999
Clinton is acquitted after his impeachment trial.

2001
World Trade Center and Pentagon are attacked by terrorists.
Hijacked plane crashes in Pennsylvania.
United States leads war on terrorism.

1994   **1998**   **2002**

1993 William Clinton   2001 George W. Bush

1994   **1998**   **2002**

1994
Nelson Mandela is elected president of South Africa.

1999
NATO countries take action against Serbia.

2000
USS *Cole* is attacked in Yemen by terrorists.

The Reagan Years 1981–1989

I

Terms to Know

deregulation the loosening of government controls

federal deficit the difference produced when the government spends more than it collects during a year

national debt the total amount of money the federal government owes to individuals, institutions, and itself

Main Ideas

A. Ronald Reagan, the new conservative President, faced a number of crises early in his presidency.

B. President Reagan carried out conservative policies at home.

C. Reagan's foreign policy was based on a strong defense and a focus on communism and the Soviet Union.

Active Reading

ANALYZE PROBLEMS AND SOLUTIONS
Understanding problems and how people deal with them can help us to understand people themselves. As you read this section, pay attention to how Reagan dealt with problems in the 1980s.

A. Reagan's First Year

The 1960s and 1970s had been decades of social and cultural turbulence in the United States. When President Ronald Reagan took office in 1981, many Americans were ready for stability. However, even after the return of the hostages from Iran, Reagan faced many early crises.

The New Right

During the 1980 election, Reagan gained the support of conservative groups known as the New Right. Some of these groups pushed for smaller government and lower taxes. Others focused on social issues.

One group, called the Moral Majority, promoted "family values"—an emphasis on family life, patriotism, and hard work—and social reforms, such as allowing prayer in public schools. This group, led by Reverend Jerry Falwell and others, raised millions of dollars to help elect conservatives in the 1980s. Generally, conservatives believe in smaller government.

A Rough Start

On March 30, 1981, about two months after his inauguration, President Reagan and others were shot by John Hinckley Jr. One bullet entered Reagan's chest and barely missed his heart. Fortunately, the President recovered quickly. The assassination attempt would eventually have an effect on gun laws in the United States.

President Ronald Reagan and First Lady Nancy Reagan

Sarah Brady and her husband James, who was a Reagan staff member and a victim of the shooting, led the fight to make buying a handgun more difficult. Congress finally passed the Brady Handgun Violence Prevention Bill in 1993.

Reagan faced another crisis during the first year of his presidency —a strike by federal air traffic controllers. Strikes by workers whose services are critical to public safety are illegal in the United States, so Reagan ordered the controllers back to work. When they refused, he fired thousands of controllers in August 1981. Reagan's action sent a tough message that he would firmly act on policies he thought were good for the nation.

 What groups supported Ronald Reagan for President?

B. Conservative Policies at Home

Reagan said the federal government was too big. He argued that less government interference in business and in people's lives would help the economy. Reagan's plan to help the economy was a major part of the "Reagan Revolution," or the return to conservative values and government policies.

Reagan's Economic Plan

Reagan believed that reducing tax rates would help the economy by giving people and businesses more money to spend. For example, a business might use money from a tax cut to invest in a new factory. A new factory might provide jobs for many people. Reagan's ideas were known as supply-side economics because they were meant to increase the supply of money to invest and create new goods and services.

The prospect of tax cuts was so popular that both Republicans and Democrats in Congress supported Reagan's plan. In 1981, Congress enacted the biggest tax cut in the nation's history. Tax rates were reduced for all Americans, but critics charged that high-income people benefited most. Tax cuts for the wealthy supported an idea called the trickle-down theory. According to this theory, more money spent by wealthy Americans would "trickle down," creating jobs and opportunities for middle- and low-income Americans. For example, if wealthy Americans bought more boats, then more people would need to be employed to design, build, and sell them.

Along with cutting taxes, Reagan wanted to reduce some government regulations on businesses. This **deregulation** was meant to help businesses become more profitable, thus strengthening the economy. Reagan also favored less federal spending on education, the environment, and housing. He wanted states, charities, businesses, and individuals to help more in these areas.

Meet the President

Ronald Wilson Reagan

Born 1911

Years in office 1981–1989

Political Party Republican

Birthplace Illinois

Age when elected 69

Occupations Sports Announcer, Actor, Governor of California

Nicknames The Great Communicator, Dutch

Did you know? Reagan had been a Democrat before he went into politics.

Quote "It is not my intention to do away with government. It is, rather, to make it work."

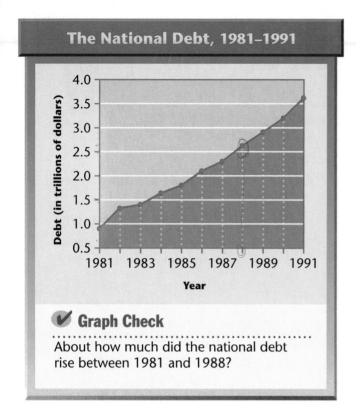

The National Debt, 1981–1991

Debt (in trillions of dollars) vs. *Year*

✔ **Graph Check**

About how much did the national debt rise between 1981 and 1988?

Mixed Results

Reagan's economic policies had some positive effects. Under President Carter, inflation had soared to 13.5 percent in 1980. Under Reagan, it was less than 5 percent in 1988. Jobs were created at a rapid pace—20 million people were added to the employment rolls during Reagan's two terms in office.

The government had been operating with a **federal deficit** for years. A federal deficit occurs when the government spends more than it takes in from taxes, fees, and other sources during a year. During Reagan's presidency, deficits increased. By 1988, the **national debt**—the total of all the money the government owed to the public and itself—was more than $2.6 trillion. One reason for this huge debt was that Reagan's policies required a great deal of military spending. Many Americans began to wonder if this kind of debt was wise. How would it ever be repaid?

Changes on the Supreme Court

Another way that Reagan extended his conservative policies was by reshaping the Supreme Court. He did this by appointing conservative justices. In 1981, Reagan appointed the first woman justice to the Supreme Court—Sandra Day O'Connor. Next, he promoted Justice William Rehnquist to the position of Chief Justice. During Rehnquist's tenure as Chief Justice, he improved the efficiency of the Court, cut its caseload, and led the Court in making many conservative rulings. Then, Reagan appointed two more conservative justices: Antonin Scalia in 1986 and Anthony Kennedy in 1988. As a result of Reagan's appointments, the Supreme Court developed a strong conservative voice.

The Election of 1984

Reagan ran for re-election in 1984. The Democratic Party's candidate was Walter Mondale, Jimmy Carter's Vice President. Mondale chose Geraldine Ferraro as his running mate. Ferraro was the first woman to run for Vice President on the ticket of a major political party. In the election, Reagan won 59 percent of the popular vote. He won every state except Mondale's home state of Minnesota and the District of Columbia.

★ **What is supply-side economics?**

C. Reagan and Foreign Affairs

Ronald Reagan believed in a strong military and an active foreign policy. He felt that communism and the Soviet Union were threats to the United States. During Reagan's first term, he called the Soviet Union "an evil empire." In his second term, however, he participated in changing U.S.-Soviet relations in surprising ways.

Foreign Policy in Latin America and the Middle East

Reagan fought communism in Central America. In Nicaragua, he supported the Contras, a rebel group fighting against the Sandinistas, a Communist group in power. In 1984, Congress banned U.S. help to the Contras. However, some members of the Reagan administration arranged secret sales of weapons to Iran, in the Middle East, and then gave the money to the Contras. After news of these deals came out in 1986, Congress held televised hearings. The secret deals became known as the Iran-Contra scandal. Reagan, however, was never proven to have been directly involved.

In the Middle East, Reagan tried to keep the peace in war-torn Lebanon. However, after American soldiers were attacked and killed in their barracks there, he withdrew the U.S. troops.

Reagan and his missile defense plan were featured on a magazine cover in 1983.

The Arms Race and Changes in the Soviet Union

Reagan encouraged Congress to approve large spending increases for defense. He asked for billions of dollars for the B-1 bomber, the MX missile, and the Strategic Defense Initiative (SDI). The purpose of the SDI project, sometimes nicknamed "Star Wars," was to create a space- and Earth-based defense system to protect the United States against missile attacks from the Soviet Union.

As U.S. military strength increased, the Soviets were forced to spend more on their military. This speeding up of the arms race between the two superpowers put a huge strain on the Soviet economy. The Soviet Union could not afford to keep up with U.S. military spending without causing severe shortages in basic consumer goods, such as food, shoes, and paper products.

Early in Reagan's second term, Mikhail Gorbachev became the new leader of the Soviet Union. Economic conditions in the Soviet Union were poor. Gorbachev believed that in order to preserve communism he would need to make changes to it. Gorbachev surprised the world with his ideas about reforming the Soviet government. In 1985, he called for a policy of glasnost, or openness to new ideas and freedom of expression. He also promoted reforms that would make the economy respond to the needs of the Soviet people. Gorbachev also wanted to establish a better relationship with the United States and to reduce military spending. Reagan and Gorbachev met several times and eventually developed a good relationship. Finally, in 1987, the two leaders signed the Intermediate-Range Nuclear Forces (INF) Treaty, an agreement aimed at reducing the number of nuclear missiles in both countries.

Today, several of the world's nations have nuclear weapons. Reagan's SDI project, developed to defend the United States against the Soviet Union, is now led by the Ballistic Missile Defense Organization (BMDO). BMDO's programs focus on intercepting possible attacks by terrorists or nations that use or support terrorism as well as on ballistic missiles launched accidentally. Beginning in March 1999, several tests resulted in the successful destruction of ballistic missile targets.

 Who were the Contras?

I Review

Review History
A. What crises did Reagan face in 1981?
B. What were some effects of Reagan's economic plan?
C. How did Reagan deal with the Soviet Union during his first and second terms?

Define Terms to Know
Provide a definition for each of the following terms. **deregulation, federal deficit, national debt**

Critical Thinking
What were the positive and negative aspects of increased military spending?

Write About Government
Write a letter to President Reagan about the country's new relationship with the Soviet Union.

Get Organized
SPIDER DIAGRAM
Use a spider diagram to organize information from this section. Choose a topic and then find related facts. For example, what were some of the main concerns of the New Right?

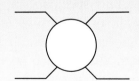

Build Your Skills

IMPROVE YOUR TEST-TAKING SKILLS

You have taken many tests. In some tests, you answered true-or-false, multiple-choice, fill-in-the-blank, or matching questions. In other tests, you answered essay questions. By following some basic test-taking tips, you can improve your scores on all kinds of tests.

Here's How

Follow these steps to improve your scores.

1. Take notes on your reading. With a partner, practice asking and answering questions that may be on the test.

2. When you get the test, skim it quickly. Decide how long you will take to do each part.

3. Read the directions carefully. Be sure you know where and how to mark the answers. In an essay test, pay special attention to key direction words, such as *compare*, *list*, and *define*.

4. Read all the choices in multiple-choice questions. If you are unsure of an answer, eliminate the wrong answers, then choose the best answer that is left.

5. Look over your work. Do not change answers unless you are certain you made a mistake.

Here's Why

Improving your test-taking skills is a good way to improve your test scores.

Practice the Skill

With a partner, skim Section I of this chapter. Write a question using each direction word in the chart. Exchange questions with another pair of students and answer them. Check each other's answers.

Extend the Skill

Look at some old tests. What answers did you get wrong? What tip in *Here's How* might help you avoid the mistakes you made? Write new test-taking tips if you need them.

Apply the Skill

As you read the remaining sections of this chapter, write a question using each direction word in the chart. Exchange questions with another student and answer them.

Key Direction Words	
DIRECTION WORDS	**WHAT TO DO**
Compare	Show how things are alike.
Contrast	Show how things are different.
Define	Tell what something means.
Discuss	Present your ideas.
Illustrate	Give examples.
Evaluate	Give good and bad points; then draw a conclusion.

II A Changing World 1987–1993

Terms to Know

downsize lay off or fire workers to cut costs

apartheid a policy in South Africa of complete separation of the races

Main Ideas

A. President George Bush tackled a troubled economy by agreeing to raise taxes.

B. Congress passed legislation to help disabled Americans and the environment.

C. President Bush faced foreign crises in Europe, the Middle East, Central America, and Africa.

 **Active Reading**

SUMMARIZE
To summarize is to find the key ideas, those most important to remember. As you read this section, summarize the key ideas you want to remember about the Bush administration.

★★★★★★★
Meet
the President
★★★★★★★★★★★★★

George H. W. Bush

Born 1924

Years in office 1989–1993

Political Party Republican

Birthplace Massachusetts

Age when elected 64

Occupations Navy Pilot, Oil Executive, C.I.A. Director

Nickname Poppy

Did you know? George H. W. Bush and his son George W. Bush are the second father-son Presidents. John Adams and his son John Q. Adams were the first.

Quote "We know what works: freedom works. We know what's right: freedom is right."

A. The Economy Under Bush

When Ronald Reagan's term as President ended in 1988, his Vice President, George Herbert Walker Bush, ran for election. Bush defeated Democrat Michael Dukakis easily. However, Bush inherited the economic difficulties of high federal deficits.

The Stock Market

During Reagan's administration, the country had gone deeply into debt. The interest on the debt strained the federal budget. American consumers also went into debt. Many people used credit cards and loans to buy items like TVs and cars. With high consumer and federal debt, the economy began to show signs of trouble.

In October 1987, the stock market suffered a large drop. The crash was called "Black Monday." Prices soon rebounded, but people were nervous. They wondered whether another crash would occur.

"No New Taxes"

Bush had made a promise during his 1988 campaign that if Congress pushed for higher taxes, his reply would be, "Read my lips: No new taxes." The slow economy, however, and the anxiety over the stock market forced Bush to take back that promise. To deal with the high deficit, Bush agreed in 1990 to raise taxes and cut federal spending. Many Americans were outraged. They felt that Bush had lied to them.

 Why did George Bush change his mind about raising taxes?

B. New Laws Helping Americans

Like Reagan, President Bush believed in conservative ideas. He promised that his policies would help Americans and the world. During his inaugural speech, Bush said:

> ❝America is never wholly herself unless she is engaged in high moral principle. We as a people have such a purpose today. It is to make kinder the face of the nation and gentler the face of the world.❞

ANALYZE PRIMARY SOURCES

DOCUMENT-BASED QUESTION
What was Bush's goal for the United States?

In two important areas, Bush and Congress cooperated to produce laws that improved the lives of Americans. Bush signed these laws even though there would be costs to business.

The Americans With Disabilities Act

In 1990, Bush supported passage of the Americans With Disabilities Act (ADA). This new civil rights law protected the rights of more than 43 million people with disabilities. The law's intent was to make all areas of American life more open to people with disabilities. It required businesses and governments to build ramps, widen doors, and make other changes.

The law covered employment, public services such as transportation, public accommodations such as stores and theaters, and telephone service. The ADA has enabled many disabled people to travel to school and work and to live independently.

Cleaning the Air

President Bush also signed amendments to the Clean Air Act of 1970. These amendments focused on three main environmental problems:

1. acid rain, mostly caused by emissions from coalburning factories
2. smog, from a combination of pollutants
3. hazardous pollutants from cars and other vehicles

⭐ **What were some effects of the Americans With Disabilities Act?**

Because of the ADA, this businessperson can travel to work by bus.

People celebrated the opening of the Berlin Wall in 1989.

C. Dramatic World Events

The world changed in dramatic and surprising ways during the presidency of George Bush. Movements toward democracy spread to many countries. The Cold War between the United States and the Soviet Union ended after almost 50 years, leaving the United States as the only superpower. However, in some parts of the world, violence erupted and freedom was suppressed.

The End of the Cold War

Since the end of World War II, the world had been divided between Communist and non-Communist nations. Ronald Reagan had worked to defeat the Soviet Union and then to support its efforts at reform. As greater freedoms spread across the country during the mid-1980s, unrest in Soviet satellite countries increased. During the late 1980s, communism began to collapse in Eastern Europe. Movements toward democracy swept through Poland, Czechoslovakia, Hungary, and other parts of Eastern Europe. Huge demonstrations against Communist governments took place, and Communist leaders fled. Free elections were held, and borders were opened. The Berlin Wall separating East and West Berlin was opened in 1989, and East and West Germany were reunited in 1990.

In 1991, the Soviet Union broke apart into one huge republic, Russia, and 14 smaller republics. An era had ended: The Cold War between the Soviet Union and the United States was over. Whether the world would eventually be a safer place than before was not yet clear.

Protests in China

In the Communist country of China, in Asia, students and workers also called for greater democracy during the late 1980s. In May 1989, thousands of Chinese students held a peaceful demonstration in Tiananmen Square in the capital city, Beijing. They were there to support a move toward democracy in China. They stayed in the square for more than a month. Then, on June 3–4, the Chinese government rolled out tanks and guns to clear the square. Several hundred demonstrators were killed. The Communist government of China was not ready to accept democracy. President Bush reacted to the events in Tiananmen Square by stopping sales of military supplies to China. Other trade with China was allowed to grow.

Sending Troops to Panama

President Bush also had to deal with issues closer to home. Manuel Noriega, the ruler of Panama, was heavily involved in international drug trading. He also refused to honor his country's national elections. In December 1989, Bush sent U.S. troops to Panama to capture Noriega. After brief but bloody fighting, Noriega surrendered. He was brought to trial in the United States and sentenced to 40 years in prison. Despite American loss of life, the effort was popular at home. Bush's approval rating soared.

War in the Persian Gulf

Another crisis arose in the Middle East. In August 1990, Iraq invaded oil-rich Kuwait. President Bush sent U.S. troops to the neighboring country of Saudi Arabia to prevent a takeover there. Saudi Arabia was important because it sold oil to the United States.

At the United Nations, the Security Council voted to use armed force if Kuwait was not freed by January 15, 1991. The Iraqi leader, Saddam Hussein, refused to leave. On January 16, the United States and its allies launched an attack called Operation Desert Storm. The attack began with a bombing campaign against Iraq. In February, the allies began a ground attack while continuing their air raids. A few days later, the allied troops claimed victory. Two heroes of the war were General H. Norman Schwarzkopf, commanding general, and General Colin Powell, Chairman of the Joint Chiefs of Staff.

Do You Remember?
In Chapter 22, you learned that the United States built the Panama Canal.

The Persian Gulf War, 1991

Legend:
- Iraqi forces
- Allied ground attacks
- Allied naval forces
- Allied air and missile strikes
- Iraqi missile strikes
- Capital cities

LEBANON, SYRIA, ISRAEL, JORDAN, IRAN, IRAQ, Baghdad, EGYPT, Mediterranean Sea, Kuwait City, SAUDI ARABIA, KUWAIT, BAHRAIN, Persian Gulf, Red Sea, Riyadh, QATAR, UNITED ARAB EMIRATES

0 200 400 mi
0 200 400 km

✔ **Map Check**

1. **LOCATION** In which bodies of water were allied naval forces located?

2. **MOVEMENT** Where did allied ground attacks begin?

After the Persian Gulf War, there seemed to be no question that Bush would be re-elected in 1992. However, a weakened economy and continued deficits hurt his chances. Some businesses, banks, and savings and loan associations were in trouble. A number of companies had started to **downsize**, or lay off workers to save money. Many Americans felt that Bush had spent too much time and energy on problems abroad and not enough in solving problems at home.

Democracy in South Africa

While Bush was President, Americans celebrated a dramatic change in another part of the world—South Africa. For more than 50 years, South Africa had a policy of **apartheid**, or separation. This official policy of racial segregation left black South Africans with no political voice. Black citizens were forced to live in separate areas and were restricted to low-paying jobs. In the early 1960s, Nelson Mandela and the other leaders of the African National Congress (ANC), were arrested. The ANC worked to end apartheid. For the next 28 years Mandela continued to lead the ANC from prison. In the early 1990s, under pressure from protesters within South Africa and from trade boycotts by other countries, South Africa began changing its apartheid laws.

★ **What major events took place in Eastern Europe and South Africa during the late 1980s and the 1990s?**

II Review

Review History
A. Why was raising taxes a special problem for President Bush?
B. What two important laws helped disabled Americans and the environment?
C. What were two of Bush's foreign policy successes?

Define Terms to Know
Provide a definition for each of the following terms.
downsize, apartheid

Critical Thinking
During the 1990s, U.S. troops were sent to foreign countries. In what situations do you think U.S. troops should be sent overseas?

Write About Economics
President Bush felt forced to raise taxes after he had promised not to. Write a speech to the American public explaining why a tax increase was necessary.

Get Organized
SPIDER DIAGRAM
Use a spider diagram to organize information from this section. Choose a topic, and then find related facts. For example, what were some foreign crises in the late 1980s?

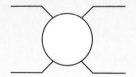

CONNECT
History & the Environment

Exxon Valdez Oil Spill

Most of the energy the world uses today comes from fossil fuels, such as oil. For more than 20 years, energy companies have drilled for oil in the state of Alaska. Many Americans support the drilling because they feel it makes the United States less dependent on foreign oil. Environmentalists, however, worry about possible damage to the land, wildlife, and people of Alaska.

THE DISASTER On March 24, 1989, the largest oil spill in U.S. history occurred in Alaska. The *Exxon Valdez*, a giant oil tanker, ran aground on a reef in Prince William Sound. About 11 million gallons of crude oil spilled into the sound.

The National Transportation Safety Board, the U.S. Coast Guard, and the state of Alaska investigated the accident. Government agencies, private companies, and environmental groups tried to clean up the site and save the wildlife. However, within a few days, strong winds scattered the oil far beyond the accident site. The oil combined with seawater to form mousse, a mixture that is difficult to remove from the water's surface or the shore.

THE IMPACT OF THE DISASTER Hundreds of thousands of animals—including fish, sea otters, and bald eagles—were killed as a result of the oil spill. Ten years later, many species had not recovered from the damage. In addition to the environmental damage, there were economic consequences. Property values and fishing and hunting grounds were affected.

After the *Exxon Valdez* oil spill, Congress passed the Oil Pollution Act of 1990. The act required stronger tanker hulls. The hull is the body of a ship.

Critical Thinking
Answer the following questions. Then, complete the activity.

1. What made the cleanup process so difficult in Prince William Sound?

2. Should U.S. oil companies expand drilling for oil in Alaska? Why or why not?

Write About It
Go to the following Web site to learn more about drilling and transporting oil in Alaska and other areas: www.gfamericanhistory.com. Then, research an animal that lives in an area in which oil is found. Write a paragraph that describes one way to protect the animal's environment, with or without oil drilling.

This seabird with oil-matted feathers is being rinsed with a powerful hose.

III

Americans Respond to Crises
1992–Present

Terms to Know

nation-building the support of developing governments in foreign countries

ethnic cleansing the act of ridding a region or society of one or more ethnic groups

terrorism the use of violence or threats to achieve a goal

grand jury a jury that decides if the charges against a person are strong enough for a trial

Main Ideas

A. During most of Bill Clinton's presidency, the economy improved.

B. Clinton used diplomacy and U.S. forces to try to solve problems abroad.

C. Terrorism, impeachment, and a close election disturbed many Americans.

D. The United States responded to terrorist attacks on American soil.

Active Reading

PREDICT
When you predict, you make an educated guess about what will happen next. As you read this section, identify the main concerns of Americans from the 1990s to 2002. Then, predict the topics of major concern ten years from now.

A. Clinton Takes Command

During the 1992 presidential election, President Bush emphasized his achievements in foreign policy. However, voters worried about having enough money in their pockets. They were afraid Bush did not have the answers to high federal deficits and rising unemployment.

Three Presidential Candidates

The Democratic candidate, Arkansas Governor William Jefferson Clinton, and his running mate, Tennessee Senator Albert Gore Jr., challenged President Bush and Vice President Dan Quayle. However, Americans did not strongly support either major-party ticket in the 1992 campaign. As a result, a third candidate, businessman H. Ross Perot, gained supporters and later founded the Reform Party.

Perot promised to deal with the national debt and clean up the federal government. His energy and enthusiastic supporters got him on the ballot in every state. In the end, however, most Americans voted for the two major-party candidates. On election day, Perot won no electoral votes. He did, however, receive almost 20 million popular votes—more than any other third-party candidate in history.

Bush (left), Clinton, and Perot (right) explained their views during a 1992 debate.

Hillary Clinton led the task force on healthcare. Later, in 2000, she was elected U.S. senator from New York, becoming the first First Lady elected to the U.S. Senate.

Successes and Failures

During the 1992 campaign, Clinton's main issue was the economy. This strategy worked, and he won the election. Early in Clinton's presidency, an ambitious plan for national health insurance failed to win approval in the Congress. However, later in his term, the nation experienced a low unemployment rate and the lowest inflation in 30 years. He submitted the first balanced budget in decades and even achieved a budget surplus. Clinton supported welfare reform, and the number of people on welfare dropped. He also worked hard to end racial discrimination.

President Bush had signed a free trade agreement between the United States and its neighbors. Like Bush, Clinton supported the North American Free Trade Agreement (NAFTA) with Canada and Mexico. The agreement went into effect in January 1994. It removed tariffs and other barriers to trade among the three countries.

During the Clinton years, good economic times caused some people to invest unwisely in the stock market. However, others became rich from their investments. Some started Internet businesses that prospered rapidly. Many of these businesses, however, eventually failed, and by 2000, there were signs of a weakening economy.

⭐ What was Clinton's main issue in the 1992 election?

B. Clinton's Foreign Policy

Clinton's approach to foreign policy was affected by the end of the Cold War and the breakup of the Soviet Union. Clinton did not need to focus on containing or defeating communism around the world. Instead, he used diplomacy and U.S. armed forces to try to resolve a variety of problems abroad. He also tried to assist in the development of democratic governments. This strategy came to be called **nation-building**.

★★★★★★★
Meet
the President
★★★★★★★★★★★★★★★

William J. Clinton
Born 1946

Years in office 1993–2001

Political Party Democratic

Birthplace Arkansas

Age when elected 46

Occupations Lawyer, Governor of Arkansas

Nickname Bill, The Comeback Kid

Did you know? When Clinton was a teenager, he met President John Kennedy at the White House.

Quote "The sun is rising on America again."

Troubles in Bosnia and Kosovo

The end of the Cold War brought conflicts in the Balkan countries of southeastern Europe. In Bosnia, in the former Yugoslavia, three main ethnic groups—Croats, Muslims, and Serbs—were fighting for control. Serbian troops engaged in **ethnic cleansing**. They hoped to kill or expel all Muslims and Croats from their villages so that only Serbs would be left.

In 1994, after years of fighting, the United States and other countries of the North Atlantic Treaty Organization (NATO) launched air attacks on the Serbs. Clinton brought the opposing groups together in 1995, and the Dayton Peace Agreement was signed. With the peace agreement, the air attacks ended.

In 1998, more trouble occurred in the Balkans. This time Serbs applied ethnic cleansing policies against Albanians living in Kosovo. In 1999, the United States and other NATO countries bombed the Serbs again. Then they began a peacekeeping mission to try to bring safety and supplies to the devastated region.

Problems in Africa and the Caribbean

In Somalia, in Africa, a drought and fighting among different groups caused widespread starvation. President Bush had sent U.S. troops to Somalia to help ensure that food and medical supplies were safely delivered. In 1993, Clinton sent soldiers to capture a Somali warlord. Eighteen soldiers were killed, and the warlord was not captured. The United States withdrew from Somalia in March 1994.

A civil war was also causing mass starvation in Rwanda, in Africa. Because of the U.S. failure in Somalia, Clinton did not send troops to help. In a trip to Rwanda in 1998, Clinton apologized for the international community, which "did not act quickly enough after the killing began."

Still more foreign conflict drew U.S. forces to Haiti, in the Caribbean. In 1994, U.S. troops were sent to return power to Haiti's elected president, Jean-Bertrand Aristide. Former President Jimmy Carter negotiated the peaceful departure of military leaders who had seized power.

An Election in South Africa

In 1990, the South African government released Nelson Mandela from prison. In 1994, South Africa held its first truly democratic election. A government was elected with a black majority, including the president, Nelson Mandela. Mandela's election marked the end of legalized apartheid in South Africa.

Nelson Mandela cast his vote in South Africa's first democratic election.

Clinton is shown here with Prime Minister Yitzhak Rabin (left) of Israel and PLO Chairman Yasser Arafat (right) of Palestine. The two Middle Eastern leaders had just signed the Oslo accords.

Israelis and Palestinians

Clinton made many efforts to bring peace to the Middle East. He witnessed the signing of the Oslo accords in 1993. The accords laid out long-term goals, including the withdrawal of Israeli troops from the Gaza Strip and the West Bank and Palestinian self-rule in those areas. Clinton also worked on a later peace agreement, but talks between the Israelis and Palestinians broke down, and violence continued to erupt in the region.

 How did Clinton respond to the conflict in Bosnia?

Do You Remember?
In Chapter 27, you learned that the state of Israel was formed in 1948 when Palestine was divided.

C. Into the New Millennium

As Americans approached the year 2000, they faced several new problems at home. Acts of violence against the United States shook the country. Also, for the second time in U.S. history, a President was impeached. Then, a close presidential election caused concerns.

Terrorism at Home and Abroad

In the late twentieth century, political violence against the United States increased. A terrible act of **terrorism**, or the use of violence to promote a cause, took place in December 1988 when a jumbo jet, Pan Am Flight 103, was blown up as it flew over Scotland. The explosion killed everyone onboard, including 189 Americans. The bombing of this airplane was the work of Libyan terrorists. In January 2001, one of the men charged with the crime was found guilty of 270 counts of murder.

In 1993, a bomb exploded in a parking garage beneath the World Trade Center in New York City. Six people were killed, and about 1,000 were injured. A group of foreign terrorists were charged with the crime. Six were eventually tried, convicted, and sentenced to 240-year prison terms.

In Oklahoma City in 1995, a bomb inside a van exploded at the Alfred P. Murrah Federal Building. One hundred sixty-eight people, including some children at a day-care center, were killed. Two American men were responsible for this terrorist act. One received the death penalty, while the other was sent to prison for life.

In 1998, terrorists attacked U.S. embassies in Kenya and Tanzania, in Africa. Then, the Navy destroyer USS *Cole* was attacked in October 2000. The ship was refueling in Yemen, in the Middle East. Seventeen crewmembers were killed, and 39 were injured.

Clouds Over the Presidency

As President, Bill Clinton had some successes. The economy was stronger than it had been in decades. Clinton supported civil rights and appointed a second woman to the Supreme Court—Ruth Bader Ginsburg— in 1993. However, scandals during his presidency sometimes overshadowed these successes.

In 1998, a **grand jury** questioned President Clinton about some personal behavior while he was President. A grand jury decides if evidence is strong enough to take a case to court. Many thought that Clinton lied to the grand jury. As a result, Congress adopted two articles of impeachment against him for lying to a grand jury and obstructing justice. This was the second impeachment of a U.S. President—Andrew Johnson was impeached in 1868. In both cases, the Presidents were found not guilty. Clinton completed his term.

The Election of 2000

The election of 2000 saw Clinton's Vice President, Albert Gore Jr., run against George Bush's son, George W. Bush. Gore received the majority of the popular votes. However, the electoral vote was very close. The election hinged on the electoral votes in Florida. Many people thought Florida's ballots should be recounted.

Five weeks of legal battles concerning Florida's electoral votes followed election day. Finally, the U.S. Supreme Court made a decision. The justices voted 5–4 that hand counting of Florida ballots to confirm the number of popular votes could not continue. Time had run out for the entire process. George W. Bush became the forty-third President of the United States.

 **What was unique about the election of 2000?**

★★★★★★★
Meet
the President
★★★★★★★★★★★★★★

George Walker Bush
Born 1946

Years in office 2001–

Political Party Republican

Birthplace Connecticut

Age when elected 54

Occupations Business Owner, Governor of Texas

Nickname "W"

Did you know? Before he became governor of Texas, Bush was managing general partner of a baseball team, the Texas Rangers.

Quote "We have seen the strength of America in countless acts of kindness, compassion, and courage."

D. Terrorist Attacks and U.S. Response

When George W. Bush took office in January 2001, a weakened American economy seemed to be the biggest problem he would face. Americans did not know that nine months into his presidency, foreign terrorists would attack the United States. President Bush would lead the nation's recovery and its response.

A Morning of Terror

On the morning of September 11, 2001, terrorists hijacked four passenger airplanes after their departure from three U.S. airports. The hijackers flew two planes into the 110-story Twin Towers of the World Trade Center, in New York City. Explosions and fires broke out, and the towers fell, releasing giant clouds of ash, glass, smoke, and paper. About an hour after the first attack on the World Trade Center, a third hijacked airliner struck the Pentagon building, near Washington, D.C. The Pentagon is the headquarters of the U.S. Department of Defense. Thirty minutes later, a fourth plane crashed in the countryside near Pittsburgh, Pennsylvania. On that plane, passengers fought with hijackers to take control of the plane and prevent another attack.

Thousands of people died in the attacks of September 11, and thousands of others were injured. The prime suspect of what President Bush called "evil, despicable acts of terror" was Osama bin Laden. From his hiding places in Afghanistan, in Central Asia, bin Laden ran a worldwide network of terrorists called al Qaeda. Osama bin Laden and al Qaeda hated the United States for its policies in the Arab world.

Terrorists attacked the Twin Towers of the World Trade Center, symbols of U.S. economic power.

The Pentagon, near Washington, D.C., after the attacks

They Made History

American Heroes, September 11, 2001

In a speech to Congress and to all Americans on September 20, 2001, President George W. Bush described the courage of the American people in response to the terrorist attacks of September 11. He praised airplane passengers who fought with hijackers over Pennsylvania, as well as rescuers who risked their lives to save fellow Americans in New York City and at the Pentagon. Bush noted the spirit of a "loving and giving people who have made the grief of strangers their own." The people in these photographs reveal that spirit.

Following the attacks at the World Trade Center, firefighters and other rescuers worked around the clock in search of survivors.

Many thousands of workers escaped from the World Trade Center before the towers fell. Fleeing dangerous clouds of dust and falling debris, they often risked their own safety to help others. When the towers finally collapsed, however, several thousand workers and rescuers trapped in the towers died.

New York Mayor Rudolph Giuliani (right) provided encouragement and guidance after the attacks. Here, Giuliani speaks to workers at the World Trade Center site, now called Ground Zero.

Americans across the country shared their grief at candlelight vigils. This one took place in Greenwich Village, in New York City.

At Ground Zero President Bush (left) comforted a weary firefighter. The volunteer (below) traveled from Providence, Rhode Island, to help prepare food for rescue workers at Ground Zero.

In December 2001, the Olympic torch made its way toward Salt Lake City, Utah, for the February 2002 games. The torch arrived at the Pentagon, carried by Chief Petty Officer Bernard Brown. His son was killed in the terrorist attack on the Pentagon.

Critical Thinking Why do you think so many Americans wanted to find ways to help after September 11, 2001?

Many Americans wore ribbons to show support for the country and the war on terrorism.

The War on Terrorism at Home

After the terrorist attacks, Americans reached out to help each other and the victims of the terrorist attacks. At the same time, they wondered if a new attack would come, and when.

The President and other leaders worked hard to make Americans secure. On September 11, the U.S. government reacted quickly, grounding commercial airplanes and closing landmarks and government offices. Soon, military aircraft and ships were dispatched to cities, and National Guard troops were stationed at airports. Then, on October 8, Tom Ridge (the former governor of Pennsylvania) was appointed Director of Homeland Security, a new Cabinet-level office. His job was to coordinate efforts to make Americans safe at home.

As Americans tried to get back to near-normal life after September 11, they faced other challenges. First, some media companies and political leaders received letters containing anthrax, a dangerous form of bacteria, from an unknown source. Several people, including postal workers, died from a serious disease caused by the bacteria. Second, several airplane incidents added to worries about airline security. On one plane, passengers prevented a man from trying to light a shoe bomb.

The Bush administration and Congress took further actions to reassure Americans. They worked to provide medications to those exposed to anthrax, purchase machines to sanitize the U.S. mail, increase airline security, and help Americans learn how to protect themselves from terrorist attacks.

U.S. soldiers were deployed to lead the fight against terrorism in Afghanistan.

The War on Terrorism Abroad

Following the attacks of September 11, President George W. Bush promised to use every effort to disrupt and defeat the global terrorist network. He said that the United States would punish terrorists and the governments that protected them. Great Britain and other countries quickly promised to support U.S. efforts.

The United States began the war on terrorism abroad in the country of Afghanistan. There, the Taliban government protected the terrorist Osama bin Laden and his al Qaeda followers. The United States wanted the Taliban to hand over bin Laden, but the Taliban refused. As a result, the United States began Operation Enduring Freedom by bombing targets in Afghanistan on October 7. U.S. soldiers on the ground helped the Northern Alliance, Afghan opponents of the Taliban, search for and defeat terrorists.

By the end of 2001, the Taliban and al Qaeda had been driven from power. A number of terrorist training camps had been destroyed. Millions of U.S. aid packages had been dropped from planes to help the Afghan people.

As the Taliban left Afghan cities, many residents rejoiced. The Taliban government had enforced an extreme form of Islam. Movies and music were banned. Women were not allowed to work, and girls were forbidden to go to school.

President Bush had warned Americans that the war against terrorism would be difficult and long. It would be fought on the homefront and in a number of places abroad. In his speech of September 20, 2001, he had said,

> " Our nation—this generation—will lift a dark threat of violence from our people and our future. We will rally the world to this cause by our efforts, by our courage. We will not tire, we will not falter, and we will not fail. "

ANALYZE PRIMARY SOURCES

DOCUMENT-BASED QUESTION
How did President Bush plan to gain the support of other countries?

Most Americans expressed support for President Bush and the war on terrorism. They united in support of the victims and rescue workers of the September 11, 2001, attack. Americans carried on with their lives, but they would never forget.

★ **How was the United States attacked on September 11, 2001?**

III Review

Review History
A. What happened to the U.S. economy during the Clinton years?
B. Why did Clinton send troops to other countries?
C. What were some crises at home in the 1990s?
D. How did Americans react to the events of September 11, 2001?

Define Terms to Know
Provide a definition for each of the following terms. **nation-building, ethnic cleansing, terrorism, grand jury**

Critical Thinking
What is the best way for Americans to protect themselves against terrorism?

Write About Government
Write a letter to the editor stating your opinion regarding whether the President should be elected based only on the popular vote. Tell why or why not.

Get Organized
SPIDER DIAGRAM
Use a spider diagram to organize information from this section. Choose a topic, and then find related facts. For example, in which countries did President Clinton practice nation-building?

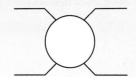

CHAPTER 31 Review

Chapter Summary

In your notebook, complete the following outline. Then, use your outline to write a brief summary of the chapter.

New Challenges for the Nation

I. The Reagan Years 1981-1989

    A. Reagan's First Year

    B.

    C.

II. A Changing World 1987-1993

    A.

    B.

    C.

III. Americans Respond to Crises 1992-Present

    A.

    B.

    C.

    D.

Interpret the Timeline

Use the timeline on pages 724–725 to answer the following questions.

1. Which two Presidents appointed women to the United States Supreme Court?

2. **Critical Thinking** Which world event affected the United States the most? Explain your answer.

Use Terms to Know

Match each term with its definition.

a. apartheid   d. federal deficit

b. deregulation   e. nation-building

c. ethnic cleansing   f. terrorism

1. the act of ridding a region or society of one or more ethnic groups

2. the support of developing governments in foreign countries

3. the loosening of government controls placed on businesses

4. a policy in South Africa of complete separation of the races

5. the difference produced when the government spends more than it collects during a year

6. the use of violence or threats of violence to achieve a goal

Check Your Understanding

1. **Summarize** Reagan's approach to the economy.

2. **Explain** what happened to U.S.-Soviet relations during the Reagan administration.

3. **Define** the difference between the federal deficit and the national debt.

4. **Identify** three events that signaled the fall of communism.

5. **Contrast** Reagan's and Clinton's approaches to foreign policy.

6. **Explain** how the United States fought a war on terrorism at home and abroad.

Critical Thinking

1. **Analyze Primary Sources** What was the weapon that Reagan described in his speech on page 724?

2. **Compare and Contrast** What were the similarities and differences between the administrations of Ronald Reagan (1981–1989) and George Bush (1989–1993)?

3. **Make Inferences** Why did the United States wait until 2001 to fight a war on terrorism?

Put Your Skills to Work
IMPROVE YOUR TEST-TAKING SKILLS

You have learned that following test-taking tips can improve your test scores. You learned that it is important to pay attention to key direction words, such as *compare*, *contrast*, *define*, *discuss*, *illustrate*, and *evaluate*.

Choose a person from the chapter. Write three essay questions about that person, using three different direction words listed above. Then, write answers to the questions. Review the chart on page 731 to see if you followed "What To Do." If not, rewrite your answers.

Then, choose an event from the chapter. Again, write three questions, using three different direction words. This time, exchange questions with a partner. Read and discuss each other's answers.

In Your Own Words
JOURNAL WRITING

Many dramatic U.S. and world events occurred between 1980 and the present. People will always remember where they were and what they were doing when they heard the news of those events. Write a journal entry about a major U.S. or world event in your lifetime. Where were you when it happened? What were you doing?

Net Work
INTERNET ACTIVITY

Working with a partner, use the Internet as a resource to make a chart about the 2000 election. Begin with election night, and then list each major development, ending with the U.S. Supreme Court decision. Write a brief description of each event. Illustrate your chart with photographs or your own drawings.

For help in starting this activity, visit the following Web site: www.gfamericanhistory.com.

Look Ahead

In the next chapter, learn about new and possible future developments in the United States and the world.

CHAPTER 32

Looking to the Future 1990–Present

I. Advances in Technology and Science
II. Life in the Twenty-First Century
III. The Future of Our Planet

*W*hat lies ahead for the United States? What does the future hold for this country? Charles Franklin Kettering, an American engineer and inventor, once said,

"We should all be concerned about the future because we will have to spend the rest of our lives there."

Technology has revolutionized American life. It has led to advances in communication, transportation, medicine, space exploration, and entertainment. The future will bring new challenges. By examining the past and adapting to new conditions, Americans can shape the world of tomorrow.

Robot

1990
Hubble Space Telescope is launched.
Human Genome Project begins.

U.S. Events	1990	1994
Presidential Term Begins		1993 William Jefferson Clinton
World Events	1990	1994

1991
Boris Yeltsin is elected president of Russia.
World Wide Web is introduced.

1992
Number of Internet providers tops 1,000,000.

1994
North American Free Trade Agreement eliminates trade barriers between Canada, U.S., and Mexico.

VIEW HISTORY The International Space Station, to be completed in 2004, is being developed by 16 nations in order to promote scientific advancement. Technology, including robots (left), alter life in the workplace and at home.

★ How do you think new technology in the twenty-first century will change life?

Get Organized

FIVE Ws CHART

Reporters use the Five *Ws* to gather information. They ask *Who? What? Where? When?* and *Why?* You can use this system when reading about history. Make a chart like the one below. Ask yourself the Five *Ws* as you read Chapter 32. Write the answer to each question in the correct column on your chart. Here is an example from this chapter.

Who?	NASA
What?	Launched the Hubble Telescope
Where?	Into outer space
When?	1990
Why?	To better observe outer space

1997 Mars Pathfinder Mission successfully lands a robot on Mars.

2000 First stage at mapping the human genome is completed.

2001 Terrorists strike the World Trade Center in New York City and the Pentagon near Washington, D.C.

1998

2002

2001 George Walker Bush

1998

2002

1996 First mammal— a sheep named Dolly— is cloned successfully.

1997 Kyoto environmental conference is held in Japan.

1998 Construction of the International Space Station begins.

2002 Euro becomes official currency of many Western European nations.

I Advances in Technology and Science

Main Ideas

A. The computer has changed the way people work and live.

B. New technologies have led to advances in space exploration.

C. Learning more about genes has led to challenges and advances in medicine and agriculture.

 Active Reading

PROBLEMS AND SOLUTIONS
Identifying problems and solutions is an important part of the human story. In this section, take note of some of the problems and solutions that scientists are working on today.

A. The Age of the Computer

Advances in science and technology have drastically changed the way people work and live. One of the most far-reaching advances of the twentieth century has been the computer. Today, computers are used in almost every aspect of life.

Development of the Modern Computer

The idea of a modern machine that could compute, or do arithmetic, was first thought of in the 1880s by an Englishman named

Early computers could weigh as much as 60,000 pounds and fill the space of a large room.

Charles Babbage. Babbage's machine, while never built, would have been powered by steam and would have been as large as a locomotive engine.

A major breakthrough in building a workable computer came in 1946 with the Electronic Numerical Integrator and Computer (ENIAC). Occupying more than 1,500 square feet of office space, ENIAC could do up to 5,000 addition calculations per second.

Compared with today's computers, ENIAC was slow, huge, and expensive. The average desktop computer of today is 400 times faster, 3,000 times lighter in weight, and millions of dollars cheaper. Laptop and palm-sized computers are even smaller.

Over the last few decades, the number of computers in use has skyrocketed. In 1985, there were about 21 million computers in the United States.

In 2000, the number jumped to more than 160 million. Computers have become so much a part of society that most people need to be **computer literate**, or know how to use a computer, to do their jobs, communicate, or access information. This knowledge will be even more important as computers continue to become a vital part of schools, the workplace, and the home.

Computers and Communications

Computers have greatly changed communication. Almost all telephones, televisions, VCRs, CD players, cameras, and office machines use computer technology. Many movies also use special effects created by computers. Some books are available as electronic books, or e-books.

Computers have also allowed people greater access to information and to each other. Through electronic mail, known as e-mail, people can keep in touch with family, friends, and co-workers.

These changes in communications have made it possible for people to work at home. Telecommuters stay in touch with their offices by e-mail. Important memos and files are sent electronically from a person's home to their office within seconds.

The Information Superhighway

Computers around the world are connected to one another. This network of computers is called the Internet, and it is truly an "information superhighway."

The World Wide Web, introduced in 1991, has made it easier for people to use the Internet. The Web contains all the documents on the Internet. It enables people to send pictures and sound over the Internet as well as create links from one site to another.

The Internet is still young. In 2000, Arun Netravlai, the president of a leading technology company, predicted that more advances are coming:

> 66 [The Internet of the future] will respond to spoken commands without regard to language or accent and will be able to find the information and services you want, even if you only have a vague idea of what you're looking for. 99

 What are some ways that computers have changed daily life?

This technology professional is preparing to divide microchips to be used in computers. Protective clothing helps to prevent dust from damaging the microchips.

ANALYZE PRIMARY SOURCES

DOCUMENT-BASED QUESTION What advantages will the Internet offer to users in the future?

Then & Now

In 1961, Alan B. Shepard became the first American to orbit Earth. Today, space exploration has come even further. NASA's *Pathfinder* mission succeeded in landing a robotic craft on Mars to help explore the planet. In 2001, NASA sent the *Odyssey* into orbit around Mars to search for water and examine the climate of the planet for future explorers.

The parts of the Hubble Telescope include solar panels and communication antennae which are designed to be replaced by visiting astronauts.

B. Space Technology

Technology has allowed people to see places that have never been explored before. Scientists can search many kinds of places, from the tiniest inner spaces of the human body to the vast reaches of outer space.

Challenges to Space Exploration

During the 1970s researchers at the National Aeronautics and Space Administration (NASA) created the technology of the space shuttle. The space shuttle served as a reusable rocket and spacecraft, allowing astronauts to use the same craft to enter orbit repeatedly. The first successful space shuttle, *Columbia*, was launched in April 1981.

However, NASA suffered a major setback in January 1986, when the space shuttle *Challenger* exploded after liftoff. Seven astronauts, and a school teacher who was chosen to travel with them, were killed in the accident. It was later discovered that a problem with one of the rocket boosters had led to the fatal accident. After extensive research, many changes were made to the shuttle system, and shuttle flights resumed to perform important scientific experiments.

Advances in Space Exploration

Aboard space shuttle flights, astronauts conduct experiments about the space environment. In 1998, the United States began working with 14 other countries to build an International Space Station. Today, the station is visited by crews of astronauts who conduct experiments and undertake space walks from the station.

Another advance in space technology is the use of high-powered telescopes that operate in space. The Hubble Space Telescope, launched in 1990, sends pictures of events and objects in space back to Earth. Scientists hope to learn more about our own planet and galaxy by studying the formation and behavior of other objects within the galaxy.

One problem in space exploration is the large amount of fuel required to travel through space. NASA is studying one possible solution: a solar-sail spacecraft. Such a vehicle would use the power of the sun and be able to travel long distances on a small amount of fuel.

★ **What are some recent advances in space exploration?**

This cartoon calls attention to the possible dangers of genetic engineering.

ANALYZE PRIMARY SOURCES

DOCUMENT-BASED QUESTION
What does this cartoon suggest about scientists' efforts to decode the human genome?

C. The Genetic Frontier

Genes are the building blocks of all living organisms. Studying genes can unlock new doors to understanding the human body and other living organisms.

Mapping the Human Genome

Every cell in the human body is made up of genes that are passed on from parent to child. They determine how a person's cells will function. This determines many physical traits of the person.

In 1990, scientists began the Human Genome Project to identify and sequence every human gene. The **human genome** is the complete genetic makeup of human beings. Scientists discovered that about 30,000 genes exist in the human body. They identified many genes, including some connected to deafness, diabetes, kidney disease, certain cancers, and other diseases. The first working draft of the complete human genome was published in 2001.

Genetic Engineering

Scientists can now remove genes, take them apart, put them back together, and copy them. Called **genetic engineering**, this research may lead to new medicines and cures. Experiments have been conducted whereby imperfect genes are replaced with normal genes in order to rid the body of disease.

Dolly, the sheep, was the first mammal to be cloned from a body cell of an adult sheep.

Genetic engineering is also changing agriculture. Scientists can grow corn, tomatoes, and other foods that resist insects and diseases. Some genetically altered foods are available in supermarkets. However, questions have been raised as to whether these foods are safe to eat. There is also concern about the impact of such foods on the environment. For example, genetically engineered salmon that escape from fish farms might accidentally cause harm to natural salmon.

By working with genes, scientists can now **clone**, or copy, cells and entire organisms. In 1996, a sheep named Dolly was born in Scotland. She was a clone of an adult sheep. However, there are concerns about the safety of cloning and the transmission of diseases and defects to cloned animals. Because of these concerns, the topic of cloning is currently being debated in the United States. In fact, the latest cloning research involves human beings. However, some governments have banned such research until solid guidelines are established for the use of cloning.

The science of genetic engineering—especially in humans—is made possible because of increased knowledge of DNA. Scientists know that DNA is the molecule that encodes genetic information that makes up each individual's inherited characteristics.

 What is the human genome?

 **Review**

Review History

A. How have changes in computer design helped to make computers part of our daily lives?

B. What challenges did NASA face for its space program in the 1980s?

C. In what way can mapping the human genome benefit people?

Define Terms to Know
Provide a definition for each of the following terms.
computer literate, human genome, genetic engineering, clone

Critical Thinking
In what ways do advances in medical and space technology pose new challenges?

Write About History
Great advances have been made in space exploration. Write a paragraph stating your thoughts on the future of space exploration based on what you have read.

Get Organized
FIVE Ws CHART
Think about some of the facts you learned in this section. Use the Five Ws chart to organize the information. For example, who introduced the idea of computers? Where? When? Why?

Who?	
What?	
Where?	
When?	
Why?	

Build Your Skills

DEVELOP A MULTIMEDIA PRESENTATION

Multimedia presentations are often used in the workplace, at conferences, and by public speakers. In addition to using words to talk about the information, the presenter displays information in pictures using an overhead projector with transparencies, a videotape, a film, or slides. Multimedia presentations are also created by using computer software. Your choices of media will depend on which most effectively helps you to make your point.

In history class, you may be asked to make a presentation. A multimedia presentation can make your information more interesting. For example, a report on computers might include computer-generated charts and graphs to illustrate your ideas.

Here's How

Follow these directions to create your presentation.

1. Identify and research your topic. Use information from several different sources.

2. Determine what media will best convey your message. You may wish to combine several types of media.

3. Use the media resources to make your presentation interesting.

Here's Why

You have just read about the effects computers have had on communications. Creating a multimedia presentation on this topic would give you many options for demonstrating what you have learned.

Practice the Skill

Copy the chart on the right on a sheet of paper. Identify a presentation topic from the information in Section I. Write the topic in the top box. Then, list four types of media you could use to develop the presentation and how you would use each type.

Extend the Skill

Choose at least one type of media listed in your chart. Develop a short presentation using that media. Share your presentation with the class.

Apply the Skill

As you read the remaining sections of this chapter, think about how you would present the information if you were asked to develop a multimedia presentation. List your ideas.

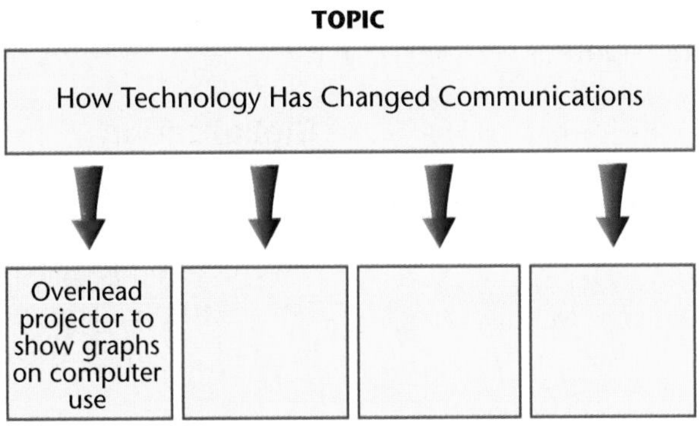

TOPIC

How Technology Has Changed Communications

Overhead projector to show graphs on computer use			

II Life in the Twenty-First Century

Terms to Know

globalization a condition in which countries are members of a world community

bilingual using two languages

Main Ideas

A. The U.S. economy is affected by events in the world economy.

B. The kinds of jobs and the way people work will keep changing in the future.

C. Immigration to the United States continues, but patterns are changing.

D. Providing affordable healthcare for all Americans continues to be a challenge.

 Active Reading

SUMMARIZE
Summarizing information helps you identify important facts from what you learn. As you read this chapter, select and summarize the most important ideas.

Spotlight on Economics

In 1951, several European countries joined together to form an economic community known as the European Union (EU). On January 1, 2002, most of the member countries officially adopted one currency, the euro. Euro coins and paper money can be used in any of the participating countries.

A. A Shifting Economy

The United States' role as a world power has affected its domestic economy. In the second half of the 1990s, foreign trade increased. The U.S. economy became increasingly connected with the economies of other countries.

Economic Slowdown

Starting in 1995, the United States experienced a growing economy. The stock market soared even though it had minor setbacks at times. Inflation, unemployment figures, and interest rates stayed low.

In 2001, however, the United States economy began to decline. Unemployment rates rose, and stock prices fell. People felt uneasy about the economy. President George W. Bush proposed federal tax cuts to help the economy grow, and Congress eventually supported a tax cut. In addition, the U.S. economy reached low levels after the terrorist attacks of September 11, 2001. The slowdown led to a recession in the economy that continued in 2002.

Globalization

The U.S. economy has been changed by **globalization**, or the creation of a world community. Governments and businesses now have economic partnerships and ties in many parts of the world. For example, some factories that produce U.S. goods are now located in other areas of the world where labor is less expensive.

Another example of globalization involves trade among nations. Today, the United States has many formal trade agreements. The North American Free Trade Agreement (NAFTA) eliminated trade barriers between the United States, Canada, and Mexico in 1994. That same year, the General Agreement on Tariffs and Trade (GATT) cut tariffs among more than 100 trading nations.

One major effect of globalization is that it ties together the economies of many countries. This means that when economic problems arise in one country, the United States may be affected. The reverse is also true. When the economy of the United States is strong, its global partners tend to be strong, too.

★ **How do the economies of other countries affect the U.S. economy?**

B. A Changing Workforce

Jobs in the twenty-first century will be different from jobs in the past. More occupations will involve taking care of an aging population, and more will be created by the recent advances in technology. Many jobs today did not exist 100 years ago, and many jobs of the future do not exist now.

Jobs in Healthcare

As the population ages and medical technology improves, jobs in the field of healthcare will increase. Traditional professions, such as doctors, nurses, and health aides, will grow in demand.

Do You Remember?
In Chapter 31, you learned that Presidents George H. W. Bush and Bill Clinton both supported free trade.

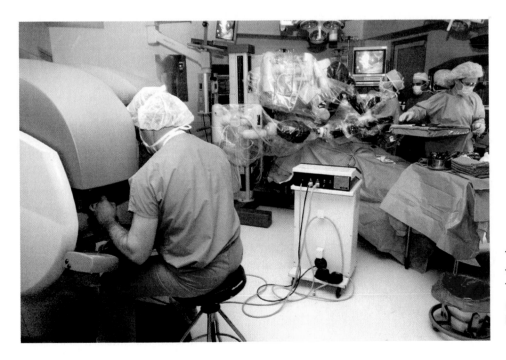

Technology has changed the medical profession. Today, surgeons can perform some operations by using computers and laser beams.

Professions in healthcare will also make use of new inventions to care for people. Other healthcare jobs that are expected to grow are physical therapists, respiratory therapists, and medical records technicians.

Technology At Home and Work

Changes in technology and science are creating the need for a better educated, more technically trained workforce. Think of some of the machines in your home—such as computers, DVD players, and cellular phones—that did not exist 50 years ago. All these machines have created new types of jobs. Positions that require expertise with computers, such as computer engineers, computer scientists, and computer programmers, will probably continue to be in demand.

★ **What are some areas of the workforce that can be expected to grow in the future?**

C. Immigration in a New Century

The United States has always been a nation of immigrants. People worldwide have come to the United States and made this country their home. They continue to do so even in the twenty-first century.

Immigration Continues

Most immigrants from the colonial period to the early part of the twentieth century were from European countries. However, today most immigrants are from Latin American countries. People from Asian countries make up the second largest group of U.S. immigrants.

Immigrants have tended to live in major cities where people from their homeland already live. Many live near the area where they entered the country. For example, many people from Poland settled in Chicago around the turn of the century. For this reason, many Polish people continue to immigrate to Chicago today. However, in recent years, many immigrants have also flocked to suburbs.

Immigrants make up a large part of the American workforce in a variety of professions. Some work in technical or professional positions. Others work in factory jobs located in urban areas. However, the number of manufacturing jobs is declining because some work has become automated, and positions have been eliminated. Also, factories are relying more on skilled workers with technical educations.

Each year, many immigrants become naturalized citizens of the United States.

Educating New Americans

Educating the diverse population of the United States has become a key challenge. One area of concern is whether non-English-speaking children should be taught school subjects in separate classes in their own language or taught only in English so they can learn the language more quickly.

Traditionally, learning English is one way that immigrants have assimilated into, or have become part of, American society. Many people, including many immigrants, believe that learning English early is important for success in school and in the workplace. Others argue that **bilingual** education, or classes taught using two languages, promotes better learning.

★ How have immigration patterns changed since the early twentieth century?

D. Healthcare Reform and Senior Citizens

People are living longer because of advances in medicine and healthier lifestyles. However, longer life expectancies lead to concerns over the cost of affordable healthcare.

Healthcare Issues

Affordable healthcare is a challenge that the United States faces in the twenty-first century. Many working people in the United States have some health insurance through the company where they work. However, Americans who work for small companies, work part-time, or are self-employed usually need to pay for their own health insurance. People can also lose their health insurance if they become unemployed.

A problem for people who have some health insurance is paying for expenses that are not covered by insurance. This problem is especially true of the cost of prescription medicines. Many of the newer prescription medications, while extremely effective, are also very expensive. Some healthcare plans cover only a small part of the cost, and other plans do not cover any of the costs.

Some people believe that the government needs to play a role in solving the healthcare issue. Some states offer low or no-cost insurance for low-income families. This insurance helps to ensure that children receive the vaccines they need to stay healthy and that their families can afford to send them to a doctor when they are ill. Others believe that competition between healthcare companies would lower the prices of medications and medical services, making healthcare more affordable.

Persons Age 65 and Older in the United States, 1995–2005

*projected numbers, 2001–2005   Source: U.S. Census Bureau

✔ **Graph Check**
....

By how much will the number of people age 65 and older increase between 1995 and 2005?

An Aging Population

By the end of the twentieth century, almost 35 million Americans were over 65 years of age. This number is expected to grow as the huge generation of baby boomers from the 1950s and 1960s reaches retirement age.

An ever-growing senior population poses many challenges. Increased spending for Social Security and Medicare benefits is an option being debated by the government. Many people are asking the government to provide relief to seniors who face large bills for prescription drugs.

Housing for seniors is also a key concern. Because people now live longer and healthier lives, they can remain independent for a longer period of time. Housing, however, can be very expensive for senior citizens on fixed incomes. One way to accommodate seniors' housing needs is through planned senior communities, which often provide medical help, food, and transportation at a reduced cost.

★ **Why do many Americans have a hard time paying for healthcare?**

II Review

Review History
A. How does globalization affect the United States?
B. Why have the types of jobs changed over time?
C. What groups make up the largest number of recent immigrants to the United States?
D. What are some current healthcare issues?

Define Terms to Know
Provide a definition for each of the following terms.
globalization, bilingual

Critical Thinking
How might the increasing number of senior citizens affect this country?

Write About Culture
Write a short paragraph explaining the advantages of having so many different immigrant cultures in the United States.

Get Organized
FIVE Ws CHART
Use the Five Ws chart to organize the information you learned in this section. For example, what is the effect of the high costs of prescription medicines? Who is affected? Where? When? Why?

Who?	
What?	
Where?	
When?	
Why?	

Points of View

Technology in the Classroom

Today, the use of technology, especially computers, is widespread. Most schools have computers that are connected to the Internet. Now, students can learn from a distance, using the World Wide Web.

Not everyone, however, thinks that computer learning is appropriate for students. They believe that computer learning should not replace learning through human contact.

Other people disagree. They believe that technology will enhance learning. The following quotes present both sides of this issue.

Many students use computers today.

> "The Internet is bringing us closer than we ever thought possible to make learning—of all kinds, at all levels, at any time, any place, any pace—a practical reality. The World Wide Web is a tool that empowers society to school the illiterate, bring job training to the unskilled, open a universe of wondrous images and knowledge to all students, and enrich the understanding of the lifelong learner. The issue before us now is how to make good on the Internet's promise for learning."
>
> —Web-Based Education Commission, 2001

> "Too often . . . computers . . . connect children to . . . games, inappropriate adult material, and . . . advertising. They can also isolate children . . . from direct experience. The "distance" education they promote is the opposite of what all children . . . need most—close relationships with caring adults. . . . Children need live lessons that engage their hands, hearts, bodies, and minds. . . . Even in high school . . . too few technology classes emphasize the ethics or dangers of online research and communication."
>
> —Alliance for Childhood, 2000

ANALYZE PRIMARY SOURCES

DOCUMENT-BASED QUESTIONS

1. According to the Web-Based Education Commission, how can technology benefit students?

2. According to the Alliance for Childhood, how can technology harm students?

3. **Critical Thinking** How might both traditional teaching and computer learning be used together to benefit both students and teachers?

III The Future of Our Planet

A. Earth's Changing Environment

Over the past century, people have made great advances in technology. However, these advances have had some negative effects on the planet as a whole.

Earth's Rising Temperatures

In the 1980s, scientists documented that temperatures on Earth were slowly rising, with the potential to cause climate changes. This increase has become known as **global warming**. It is known that the twentieth century was the warmest century of the millennium. It is also known that the 1990s was the warmest decade.

Rising temperatures pose several dangers. If the polar ice caps were to melt, sea levels might rise. Many islands and low-lying coastal areas around the world could experience flooding. Agriculture would be affected. Changing climate patterns could also produce more severe weather.

Scientists believe that global warming is caused by the release of excess amounts of carbon dioxide and other gases into the atmosphere. These gases stay in the upper atmosphere, trapping Earth's heat. This condition is known as the **greenhouse effect**.

Carbon dioxide occurs naturally in the air, but human activities add large amounts of this gas to the environment. One source of carbon dioxide is the burning of fossil fuels, such as oil, gas, and coal. In developed countries, carbon dioxide and other gases come from cars, homes, and factories. In developing countries, these gases are produced by activities such as burning rain forests to clear land.

Efforts to Protect Earth's Atmosphere

People in many countries believe it is time to take action on global warming. In 1997, more than 150 countries met in Kyoto, Japan, for a conference on the environment. One of the conference goals was to reduce the amount of greenhouse gases being produced worldwide. As a result of this conference, a treaty called the Kyoto Protocol was written to try to slow global warming.

While President Clinton supported the Protocol, many U.S. business owners objected to it. They claimed that the requirements to meet new regulations would result in greater costs, unemployment, and possible economic recession. As a result, the U.S. Senate, as well as President George W. Bush, did not confirm the treaty.

Another environmental problem is damage to Earth's ozone layer, a thin layer of gas that surrounds Earth and shields it against harmful radiation from the Sun. Ozone levels are measured in Dobson units. Scientists discovered that certain chemicals, called chlorofluorocarbons (CFCs), caused damage to the ozone layer when released into Earth's atmosphere. CFCs, once used in air conditioner and refrigerator coolants, created a hole in the ozone layer over Antarctica.

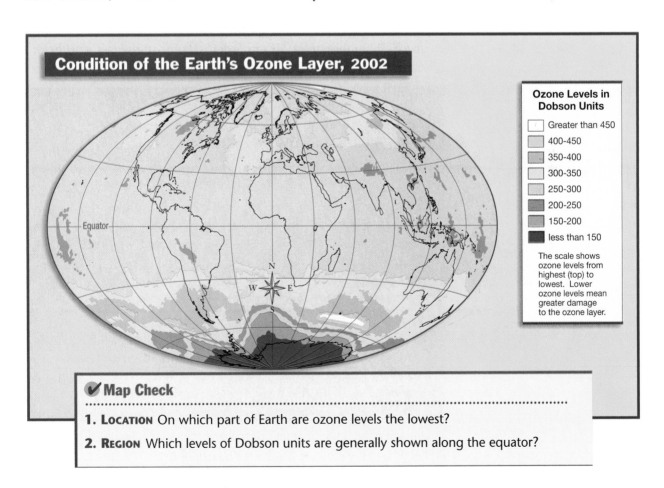

Condition of the Earth's Ozone Layer, 2002

Ozone Levels in Dobson Units

- Greater than 450
- 400–450
- 350–400
- 300–350
- 250–300
- 200–250
- 150–200
- less than 150

The scale shows ozone levels from highest (top) to lowest. Lower ozone levels mean greater damage to the ozone layer.

✔ **Map Check**

1. **LOCATION** On which part of Earth are ozone levels the lowest?

2. **REGION** Which levels of Dobson units are generally shown along the equator?

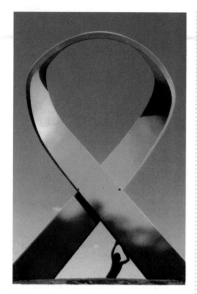

This ribbon sculpture was unveiled in 2000 during the World AIDS Conference in South Africa. It represents world unity toward the goal of eliminating AIDS.

In 1987, governments worldwide banned the use of CFCs. Due to these efforts, the hole has stabilized and is expected to shrink.

★ **What are some ways that global warming might affect people?**

B. Working Together in a New Century

In the twenty-first century, people around the world wonder what new challenges await them. The United States faces many challenges in a changing world.

Our Good Health

Despite many advances in healthcare, diseases continue to threaten the well-being of people around the world. For example, AIDS (Acquired Immune Deficiency Syndrome) and the related infection, HIV (Human Immunodeficiency Virus), are diseases for which healthcare professionals have been working to find a cure.

Steps are being taken to combat other diseases as well. The World Health Organization (WHO), a part of the United Nations, works everywhere in the world to help people achieve a decent level of health. It promotes cooperation among nations and provides access to medicines and healthcare. In the year 2001, the United States agreed to give $200 million to WHO in order to combat diseases worldwide.

Americans often come together at times of national celebration, such as taking part in a parade to celebrate Independence Day.

Challenges and Hopes

The world is always changing. We cannot know what the future will bring. We do know, however, that in order to grow and prosper the United States depends on the friendship of countries around the world. Along with its allies, the United States continues to defend the common goals of global peace and security.

When faced with new challenges, the people of the United States come together as a nation. This was particularly true after the September 11, 2001 terrorist attacks on the United States. Again and again, Americans have proven that they can overcome obstacles and adapt to new conditions. In the future, as in the past, Americans will draw strength from their diversity and their commitment to freedom and equality. President George W. Bush recognized this ability to face challenges in 2001 when he remarked,

> **"** Americans are generous and strong and decent, not because we believe in ourselves, but because we hold beliefs beyond ourselves. When this spirit of citizenship is missing, no government program can replace it. When this spirit is present, no wrong can stand against it. **"**

ANALYZE PRIMARY SOURCES

DOCUMENT-BASED QUESTION
According to President George W. Bush, what is a strength of the people of the United States?

★ **How might the United States be expected to face future challenges?**

III Review

Review History
A. What steps have people taken to stop or slow damage to the environment?
B. What steps are being taken to combat diseases?

Define Terms to Know
Provide a definition for each of the following terms.
global warming, greenhouse effect

Critical Thinking
What problems might an industrialized nation such as the United States have in trying to protect the environment?

Write About Government
Write a paragraph explaining your opinion on whether the United States should have passed the Kyoto Protocol.

Get Organized
FIVE Ws CHART
Think about some of the facts you learned in this section. Use a Five Ws chart to organize the information. For example, what actions have countries taken to protect the environment? Who? When? Where? Why?

Who?	
What?	
Where?	
When?	
Why?	

CHAPTER 32 Review

Chapter Summary

In your notebook, complete the following outline. Then, use your outline to write a brief summary of the chapter.

Looking to the Future

I. Advances in Technology and Science

   A. The Age of the Computer
   B.
   C.

II. Life in the Twenty-First Century

   A.
   B.
   C.
   D.

III. The Future of Our Planet

   A.
   B.

Interpret the Timeline

Use the timeline on pages 750–751 to answer the following questions.

1. How long after beginning the project to map the human genome was the first stage completed?

2. **Critical Thinking** What examples of advances in space exploration can be found on the timeline?

Use Terms to Know

Select the term that best completes each sentence.

bilingual   globalization
clone   greenhouse effect
genetic engineering   human genome

1. An exact genetic duplicate of another organism is called a _____.

2. Gases that stay in Earth's atmosphere and trap heat is a condition called the _____.

3. Many students attend _____ classes, in which two languages are used.

4. A map showing the genetic makeup of people is called the _____.

5. The creation of a world community is called _____.

6. Research into _____ may lead to new medicines and cures.

Check Your Understanding

1. **Describe** two important space projects from the 1990s and their purposes.

2. **Discuss** the controversy surrounding genetically engineered food.

3. **Describe** the effects of globalization.

4. **Explain** why there is pressure to meet the needs of senior citizens.

5. **Describe** the impact that CFCs have on Earth's atmosphere.

6. **Identify** steps being taken to combat global diseases.

Critical Thinking

1. **Analyze Primary Sources** Do you think the person who drew the cartoon on page 755 supports the Human Genome Project? Why or why not?

2. **Predict** What new inventions or changes in lifestyles may result in new types of jobs?

3. **Generalize** In what ways will this country's future challenges be different from those of the past?

Put Your Skills to Work

DEVELOP A MULTIMEDIA PRESENTATION

You have learned how the use of a variety of media can add interest to a presentation. Copy the chart below. In the top rectangle, write a topic for a presentation you could create using the information in this chapter. Then, list four types of media you would use to develop your presentation.

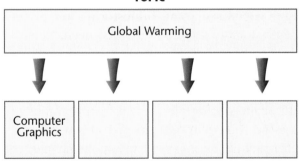

TOPIC

Global Warming

Computer Graphics

In Your Own Words

JOURNAL WRITING

What changes in technology and science do you think will occur in your lifetime? What inventions do you expect to see in the future? Where will space exploration take us in the future? Write a journal entry predicting what life will be like in 50 years.

Net Work

INTERNET ACTIVITY

Working with a group of classmates, choose one challenge that the United States faces. Research your topic, using the Internet to gather information on both sides of the issue. Then, with your team, prepare an oral presentation using the material you found online. Possible issues include healthcare, the environment, genetics, and the economy. Have your team prepare handouts to help the class understand your topic. On the handouts, include information found online as well as informative charts or other visuals created by your team.

For help in starting this activity, visit the following Web site: www.gfamericanhistory.com.

Unit 10 Portfolio Project

Visual Essay

YOUR ASSIGNMENT

What is life like in the twenty-first century? In your class, form teams to work on a visual essay. Each team will collect pictures found in magazines and newspapers, as well as photographs dealing with different areas of modern life. When all the photos and pictures are collected, each team will mount them on a sheet of poster board to create a visual essay of life in the United States.

THE BRAINSTORMING SESSION

Choose Your Subject Each team will focus on one area. Choose from the following topics.

technology/space	entertainment	transportation
medicine	business	recreation
communications	government	school

Plan Your Essay After choosing a topic, discuss some of the pictures that might be included in your visual essay. Brainstorm some places where you can find the photographs and pictures you need. Refer to this Web site for ideas: www.gfamericanhistory.com.

THE ASSEMBLY LINE

Snoop and Snip Search for interesting pictures and photographs to include in your visual essay. Take photographs of your own if you have a camera. Look for pictures in newspapers and magazines. Choose at least seven good visuals.

Meet and Select As a team, select the five best visuals from each team member. Remember that the visuals must be relevant to the topic you have selected.

Cut and Paste Trim all pictures and photos so that they are neat and focus clearly on the object. When the visuals are trimmed, paste them onto poster board. Leave space to put a title at the top. Use colorful markers or glue pens to write the title.

Multimedia Presentation

Now, turn your visual essay into a video essay. Use a video recorder to collect images related to your subject. Show real people performing real activities. Select images that represent modern life in the United States. When you have finished, show your video essay to your classmates.

Handbook Section

Declaration of Independence
HANDBOOK

Document Dictionary
endowed provided
unalienable unable to
be taken away
prudence care

The text of the Declaration of Independence, using modern spelling, punctuation, and capitalization appears on the following pages. The titles in red and notes in the margin have been added to help you understand the document.

Declaration of Independence

Action of the Second Continental Congress, July 4, 1776

Preamble

When in the course of human events, it becomes necessary for one people to dissolve the political bands which have connected them with another, and to assume among the powers of the earth, the separate and equal station to which the laws of nature and of nature's God entitle them, a decent respect to the opinions of mankind requires that they should declare the causes which impel them to the separation.

A New Theory of Government

We hold these truths to be self-evident, that all men are created equal, that they are **endowed** by their Creator with certain **unalienable** rights, that among these are life, liberty, and the pursuit of happiness. That to secure these rights, governments are instituted among men, deriving their just powers from the consent of the governed, that whenever any form of government becomes destructive of these ends, it is the right of the people to alter or to abolish it, and to institute new government, laying its foundation on such principles, and organizing its powers in such form, as to them shall seem most likely to effect their safety and happiness. **Prudence**, indeed, will dictate that governments long established should not be changed for light and transient causes; and accordingly all experience hath shown, that mankind are more disposed to suffer, while evils are sufferable, than to right themselves by abolishing the forms to which they are accustomed. But when a long train of abuses and

> **The Main Idea**
>
> **A New Theory of Government**
> The colonists believed that humans are created equal and have equal rights to life, liberty, and the pursuit of happiness. Governments are formed to protect these rights. When a government threatens or takes away these rights, then the people have the right to change or do away with that government.

The Main Idea

Abuses by King George III

This part of the Declaration lists offenses by the British king and Parliament against the colonies. This list explains why the colonists wanted to be free from Britain. It includes some of the following:

- ignoring laws that the colonies needed

- refusing to set up courts in the colonies

- refusing to let settlers move west

- housing troops in colonists' homes

- blocking trade with other countries

usurpations, pursuing invariably the same object, evinces a design to reduce them under absolute **despotism**, it is their right, it is their duty, to throw off such government, and to provide new guards for their future security.

Such has been the patient sufferance of these colonies; and such is now the necessity which constrains them to alter their former systems of government. The history of the present king of Great Britain is a history of repeated injuries and usurpations, all having in direct object the establishment of an absolute tyranny over these states. To prove this, let facts be submitted to a candid world.

Abuses by King George III

He has refused his **assent** to laws, the most wholesome and necessary for the public good.

He has forbidden his governors to pass laws of immediate and pressing importance, unless suspended in their operation till his assent should be obtained; and when so suspended, he has utterly neglected to attend to them.

He has refused to pass other laws for the accommodation of large districts of people, unless those people would **relinquish** the right of representation in the legislature, a right inestimable to them, and formidable to tyrants only.

He has called together legislative bodies at places unusual, uncomfortable, and distant from the depository of their public records, for the sole purpose of fatiguing them into compliance with his measures.

He has **dissolved** representative houses repeatedly, for opposing with manly firmness his invasions on the rights of the people.

He has refused for a long time, after such dissolutions, to cause others to be elected; whereby the legislative powers, incapable of **annihilation**, have returned to the people at large for their exercise; the state remaining in the meantime exposed to all the dangers of invasion from without, and **convulsions** within.

He has endeavored to prevent the population of these states; for that purpose obstructing the laws for naturalization of foreigners; refusing to pass others to encourage their migrations hither, and raising the conditions of new appropriations of lands.

He has obstructed the administration of justice, by refusing his assent to laws for establishing judiciary powers.

He has made judges dependent on his will alone, for the tenure of their offices, and the amount and payment of their salaries.

He has erected a multitude of new offices, and sent hither swarms of officers to harass our people, and eat out their substance.

He has kept among us, in times of peace, standing armies, without the consent of our legislatures.

He has affected to render the military independent of and superior to the civil power.

He has combined with others to subject us to a jurisdiction foreign to our constitution, and unacknowledged by our laws; giving his assent to their acts of pretended legislation:

For quartering large bodies of armed troops among us;

For protecting them, by a mock trial, from punishment for any murders which they should commit on the inhabitants of these states;

For cutting off our trade with all parts of the world;

For imposing taxes on us without our consent;

For depriving us, in many cases, of the benefits of trial by jury;

For transporting us beyond seas to be tried for pretended offenses;

For abolishing the free system of English laws in a neighbouring province, establishing therein an arbitrary government, and enlarging its boundaries, so as to render it at once an example and fit instrument for introducing the same absolute rule into these colonies;

For taking away our charters, abolishing our most valuable laws, and altering fundamentally the forms of our governments;

For suspending our own legislatures, and declaring themselves invested with power to legislate for us in all cases whatsoever.

Acts of War Against the Colonies

He has **abdicated** government here, by declaring us out of his protection and waging war against us.

He has plundered our seas, ravaged our coasts, burnt our towns, and destroyed the lives of our people.

He is, at this time, transporting large armies of foreign mercenaries to compleat the works of death, desolation, and tyranny, already begun with circumstances of cruelty and **perfidy**, scarcely paralleled in the most barbarous ages, and totally unworthy the head of a civilized nation.

He has **constrained** our fellow citizens taken captive on the high seas to bear arms against their country, to become the executioners of their friends and brethren, or to fall themselves by their hands.

He has excited domestic **insurrections** amongst us, and has endeavored to bring on the inhabitants of our frontiers, the merciless Indian savages, whose known rule of warfare, is an undistinguished destruction, of all ages, sexes, and conditions.

Taking Action

In every stage of these oppressions we have petitioned for **redress** in the most humble terms: Our repeated petitions have been answered only by repeated injury. A prince, whose character is thus marked by every act which may define a tyrant, is unfit to be the ruler of a free people.

Nor have we been wanting in attentions to our British brethren. We have warned them from time to time of attempts by their legislature to extend an **unwarrantable** jurisdiction over us. We have reminded them of the circumstances of our emigration and settlement here. We have appealed to their native justice and **magnanimity**, and we have conjured them by the ties of our common kindred to disavow these usurpations, which, would inevitably interrupt our connections and correspondence. They too have been deaf to the voice of justice and of **consanguinity**. We must, therefore, acquiesce in the necessity, which denounces our separation, and hold them, as we hold the rest of mankind, enemies in war, in peace, friends.

A Proclamation of Independence

We, therefore, the representatives of the United States of America, in General Congress, assembled, appealing to the Supreme Judge of the world for the rectitude of our intentions, do, in the name, and by authority of the good people of these colonies, solemnly publish and declare, that these united colonies are, and of right ought to be, free and independent states; that they are absolved from all allegiance to the British Crown, and that all political connection between them and the state of Great Britain, is and ought to be totally dissolved; and that as free and independent states, they have full power to **levy** war, conclude peace, contract alliances, establish commerce, and to do all other acts and things which independent states may of right do. And for the support of this declaration, with a firm reliance on the protection of Divine Providence, we mutually pledge to each other our lives, our fortunes, and our sacred honor.

Signed by John Hancock of Massachusetts, President of the Congress, and by the fifty-five other Representatives of the thirteen United States of America.

> ### The Main Idea
> **A Proclamation of Independence**
> The final paragraph was a formal declaration of independence. It states that the colonies are free, and should be free, from the control of Britain and should have all the rights of an independent nation. These rights include the rights to
>
> • make war and peace.
>
> • create treaties with other nations.
>
> • regulate trade.

ANALYZE PRIMARY SOURCES

DOCUMENT-BASED QUESTIONS

1. What is the purpose of the Declaration of Independence as stated in the Preamble?

2. According to the Declaration, when are people allowed to change their government?

3. How were the colonists' unalienable rights taken away by King George III?

4. How do you think the signers of the Declaration felt about making a formal declaration of independence from Britain?

5. How did the British citizens react when the American colonists asked them for help?

6. **Critical Thinking** In what ways would declaring formal independence benefit the American colonies?

Constitution
HANDBOOK

What the Constitution Is

More than 200 years after it was written, the Constitution still provides the rules by which the people of the United States live together. The Founding Fathers of the Constitution constructed a document flexible enough to be used in today's world. The newspapers and magazines that you read are free to print the news because freedom of speech and the press are protected in the Constitution. Even the right to have clubs and sports teams is guaranteed in the Constitution.

Contents

Goals of the Constitution

The Founding Fathers of the Constitution wanted to create a single, united nation with a fair government and a fair system of laws. Their goals are stated in the Preamble, or beginning, of the Constitution:

> " . . . to form a more perfect union, establish justice, insure domestic tranquility, provide for the common defense, promote the general welfare, and secure the blessing of liberty to ourselves . . . "

Principles of the Constitution

The Founding Fathers of our nation, as well as most colonists, opposed the harsh rule of the British king. They wanted a government that was fairer and less cruel. However, the weaknesses of the Articles of Confederation made them realize that a strong national government was necessary to run a country.

The Founders faced many questions:

- How could they create a government that was strong but that still allowed its citizens the liberty for which they had fought so hard?

- How could they make sure that the country was well led but that power would not fall into the hands of a few?

- How could power be balanced between the people who made the rules and those who had to live by them?

Their solutions can be found in the basic principles of the Constitution: popular sovereignty, federalism, limited government, separation of powers, and checks and balances.

Popular Sovereignty

The opening words of the Constitution, "We the people of the United States," express the principle of popular sovereignty. In a government based on popular sovereignty, the people rule. The citizens have the right to elect the people who make the laws and other decisions for them.

Federalism

The Founding Fathers wanted to create a strong national government. They also wanted to give the state governments some authority. The principle of federalism divides power between the federal government and the state governments. The federal government deals with national issues. The state governments have the power to make decisions on local matters. Some powers are shared by the federal and the state governments. The chart below shows how some of the powers are shared under federalism.

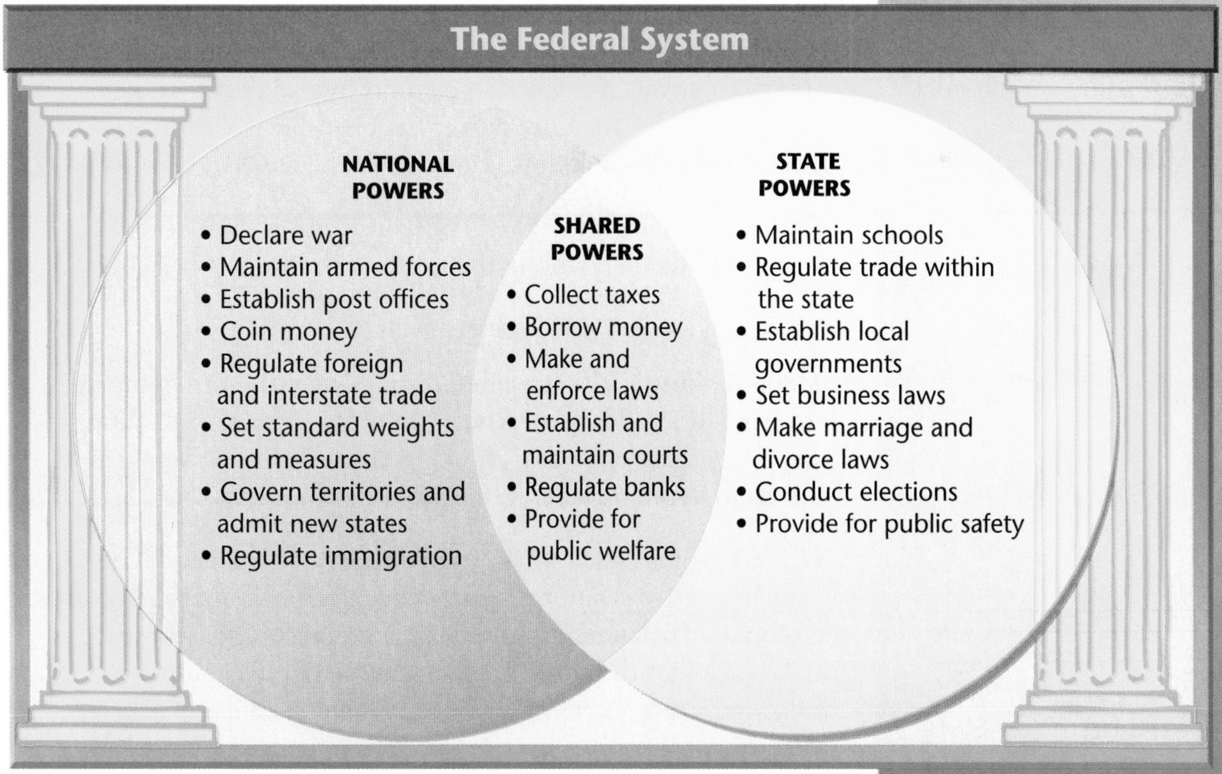

The Federal System

NATIONAL POWERS

- Declare war
- Maintain armed forces
- Establish post offices
- Coin money
- Regulate foreign and interstate trade
- Set standard weights and measures
- Govern territories and admit new states
- Regulate immigration

SHARED POWERS

- Collect taxes
- Borrow money
- Make and enforce laws
- Establish and maintain courts
- Regulate banks
- Provide for public welfare

STATE POWERS

- Maintain schools
- Regulate trade within the state
- Establish local governments
- Set business laws
- Make marriage and divorce laws
- Conduct elections
- Provide for public safety

Limited Government

The Founding Fathers of the Constitution remembered the harsh rule of the British king and feared misuse of power. They wanted to prevent the government from using its power to give one group special advantages. They also wanted to make sure that no group's rights could be taken away. Article I of the Constitution defines the powers that the government has and the powers that it does not have.

The Bill of Rights states the most important limit on government. It guarantees that the federal government may not take away the individual freedoms of the people.

Limited government is also known as "rule of the law." In the U.S. government, everyone—whether citizens or powerful leaders—must obey the law.

Separation of Powers

The Constitution divides the federal government into three branches: the legislative, the executive, and the judicial. Each branch of government has its own powers and its own duties. No one branch has more power than another. This division of the federal government is known as the separation of powers.

Articles I, II, and III of the U.S. Constitution state how the powers are divided among the three branches.

Checks and Balances

The Founding Fathers wanted to be certain that no branch of government could abuse power. To do so, they set up a system that makes sure each branch of government has powers that limit and control the powers of the two other branches.

This control is called a system of checks and balances. The three branches of government keep a "check" on one another, making sure that a "balance" of power is maintained. This system helps make sure that the three branches work together fairly. The following chart shows how the checks and balances work.

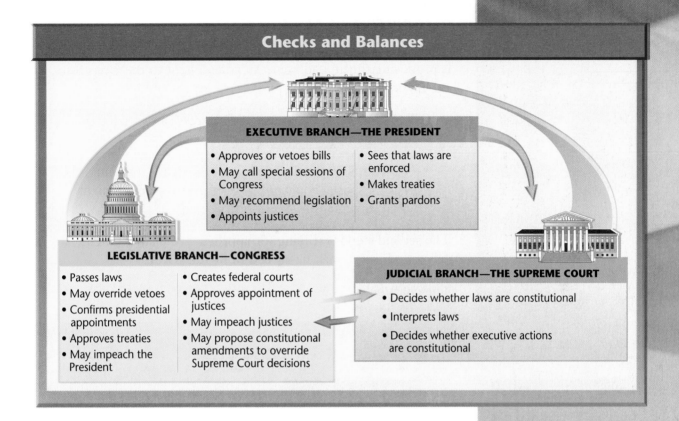

Checks and Balances

EXECUTIVE BRANCH—THE PRESIDENT
- Approves or vetoes bills
- May call special sessions of Congress
- May recommend legislation
- Appoints justices
- Sees that laws are enforced
- Makes treaties
- Grants pardons

LEGISLATIVE BRANCH—CONGRESS
- Passes laws
- May override vetoes
- Confirms presidential appointments
- Approves treaties
- May impeach the President
- Creates federal courts
- Approves appointment of justices
- May impeach justices
- May propose constitutional amendments to override Supreme Court decisions

JUDICIAL BRANCH—THE SUPREME COURT
- Decides whether laws are constitutional
- Interprets laws
- Decides whether executive actions are constitutional

A Living Document

When the Constitution was written, only white men over age 21 who owned property were allowed to vote in national elections. Today, citizens over the age of 18 are permitted to vote. How did this change come about?

The Founding Fathers of the Constitution realized that the United States would grow and change. They realized that the Constitution would have to change to meet new circumstances and challenges. That is why it is called a "living document."

The Founding Fathers outlined a process by which amendments, or written changes, could be added to the Constitution. However, the amendment process was set up to be difficult in order to discourage minor or frequent changes.

How to Amend the Constitution

There are two steps to amending the Constitution. The first step is proposing the amendment. An amendment to the Constitution can be proposed in two ways:

- Two-thirds of each house of Congress can vote for the amendment.

- Two-thirds of the state legislatures can ask for Congress to call a special convention to suggest the amendment. So far, this method has not been used.

The second step is ratifying, or approving, the amendment. All amendments must be agreed to by the states.

The chart below shows how the amendment process works.

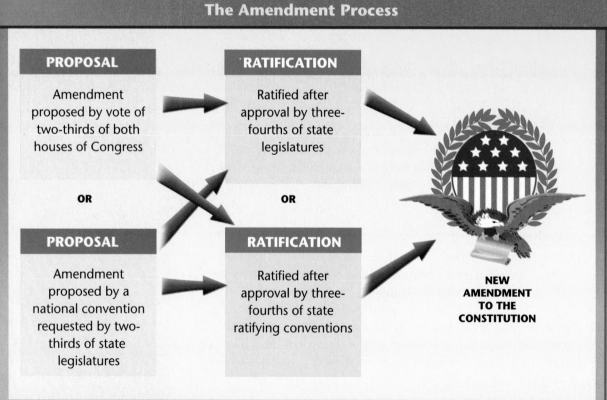

The Amendment Process

PROPOSAL

Amendment proposed by vote of two-thirds of both houses of Congress

OR

PROPOSAL

Amendment proposed by a national convention requested by two-thirds of state legislatures

RATIFICATION

Ratified after approval by three-fourths of state legislatures

OR

RATIFICATION

Ratified after approval by three-fourths of state ratifying conventions

NEW AMENDMENT TO THE CONSTITUTION

Citizenship

As a citizen of the United States, you are entitled to all the rights in the U.S. Constitution. A democratic society also needs its citizens to carry out certain duties and responsibilities in order to run smoothly.

Duties

Duties are actions required by law. Here are some duties to keep in mind:

- It is each person's duty to obey the law and to respect everyone's rights equally.

- Americans also have a duty to pay taxes. The federal government uses tax money to build roads and bridges, maintain the armed forces, support education, and provide health insurance for the elderly.

- Another duty of citizens is to defend their country. Eighteen-year-old males must register with the federal government in case the nation may need to call on them for military service.

Responsibilities

A healthy democracy depends on its citizens to accept certain responsibilities in their communities. Here are some responsibilities to keep in mind:

- Become well informed. Know what is happening in your community, your state, your country, and the world.

- Know your rights. You cannot protect your rights unless you know what they are. You can get information about your rights from books and from government publications.

- Vote. All American citizens can vote when they are 18 years of age. Voting is probably your most important responsibility as a citizen. When you vote, you choose people to represent you in government. You exercise your right of self-government—the very principle upon which the United States was founded.

The text of the Constitution, using modern spelling, punctuation, and capitalization, appears on the following pages. Portions which no longer apply or have been changed are crossed out. The titles in bold and notes in the margin have been added to help you understand the document.

Document Dictionary

tranquility peace

posterity future generations

ordain to establish by law

vested held completely

requisite required

enumeration an official count, such as a census

impeachment the constitutional process of accusing the President or other high officials of a crime

The Main Idea

Section 2. House of Representatives

States must hold elections for the House of Representatives every two years.

A representative must

- be at least 25 years old.
- have been a citizen of the United States for seven years.
- be a resident of the state that elects the representative.

The total number of representatives in the House is limited to 435.

The Constitution
of the United States of America

Preamble

We the people of the United States, in order to form a more perfect Union, establish justice, insure domestic **tranquility**, provide for the common defense, promote the general welfare, and secure the blessings of liberty to ourselves and our **posterity**, do **ordain** and establish this Constitution for the United States of America.

Article I. The Legislative Branch

Section 1. Congress All legislative powers herein granted shall be **vested** in a Congress of the United States, which shall consist of a Senate and House of Representatives.

Section 2. House of Representatives

1. ELECTIONS The House of Representatives shall be composed of members chosen every second year by the people of the several states, and the electors in each state shall have the qualifications **requisite** for electors of the most numerous branch of the state legislature.

2. QUALIFICATIONS No person shall be a representative who shall not have attained to the age of twenty-five years, and been seven years a citizen of the United States, and who shall not, when elected, be an inhabitant of that state in which he shall be chosen.

3. NUMBER OF REPRESENTATIVES Representatives and direct taxes shall be apportioned among the several states which may be included within this Union, according to their respective numbers, which shall be determined by adding to the whole number of free persons, including those bound to service for a term of years, and excluding Indians not taxed, three-fifths of all other persons. The actual **enumeration** shall be made within three years after the first meeting of the Congress of the United States, and within every subsequent term of ten years, in such manner as they shall by law direct. The number of representatives shall not exceed one for every thirty thousand, but each state shall have at least one representative; and until such enumeration shall be made, the state of New Hampshire shall be entitled to choose 3, Massachusetts 8, Rhode Island and Providence Plantations 1, Connecticut 5, New York 6, New Jersey 4, Pennsylvania 8, Delaware 1, Maryland 6, Virginia 10, North Carolina 5, South Carolina 5, and Georgia 3.

4. VACANCIES When vacancies happen in the representation of any state, the executive authority thereof shall issue writs of election to fill such vacancies.

5. OFFICERS AND IMPEACHMENT The House of Representatives shall choose their speaker and other officers; and shall have the sole power of **impeachment**.

Section 3. The Senate

1. NUMBER OF SENATORS The Senate of the United States shall be composed of two senators from each state, chosen by the legislature thereof, for six years; and each senator shall have one vote.

2. CLASSIFYING TERMS Immediately after they shall be assembled in consequence of the first election, they shall be divided as equally as may be into three classes. The seats of the senators of the first class shall be vacated at the expiration of the second year, of the second class at the expiration of the fourth year, and of the third class at the expiration of the sixth year, so that one-third may be chosen every second year; and if vacancies happen by resignation, or otherwise, during the recess of the legislature of any state, the executive thereof may make temporary appointments until the next meeting of the legislature, which shall then fill such vacancies.

3. QUALIFICATIONS No person shall be a senator who shall not have attained to the age of thirty years, and been nine years a citizen of the United States, and who shall not, when elected, be an inhabitant of that state for which he shall be chosen.

> **The Main Idea**
>
> **Section 3. The Senate**
>
> Senators are elected every six years. The Founding Fathers of the Constitution made Senate terms longer than House terms to make the Senate more stable.
>
> A Senator must
>
> - be at least 30 years old.
> - have been a citizen of the United States for nine years.
> - live in the state he or she will represent.

pro tempore for the time being

concurrence agreement

indictment accusation

quorum the minimum number of members who must be present in order to conduct business

adjourn stop a meeting

felony a serious crime

breach break

emolument a payment

The Main Idea

Section 4. Congressional Elections and Meetings

Each state makes its own rules about electing senators and representatives. However, Congress may change these rules at any time. The Constitution requires the Congress to meet at least once a year.

The Main Idea

Section 5. Rules and Procedures

Each house is responsible for overseeing its elections, determining its rules, and punishing its members for violation of such rules. Each house must keep a record of its proceedings and votes so that people know how their representatives voted on bills.

---

4. ROLE OF VICE PRESIDENT The Vice President of the United States shall be President of the Senate, but shall have no vote, unless they be equally divided.

5. OFFICERS The Senate shall choose their other officers, and also a president **pro tempore**, in the absence of the Vice President, or when he shall exercise the office of President of the United States.

6. IMPEACHMENT TRIALS The Senate shall have the sole power to try all impeachments. When sitting for that purpose, they shall be on oath or affirmation. When the President of the United States is tried, the Chief Justice shall preside: And no person shall be convicted without the **concurrence** of two-thirds of the members present.

7. PUNISHMENT FOR IMPEACHMENT Judgment in cases of impeachment shall not extend further than to removal from office, and disqualification to hold and enjoy any office of honor, trust, or profit under the United States; but the party convicted shall nevertheless be liable and subject to **indictment**, trial, judgment, and punishment, according to law.

Section 4. Congressional Elections and Meetings

1. REGULATIONS The times, places, and manner of holding elections for senators and representatives, shall be prescribed in each state by the legislature thereof; but the Congress may at any time by law make or alter such regulations, except as to the places of choosing senators.

2. SESSIONS The Congress shall assemble at least once in every year, and such meeting shall be on the first Monday in December, unless they shall by law appoint a different day.

Section 5. Rules and Procedures

1. QUORUM Each house shall be the judge of the elections, returns, and qualifications of its own members, and a majority of each shall constitute a **quorum** to do business; but a smaller number may **adjourn** from day to day, and may be authorized to compel the attendance of absent members, in such manner, and under such penalties as each house may provide.

2. RULES AND CONDUCT Each house may determine the rules of its proceedings, punish its members for disorderly behavior, and, with the concurrence of two-thirds, expel a member.

3. RECORD KEEPING Each house shall keep a journal of its proceedings, and from time to time publish the same, excepting such parts as may in their judgment require secrecy; and the yeas and nays of the members of either house on any question shall, at the desire of one-fifth of those present, be entered on the journal.

4. ADJOURNMENT Neither house, during the session of Congress, shall, without the consent of the other, adjourn for more than three days, nor to any other place than that in which the two houses shall be sitting.

Section 6. Payment and Privileges

1. SALARY The senators and representatives shall receive a compensation for their services, to be ascertained by law, and paid out of the treasury of the United States. They shall in all cases, except treason, **felony**, and **breach** of the peace, be privileged from arrest during their attendance at the session of their respective houses, and in going to and returning from the same; and for any speech or debate in either house, they shall not be questioned in any other place.

2. RESTRICTIONS No senator or representative shall, during the time for which he was elected, be appointed to any civil office under the authority of the United States, which shall have been created, or the **emoluments** whereof shall have been increased during such time; and no person holding any office under the United States, shall be a member of either house during his continuance in office.

Section 7. How a Bill Becomes a Law

1. TAX BILLS All bills for raising revenue shall originate in the House of Representatives; but the Senate may propose or concur with amendments as on other bills.

The Main Idea

Section 6. Payment and Privileges

Members of Congress are paid by the federal government. Congressional immunity protects members from punishment for anything said in Congress. This protection allows the members to speak freely. However, it does not protect them from arrest for criminal offenses.

The Main Idea

Section 7. How a Bill Becomes a Law

All taxation bills must start in the House of Representatives. Bills have to be passed by both houses of Congress.

2. APPROVING A BILL Every bill which shall have passed the House of Representatives and the Senate, shall, before it become a law, be presented to the President of the United States; if he approve he shall sign it, but if not he shall return it, with his objections to that house in which it shall have originated, who shall enter the objections at large on their journal, and proceed to reconsider it. If after such reconsideration two-thirds of that house shall agree to pass the bill, it shall be sent, together with the objections, to the other house, by which it shall likewise be reconsidered, and if approved by two-thirds of that house, it shall become a law. But in all such cases the votes of both houses shall be determined by yeas and nays, and the names of the persons voting for and against the bill shall be entered on the journal of each house respectively. If any bill shall not be returned by the President within ten days (Sundays excepted) after it shall have been presented to him, the same shall be law, in like manner as if he had signed it, unless the Congress by their adjournment prevent its return, in which case it shall not be a law.

3. ROLE OF THE PRESIDENT Every order, resolution, or vote to which the concurrence of the Senate and House of Representatives may be necessary (except on a question of adjournment) shall be presented to the President of the United States; and before the same shall take effect, shall be approved by him, or being disapproved by him, shall be repassed by two-thirds of the Senate and House of Representatives, according to the rules and limitations prescribed in the case of a bill.

Section 8. Powers of Congress

1. TAXATION The Congress shall have the power to lay and collect taxes, duties, imposts, and excises, to pay the **debts** and provide for the common defense and general welfare of the United States; but all duties, imposts, and excises shall be uniform throughout the United States;

2. BORROW MONEY To borrow money on the credit of the United States;

3. TRADE To regulate commerce with foreign nations, and among the several states, and with the Indian tribes;

The Main Idea

Section 8. Powers of Congress

The powers and duties of Congress are listed here. They are specific powers that include the right to

- tax.
- borrow money.
- regulate trade.
- coin money.
- set up post offices.
- declare war.
- raise an army and a navy.

4. NATURALIZATION, BANKRUPTCY To establish a uniform rule of naturalization, and uniform laws on the subject of bankruptcies throughout the United States;

5. MONEY To coin money, regulate the value thereof, and of foreign coin, and fix the standard of weights and measures;

6. COUNTERFEITING To provide for the punishment of **counterfeiting** the securities and current coin of the United States;

7. POST OFFICES To establish post offices and post roads;

8. COPYRIGHTS AND PATENTS To promote the progress of science and useful arts, by securing for limited times to authors and inventors the exclusive right to their respective writings and discoveries;

9. FEDERAL COURTS To constitute **tribunals** inferior to the Supreme Court;

10. INTERNATIONAL LAW To define and punish piracies and felonies committed on the high seas, and offenses against the law of nations;

11. WAR To declare war, ~~grant letters of marque and reprisal,~~ and make rules concerning captures on land and water;

12. ARMY To raise and support armies, but no appropriation of money to that use shall be for a longer term than two years;

13. NAVY To provide and maintain a navy;

14. RULES FOR ARMED FORCES To make rules for the government and regulation of the land and naval forces;

15. MILITIA To provide for calling forth the militia to execute the laws of the Union, suppress insurrections and repel invasions;

16. RULES FOR MILITIA To provide for organizing, arming, and disciplining the militia, and for governing such part of them as may be employed in the service of the United States, reserving to the states respectively, the appointment of the officers, and the authority of training the militia according to the discipline prescribed by Congress;

Document Dictionary

attainder to punish a person without a trial

ex post facto law a law that punishes a person for an action that was legal when the action was performed

tender money

duty of tonnage charge per ton

The Main Idea

Section 9. Powers Denied to Congress

Congress does not have the powers listed in this section. This clause reflects the Founding Fathers' fear of creating a government that was too powerful. Congress cannot

- set a direct tax on people unless it is in proportion to the total population.
- tax goods sent from one state to another or from a state to another country.
- favor one state over another in making trade laws.

17. DISTRICT OF COLUMBIA To exercise exclusive legislation in all cases whatsoever, over such district (not exceeding ten miles square) as may, by cession of particular states, and the acceptance of Congress, become the seat of the government of the United States, and to exercise like authority over all places purchased by the consent of the legislature of the state in which the same shall be, for the erection of forts, magazines, arsenals, dockyards, and other needful buildings; and

18. ELASTIC CLAUSE To make all laws which shall be necessary and proper for carrying into execution the foregoing powers, and all other powers vested by this Constitution in the government of the United States, or in any department or officer thereof.

Section 9. Powers Denied to Congress

1. SLAVERY ~~The migration or importation of such persons as any of the states now existing shall think proper to admit, shall not be prohibited by the Congress prior to the year one thousand eight hundred and eight, but a tax or duty may be imposed on such importation, not exceeding ten dollars for each person.~~

2. HABEAS CORPUS The privilege of the writ of habeas corpus shall not be suspended, unless when in cases of rebellion or invasion the public safety may require it.

3. ILLEGAL PUNISHMENT No bill of **attainder** or **ex post facto law** shall be passed.

4. DIRECT TAX No capitation, ~~or other direct,~~ tax shall be laid, unless in proportion to the census or enumeration herein before directed to be taken.

5. EXPORT TAXES No tax or duty shall be laid on articles exported from any state.

6. TRADE PREFERENCES No preference shall be given by any regulation of commerce or revenue to the ports of one state over those of another; nor shall vessels bound to, or from, one state, be obliged to enter, clear, or pay duties in another.

7. SPENDING PUBLIC MONEY No money shall be drawn from the treasury, but in consequence of appropriations made by law; and a regular statement and account of the receipts and expenditures of all public money shall be published from time to time.

8. TITLES OF NOBILITY No title of nobility shall be granted by the United States; and no person holding any office of profit or trust under them, shall, without the consent of the Congress, accept of any present, emolument, office, or title, of any kind whatever, from any king, prince, or foreign state.

Section 10. Powers Denied to the States

1. RESTRICTIONS No state shall enter into any treaty, alliance, or confederation; grant letters of marque and reprisal; coin money; emit bills of credit; make anything but gold and silver coin as **tender** in payment of debts; pass any bill of attainder, ex post facto law, or law impairing the obligation of contracts, or grant any title of nobility.

2. IMPORT AND EXPORT TAXES No state shall, without the consent of the Congress, lay any imposts or duties on imports or exports, except what may be absolutely necessary for executing its inspection laws; and the net produce of all duties and imposts, laid by any state on imports or exports, shall be for the use of the treasury of the United States; and all such laws shall be subject to the revision and control of the Congress.

3. PEACETIME AND WAR RESTRAINTS No state shall, without the consent of Congress, lay any **duty of tonnage**, keep troops, or ships of war in time of peace, enter into any agreement or compact with another state, or with a foreign power, or engage in war, unless actually invaded, or in such imminent danger as will not admit of delay.

Article II. The Executive Branch

Section 1. The Presidency

1. TERMS OF OFFICE The executive power shall be vested in a President of the United States of America. He shall hold his office during the term of four years, and, together with the Vice President, chosen for the same term, be elected, as follows:

The Main Idea

Section 10. Powers Denied to the States

The Founding Fathers of the Constitution understood the dangers of a powerful federal government, but they also wanted to prevent the 13 states from acting like independent nations. The states may not assume any of the powers that are specifically given to Congress. These powers include the right to

- make treaties with other nations.
- coin money.
- declare war.
- tax trade.

The Main Idea

Section 1. The Presidency

Article II of the Constitution gives the President "executive power." This power includes the right to enforce the laws of the U.S. government. The first clause sets the term of office at four years.

A President must

- have been born in the United States.
- be at least 35 years old.
- have lived in the United States for at least 14 years.

2. ELECTORAL COLLEGE Each state shall appoint, in such manner as the legislature thereof may direct, a number of electors, equal to the whole number of senators and representatives to which the state may be entitled in the Congress; but no senator or represen-tative, or person holding an office of trust or profit under the United States, shall be appointed an elector.

3. FORMER METHOD OF ELECTING PRESIDENT The electors shall meet in their respective states, and vote by ballot for two persons, of whom one at least shall not be an inhabitant of the same state with themselves. And they shall make a list of all the persons voted for, and of the number of votes for each; which list they shall sign and certify, and transmit sealed to the seat of the government of the United States, directed to the president of the Senate. The presi-dent of the Senate shall, in the presence of the Senate and House of Representatives, open all the certificates, and the votes shall them be counted. The person having the greatest number of votes shall be the President, if such number be a majority of the whole num-ber of electors appointed; and if there be more than one who have such majority, and have an equal number of votes, then the House of Representatives shall immediately choose by ballot one of them for President; and if no person have a majority, then from the five highest on the list the said House shall in like manner choose the President. But in choosing the President, the votes shall be taken by states, the representation from each state having one vote; a quorum for this purpose shall consist of a member or members from two-thirds of the states, and a majority of all the states shall be necessary to a choice. In every case, after the choice of the President, the person having the greatest number of votes of the electors shall be the Vice President. But if there should remain two or more who have equal votes, the Senate shall choose from them by ballot the Vice President.

4. TIME OF ELECTIONS The Congress may determine the time of choosing the electors, and the day on which they shall give their votes; which day shall be the same throughout the United States.

5. REQUIREMENTS FOR PRESIDENT No person except a **natural-born citizen,** or a citizen of the United States, at the time of the adoption of this Constitution, shall be eligible to the office of President; neither shall any person be eligible to that office who shall not have attained to the age of thirty-five years, and been fourteen years a resident within the United States.

6. SUCCESSION In case of the removal of the President from office, or of his death, resignation, or inability to discharge the powers and duties of the said office, the same shall devolve on the Vice President, and the Congress may by law provide for the case of removal, death, resignation or inability, both of the President and Vice President, declaring what officer shall then act as President, and such officer shall act accordingly, until the disability be removed, or a President shall be elected.

7. SALARY The President shall, at stated times, receive for his services, a compensation, which shall neither be increased nor diminished during the period for which he shall have been elected, and he shall not receive within that period any other emolument from the United States, or any of them.

8. OATH OF OFFICE Before he enter on the execution of his office, he shall take the following oath or **affirmation**: "I do solemnly swear (or affirm) that I will faithfully execute the office of President of the United States, and will to the best of my ability, preserve, protect, and defend the Constitution of the United States."

Section 2. Powers of the President

1. MILITARY POWERS The President shall be commander in chief of the Army and Navy of the United States, and of the militia of the several states, when called into the actual service of the United States; he may require the opinion, in writing, of the principal officer in each of the executive departments, upon any subject relating to the duties of their respective offices, and he shall have power to grant reprieves and pardons for offenses against the United States, except in cases of impeachment.

2. CHECKS AND BALANCES He shall have power, by and with the advice and consent of the Senate, to make treaties, provided two-thirds of the senators present concur; and he shall nominate, and by and with the advice and consent of the Senate, shall appoint

The Main Idea

Section 2. Powers of the President

This section gives the President the power to

- command the nation's armed forces.

- obtain information from the head of each executive.

- grant pardons for federal offenses.

- make treaties and appoint government officials with the advice and consent of the Senate.

The Main Idea

Section 3. Presidential Duties

The President shall deliver a state of the Union message to Congress shortly after the beginning of each congressional session. In this message, the President can suggest laws that should be made. The President must see that laws are executed.

The Main Idea

Section 1. The Court System

The Supreme Court is the nation's highest court. Its judges are appointed by the President, with the approval of the Senate, and they may hold office for life. Congress has the power to establish other federal courts.

ambassadors, other public ministers and consuls, judges of the Supreme Court, and all other officers of the United States, whose appointments are not herein otherwise provided for, and which shall be established by law; but the Congress may by law vest the appointment of such inferior officers, as they think proper, in the President alone, in the courts of law, or in the heads of departments.

3. FILLING VACANCIES The President shall have power to fill up all vacancies that may happen during the recess of the Senate, by granting commissions which shall expire at the end of their next session.

Section 3. Presidential Duties He shall from time to time give to the Congress information of the state of the Union, and recommend to their consideration such measures as he shall judge necessary and expedient; he may, on extraordinary occasions, convene both houses, or either of them, and in case of disagreement between them, with respect to the time of adjournment, he may adjourn them to such time as he shall think proper; he shall receive ambassadors and other public ministers; he shall take care that the laws be faithfully executed, and shall commission all the officers of the United States.

Section 4. Impeachment The President, Vice President, and all civil officers of the United States, shall be removed from office on impeachment for, and conviction of, treason, bribery, or other high crimes and **misdemeanors.**

Article III. The Judicial Branch

Section 1. The Court System The judicial power of the United States, shall be vested in one Supreme Court, and in such inferior courts as the Congress may from time to time ordain and establish. The judges, both of the Supreme and inferior courts, shall hold their offices during good behavior, and shall, at stated times, receive for their services, a compensation, which shall not be diminished during their continuance in office.

Section 2. Authority of the Courts

1. FEDERAL COURTS AND JUDGES The judicial power shall extend to all cases, in law and **equity**, arising under this Constitution, the laws of the United States, and treaties made, or which shall be made, under their authority; to all cases affecting ambassadors, other public ministers and **consuls**; to all cases of **admiralty** and maritime jurisdiction; to controversies to which the United States shall be a party; to controversies between two or more states; ~~between a state and citizens of another state;~~ between citizens of different states; between citizens of the same state claiming lands under grants of different states, and between a state, or the citizens thereof, and foreign states, ~~citizens or subjects~~.

2. SUPREME COURT In all cases affecting ambassadors, other public ministers and consuls, and those in which a state shall be party, the Supreme Court shall have original jurisdiction. In all the other cases before mentioned, the Supreme Court shall have appellate jurisdiction, both as to law and fact, with such exceptions, and under such regulations as the Congress shall make.

3. TRIAL BY JURY The trial of all crimes, except in cases of impeachment, shall be by jury; and such trial shall be held in the state where the said crimes shall have been committed; but when not committed within any state, the trial shall be at such place or places as the Congress may by law have directed.

Section 3. Treason

1. DEFINITION Treason against the United States, shall consist only in **levying** war against them, or in adhering to their enemies, giving them aid and comfort. No person shall be convicted of treason unless on the testimony of two witnesses to the same overt act, or on confession in open court.

2. PUNISHMENT The Congress shall have power to declare the punishment of treason, but no attainder of treason shall work corruption of blood, or forfeiture except during the life of the person attainted.

The Main Idea

Section 2. Authority of the Courts

Federal courts handle certain kinds of cases. Only a few are handled directly by the Supreme Court. The judgment of the Supreme Court is final.

The Main Idea

Section 3. Treason

Treason is a serious act of disloyalty against the United States. It is the only crime defined in the Constitution.

Article IV. Relations Among the States

Section 1. State Acts and Records Full faith and credit shall be given in each state to the public acts, records, and judicial proceedings of every other state. And the Congress may by general laws prescribe the manner in which such acts, records, and proceedings shall be proved, and the effect thereof.

Section 2. Rights of Citizens

1. CITIZENSHIP The citizens of each state shall be entitled to all privileges and **immunities** of citizens in the several states.

2. CRIMINAL JURISDICTION A person charged in any state with treason, felony, or other crime, who shall flee from justice, and be found in another state, shall on demand of the executive authority of the state from which he fled, be delivered up, to be removed to the state having jurisdiction of the crime.

3. FUGITIVE SLAVES ~~No person held to service or labor in one state, under the laws thereof, escaping into another, shall, in consequence of any law or regulation therein, be discharged from such service or labor, but shall be delivered up on claim of the party to whom such service or labor may be due.~~

Section 3. New States

1. ADMISSION New states may be admitted by the Congress into this Union; but no new state shall be formed or erected within the jurisdiction of any other state; nor any state be formed by the junction of two or more states, or parts of states, without the consent of the legislatures of the states concerned as well as of the Congress.

2. CONGRESSIONAL AUTHORITY The Congress shall have power to dispose of and make all needful rules and regulations respecting the territory of other property belonging to the United States; and nothing in this Constitution shall be so **construed** as to prejudice any claims of the United States, or of any particular state.

Section 4. Guarantees to the States The United States shall guarantee to every state in this Union a republican form of government, and shall protect each of them against invasion; and on

---

The Main Idea

Section 2. Rights of Citizens

A citizen of one state must be given the same rights as a citizen of another state when visiting that other state. The governor of a state has the power to send someone accused of a crime in another state back to that other state for trial.

The Main Idea

Section 3. New States

Only Congress can admit new states to the Union.

The Main Idea

Section 4. Guarantees to the States

The U.S. government will protect all states from enemies and help the states deal with rebellion or local violence.

application of the legislature, or of the executive (when the legislature cannot be convened) against domestic violence.

Article V. Amending the Constitution

The Congress, whenever two-thirds of both houses shall deem it necessary, shall propose amendments to this Constitution, or, on the application of the legislatures of two-thirds of the several states, shall call a convention for proposing amendments, which, in either case, shall be valid to all intents and purposes, as part of this Constitution, when ratified by the legislatures of three-fourths of the several states, or by conventions in three-fourths thereof, as the one or the other mode of ratification may be proposed by the Congress; provided that no amendment which may be made prior to the year one thousand eight hundred and eight shall in any manner affect the first and fourth clauses in the ninth section of the first article; and that no state, without its consent, shall be deprived of its equal suffrage in the Senate.

Article VI. National Debts and Ratification

Section 1. Debts All debts contracted and engagements entered into, before the adoption of this Constitution, shall be as valid against the United States under this Constitution, as under the Confederation.

Section 2. Supreme Law This Constitution, and the laws of the United States which shall be made in pursuance thereof; and all treaties made, or which shall be made, under the authority of the United States, shall be the supreme law of the land; and the judges in every state shall be bound thereby, anything in the constitution or laws of any state to the contrary notwithstanding.

Section 3. Loyalty to the Constitution The senators and representatives before mentioned, and the members of the several state legislatures, and all executive and judicial officers, both of the United States and of the several states, shall be bound by oath or affirmation, to support this Constitution; but no religious test shall ever be required as a qualification to any office or public trust under the United States.

The Main Idea

Article V. Amending the Constitution

These procedures are necessary to amend, or change, the Constitution. The process is very difficult. Since 1789, only 33 amendments have been proposed, and 27 have been ratified. There are two ways of proposing an amendment:

• by a two-thirds vote in Congress

• by a national convention called by Congress at the request of two-thirds of the individual state legislatures

The Main Idea

Article VI. National Debts and Ratification

The Constitution is the highest law of the land. All national and state lawmakers must support the Constitution.

The Main Idea

**Article VII. Ratification of
the Constitution**

The last article says that the
Constitution was to become
law when 9 of 13 states
approved it. The members of
the Constitutional Convention
present on September 17,
1787, witnessed and signed
the Constitution.

Article VII. Ratification of the Constitution

The ratification of the conventions of nine states, shall be
sufficient for the establishment of this Constitution between
the states so ratifying the same.

Done in convention by the unanimous consent of the states
present the seventeenth day of September in the year of our
Lord one thousand seven hundred and eighty-seven and of the
independence of the United States of America the twelfth. In
witness whereof, we have hereunto subscribed our names,

George Washington—*President and deputy from Virginia*

New Hampshire
John Langdon
Nicholas Gilman

Massachusetts
Nathaniel Gorham
Rufus King

Connecticut
William Samuel
  Johnson
Roger Sherman

New York
Alexander Hamilton

New Jersey
William Livingston
David Brearley
William Paterson
Jonathan Dayton

Pennsylvania
Benjamin Franklin
Thomas Mifflin
Robert Morris
George Clymer
Thomas FitzSimons
Jared Ingersoll
James Wilson
Gouverneur Morris

Delaware
George Read
Gunning Bedford,
  Jr.
John Dickinson
Richard Bassett
Jacob Broom

Maryland
James McHenry
Daniel of St.
  Thomas Jenifer
Daniel Carroll

Virginia
John Blair
James Madison, Jr.

North Carolina
William Blount
Richard Dobbs
  Spaight
Hugh Williamson

South Carolina
John Rutledge
Charles Cotesworth
  Pinckney
Charles Pinckney
Pierce Butler

Georgia
William Few
Abraham Baldwin

Amendments to the Constitution

Amendment 1. Religious and Political Freedom

Ratified December 15, 1791

Congress shall make no law respecting an establishment of religion, or prohibiting the free exercise thereof; or **abridging** the freedom of speech, or of the press; or the right of the people peaceably to assemble, and to petition the government for a **redress** of grievances.

Amendment 2. Right to Keep Arms

Ratified December 15, 1791

A well-regulated militia, being necessary to the security of a free state, the right of the people to keep and bear arms, shall not be infringed.

Amendment 3. Housing of Soldiers

Ratified December 15, 1791

No soldier shall, in time of peace, be quartered in any house, without the consent of the owner; nor in time of war, but in a manner to be prescribed by law.

Amendment 4. Search and Arrest Warrant

Ratified December 15, 1791

The right of the people to be secure in their persons, houses, papers, and effects, against unreasonable searches and seizures, shall not be violated; and no warrants shall issue, but upon probable cause, supported by oath or affirmation, and particularly describing the place to be searched, and the persons or things to be seized.

Amendment 5. Rights of Accused Persons

Ratified December 15, 1791

No person shall be held to answer for a capital, or otherwise infamous crime, unless on a presentment or indictment of a grand jury, except in cases arising in the land or naval forces, or in the militia, when in actual service in time of war or public danger; nor shall any person be subject for the same offense to be twice put in jeopardy of life or limb; nor shall be compelled in any criminal

The Main Idea

Amendments 1–10. The Bill of Rights

The first ten amendments, which became part of the Constitution in 1791, are known as the Bill of Rights. They protect the basic freedoms of the American people.

The Main Idea

Amendment 4. Search and Arrest Warrant

This amendment protects people's privacy and safety. A law officer cannot search a person or a person's home unless a judge has issued a valid search warrant.

The Main Idea

Amendment 6. Rights to a Fair Trial

Persons accused of serious crimes have the right to a speedy and public trial. They must be told of what they are accused. They have the right to have a lawyer and to see and question those who accuse them.

The Main Idea

Amendment 10. Powers Reserved to the States

This amendment limits federal powers. It states that powers not given to the federal government and not denied to the states belong to the states or to the people who live in them.

case to be a witness against himself; nor be deprived of life, liberty, or property, without due process of law; nor shall private property be taken for public use, without just compensation.

Amendment 6. Rights to a Fair Trial

Ratified December 15, 1791

In all criminal prosecutions, the accused shall enjoy the right to a speedy and public trial, by an impartial jury of the state and district wherein the crime shall have been committed, which district shall have been previously ascertained by law, and to be informed of the nature and cause of the accusation; to be confronted with the witnesses against him; to have compulsory process for obtaining witnesses in his favor, and to have the assistance of counsel for his defense.

Amendment 7. Rights in Civil Cases

Ratified December 15, 1791

In suits at **common law**, where the value in controversy shall exceed twenty dollars, the right of trial by jury shall be preserved; and no fact tried by a jury, shall be otherwise reexamined in any court of the United States, than according to the rules of the common law.

Amendment 8. Limits on Bails, Fines, and Punishments

Ratified December 15, 1791

Excessive **bail** shall not be required, nor excessive fines imposed, nor cruel and unusual punishments inflicted.

Amendment 9. Rights Retained by the People

Ratified December 15, 1971

The enumeration in the Constitution of certain rights shall not be construed to deny or disparage others retained by the people.

Amendment 10. Powers Reserved to the States

Ratified December 15, 1971

The powers not delegated to the United States by the Constitution, nor prohibited by it to the states, are reserved to the states respectively, or to the people.

Amendment 11. Lawsuits Against States

Ratified February 7, 1795

The judicial power of United States shall not be construed to extend to any suit in law or equity, commenced or prosecuted against one of the United States by citizens of another state, or by citizens or subjects of any foreign state.

Amendment 12. Election of the President and Vice President

Ratified June 15, 1804

The electors shall meet in their respective states and vote by ballot for President and Vice President, one of whom, at least, shall not be an inhabitant of the same state with themselves; they shall name in their ballots the person voted for as President, and in distinct ballots the person voted for as Vice President, and they shall make distinct lists of all persons voted for as President, and of all persons voted for as Vice President; and of the number of votes for each, which lists they shall sign and certify, and transmit sealed to the seat of the government of the United States, directed to the President of the Senate; the President of the Senate shall, in the presence of the Senate and House of Representatives, open all the certificates and the votes shall then be counted; the person having the greatest number of votes for President, shall be the President, if such number be a majority of the whole number of electors appointed; and if no person have such majority, then from the persons having the highest numbers not exceeding three on the list of those voted for as President, the House of Representatives shall choose immediately, by ballot, the President. But in choosing the President, the votes shall be taken by states, the representation from each state having one vote; a quorum for this purpose shall consist of a member or members from two-thirds of the states, and a majority of all the states shall be necessary to a choice. And if the House of Representatives shall not choose a President whenever the right of choice shall devolve upon them, ~~before the fourth day of March next following,~~ then the Vice President shall act as President, as in the case of the

The Main Idea

Amendment 12. Election of the President and Vice President

Electors vote for the President and Vice President separately. An elector is a person chosen by the state legislature to elect the President and Vice President.

death or other constitutional disability of the President. The person having the greatest number of votes as Vice President, shall be the Vice President, if such number be a majority of the whole number of electors appointed, and if no person have a majority, then from the two highest numbers on the list, the Senate shall choose the Vice President; a quorum for the purpose shall consist of two-thirds of the whole number of senators, and a majority of the whole number shall be necessary to a choice. But no person constitutionally ineligible to the office of President shall be eligible to that of Vice President of the United States.

Amendment 13. Abolition of Slavery

Ratified December 6, 1865

SECTION 1. Neither slavery nor involuntary servitude, except as a punishment for crime whereof the party shall have been duly convicted, shall exist within the United States, or any place subject to their jurisdiction.

SECTION 2. Congress shall have power to enforce this article by appropriate legislation.

Amendment 14. Rights of Citizens

Ratified July 9, 1868

SECTION 1. All persons born or naturalized in the United States, and subject to the jurisdiction thereof, are citizens of the United States and of the state wherein they reside. No state shall make or enforce any law which shall abridge the privileges or immunities of citizens of the United States; nor shall any state deprive any person of life, liberty, or property, without due process of law; nor deny to any person within its jurisdiction the equal protection of the laws.

SECTION 2. Representatives shall be apportioned among the several states according to their respective numbers, counting the whole number of persons in each state, ~~excluding Indians not taxed.~~ But when the right to vote at any election for the choice of electors for President and Vice President of the United States, representatives in Congress, the executive and judicial officers of a state, or the members of the legislature thereof, is denied to any

The Main Idea

Amendment 14. Rights of Citizens

People who are born in the United States or who are granted citizenship are U.S. citizens. They are also citizens of the states in which they live. States may not make laws that overrule the rights given to citizens by the U.S. Constitution. States may not take away a person's life, freedom, or property unfairly. They must treat all people equally under the law.

of the ~~male~~ inhabitants of such state, ~~being twenty-one years of age,~~ and citizens of the United States, or in any way abridged, except for participation in rebellion, or other crime, the basis of representation therein shall be reduced in the proportion which the number of such male citizens shall bear to the whole number of ~~male~~ citizens ~~twenty-one years of age~~ in such state.

SECTION 3. No person shall be a senator or representative in Congress, or elector of President and Vice President, or hold any office, civil or military, under the United States, or under any state, who, having previously taken an oath, as a member of Congress, or as an officer of the United States, or as a member of any state legislature, or as an executive or judicial officer of any state, to support the Constitution of the United States, shall have engaged in insurrection or rebellion against the same, or given aid or comfort to the enemies thereof. But Congress may by a vote of two-thirds of each house, remove such disability.

SECTION 4. The validity of the public debt of the Untied States, authorized by law, including debts incurred for payment of pensions and bounties for services in suppressing insurrection or rebellion, shall not be questioned. But neither the United States nor any state shall assume or pay any debt or obligation incurred in aid of insurrection or rebellion against the United States, or any claim for the loss or emancipation of any slave, but all such debts, obligations, and claims shall be held illegal and void.

SECTION 5. The Congress shall have power to enforce, by appropriate legislation, the provisions of this article.

Amendment 15. African American Suffrage

Ratified February 3, 1870

SECTION 1. The right of citizens of the United States to vote shall not be denied or abridged by the United States or by any state on account of race, color, or **previous condition of servitude**.

SECTION 2. The Congress shall have power to enforce this article by appropriate legislation.

The Main Idea

Amendment 16. Income Tax

Congress has the power to collect taxes on its citizens based on their personal incomes rather than on the number of people living in a state.

The Main Idea

Amendment 17. Direct Election of Senators

Senators are elected directly by the voters and not by state legislatures. This is to make senators more responsible to the people they represent.

Amendment 16. Income Tax

Ratified February 3, 1913

The Congress shall have power to lay and collect taxes on incomes, from whatever source derived, without **apportionment** among the several states, and without regard to any census or enumeration.

Amendment 17. Direct Election of Senators

Ratified April 8, 1913

SECTION 1. The Senate of the United States shall be composed of two senators from each state, elected by the people thereof for six years; and each senator shall have one vote. The electors in each state shall have the qualifications requisite for electors of the most numerous branch of the state legislatures.

SECTION 2. When vacancies happen in the representation of any state in the Senate, the executive authority of such state shall issue writs of election to fill such vacancies: Provided, that the legislature of any state may empower the executive thereof to make temporary appointments until the people fill the vacancies by election as the legislature may direct.

SECTION 3. This amendment shall not be so construed as to affect the election or term of any senator chosen before it becomes valid as part of the Constitution.

Amendment 18. Prohibition

Ratified January 16, 1919

SECTION 1. After one year from the ratification of this article the manufacture, sale, or transportation of intoxicating liquors within, the importation thereof into, or the exportation thereof from the United States and all territory subject to the jurisdiction thereof for beverage purposes is hereby prohibited.

SECTION 2. The Congress and the several states shall have concurrent power to enforce this article by appropriate legislation.

SECTION 3. ~~This article shall be inoperative unless it shall have been ratified as an amendment to the Constitution by the legislatures of the several states, as provided in the Constitution, within seven years from the date of the submission hereof to the states by the Congress.~~

Amendment 19. Women's Right to Vote

Ratified August 18, 1920

SECTION 1. The right of citizens of the United States to vote shall not be denied or abridged by the United States or by any state on account of sex.

SECTION 2. Congress shall have power to enforce this article by appropriate legislation.

Amendment 20. Terms of the President and Congress

Ratified January 23, 1933

SECTION 1. The terms of the President and Vice President shall end at noon on the 20th day of January, and the terms of senators and representatives at noon on the third day of January, of the year in which such terms would have ended if this article had not been ratified; and the terms of their successors shall then begin.

SECTION 2. The Congress shall assemble at least once in every year, and such meeting shall begin at noon on the third day of January, unless they shall by law appoint a different day.

SECTION 3. If, at the time fixed for the beginning of the term of the President, the President elect shall have died, the Vice President elect shall become President. If a President shall not have been chosen before the time fixed for the beginning of his term, or if the President elect shall have failed to qualify, then the Vice President elect shall act as President until a President shall have qualified; and the Congress may by law provide for the case wherein neither a President elect nor a Vice President elect shall have qualified, declaring who shall then act as President, or the manner in which one who is to act shall be selected, and such person shall act accordingly until a President or Vice President shall have qualified.

The Main Idea

Amendment 19. Women's Right to Vote

In 1920, women finally won the right to vote in both national and state elections. The struggle went on for almost 75 years before passage of the Nineteenth Amendment.

The Main Idea

Amendment 20. Terms of the President and Congress

Presidents start their new terms on January 20. Congress starts its new term on January 3.

SECTION 4. The Congress may by law provide for the case of the death of any of the persons from whom the House of Representatives may choose a President whenever the right of choice shall have devolved upon them, and for the case of the death of any of the persons from whom the Senate may choose a Vice President whenever the right of choice shall have devolved upon them.

SECTION 5. Sections 1 and 2 shall take effect on the 15th day of October following the ratification of this article.

SECTION 6. This article shall be **inoperative** unless it shall have been ratified as an amendment to the Constitution by the legislatures of three-fourths of the several states within seven years from the date of its submission.

Amendment 21. Repeal of Prohibition

Ratified December 5, 1933

SECTION 1. The eighteenth article of amendment to the Constitution of the United States is hereby repealed.

SECTION 2. The transportation or importation into any state, territory, or possession of the United States for delivery or use therein of intoxicating liquors, in violation of the laws thereof, is hereby prohibited.

SECTION 3. This article shall be inoperative unless it shall have been ratified as an amendment to the Constitution by conventions in the several states, as provided in the Constitution, within seven years from the date of the submission hereof to the states by the Congress.

Amendment 22. Limitation of Presidential Terms

Ratified February 27, 1951

SECTION 1. No person shall be elected to the office of President more than twice, and no person who has held the office of President, or acted as President, for more than two years of a term to which some other person was elected President shall be elected to the office of the President more than once. But this article shall not apply to any person holding the office of President when this article was proposed by the Congress, and shall not prevent any person

The Main Idea

Amendment 21. Repeal of Prohibition

This amendment repealed the Eighteenth Amendment, which prohibited the manufacture, sale, and transportation of alcohol.

The Main Idea

Amendment 22. Limitation of Presidential Terms

A President is limited to two terms in office. Any President who serves less than two years of a previous President's term may be elected for two more terms.

~~who may be holding the office of President, or acting as President, during the term within which this article becomes operative from holding the office of President or acting as President during the remainder of such term.~~

SECTION 2. This article shall be inoperative unless it shall have been ratified as an amendment to the Constitution by the legislatures of three-fourths of the several states within seven years form the date of its submission to the states by the Congress.

Amendment 23. Presidential Electors in the District of Columbia

Ratified March 29, 1961

SECTION 1. The district constituting the seat of government of the United States shall appoint in such manner as the Congress may direct: A number of electors of President and Vice President equal to the whole number of senators and representatives in Congress to which the district would be entitled if it were a state, but in no event more than the least populous state; they shall be in addition to those appointed by the states, but they shall be considered, for the purposes of the election of President and Vice President, to be electors appointed by a state; and they shall meet in the district and perform such duties as provided by the twelfth article of amendment.

SECTION 2. The Congress shall have power to enforce this article by appropriate legislation.

Amendment 24. Abolition of Poll Taxes in National Elections

Ratified January 23, 1964

SECTION 1. The right of citizens of the United States to vote in any **primary** or other election for President or Vice President, for electors for President or Vice President, or for senator or representative in Congress, shall not be denied or abridged by the United States or any state by reason of failure to pay any poll tax or other tax.

SECTION 2. The Congress shall have power to enforce this article by appropriate legislation.

The Main Idea

Amendment 23. Presidential Electors in the District of Columbia

By the time this amendment was ratified in 1960, more than 760,000 people lived in Washington, D.C. However, the Constitution had no provisions for allowing residents of the District of Columbia to vote in presidential elections. Now the District of Columbia has three electoral college votes.

The Main Idea

Amendment 25. Presidential Disability and Succession

This amendment establishes procedures for how the U.S. government will continue to work if the President dies, resigns, or is temporarily disabled. This amendment also states that if a vacancy exists in the office of Vice President, the President nominates a Vice President, and a majority of both houses of Congress must approve the nominee.

Amendment 25. Presidential Disability and Succession

Ratified February 10, 1967

SECTION 1. In case of the removal of the President from office or of his death or resignation, the Vice President shall become President.

SECTION 2. Whenever there is a vacancy in the office of the Vice President, the President shall nominate a Vice President who shall take office upon confirmation by a majority vote of both houses of Congress.

SECTION 3. Whenever the President transmits to the President pro tempore of the Senate and the Speaker of the House of Representatives his written declaration that he is unable to discharge the powers and duties of his office, and until he transmits to them a written declaration to the contrary, such powers and duties shall be discharged by the Vice President as Acting President.

SECTION 4. Whenever the Vice President and a majority of either the principal officers of the executive departments or of such other body as Congress may by law provide, transmit to the President pro tempore of the Senate and the Speaker of the House of Representatives their written declaration that the President is unable to discharge the powers and duties of his office, the Vice President shall immediately assume the powers and duties of the office as Acting President. Thereafter, when the President transmits to the President pro tempore of the Senate and the Speaker of the House of Representatives his written declaration that no inability exists, he shall resume the powers and duties of his office unless the Vice President and a majority of either the principal officers of the executive department or of such other body as Congress may by law provide, transmit within four days to the President pro tempore of the Senate and the Speaker of the House of Representatives their written declaration that the President is unable to discharge the powers and duties of his office. Thereupon Congress shall decide the issue, assembling within forty-eight hours for that purpose if not in session. If the Congress, within twenty-one days after receipt of the latter written declaration, or, if

Congress is not in session within twenty-one days after Congress is required to assemble, determines by two-thirds vote of both houses that the President is unable to discharge the powers and duties of his office, the Vice President shall continue to discharge the same as Acting President; otherwise, the President shall resume the powers and duties of his office.

Amendment 26. Eighteen-Year-Old Vote

Ratified July 1, 1971

SECTION 1. The right of citizens of the United States, who are eighteen years of age or older, to vote shall not be denied or abridged by the United States or by any state on account of age.

SECTION 2. The Congress shall have power to enforce this article by appropriate legislation.

Amendment 27. Congressional Compensation

Ratified May 7, 1992

No law, varying the **compensation** for the services of the senators and representatives, shall take effect until an election of representatives shall have intervened.

The Main Idea

Amendment 27. Congressional Compensation

Congress may raise members' salaries, but the raise takes effect only after the next congressional elections. This delay allows voters to speak out on the proposed raises.

ANALYZE PRIMARY SOURCES

DOCUMENT-BASED QUESTIONS

1. What are three differences between the House of Representatives and the Senate?

2. Why do you think a person must have been born in the United States in order to be eligible to be President?

3. If a person charged with a crime flees to another state, what action is that state required to take?

4. How many states were needed to ratify the Constitution in order for it to take effect?

5. **Critical Thinking** How would you describe the impact of the Fourteenth, Fifteenth, and Sixteenth amendments on life in the United States?

6. **Critical Thinking** Which three amendments passed since 1800 do you think have had the most significant impact on American society today?

Reference Section

Primary Source Documents

From The Magna Carta (1215)

This charter, granted by King John of England, limited the powers of a king and protected the basic rights of some individuals. More than 500 years later, American colonists fought against the British for the same rights listed in the Magna Carta.

1. . . . we have granted . . . that the English Church shall be free, and shall have its rights undiminished, and its liberties unimpaired. . . . To all free men of our kingdom, we have also granted, for us and our heirs forever, all the liberties written out below, to have and to keep for them and their heirs, of us and our heirs. . . .

38. In future no official shall place a man on trial upon his own unsupported statement, without producing credible witnesses to the truth of it.

39. No free man shall be seized or imprisoned, or stripped of his rights or possessions, or outlawed or exiled, . . . except by the lawful judgment of his equals or by the law of the land.

40. To no one will we sell, to no one deny or delay, right or justice.

41. All merchants may enter or leave England, unharmed and without fear, and may stay or travel within it, by land or water, for purposes of trade. . . .

42. In future it shall be lawful for any man to leave and return to our kingdom unharmed and without fear, by land or water. . . .

60. All these customs and liberties that we have granted shall be observed in our kingdom in so far as concerns our own relations with our subjects. . . .

63. . . . the English Church be free, and that the men in our kingdom shall have and keep all these liberties, rights, and concessions, well and peaceably, in their fullness and entirety for them and their heirs, of us and our heirs, in all things and all places forever.

From The Mayflower Compact (1620)

The Pilgrims, sailing aboard the Mayflower, *left England behind to begin a new life in North America. The Mayflower Compact was a step toward self-government in the English colonies.*

. . . Having undertaken, for the glory of God, and advancement of the Christian faith, and honor of our King and country, a voyage to plant the first colony in the northern parts of Virginia, do by these presents solemnly and mutually, in the presence of God, and one of another, covenant and combine our selves together into a civil body politic; for our better ordering, and preservation and furtherance of the ends aforesaid; and by virtue hereof to enact, constitute, and frame such just and equal laws, ordinances, acts, constitutions and offices, from time to time, as shall be thought most meet and convenient for the general good of the Colony, unto which we promise all due submission and obedience.

From James Monroe, The Monroe Doctrine (1823)

The Monroe Doctrine stated that the United States would not allow European nations to form new colonies in the Americas. It also declared that the United States would help former colonies to maintain their independence. The doctrine guided U.S. policy in the Western Hemisphere for many years.

. . . the occasion has been judged proper for asserting, as a principle in which the rights and interests of the United States are involved, that the American continents, by the free and independent condition which they have assumed and maintain, are henceforth not to be considered as subjects for future colonization by any European powers. . . .

The citizens of the United States cherish sentiments the most friendly in favor of the liberty and happiness of their fellow-men on that side of the Atlantic. In the wars of the European powers in matters relating to themselves we have never taken any part, nor does it comport with our policy to do so. It is only when our rights are invaded or seriously menaced that we resent injuries or make preparation for our defense. With the movements in this hemisphere we are of necessity more immediately connected, and by causes which must be obvious to all enlightened and impartial observers. . . . We owe it, therefore, to . . . declare that we should consider any attempt on their part to extend their system to any portion of this hemisphere as dangerous to our peace and safety. With the existing colonies or dependencies of any European power we have not interfered and shall not interfere. But with the Governments who have declared their independence and maintain it, and whose independence we have, on great consideration and on just principles, acknowledged, we could not view any interposition for the purpose of oppressing them, or controlling in any other manner their destiny, by any European power in any other light than as the manifestation of an unfriendly disposition toward the United States.

From Appeal of the Cherokee Nation (1830)

In 1830, the U.S. Congress passed the Indian Removal Act. According to this act, Native Americans with homelands in the East would be forced to move to the West. In response, Cherokee leaders wrote this appeal declaring their right to stay on their land. Despite their efforts, most Cherokees were removed to Oklahoma Territory in 1838–1939.

. . . We are aware, that some persons suppose it will be for our advantage to remove beyond the Mississippi. We think otherwise. Our people universally think otherwise. Thinking that it would be fatal to their interests, they have almost to a man sent their memorial to congress, deprecating the necessity of a removal. . . . We are not willing to remove; and if we could be brought to this extremity, it would be not by argument, nor because our judgment was satisfied, not because our condition will be improved; but only because we cannot endure to be deprived of our national and individual rights and subjected to a process of intolerable oppression.

We wish to remain on the land of our fathers. We have a perfect and original right to remain without interruption or molestation. The treaties with us, and laws of the United States made in pursuance of treaties, guaranty our residence and our privileges, and secure us against intruders. Our only request is, that these treaties may be fulfilled, and these laws executed.

But if we are compelled to leave our country, we see nothing but ruin before us. The country west of the Arkansas territory is unknown to us. . . . All the inviting parts of it, as we believe, are preoccupied by various Indian nations, to which it has been assigned. They would regard us as intruders. . . . The far greater part of that region is, beyond all controversy, badly supplied with wood and water; and no Indian tribe can live as agriculturists without these articles.

From The Declaration of Sentiments (1848)

The first women's rights convention was held at Seneca Falls, New York, in 1848. Elizabeth Cady Stanton and other women presented the Declaration of Sentiments to the convention. This document showed that women did not have all the rights listed in the Declaration of Independence.

When, in the course of human events, it becomes necessary for one portion of the family of man to assume among the people of the earth a position different from that which they have hitherto occupied, but one to which the laws of nature and of nature's God entitle them, a decent respect to the opinions of mankind requires that they should declare the causes that impel them to such a course.

We hold these truths to be self-evident: that all men and women are created equal; that they are endowed by their Creator with certain inalienable rights; that among these are life, liberty, and the pursuit of happiness; that to secure these rights governments are instituted, deriving their just powers from the consent of the governed. Whenever any form of government becomes destructive of these ends, it is the right of those who suffer from it to refuse allegiance to it, and to insist upon the institution of a new government, laying its foundation on such principles, and organizing its powers in such form, as to them shall seem most likely to effect their safety and happiness. . . .

He has never permitted her to exercise her inalienable right to the elective franchise.

He has compelled her to submit to laws, in the formation of which she had no voice. . . .

He has made her, if married, in the eye of the law, civilly dead.

He has taken from her all right in property . . .

He has denied her the facilities for obtaining [an] . . . education . . .

He has endeavored, in every way that he could, to destroy her confidence in her own powers, to lessen her self-respect, and to make her willing to lead a dependent and abject life.

Now, in view of this entire disfranchisement of one-half the people of this country, their social and religious degradation—in view of the unjust laws above mentioned, and because women do feel themselves aggrieved, oppressed, and fraudulently deprived of their most sacred rights, we insist that they have immediate admission to all the rights and privileges which belong to them as citizens of the United States.

From Abraham Lincoln, The Emancipation Proclamation (1862)

Abraham Lincoln issued the Emancipation Proclamation during the Civil War. In it, he declared that slaves in areas controlled by the Confederacy were free. Lincoln felt certain that he was doing the right thing when he signed this paper. Although no slaves were freed immediately, the Emancipation Proclamation was a promise that enslaved people in the South would be free when the Union won the war.

. . . I do order and declare that all persons held as slaves within said designated States and parts of States are, and henceforward shall be, free; and that the Executive Government of the United States, including the military and naval authorities thereof, will recognize and maintain the freedom of said persons.

And I hereby enjoin upon the people so declared to be free to abstain from all violence, unless in necessary self-defence; and I recommend to them that, in all case when allowed, they labor faithfully for reasonable wages.

And I further declare and make known that such persons of suitable condition will be received into the armed service of the United States to garrison forts, positions, stations, and other places, and to man vessels of all sorts in said service.

And upon this act, sincerely believed to be an act of justice, warranted by the Constitution upon military necessity, I invoke the considerate judgment of mankind and the gracious favor of Almighty God.

Abraham Lincoln, The Gettysburg Address (1863)

During the Civil War, more than 50,000 soldiers were killed, wounded, or captured at the Battle of Gettysburg. Afterward, Abraham Lincoln went to the battlefield to attend a dedication ceremony for a cemetery. He gave a short speech that lasted just over two minutes. Today the Gettysburg Address is considered one of the greatest speeches in American history.

Four score and seven years ago our fathers brought forth on this continent a new nation, conceived in liberty and dedicated to the proposition that all men are created equal. Now we are engaged in a great civil war, testing whether that nation or any nation so conceived and so dedicated can long endure. We are met on a great battle-field of that war. We have come to dedicate a portion of that field as a final resting-place for those who here gave their lives that that nation might live. It is altogether fitting and proper that we should do this. But in a larger sense, we cannot dedicate, we cannot con-secrate, we cannot hallow this ground. The brave men, living and dead who struggled here have consecrated it far above our poor power to add or detract. The world will little note nor long remem-ber what we say here, but it can never forget what they did here. It is for us the living rather to be dedicated here to the unfinished work which they who fought here have thus far so nobly advanced. It is rather for us to be here dedicated to the great task remaining before us—that from these honored dead we take increased devotion to that cause for which they gave the last full measure of devotion—that we here highly resolve that these dead shall not have died in vain, that this nation under God shall have a new birth of freedom, and that government of the people, by the people, for the people shall not perish from the earth.

From Chief Joseph, I Will Fight No More Forever (Speech to the U.S. Army, 1877)

In 1877, the U.S. government ordered the Nez Percé Native Americans to a reservation. Chief Joseph and a group of followers fled toward Canada. U.S. soldiers chased them and fought several battles with them. Finally, Chief Joseph surrendered to the army with these words:

Tell General Howard I know his heart. What he told me before, I have it in my heart. I am tired of fighting. Our chiefs are killed. Looking Glass is dead. Ta Hool Hool Shute is dead. The old men are all dead. It is the young men who say, Yes or No. He who led the young men is dead. It is cold, and we have no blankets. The little children are freezing to death. My people, some of them, have run away to the hills, and have no blankets, no food. No one knows where they are—perhaps freezing to death. I want to have time to look for my children, and see how many of them I can find. Maybe I shall find them among the dead. Hear me, my Chiefs! I am tired. My heart is sick and sad. From where the sun now stands I will fight no more forever.

From Woodrow Wilson, The Fourteen Points (Address to Congress, 1918)

As World War I was coming to an end, President Wilson believed that a peace treaty calling for severe punishment of the Central Powers would only lead to future conflicts. In an effort to maintain world peace, he proposed the following ideas in the Fourteen Points.

Gentlemen of the Congress:

. . . We entered this war because violations of right had occurred which touched us to the quick and made the life of our own people impossible unless they were corrected and the world secure once for all against their recurrence. What we demand in this war . . . is that the world be made fit and safe to live in; and particularly that it be made safe for every peace-loving nation which, like our own, wishes to live its own life, determine its own institutions, be assured of justice and fair dealing by the other peoples of the world as against force and selfish aggression. All the peoples of the world are in effect partners in this interest. . . . The program of the world's peace, . . . as we see it, is this:

I. Open covenants of peace, openly arrived at, after which there shall be no private international understandings of any kind but diplomacy shall proceed always frankly and in the public view.

II. Absolute freedom of navigation upon the seas . . . .

III. The removal, so far as possible, of all economic barriers and the establishment of an equality of trade conditions among all the nations consenting to the peace and associating themselves for its maintenance.

IV. Adequate guarantees given and taken that national armaments will be reduced to the lowest point consistent with domestic safety. . . .

XIV. A general association of nations must be formed under specific covenants for the purpose of affording mutual guarantees of political independence and territorial integrity to great and small states alike. . . .

An evident principle runs through the whole program I have outlined. It is the principle of justice to all peoples and nationalities, and their right to live on equal terms of liberty and safety with one another.

From Martin Luther King Jr., I Have a Dream
(Address at the March on Washington, 1963)

On August 28, 1963, Martin Luther King Jr. led a civil rights march on Washington, D.C. On the steps of the Lincoln Memorial, he gave a powerful speech expressing his hopes for the nation's future.

. . . Five score years ago, a great American, in whose symbolic shadow we stand signed the Emancipation Proclamation. . . . But one hundred years later, the Negro is still not free. . . . So we've come here today to dramatize a shameful condition. . . . I say to you today, my friends, so even though we face the difficulties of today and tomorrow, I still have a dream. It is a dream deeply rooted in the American dream.

I have a dream that one day this nation will rise up and live out the true meaning of its creed: "We hold these truths to be self-evident: that all men are created equal." . . . I have a dream that my four little children will one day live in a nation where they will not be judged by the color of their skin but by the content of their character. . . .

This is our hope. This is the faith that I go back to the South with. . . . With this faith, we will be able to work together, to pray together, to struggle together, to go to jail together, to stand up for freedom together, knowing that we will be free one day!

This will be the day when all of God's children will be able to sing with a new meaning, "My country 'tis of thee, sweet land of liberty, of thee I sing. Land where my fathers died, land of the pilgrim's pride, from every mountainside, let freedom ring," and if America is to be a great nation, this must become true. . . .

When we allow freedom to ring, when we let it ring from every village and every hamlet, from every state and every city, we will be able to speed up that day when all of God's children, black men and white men, Jews and Gentiles, Protestants and Catholics, will be able to join hands and sing in the words of the old Negro spiritual, "Free at last! Free at last! Thank God Almighty, we are free at last!"

PRESIDENTS
of the United States

	Years in Office	Vice President	State◆
1. George Washington (1732–1799)	1789–1797	John Adams	Virginia
2. John Adams (1735–1826)	1797–1801	Thomas Jefferson	Massachusetts
3. Thomas Jefferson (1743–1826)	1801–1809	Aaron Burr, George Clinton	Virginia
4. James Madison (1751–1836)	1809–1817	George Clinton, Elbridge Gerry	Virginia
5. James Monroe (1758–1831)	1817–1825	Daniel D. Tompkins	Virginia
6. John Quincy Adams (1767–1848)	1825–1829	John C. Calhoun***	Massachusetts
7. Andrew Jackson (1767–1845)	1829–1837	John C. Calhoun, Martin Van Buren	Tennessee (SC)
8. Martin Van Buren (1782–1862)	1837–1841	Richard M. Johnson	New York
9. William Henry Harrison* (1773–1841)	1841	John Tyler	Ohio (VA)
10. John Tyler (1790–1862)	1841–1845	None	Virginia
11. James K. Polk (1795–1849)	1845–1849	George M. Dallas	Tennessee (NC)
12. Zachary Taylor* (1784–1850)	1849–1850	Millard Fillmore	Louisiana (VA)
13. Millard Fillmore (1800–1874)	1850–1853	None	New York
14. Franklin Pierce (1804–1869)	1853–1857	William R. King	New Hampshire

◆State of residence at time of election. If state of birth is different, it is shown in parentheses.
*Died while in office   **Assassinated while in office   ***Resigned while in office

		Years in Office	Vice President	State♦
15. James Buchanan (1791–1868)		1857–1861	John G. Breckinridge	Pennsylvania
16. Abraham Lincoln** (1809–1865)		1861–1865	Hannibal Hamlin, Andrew Johnson	Illinois (KY)
17. Andrew Johnson (1808–1875)		1865–1869	None	Tennessee (NC)
18. Ulysses S. Grant (1822–1885)		1869–1877	Schuyler Colfax, Henry Wilson	Illinois (OH)
19. Rutherford B. Hayes (1822–1893)		1877–1881	William A. Wheeler	Ohio
20. James A. Garfield** (1831–1881)		1881	Chester A. Arthur	Ohio
21. Chester A. Arthur (1830–1886)		1881–1885	None	New York (VT)
22. S. Grover Cleveland (1837–1908)		1885–1889	Thomas A. Hendricks	New York (NJ)
23. Benjamin Harrison (1833–1901)		1889–1893	Levi P. Morton	Indiana (OH)
24. S. Grover Cleveland (1837–1908)		1893–1897	Adlai E. Stevenson	New York (NJ)
25. William McKinley** (1843–1901)		1897–1901	Garret A. Hobart, Theodore Roosevelt	Ohio
26. Theodore Roosevelt (1858–1919)		1901–1909	Charles W. Fairbanks	New York
27. William H. Taft (1857–1930)		1909–1913	James S. Sherman	Ohio
28. T. Woodrow Wilson (1856–1924)		1913–1921	Thomas R. Marshall	New Jersey (VA)
29. Warren G. Harding* (1865–1923)		1921–1923	J. Calvin Coolidge	Ohio

Portrait numbers: 15, 16, 17, 18, 19, 20, 21, 22, 24, 23, 25, 26, 27, 28, 29

			Years in Office	Vice President	State♦
30	31	**30. J. Calvin Coolidge** (1872–1933)	1923–1929	Charles G. Dawes	Massachusetts (VT)
		31. Herbert C. Hoover (1874–1964)	1929–1933	Charles Curtis	California (IA)
32	33	**32. Franklin D. Roosevelt*** (1882–1945)	1933–1945	John N. Garner, Henry A. Wallace, Harry S Truman	New York
		33. Harry S Truman (1884–1972)	1945–1953	Alben W. Barkley	Missouri
34	35	**34. Dwight D. Eisenhower** (1890–1969)	1953–1961	Richard M. Nixon	New York (TX)
		35. John F. Kennedy** (1917–1963)	1961–1963	Lyndon B. Johnson	Massachusetts
36	37	**36. Lyndon B. Johnson** (1908–1973)	1963–1969	Hubert H. Humphrey	Texas
		37. Richard M. Nixon** (1913–1994)	1969–1974	Spiro T. Agnew,*** Gerald R. Ford	New York (CA)
38	39	**38. Gerald R. Ford** (1913–)	1974–1977	Nelson A. Rockefeller	Michigan (NE)
		39. James E. Carter Jr. (1924–)	1977–1981	Walter F. Mondale	Georgia
40	41	**40. Ronald Reagan** (1911–)	1981–1989	George H.W. Bush	California (IL)
		41. George H.W. Bush (1924–)	1989–1993	J. Danforth Quayle	Texas (MA)
42	43	**42. William J. Clinton** (1946–)	1993–2001	Albert Gore Jr.	Arkansas
		43. George W. Bush (1946–)	2001–	Richard B. Cheney	Texas (CT)

Glossary

A

abolition the elimination of something, in this case slavery (p. 347)

affirmative action programs for reversing the effects of discrimination (p. 713)

agriculture the art or science of raising crops (p. 6)

alliance an agreement between two or more people, groups, or nations to cooperate with one another (p. 257)

ally a nation, group, or people who are friendly with other people for a common goal (p. 119)

ambush a surprise attack from a hidden position (p. 126)

amendment a change or an addition (p. 203)

amnesty a government pardon for an offense (p. 433)

annexation the act of adding to or taking possession of (p. 360)

anthem a song of praise (p. 280)

apartheid a policy in South Africa of complete separation of the races (p. 736)

appeasement an attempt to keep peace with an enemy by giving in to its demands (p. 614)

apprentice a person who works to learn a specific skill (p. 97)

armistice an agreement to stop warfare (p. 555)

arms race a competition to build weapons (p. 542)

arsenal a building used to store weapons and ammunition (p. 196)

assembly an elected group that makes laws (p. 114)

assembly line a row of factory workers who put together a product, part by part, as it passes by on a conveyor belt (p. 566)

assimilate to become absorbed into a main culture (p. 467)

astrolabe an instrument used to calculate the position of the stars (p. 36)

atomic bomb a nuclear weapon that causes large-scale destruction (p. 628)

B

baby boom the increase in the birthrate after World War II (p. 652)

backcountry an area inhabited by few people and far from more settled areas (p. 82)

barrio a community in which mostly Spanish-speaking people live (p. 594)

barter to exchange one product or service for another (p. 90)

Bessemer process a method for producing a stronger type of steel (p. 476)

bilingual using two languages (p. 761)

black codes a series of laws passed in early Reconstruction to limit the freedoms of formerly enslaved African Americans (p. 436)

Black Power a movement among African Americans to gain political and economic power (p. 688)

blitzkrieg the German method of conducting war with speed and force (p. 616)

blockade a barrier of ships or troops that prevents goods from entering or leaving an area (p. 407)

boomtown a mining camp that grew into a town almost overnight (p. 370)

bootlegger a person who made or transported alcohol illegally (p. 575)

border states four slave states located between the Union and the Confederacy that stayed in the Union during the Civil War (p. 406)

boycott a protest in which people refuse to buy certain goods (p. 139)

Cabinet a group of people chosen by the President to give advice (p. 246)

canal a waterway dug across land for ships to travel through (p. 289)

caravan a group of travelers with pack animals (p. 27)

carpetbagger a Northerner who moved to the South after the Civil War for political gain (p. 440)

cash crop a crop that is grown to be sold rather than used by a farmer (p. 58)

casualty a person wounded, captured, missing, or killed in battle (p. 167)

cede to give up or surrender land (p. 127)

censorship control of free expression (p. 423)

census an official population count (p. 245)

charter an official document in which rights are given by a government to a person or company (p. 56)

checks and balances a system to keep one part of a government from becoming stronger than other parts (p. 201)

civilian a person who is not a member of the military (p. 180)

civilization a well-developed way of life of a people in one place and time (p. 10)

civil war a war between people of the same country (p. 389)

clan a small unit of related Native American families that may be known by a common symbol, such as a bear or turtle (p. 17)

clone to make an exact copy of an organism by duplicating genetic material (p. 756)

Cold War a conflict between countries, with no actual fighting (p. 634)

collective bargaining talks between a union and an employer about working conditions (p. 485)

colony a settlement in a distant land that is governed by another country (p. 39)

commerce the buying and selling of goods (p. 34)

commune a community where people live and work together using shared resources (p. 346)

communism a theory in which the economy is controlled by the government, and property is owned by everyone equally (p. 550)

computer literate having the basic skills needed to operate a computer (p. 753)

concentration camp a place where political prisoners and members of religious and ethnic groups are sent (p. 629)

Confederacy the Confederate States of America, formed in 1861 by southern states that had seceded from the Union (p. 397)

confederation a union of countries or states for a common purpose (p. 188)

conquistador the Spanish term for conqueror, or one who gains control by winning a war (p. 49)

conscription the act of requiring people to serve in the military (p. 414)

conservation protection of natural resources (p. 510)

conservative a person who believes in limited government involvement in the economy (p. 601)

constitution the basic laws and plan of a nation's government (p. 186)

containment a policy of preventing a country from expanding its power (p. 636)

cooperative an organization that is jointly owned by those who use its services (p. 462)

corollary a statement that follows logically from another statement (p. 532)

corporation a large company usually formed by a group of investors (p. 483)

cotton gin a machine that removes seeds from cotton fibers (p. 319)

cowhand a hired person who looks after cattle (p. 457)

culture all of a group's arts, beliefs, and ways of doing things (p. 8)

D

debtor a person who owes money (p. 84)

declaration a formal statement (p. 151)

deferment a postponement, or a delaying, of having to serve in the armed forces (p. 696)

demilitarized zone an area that military forces cannot enter (p. 642)

deport to force someone to leave a country (p. 577)

depression a long period of economic decline (p. 587)

deregulation the loosening of government controls (p. 727)

détente easing tensions between unfriendly nations (p. 714)

dictator a ruler who has complete power (p. 611)

diplomacy conducting relations with the governments of foreign countries (p. 533)

direct primary an election in which members of a political party vote to choose their candidates (p. 507)

discrimination unjust treatment of someone based on prejudice (p. 440)

doctrine a set of beliefs or principles (p. 292)

domino theory the belief that if one country falls to communism, others nearby will fall, one after the other (p. 692)

downsize lay off or fire workers to cut costs (p. 736)

drought a long period without rainfall (p. 15)

dry farming a method of farming that makes use of all the water available in a dry land (p. 18)

E

economy the way in which goods and services are produced and consumed in a community (p. 73)

electoral college a group of people from each state who perform the official duty of electing the President and Vice President (p. 201)

emancipate to free (p. 392)

embargo an order stopping trade with another country (p. 273)

emigrate to leave one country to settle in another country (p. 118)

empire a large land area and population controlled by a single ruler or group (p. 11)

empresario a person who received a contract to bring settlers to Texas in the 1800s (p. 356)

encomienda system the system in which Native Americans were forced to work for Spanish landowners (p. 49)

environment the social, cultural, and natural conditions that influence a community (p. 300)

escalation an increasing involvement (p. 693)

ethnic having a common racial, national, or cultural tradition (p. 489)

ethnic cleansing the act of ridding a region or society of one or more ethnic groups (p. 740)

exclusion the act of keeping a person or group out (p. 491)

executive branch the law-enforcing branch of the federal government (p. 200)

exile a person who is forced to live away from his or her home country (p. 662)

Exoduster an African American who moved to the Great Plains in the late 1800s (p. 461)

expedition a journey made for a specific purpose (p. 38)

export to sell goods to another country (p. 93)

extinction the death of a species (p. 466)

extremist a person whose opinions are very different from those of most people (p. 388)

factory a building with workers and machines in which manufacturing takes place (p. 312)

fascism a political system that emphasizes nationalism and is ruled by a dictator (p. 611)

federal deficit the difference produced when the government spends more than it collects during a year (p. 728)

feminism the belief that women's rights should be equal to men's rights (p. 689)

filibuster to give a long speech in order to delay the vote on a bill in Congress (p. 686)

forty-niner a person who went to California in 1849 seeking gold (p. 370)

Freedmen's Bureau the federal agency created to help emancipated African Americans adjust to life as free people (p. 443)

Freedom Ride a protest against segregated buses and bus stations (p. 671)

frontier the region just beyond a settled area (p. 136)

fugitive a person who has run away (p. 383)

fundamentalist a person who believes in a strict interpretation of the Bible or another religious book (p. 578)

garrison a place where troops are stationed and weapons and ammunition are stored (p. 172)

generation gap a difference in tastes and values between young people and their parents (p. 654)

genetic engineering the act of working on genes to change, or copy them (p. 755)

genocide the deliberate destruction of a group of people based on their race, culture, or beliefs (p. 627)

globalization a condition in which countries are members of a world community (p. 758)

global warming the rise in the average temperatures of Earth over time (p. 764)

grand jury a jury that decides if the charges against a person are strong enough for a trial (p. 742)

Great Society President Johnson's goals and programs for the future of the United States (p. 681)

greenhouse effect the process by which Earth is kept warm at all times (p. 764)

guerrilla war fighting involving surprise raids (p. 663)

habeas corpus the right of a citizen to ask a court to decide if a prisoner is being held lawfully (p. 423)

Harlem Renaissance a cultural movement of African American writers, painters, and musicians, many of whom lived in the Harlem area of New York City (p. 570)

Holocaust Hitler's policy of killing European Jews and others considered "unfit to live" during World War II (p. 627)

homesteader a person who received land on which to build a house and farm (p. 460)

hostage a person who is held captive until certain demands are met (p. 721)

human genome the genetic makeup of human beings (p. 755)

human rights the basic freedoms that all people should have (p. 718)

immigrant a person who moves into a country from another country (p. 259)

immigration the act of coming into a country to live there (p. 80)

impeachment the process of charging a high public official, such as the President, with a crime (p. 441)

imperialism the practice of one nation controlling other nations through conquest and colonization (p. 518)

implied power a power that is not stated in the Constitution (p. 251)

import to buy goods from another country (p. 93)

impressment seizing someone and forcing that person into service for a country (p. 255)

inauguration a formal ceremony to induct an elected official into office (p. 244)

indentured servant person who agrees to work for another until a debt is paid (p. 61)

individualism an emphasis on the value, rights, and power of the individual (p. 341)

inflation a sharp increase in the price of goods and services (p. 180)

installment plan the payment for an item in small, regular amounts over a period of time (p. 567)

insurrection a rebellion against established authority (p. 395)

integrate to open to people of all races (p. 672)

interchangeable parts identical parts that can be substituted for each other (p. 314)

internment camp a place in which people are confined, especially during a time of war (p. 619)

ironclad warship metal or metal-covered steam-driven warship (p. 415)

iron curtain a barrier of secrecy that kept Soviet-controlled nations apart from the rest of Europe (p. 635)

irrigate to supply water to dry land for growing crops (p. 15)

isolationism the policy of staying out of the political affairs of other countries (p. 519)

isthmus a narrow strip of land separating two larger land areas (p. 530)

Jazz Age the name given to the 1920s because of the new popularity of jazz music (p. 570)

Jim Crow laws laws that enforced segregation in the South (p. 446)

joint occupation the sharing of an area of land by two or more countries (p. 364)

joint-stock company a group of investors who share both risk and profit (p. 56)

judicial branch the law-interpreting branch of the federal government (p. 200)

judicial review a court review to determine whether a law is constitutional (p. 269)

kamikaze a Japanese pilot who crashes his plane into an enemy ship (p. 626)

kinship family relationships (p. 30)

"kitchen cabinet" unofficial advisors to the President (p. 296)

L

legislative branch the lawmaking branch of the federal government (p. 200)

libel a false statement made in writing about someone (p. 98)

liberal a person who favors using government resources to bring about social and economic change (p. 601)

line item veto a veto of a portion but not all of a proposed law (p. 399)

Loyalist a person who remained loyal to the British government (p. 164)

M

Manifest Destiny the idea that the United States had the right to expand from the Atlantic Ocean to the Pacific Ocean (p. 364)

massacre the brutal killing of a large number of people (p. 144)

mass production the making of many items in a short period of time (p. 314)

McCarthyism named after Senator Joseph McCarthy, the practice of publicly accusing people of political disloyalty without regard for evidence (p. 644)

Medicaid public health program that pays medical expenses for low-income people (p. 682)

Medicare national health insurance for older Americans and people with certain disabilities (p. 682)

mercantile system an economic system that stresses increasing national wealth by selling more than buying in foreign trade (p. 93)

mercenary a hired soldier (p. 166)

migrant worker a person who moves from place to place to find work, usually harvesting crops (p. 590)

migrate to move from one place to another (p. 5)

militia a group of citizen-soldiers who volunteer when needed (p. 122)

minuteman a member of the colonial militia (p. 148)

mission a settlement built by a church for religious work (p. 50)

mobilize to organize or prepare, as for war (p. 544)

monarch a ruler (p. 112)

monopoly complete control over a supply, service, or market (p. 483)

mountain man a fur trapper or trader who went west to live in or near the mountains (p. 366)

muckraker a writer who brings attention to problems in society (p. 504)

N

napalm a sticky gasoline jelly used in bombs (p. 694)

national debt the total amount of money the federal government owes to individuals, institutions, and itself (p. 728)

nationalism pride in one's country (p. 282)

nation-building the support of developing governments in foreign countries (p. 739)

nativism the view that favors people born in a country over immigrants who come to that country (p. 336)

natural resource something provided by nature that is useful to people (p. 6)

navigate to control the direction of a boat or ship (p. 35)

neutral not taking one side or the other (p. 254)

New Frontier President Kennedy's goals and programs for the future of the United States (p. 666)

nomad a person who moves about in search of food (p. 4)

nullify to cancel (p. 259)

O

ordinance a law (p. 193)

overseer a person who is in charge of enslaved people (p. 103)

P

pacifist a person who opposes war under any circumstance (p. 543)

Parliament the British law-making branch of government (p. 112)

patent a grant that gives an inventor the sole right to make and sell an invention for a set period of time (p. 477)

Patriot a person who supported independence from Great Britain (p. 149)

patroon a Dutch landowner in the colony of New Netherland (p. 77)

Peace Corps a federal agency that sends trained volunteers to help developing countries (p. 667)

pension an income for retired workers (p. 600)

perjury telling a lie under oath (p. 643)

persecute to punish or mistreat a person because of his or her beliefs (p. 70)

petition a formal written request (p. 147)

Pilgrim a religious traveler to a new land; a founder of Plymouth Colony (p. 71)

plantation a large farm requiring many workers (p. 36)

planter a person who owns and operates a plantation (p. 320)

platform a statement of a political party's policies and beliefs (p. 463)

popular sovereignty control by the people (p. 381)

precedent an example for the future (p. 246)

presidio a Spanish fort (p. 367)

proclamation an official announcement (p. 136)

profit money gained from a business or investment after expenses have been paid (p. 586)

Progressive a person who believes in social progress through reform (p. 505)

Prohibition the ban on the making and sale of alcoholic drinks (p. 506)

propaganda the promotion of certain ideas to influence people's opinions (p. 552)

proprietary colony a colony owned and managed by one or more individuals (p. 78)

prospector a person who looks for gold or other valuable ores (p. 370)

protectorate a small country protected and controlled by a larger one (p. 528)

provisional temporary (p. 399)

public domain land owned by the government (p. 194)

public works projects paid for by the government for public use (p. 588)

pueblo an apartment-like adobe dwelling; Spanish word for village (p. 15)

Puritan a member of a religious group that wanted to simplify the practices of the Church of England (p. 70)

Q

quarantine to isolate (p. 663)

quota a fixed number of a certain group of immigrants admitted to a country (p. 577)

R

racism feelings against people because of their ethnic background or skin color (p. 501)

radical someone who favors extreme social or economic changes (p. 266)

range the vast public grasslands in the West where cattle graze freely (p. 456)

ratify to approve (p. 189)

ration to limit to small portions in order to make something last (p. 624)

recession a decline in economic activity (p. 718)

Reconstruction the period from 1865 to 1877 in which programs were created to reunite the South with the North (p. 432)

reformer a person who wants to improve society (p. 346)

refugee a person who flees to a foreign country (p. 638)

relief a direct money payment to the unemployed (p. 592)

relocate to move a person or group of people (p. 301)

reparation the payment for damages (p. 557)

repeal to take back or cancel (p. 140)

representative a person selected to act and speak in place of others (p. 125)

republic a government that receives its power from the people, who elect its leaders (p. 181)

reservation public land set aside for special use, as for Native Americans (p. 467)

resolution a formal statement of opinion (p. 143)

revenue money received by a government from taxes and other sources (p. 138)

revival a reawakening (p. 345)

royal colony a colony directly under the rule of a king or queen (p. 81)

rural having to do with the country (p. 334)

S

sanitation disposal of waste (p. 60)

satellite a nation controlled by another country (p. 635)

scalawag a white Southerner who supported the Republicans during Reconstruction (p. 440)

secede to withdraw from or leave (p. 384)

sectionalism concern for the interests of a certain region or area (p. 296)

segregation separation of the races (p. 446)

self-determination the right of people to decide on their own form of government (p. 557)

Separatist a Puritan who wished to break away, or separate, from the Church of England (p. 70)

sharecropping a system of farming in which farmers work another's land and use part of their crops as rent (p. 445)

siege a long, drawn-out attack (p. 172)

sit-in a protest in which people sit and refuse to leave a place (p. 670)

slave code a set of laws that limited the activities of enslaved people (p. 104)

sovereignty the power of self-government (p. 188)

space race the competition among countries to be the first in exploring space (p. 646)

sphere of influence a region in which one nation has influence or control over other nations (p. 522)

spiritual an expressive religious song (p. 327)

spoils system government appointments of friends by the winning party of an election (p. 295)

stagflation the economic condition of higher prices without economic growth (p. 715)

steerage a large open area beneath a ship's deck (p. 489)

stock a share of ownership in a company (p. 483)

strategy a plan (p. 407)

subsistence farming growing only enough crops to meet the needs of one household (p. 77)

suburb a community at the edge of a city (p. 652)

suffrage the right to vote (p. 508)

summit meeting a meeting between important leaders of nations (p. 649)

superpower one of the most powerful nations in the world (p. 641)

sweatshop an unhealthy workplace where people are overworked (p. 499)

tariff a tax on imported goods (p. 247)

tax money paid to a government (p. 28)

temperance a reform movement that was opposed to drinking alcohol (p. 346)

tenant farmer a person who pays for the right to farm someone else's land (p. 594)

tenement a run-down apartment building (p. 498)

terrorism the use of violence or threats to achieve a goal (p. 741)

textile cloth (p. 312)

totalitarian state a country in which one person or group has complete control (p. 612)

total war a war against civilians and resources as well as against armies (p. 424)

traitor a person who acts against his or her country (p. 150)

transcendentalism the belief that people learn truth and knowledge from their experiences with God and nature (p. 341)

transcontinental across a continent (p. 455)

trench warfare soldiers fighting from long ditches dug in the ground (p. 413)

tribute money paid for protection (p. 272)

truce a temporary agreement to stop fighting (p. 707)

trust a giant corporation made up of a group of companies (p. 510)

unconstitutional something that goes against the U.S. Constitution (p. 247)

Underground Railroad escape routes used by enslaved African Americans to reach freedom in the North (p. 327)

Union the United States of America (p. 254); also, the northern states during the Civil War era (p. 397)

urban describing a city or city life (p. 335)

urban renewal a program to rebuild run-down areas of cities (p. 682)

utopia a perfect society (p. 340)

veto to reject a law (p. 201)

victory garden a garden in which people grow their own food during a war (p. 551)

Vietnamization President Nixon's plan to train the South Vietnamese to fight the Vietnam War (p. 706)

war bond a loan from U.S. citizens to the government meant to be paid back with interest in several years (p. 551)

yellow journalism publishing exaggerated or made-up news stories to attract readers and influence their ideas (p. 524)

Index

An italic *c* indicates a chart or graph; an italic *crt*, a political cartoon; an italic *m*, a map; and an italic *p*, a picture.

Abolitionist movement, 386
Acquired immune deficiency syndrome (AIDS), 766, 766*p*
Adams, Brooks, 516
Adams, Charles Francis, 412
Adamson Act, 513
Addams, Jane, 499, 499*p*
Affirmative action, 713
Afghanistan, 746–747
African Americans. *See also* Civil rights movment; Slaves
    achievements of, 655
    black codes and, 436
    as buffalo soldiers, 468
    in Civil War, 416–417, 417*p*
    discrimination against, 440, 446, 501–502
    education of, 444, 646–647, 672
    in farmers' alliances, 463
    in Great Depression, 593–594
    on the Great Plains, 461
    Harlem Renaissance and, 570–571
    jazz music of, 570
    Ku Klux Klan and, 445–446
    marriage and, 445
    New Deal and, 602
    in 1920s, 576
    organization of, 507–508
    in Reconstruction, 430, 431, 439–440, 443–445
    rights of, 433, 438, 439, 446
    in Spanish-American War, 526
    in sports, 655
    working conditions for, 484
    in World War I, 550, 551, 556
    in World War II, 624
African National Congress (ANC), 736
Agricultural Adjustment Administration (AAA), 599
Agriculture. *See also* Farmers; Farming Airplanes
    advances in, 573
    flight of first, 479
    terrorism and, 743–745
    in World War I, 541, 541*p*, 546, 556
    in World War II, 616–617, 617*p*
Alabama Platform, 395
Alaska, purchase of, 519, 519*crt*
Aldrin, "Buzz," 713
Alliance for Progress, 668

Allied Powers
    in WWI, 543, 544, 545, 548, 550, 554–555, 557
    in WWII, 617, 618, 619–621, 625–628
Al Qaeda, 743, 747
American Civil Liberties Union (ACLU), 579
American Expeditionary Force, 550
American Federation of Labor (AFL), 485, 568
American Independent Party, 705
American Indian Movement (AIM), 691
American Protective Association, 490
American Railroad Union, 486
American Red Cross, 414, 550
Americans With Disabilities Act (1990), 733
Anaconda Plan, 407, 413, 421
Anthony, Susan B., 496, 508
Antietam, Battle of, 409*m*, 410, 422, 427*p*
Anti-Semitism, 627
Antitrust legislation, 483*crt*, 510, 513
Antiwar demonstrations, 695–696, 703, 703*p*, 704, 706
Apartheid, 736
Apollo program, 713, 713*p*
Appeasement, 614
Appomattox Court House, 425*m*, 426, 426*p*, 433
Arab-Israeli conflict, 638, 715
Arafat, Yasser, 741*p*
Arapaho people, 468
Argonne Forest, 555, 556
Aristide, Jean-Bertrand, 740
Armistice Day (1954), 556
Arms race, 542, 649, 729
Armstrong, Edwin H., 553
Armstrong, Louis, 570
Armstrong, Neil, 713, 713*p*
Asian Americans, 760. *See also* specific groups
Association of Southern Women for the Prevention of Lynching, 508
Atchison, Topeka and Santa Fe Railroad, 455
Atlanta, in Civil War, 425, 425*m*
Atlantic Charter, 626
Atomic bomb, 625*m*, 628
Austria-Hungary, in World War I, 542, 543, 544, 548
Automobiles, 479, 563*p*
Axis Powers, 616, 617, 620

Baby boom, 652
Baker v. *Carr*, 667
Banks, 512–513, 587–589, 598
Barton, Clara, 414
Bay of Pigs invasion, 661–662, 662*m*
Beecher, Henry Ward, 416
Begin, Menachem, 720
Belgium, 544, 616
Bell, Alexander Graham, 480
Bell, John, 396, 397
Belleau Wood, 554
Berlin, Germany, 626, 635, 636
Berlin airlift, 636
Berlin Wall, 662–663, 663*p*, 734, 734*p*
Bessemer, Henry, 476
Bethune, Mary McLeod, 602
Bilingual education, 761
Bin Laden, Osama, 743, 746–747
Black codes, 436, 440
Black Hand society, 543
Black Kettle, Chief, 468
Black Monday, 732
Black Muslims, 687
Black Panther party, 688
Black Power, 688
Black Tuesday, 587
Bolsheviks, 550
Bonus Army, 595, 595*p*, 596
Booth, John Wilkes, 433, 433*p*
Bootlegger, 575, 575*p*
Bosnia, 543, 740
Boxer Rebellion, 522
Bozeman Trail, 469
Brady, James and Sarah, 727
Brady, Mathew B., 427
Brady Handgun Violence Prevention Bill, 727
Brandeis, Louis D., 513
Breckinridge, John C., 395, 397
Brezhnev, Leonid I., 714
Brooks, Preston, 393
Brown, John, 389, 394–395, 395*p*
Brown v. *Board of Education of Topeka*, 646–647, 683
Bryan, William Jennings, 464, 578
Buchanan, James, 392
Buffalo soldiers, 468
Bulgaria, 543, 617
Bulge, Battle of the, 621
Bull Moose Party, 511
Bull Run, 409, 409*m*, 410
Bush, George Herbert Walker, 732, 734–736, 738
Bush, George Walker, 742, 758–759, 743–747
Business, new laws for, 512–513

Acknowledgments and Photo Credits

Text Acknowledgments

"I Have a Dream," reprinted by arrangement with The Heirs to the Estate of Martin Luther King Jr., c/o Writers House, Inc. as agent for the proprietor. *Copyright 1963 by Martin Luther King, Jr., copyright renewed 1991 by Coretta Scott King.*

NOTE: Every effort has been made to locate the copyright owner of material reprinted in this book. Omissions brought to our attention will be corrected in subsequent editions.